Church, Faith and Culture in the Medieval West

General Editors: Brenda Bolton with Anne J. Duggan and Damian J. Smith

About the series

The series Church, Faith and Culture in the Medieval West reflects the central concerns necessary for any in-depth study of the medieval Church – greater cultural awareness and interdisciplinarity. Including both monographs and edited collections, this new series draws on the most innovative work from established and younger scholars alike, offering a balance of interests, vertically though the period from *c*.400 to *c*.1500 or horizontally across Latin Christendom. Topics covered range from cultural history, the monastic life, relations between Church and State to law and ritual, palaeography and textual transmission. All authors, from a wide range of disciplinary backgrounds, share a commitment to innovation, analysis and historical accuracy.

About the volume

In the period following the collapse of the Carolingian Empire up to the Fourth Lateran Council (1215), the episcopate everywhere in Europe experienced substantial and important change. How did the medieval bishop, unquestionably one of the most powerful figures of the Middle Ages, respond to these and other historical changes? In this volume of interdisciplinary studies drawn from literary scholarship, art history, and history, the editors and contributors propose less a conventional socio-political reading of the episcopate and more of a "cultural" reading of bishops that, especially, is concerned with issues such as episcopal (self-)representation, conceptualization of office and authority, cultural production (images, texts, material objects, space), and ecclesiology/ideology.

About the editors

John S. Ott is Associate Professor of History at Portland State University, USA.

Anna Trumbore Jones is Assistant Professor of History at Lake Forest College, USA.

Church, Faith and Culture in the Medieval West

General Editors: Brenda Bolton with Anne J. Duggan and Damian J. Smith

Other titles in the series:

THE BISHOP REFORMED

The Bishop Reformed

Studies of Episcopal Power and Culture in the Central Middle Ages

Edited by

JOHN S. OTT
Portland State University, USA

and

ANNA TRUMBORE JONES
Lake Forest College, USA

ASHGATE

Published by
Ashgate Publishing Limited
Gower House
Croft Road
Aldershot
Hampshire GU11 3HR
England

Ashgate Publishing Company
Suite 420
101 Cherry Street
Burlington, VT 05401-4405
USA

Ashgate website: http://www.ashgate.com

British Library Cataloguing in Publication Data
The bishop reformed : studies of episcopal power and culture in the central Middle Ages. –
   (Church, faith and culture in the medieval West)
   1. Bishops – History – To 1500 2. Church history – Middle Ages, 600–1500
   I. Ott, John S. II. Jones, Anna Trumbore
   262.1'2'0902

Library of Congress Cataloging-in-Publication Data
The bishop reformed : studies of Episcopal power and culture in the central middle ages /
edited by John S. Ott and Anna Trumbore Jones.
      p. cm. – (Church, faith and culture in the medieval west)
   ISBN 978-0-7546-5765-1 (alk. paper)
   1. Episcopacy–History. 2. Church history–Middle Ages, 600–1500. 3. Christianity and
culture. I. Ott, John S. II. Jones, Anna Trumbore.

   BV670.3.B57 2007
   262'.12–dc22

                                                                2006034272

ISBN 978 0 7546 5765 1

Printed and bound in Great Britain by MPG Books Ltd. Bodmin, Cornwall.

Contents

List of Figures and Tables

Tables

Figures

List of Contributors

Greta Austin is Assistant Professor of Religion at the University of Puget Sound. She is the author of *Law, Theology and 'Forgery' around the Year 1000: The Decretum of Burchard of Worms*.

Bruce C. Brasington is Professor of History at West Texas A&M University and in recent years has been a visiting professor in Dresden. His most recent publications have been on the study and practice of canon law in the twelfth century.

John Eldevik received his Ph.D. at UCLA and teaches medieval history at Pomona College in Claremont, California. He is most recently the author of *Medieval Germany: Research and Resources*, Reference Guide 21, published by the German Historical Institute in Washington, D.C.

Evan A. Gatti is Assistant Professor of Art History at Elon University. After completing her dissertation on eleventh-century episcopal portraiture, she is currently researching north Italian wall painting and the Via Francigena.

Dorothy F. Glass is Professor Emerita at the University at Buffalo, Fellow of the American Academy in Rome, and formerly Richard Krautheimer Guest Professor at the Bibliotheca Hertziana, Rome (2004–2005). She has published widely on Italian Romanesque art, including: *Studies on Cosmatesque Pavements*; *Romanesque Sculpture in Campania: Patrons, Programs, and Styles*; and *Portals, Pilgrimage, and Crusade in Western Tuscany*.

Thomas Head is Professor of History at Hunter College and the Graduate Center of the City University of New York. He is the author and editor of many works on hagiography and the religious history of the central Middle Ages, including *Hagiography and the Cult of Saints: The Diocese of Orléans, 800–1200* and *The Peace of God: Social Violence and Religious Response in France around the Year 1000*.

Anna Trumbore Jones is Assistant Professor of History at Lake Forest College. She has published articles on the tenth-century church in southwestern France and is completing a book on the bishops of Aquitaine in that era.

Maureen C. Miller is Professor of History at the University of California, Berkeley. She is author of *The Bishop's Palace: Architecture and Authority in Medieval Italy*, which was awarded the 2001 Helen and Howard R. Marraro Prize of the Society for Italian Historical Studies for the best book in Italian history, and *The Formation of a Medieval Church: Ecclesiastical Change in Verona, 950–1150*, winner of the American Catholic Historical Association's John Gilmary Shea prize.

John S. Ott is Associate Professor of History at Portland State University. His research interests and publications concentrate on episcopal culture in northwestern Europe *c*.1050–1150, and he is currently working on a book on episcopal authority and community in northern France and Flanders.

Eric Palazzo is Professor of Medieval Art History at the Université de Poitiers and Director of the Centre d'Études Supérieures de Civilisation Médiévale. He is a specialist in medieval liturgy, rituals, and iconography, focusing particularly on the study of liturgical manuscripts and their decoration. He has published numerous books and articles on these themes. He was a Getty Scholar at the Getty Research Institute in Los Angeles in 2006–2007.

Valerie Ramseyer is Associate Professor of History at Wellesley College. She is the author of *The Transformation of a Religious Landscape: Medieval Southern Italy, 850–1150*.

T.M. Riches is a Teaching Fellow at the University of Birmingham (UK), working on ecclesiastical culture in France and Germany at the turn of the first millennium.

Renée R. Trilling is Assistant Professor of English and Medieval Studies at the University of Illinois at Urbana-Champaign. She has written on Old English historical poetry, Anglo-Saxon saints' lives, and the historiography of the immediate post-Conquest era.

Acknowledgments

This collection had its roots in a conference panel on "Episcopal Hagiography and Historiography in the High Middle Ages" organized by John Ott for the International Congress on Medieval Studies in Kalamazoo, Michigan, in May 2003. The quality of the papers and the discussion at dinner afterwards fed the conviction that a collection of new work on bishops, involving scholars from a variety of disciplines, was both necessary and desirable. A second panel, organized two years later for the Eightieth Annual Meeting of the Medieval Academy of America in Miami Beach, Florida, brought together several of the volume's contributors to present papers on the subject of "The Bishop Reformed: Conceptions of Episcopal Power and Office in the Central Middle Ages." From these two meetings emerged the nucleus of the present volume. In the intervening years the editors have incurred numerous debts to people and institutions, which are a pleasure to acknowledge. Above all, we must thank our contributors for their essays, their responsiveness to our numerous pleas for clarification, and their patience in the face of our reminders about deadlines. This volume would not exist without their hard work and dedication to the book. At Ashgate Publishing, we would like to thank the series editors, John Smedley and Brenda Bolton, for their belief in the project and their work in bringing it to publication. In addition, we thank Rachel Lynch, Emily Ebdon, and Anthea Lockley of Ashgate, for their scrupulous editing and oversight of various aspects of the process.

John undertook much of his initial work on the book and his contributions to it while in residence as a Mellon Fellow at the Pontifical Institute of Mediaeval Studies (Toronto) during 2004–2005, and he benefited greatly from discussions with the other fellows and faculty of the Institute, especially Diane Reilly. Additionally, John would like to thank his colleagues at Portland State University for their interest in, and support of, the book's composition. Portland State graduate student Ashlee Hill rendered valuable service tracking down and verifying references and in preparing the index. Anna thanks Lake Forest College for generous research support and leave to complete the book, as well as numerous colleagues in the history department who provided criticism and encouragement in appropriate measure. Special thanks go to Tom Head, Adam J. Kosto, and Jay Rubenstein for helpful discussions on various aspects of the project.

Our deepest and most personal thanks go to friends and family. John's family—his wife, Tever Nickerson, and daughters Madeleine and Ellery—patiently put up with him through the project's numerous phases, frustrations, and pleasures. He also thanks his parents, John and Marcia Ott, for their unstinting support over many years. Anna thanks Susan Chenelle, Joyce Shin and Michael David, Michelle Dowd, and especially Lawrence Jones and David and Linda Trumbore for their love and encouragement. Finally, we thank each other for the hard work, patience, and sense of humor that made the creation of this book not only a rewarding process but also a deeply enjoyable one.

List of Abbreviations

AASS		Acta sanctorum quotquot toto orbe coluntur, ed. Jean Bolland et al. (Antwerp and Brussels, 1643–)
CCCM		Corpus Christianorum, Continuatio Mediaevalis (Turnhout, 1971–)
CCSL		Corpus Christianorum, Series Latina (Turnhout, 1953–)
EETS		Early English Text Society
	o.s.	original series
	s.s.	supplementary series
GC		Gallia Christiana, in provincias ecclesiasticas distributa, 17 volumes (Paris, 1715–1865, repr. Westmead, 1970)
MGH		Monumenta Germaniae Historica
	DD	Diplomata regum et imperatorum Germaniae
	Ldl	Libelli de lite imperatorum et pontificum saeculi XI. et XII. conscripti, 3 volumes (Hannover, 1891–1897)
	SS	Scriptores in folio (Hannover, 1826–)
	SS rer. Germ.	Scriptores rerum Germanicarum in usum scholarum separatim editi (Hannover and Leipzig, 1846–)
	SS rer. Merov.	Scriptores rerum Merovingicarum, 7 volumes (Hannover, 1885–1920)
n.s.		new series/nova series
PL		Patrologiae cursus completus … series latina, ed. Jacques-Paul Migne, 221 volumes (Paris, 1844–1864)
s.a.		*sub anno*

Chapter 1

Introduction: The Bishop Reformed

John S. Ott and Anna Trumbore Jones

The bishop was unquestionably one of the most important individuals of the European Middle Ages. It is hard to think of an area of daily life, at any time, where his influence was not felt to some degree. From the summits of worldly power to the most remote rural pastures, in cities and on battlefields, men and women of every rank and station felt his presence in their lives. The bishop was directly responsible for every soul in his diocese, mighty and meek. His church, the cathedral, was typically the largest structure for miles around, looming over town walls, dwarfing all but the grandest abbeys in its precincts. He administered the wealthiest land-holding institution of the medieval period, overseeing its fields and streams, its produce, its free and unfree residents and servants, and its armed men. The bishop communed with God and his saints. He judged and corrected his fellow man. He did not simply stand at the center of things—he *was* the center.

In the period from *c*.900 to 1200, medieval people generally recognized that only an individual of high social standing could be entrusted to occupy so vital a position. The few cases of men elevated to the bishop's throne from non-elite ranks furnish the exception that proves the rule: the bishop was a nobleman. His bloodline and aristocratic origins endowed him with the requisite authority to defend and intercede on behalf of the bodies and souls of his fellow men. With his familial connections and accumulated wealth, the bishop could also support his church and its clergy in a fitting manner. If powerful connections and nobility were episcopal prerequisites, ideally it was necessary that he should also embody the range of virtues outlined for pastors in 1 Timothy 3.1–7. The bishop should be "above reproach," a man of high principle.[1] Church law demanded that he be educated, *litteratus*—Timothy uses the adjective *doctorem*—and so able to instruct his flock in the word of God.

Two early eleventh-century documents written shortly after the death of Harduin of Crouy, the bishop of Noyon-Tournai, illuminate how the twin ideals of noble resourcefulness and pastoral solicitude combined in the figure of the bishop.[2] The

---

[1]   1 Tim. 3.2 (Vulgate). 'Oportet ergo episcopum irreprehensibilem esse, unius uxoris virum, sobrium, prudentem, ornatum, pudicum, hospitalem, doctorem…'.

[2]   *Gallia Christiana, in provincias ecclesiasticas distributa* [hereafter *GC*], 17 vols (Paris, 1715–1865, repr. Westmead, 1970) 10, Instrumenta, cols 362–63, 365–66, and continued in *GC* 9:994; see also Michel Parisse, "The Bishop: Prince and Prelate," in *The Bishop: Power and Piety at the First Millennium*, ed. Sean Gilsdorf, Neue Aspekte der europäischen Mittelalterforschung 4 (Münster, 2004), pp. 8–16; Jeffrey Bowman, "The Bishop Builds a Bridge: Sanctity and Power in the Medieval Pyrenees," *The Catholic Historical Review* 88 (2002), 1–16.

first, a letter written on behalf of the people and cathedral chapters of Noyon and Tournai, transmitted the news of the bishop's death in July 1030 to the archbishop and bishops of the province of Reims. The missive details the sorrow of both communities and explains their reasons for electing Hugh, Harduin's successor.

> We elected him just as apostolic and canonical authority commands: [he is] catholic in faith, by nature wise, teachable, patient, temperate of mores, of chaste life, sober, humble, expressive, merciful, lettered, educated in God's law, circumspect in the meanings of the scriptures, trained in ecclesiastical doctrines, and orthodox according to the ways and tradition of scriptures . . . , hospitable, modest, a good manager of his household, not a neophyte, a man of good character, one who has followed ecclesiastical tradition at every step, who has administered good works to all and right reason to the satisfaction of all who have asked for it. . . .[3]

The letter notes in closing that the pastor should possess these virtues because his integrity was "the salvation of those subject to him" (*integritas praesidentium salus est subditorum*). The chapter portrayed Hugh as a bishop cut directly from the cloth of 1 Timothy's model, one who possessed the qualities to lead through example rather than command.

The second document, a letter composed by Gui, treasurer of Notre-Dame of Noyon, is of uncertain date but probably belongs to the period from 1045–1068.[4] In it, Gui lists the various episcopal bequests received by the cathedral chapter since the early tenth century. The largesse of Bishop Harduin—who was described as a "lover of the clergy and defender of the people committed to him"—is painstakingly detailed.[5] In addition to numerous altars, churches, and lands in the regions of Vermandois and Amiens, he bequeathed a gold chalice and paten, a gold cross studded with pearls and a copious number of precious gems, and clerical vestments of high quality. Much of this came from his own inheritance and was offered in memory of his parents and sister; Gui noted the annual dates on which the chapter recited prayers for all their souls. Harduin's family connection to Noyon was established physically as well as memorially. The bishop was buried between the tombs of his mother and

---

[3]   "Eligimus ergo eum talem qualem jubet apostolica et canonica auctoritas, fide catholicum, natura prudentem, docibilem, patientem, moribus temperatum, vita castum, sobrium, humilem, effabilem, misericordem, litteratum, in lege Dei instructum, in scripturarum sensibus cautum, in dogmatibus ecclesiasticis exercitatum, et secundum scripturarum tramitem traditionemque orthodoxum . . . , hospitalem, modestum, suae domui bene praepositum, non neophytum, habentem testimonium bonum, in gradibus singulis secundum traditionem ecclesiasticam, ministrantem ad omne opus bonum, et ad satisfactionem omni poscenti rationem": *GC* 10, Instrumenta, cols 362–63.

[4]   The editors of the *Gallia Christiana* place its date "circiter 1050," but as the same dignitaries named in Gui's letter also appear in a 1064 charter of Bishop Baldwin of Noyon (1044–1068), it may well have been composed about that time. See Olivier Guyotjeannin, *Episcopus et comes: Affirmation et déclin de la seigneurie épiscopale au nord du royaume de France (Beauvais-Noyon, Xe–début XIIIe siècle)*, Mémoires et documents publiés par la Société de l'École des chartes 30 (Geneva, 1987), p. 174.

[5]   *GC* 9:994.

sister in the cathedral chapter house.[6] There, Harduin and his blood relatives would continue to witness and attend the daily life of the cathedral clergy until the Day of Judgment, when the bishop and his kindred would arise in the company of his spiritual brethren to face their God. In every respect, Harduin's care for his church was a family concern, one that did not cease with his final breath.

Social status also meant that the bishop had the ability to defend the churches and populations under his care, and authors of the central Middle Ages often included the bishop's military capabilities—when used for proper ends—among his worthy qualities. A near contemporary of Harduin and Hugh, the chronicler Ademar of Chabannes, when describing the "good pastor" Ebles of Limoges (944–c.977), emphasized his activities in fortifying towns and monasteries as well as his membership in the powerful ruling family of Aquitaine.[7] Building walls and fighting when necessary were therefore also part of the bishop's mandate.[8]

Their contemporaries lauded prelates such as Harduin, Hugh, and Ebles for precisely those characteristics esteemed of bishops everywhere in Europe: their generosity toward the church, their quality of mind and training, their willingness to defend their flocks. Scholars have long understood these aspects of the medieval bishop; together with the papacy and monastic institutions, the episcopacy and its tenants have been the subject of countless specialized studies over the past two centuries.[9] The sheer volume of research disguises some surprising absences, however. Apart from a few essays and book chapters, no general survey of the medieval episcopate exists.[10] Only a modest handful of collected studies or anthologies have been published, and these are often confined within limited chronological or thematic frameworks.[11] With some notable exceptions, the central Middle Ages, which we

---

[6]   Ibid.

[7]   Ademar of Chabannes, *Ademari Cabannensis Chronicon*, 3.25, ed. Pascale Bourgain, Richard Landes, and Georges Pon, CCCM 129 (Turnhout, 1999), pp. 146–47.

[8]   Of course, bishops also attracted their fair share of sanction and criticism for their militaristic activities, especially in the latter part of the period surveyed in this collection. See Timothy Reuter, "*Episcopi cum sua militia*: The Prelate as Warrior in the Early Staufer Era," in *Warriors and Churchmen in the High Middle Ages: Essays Presented to Karl Leyser*, ed. Timothy Reuter (London, 1992), pp. 79–94.

[9]   See the notes below for some of the more important studies to have appeared in recent years.

[10]   Recent studies of episcopal office that survey the period around the year 1000: Michel Parisse, "The Bishop: Prince and Prelate" (above, n. 2); Timothy Reuter, "Ein Europa der Bischöfe. Das Zeitalter Burchards von Worms," in *Bischof Burchard von Worms, 1000–1025*, ed. Wilfried Hartmann, Quellen und Abhandlungen zur mittelrheinischen Kirchengeschichte 100 (Mainz, 2000), pp. 1–28; Rosamond McKitterick, "The Church," in *The New Cambridge Medieval History*, vol. 3, *c. 900–c. 1024*, ed. Timothy Reuter (Cambridge, 1999), pp. 130–62; Heinrich Fichtenau, *Living in the Tenth Century: Mentalities and Social Orders*, trans. Patrick J. Geary (Chicago, 1991), pp. 181–216, 239–41.

[11]   Most recently the volume of essays edited by Sean Gilsdorf, cited in n. 2 above, and a collection of studies edited by Natalie Fryde and Dirk Reitz, *Bischofsmord im Mittelalter/ Murder of Bishops*, Veröffentlichungen der Max-Plancks-Institut für Geschichte 191 (Göttingen, 2003). An older anthology, centered heavily on ecclesiology, is *L'épiscopat et l'Église universelle*, ed. Yves Congar and B.-D. Dupuy, Unam Sanctam 39 (Paris, 1962). There

consider here to be the period stretching from the fragmentation of the Carolingian Empire to the Fourth Lateran Council (1215), has been especially underrepresented.[12] Significantly, a recently published collection of fifteen articles exemplifying "new approaches" to the study of medieval religion contains no contribution devoted exclusively, or even primarily, to the episcopate.[13] The central figure of the bishop, by virtue of his absence in general studies, has become in some ways a marginal entity in modern scholarship covering the church and religion in the period from 900 to 1200.[14] How then might this curious paradox be explained?

The bishop's vanishing act is a by-product of the historiography of the medieval church and medieval religion of the past four decades.[15] That historiography has, on the one hand, explored episcopal office in light of prevailing social, economic, political, or cultural structures. Here, two related trends have dominated the field. The decline of the centralized power of the Carolingian state and the proliferation and expansion of territorial lordships after the year 900 has constituted one primary framework for assessing the bishop's interests and activities, especially his role in the rise to power of family and kin-networks and their political and military ambitions. The increasing organization of the papacy and the extension of its authority into the governance of local churches in the late eleventh and twelfth centuries has established another. Interest in the bishop as landed lord and in the bishop's place within the process of ecclesiastical reform has decisively influenced the course of scholarship devoted to this figure. Indeed, these two historiographical trends are intertwined: the growth of the institutional church has often been measured against the resistance of local religious cultures, especially local traditions of episcopal administrative, political, and cultic autonomy. Meanwhile, scholars considering the tenth century in light of the coming reform have long emphasized examples of the "abuses" that reformers would condemn, such as the deep involvement of the bishops in lay power

---

are also surveys of bishops of particular regions, but even these are few; see, for example, the collection of essays edited by Pierre Bouet and François Neveux, *Les évêques normands du XIe siècle: Colloque de Cerisy-la-Salle (30 septembre–3 octobre 1993)* (Caen, 1995); and David Douglas, "Les évêques de Normandie (1035–1066)," *Annales de Normandie* 8 (1958), 87–102.

[12] By contrast, studies on the bishop in Late Antiquity are positively thriving: see Claudia Rapp, *Holy Bishops in Late Antiquity: The Nature of Christian Leadership in an Age of Transition*, The Transformation of the Classical Heritage 37 (Berkeley, CA, 2005); Andrea Sterk, *Renouncing the World Yet Leading the Church: The Monk-Bishop in Late Antiquity* (Cambridge, MA, 2004); Eva Elm, *Die Macht der Weisheit: Das Bild des Bischofs in der Vita Augustini des Possidius und anderen spätantiken und frühmittelalterlichen Bischofsviten*, Studies in the History of Christian Thought 109 (Leiden, 2003); Raymond Van Dam, *Leadership and Community in Late Antique Gaul*, The Transformation of the Late Antique Heritage 8 (Berkeley, CA, 1985), to name only a few.

[13] Constance Hoffman Berman ed., *Medieval Religion: New Approaches* (New York, 2005).

[14] This assertion is not intended to diminish the numerous monographs and articles that continue to appear on the lives, works, and times of individual bishops or dioceses.

[15] Recently surveyed by John Van Engen, "The Future of Medieval Church History," *Church History* 71 (2002), 492–522.

structures. We examine each of these broader interpretive frameworks, and their implications for the representation of the episcopate, below.

Concurrently, soaring scholarly interest in the experiences and identities of religious minorities, such as heretics and dissenters, and social minorities, above all women and non-elites, appears to have fostered a general disinterest in the study of bishops and secular clergy, in part because they are frequently viewed as the exemplars of an institution that sought to silence those minorities. Obviously, bishops were likely to come face-to-face with religious dissenters when they appeared in their dioceses. Bishop Gerard I of Cambrai's (1012–1051) famous confrontation with heretics at Arras in 1025, treated in Theo Riches's essay (Chapter 7), gave him the opportunity to expound before a captive audience his theology of the church as a material and spiritual signifier of the Christian community. Where, Gerard asked the members of the heretical sect, did they think the spirit of eternal life would come to them, if not in the churchyard where the penitent are properly buried? In that very place the faithful come together to await judgment with the spiritual community of their fellow Christians. Gerard of Cambrai's altogether traditional associations between the material aspects of the church and the community of faithful came to be rejected by a growing number of people in the twelfth century, for whom religious community was created through access to sacred texts, visions, or charismatic leaders, not in the physical church or through the figure of the bishop.

As representatives of the church hierarchy, bishops are frequently alleged to have sought firm control over expressions of religiosity among the flocks under their care. In a limited sense, this is a fair assertion. In an ongoing attempt to maintain the boundaries of orthodoxy—and to keep the Muslim, heretic, or Jew safely distinct and outside the community of the faithful—bishops led crusades, presided over inquisitorial inquiries into heterodox beliefs and behaviors, and looked with suspicion or disdain on the affective mysticism and communal lifestyles of pious men and women.[16] Bishops sometimes waged this fight by channeling kinetic religious enthusiasms into "safe" environments, above all monasteries. Scholars have shown that bishops were frequently avid supporters of new religious communities and orders in the twelfth century, and that they fostered the reform of countless individual religious houses. They also tolerated—far more than is generally allowed—the presence of charismatic itinerant preachers in their midst, whom they often saw as living spectacles of spiritual devotion worthy of emulation by their parishioners. After all, was not the bishop a spectacle himself? Gregory the Great's foundational *Rule of Pastoral Care* (*Regula pastoralis*) certainly held so.[17] The willingness of some bishops to welcome the presence of preachers and hermits at their courts was even satirized quite pointedly in a poem of about 1130, penned by an archdeacon of

---

[16] R.N. Swanson, *Religion and Devotion in Europe, c. 1215–c. 1515* (Cambridge, 1995), pp. 108–16, 177–82.

[17] Gregory the Great, *Règle pastorale* [hereafter *RP*], Prologue, ed. and trans. Bruno Judic, Floribert Rommel, and Charles Morel, Sources chrétiennes 381–82, 2 vols (Paris, 1992), 1:124–27.

Chartres and widely read by contemporaries.[18] The extent to which bishops sought to control expressions of religiosity in their provinces must remain open to question and close scrutiny. The reality is that most bishops walked a tightrope between fostering the salutary example of those who had rejected the world or its institutions in the name of leading an apostolic life, and trying to ensure that rejection of the world did not mean rejection of its proper authorities. This was no easy task.

Episcopal office was, as its medieval commentators knew, an almost impossible balancing act, and the occupants of that office negotiated between competing ideals or behavior that resulted in a position best described—to borrow from the title of Thomas Head's Postscript (chapter 14)—as ambiguous. "The governance of souls" alone—let alone juggling it with secular administration—"was the art of arts."[19] The conscientious pastor negotiated countless demands: demands of parishioners and subordinate clergy, family and kin, pope and king, the powerful and the powerless, zealous believers and the religiously aloof. Gregory's *Rule of Pastoral Care*, the closest thing to a standardized text on episcopal conduct the Middle Ages possessed, likened the pastor's need to weigh his secular and spiritual obligations to the length of the hair on his head: overly long locks signified preoccupation with things external to the spirit, whereas a fastidiously shaved head signaled its bearer's attention to spiritual needs to the exclusion of quotidian demands. In contrast to both, the bishop's hair should be neither shaved nor luxurious, but sufficiently shorn to reveal his eyes, the seat of his discernment and the gaze which penetrated the souls of men.[20] If scholars are increasingly sensitive to the multiplicity of demands on bishops and the variability of regional clerical cultures, they have nevertheless directed their own eyes toward theoretical ideals (medieval and modern) or interpretive frameworks of episcopal conduct imposed from outside the bishop's immediate social context. We turn now to examine two influential and related examples of this practice.

The Bishop as Lord

Throughout Late Antiquity and the Middle Ages, the bishop functioned both as pastor and administrator of a temporal estate, with all the responsibilities that came with the latter function. Despite the long-standing nature of this arrangement, attention to the bishop's role as landed lord has predominated in scholarship of the years from *c*.900 to 1050; it is telling, for example, that in Heinrich Fichtenau's study of the tenth century, discussion of the bishop appears primarily in the section entitled "Nobilitas," rather than that concerning "Religio."[21] This emphasis results, at least in part, from the fact that bishops themselves have rarely been the focus of study. Rather, exploration of the episcopate in this period has tended to appear within the context of other subjects, particularly the fragmentation of the Carolingian Empire

---

[18]   Jean Leclercq, "Le poème de Payen Bolotin contres les faux ermites," *Revue bénédictine* 68 (1958), 52–86.

[19]   *RP*, 1.1, 1:128–29.

[20]   *RP*, 2.7, 1:220–21 and 1:228–31.

[21]   Fichtenau, *Living in the Tenth Century* (above, n. 10), pp. 181–216.

and the proliferation of smaller territorial lordships—the much-debated "feudal revolution."

The period stretching from *c*.900 to 1050, sometimes referred to as the "long tenth century," is only recently emerging from a period of general scholarly neglect, in which it was seen as a dark age both in the supposed proliferation of violence and in the lack of surviving sources.[22] The vision of the episcopacy in these years as deeply implicated in politics, before a papally-driven reform attempted to separate the church from worldly power, was enshrined in the contribution of Émile Amann and Auguste Dumas to the multi-volume church history edited by Augustin Fliche and Victor Martin, dramatically titled *L'Église au pouvoir des laïques (888–1057)*.[23] Amann and Dumas emphasized the bishops' relations with temporal powers, describing the role of princes in episcopal elections and devoting an entire chapter to "la féodalité épiscopale," which outlined the development of episcopal estates and the services owed by bishops to princes in exchange for their lands. Less attention was paid, by contrast, to other aspects of the episcopal office, such as their pastoral or intellectual activity. The tone of disapproval in the title of the volume is carried over into the text as the authors foreshadow the coming Gregorian movement; the title of one chapter, "The Vices of the Clergy and the Hope for a Reform of the Secular Church," shows much about the assumptions of the authors concerning this time period and its place in the history of the medieval church.

Following the lead of Amann and Dumas, much subsequent scholarly attention to bishops has focused on their political role and appears in studies of political and social change in western Continental Europe around the year 1000. This has been a rich field of inquiry, sparked by the publication of Georges Duby's seminal study of the Mâconnais in 1953.[24] A number of regional studies in the mold of Duby have included the activities of bishops in their discussions, but the prelates have not often

---

[22] Timothy Reuter, "Introduction: Reading the Tenth Century," in *The New Cambridge Medieval History*, vol. 3, *c. 900–c. 1024*, pp. 1–24.

[23] Émile Amann and Auguste Dumas, *L'Église au pouvoir des laïques (888–1057)*, vol. 7 in *Histoire de l'Église depuis les origines jusqu'à nos jours*, ed. Augustin Fliche and Victor Martin ([Paris], 1940).

[24] Georges Duby, *La société aux XIe et XIIe siècles dans la region mâconnaise* (Paris, 1953). Duby's model is supported in Jean-Pierre Poly and Eric Bournazel, *La mutation féodale: Xe–XIIe siècle*, 2nd edn (Paris, 1991), and most notably among the regional studies by Pierre Bonnassie, *La Catalogne du milieu du Xe à la fin du XIe siècle: Croissance et mutations d'une société*, Publications de l'Université de Toulouse-Le Mirail A23 and 29, 2 vols (Toulouse, 1975–1976). The strongest voice against *mutationnisme* has been Dominique Barthélemy, most notably in *La société dans le comté de Vendôme, de l'an mil au XIVe siècle* (Paris, 1993) and *La mutation de l'an mil a-t-elle eu lieu? Servage et chevalerie dans la France des Xe et XIe siècles* (Paris, 1997). For a recent debate on the issue, see Thomas N. Bisson, "The 'Feudal Revolution,'" *Past and Present* 142 (1994), 6–42, and responses by Dominique Barthélemy, Stephen D. White, Timothy Reuter, Chris Wickham, and Thomas Bisson, "Debate: The 'Feudal Revolution,'" *Past and Present* 152 (1996), 196–223, and 155 (1997), 177–225.

been a focus.[25] Rather, their status, their elections, and the development of their lordships have been used to chart either the persistence of public power or—if the bishoprics fell into the hands of noble families—of the rise of territorial lordships that encompassed former public offices such as count and bishop.[26] While scholars have in general paid more attention to the bishops' political activities than to other aspects of their office, it is important to note that there are exceptions: Elisabeth Magnou-Nortier's study of the interactions between the lay nobility and the church in the Narbonnais, for example, includes a long consideration of the bishop's role, including election procedures and ideals of episcopal behavior as well as the assembling of episcopal estates.[27] The fact remains, however, that even studies devoted to the bishops of this period tend to focus on their ties to aristocratic families and the development of the bishop's temporal power and property, rather than on the entirety of their office.[28]

---

[25]   Steven Fanning, in his study of the career of Bishop Hubert of Angers (1006–1047), bemoaned the almost complete absence of similar works on bishops in tenth- and early eleventh-century France: *A Bishop and his World before the Gregorian Reform: Hubert of Angers, 1006–1047*, Transactions of the American Philosophical Society 78 (Philadelphia, 1988), pp. 10–12. Fanning notes that a number of regional studies, including Duby's, do not address bishops. Others study bishops only very briefly and usually from the point of view of the development of comital power (p. 12 nn. 37–41).

[26]   For example, Christian Lauranson-Rosaz, in his chapter on the development of the Auvergnat church, looks at episcopal power in relation to that of the count, the development of episcopal lordship, and the phenomenon of the chorepiscopate, as well as devoting considerable space to the efforts of Bishop Gui of Le Puy in the early councils of the Peace of God: *L'Auvergne et ses marges (Velay, Gévaudan) du VIIIe au XIe siècle: La fin du monde antique?* (Le Puy-en-Velay, 1987), pp. 232–42, 412–30; André Debord, *La société laïque dans les pays de la Charente, Xe–XIIe siècles* (Paris, 1984), was interested primarily in the development of the episcopal domain, the bishops' role in castle building, and their relations with the counts of Angoulême (see for example pp. 92, 94, 113, and 149); Jean-Pierre Poly examines bishoprics in Provence as an example of public institutions that survived in the tenth century, but were seized by the comital families around the year 1000 (*La Provence et la société féodale (879–1166)* [Paris, 1976], pp. 56–87). In some cases, as Olivier Guyotjeannin has shown, the office of bishop was fused with that of the local lay lord; see his *Episcopus et comes* (above, n. 4).

[27]   Elisabeth Magnou-Nortier, *La société laïque et l'Église dans la province ecclésiastique de Narbonne (zone cispyrénéenne) de la fin du VIIIe à la fin du XIe siècle*, Publications de l'Université de Toulouse-Le Mirail A20 (Toulouse, 1974), pp. 315–78.

[28]   See, for example, Jean-Louis Biget, "L'épiscopat de Rouergue et de l'Albigeois (Xe-XIe siècle)," in *Catalunya i França meridional a l'entorn de l'any mil*, ed. Xavier Barral i Altet et al. (Barcelona, 1991), pp. 181–99; Reinhold Kaiser, *Bischofsherrschaft zwischen Königtum und Fürstenmacht: Studien zur bischöflichen Stadtherrschaft im westfränkisch-französischen Reich im frühen und hohen Mittelalter*, Pariser historische Studien 17 (Bonn, 1981); idem, "Les évêques neustriens du Xe siècle dans l'exercice de leur pouvoir temporel d'après l'historiographie médiévale," in *Pays de Loire et Aquitaine de Robert le Fort aux premiers Capétiens*, ed. Olivier Guillot and Robert Favreau (Poitiers, 1997), pp. 117–43; Muriel Laharie, "Évêques et société en Périgord du Xe au milieu du XII siècle," *Annales du Midi* 94 (1982), 343–68; George Dameron, *Episcopal Power and Florentine Society, 1000–1320* (Cambridge, MA, 1991).

Scholarship on episcopal lordship (*Bischofsherrschaft*) has been a particular focus of the historiography of the German church in the long tenth century. The Carolingian and Ottonian kings and emperors leaned heavily on episcopal support to administer their kingdoms, to carry Christianity to non-Christian peoples at the peripheries of their realms, to serve as diplomats and emissaries, to oversee the religious discipline of their subjects, and to keep in check ambitious noble families. The co-dependency between bishop and monarch grew so strong that German historians coined the term *Reichskirchensystem* as a shorthand way of indicating this dominant characteristic of the Carolingian and Ottonian churches.[29] Early historians of *Bischofsherrschaft* probed the origins of the episcopate's administrative, jurisdictional, or secular features, often looking backward from the Ottonian and Salian kingdoms, when these facets of episcopal governance were well established, to uncover their origins.[30] The *Reichskirchensystem*, so the earlier thesis held, remained intact until the Gregorian reform undermined its harmonious operation by opening an ideological fissure between secular government and the church.[31] It even spawned a particular kind of prelate, the so-called courtier bishop, whose career took root in the imperial chapel, and whose written biographies formed a distinct sub-genre of episcopal biography.[32]

---

[29] Timothy Reuter, "The 'Imperial Church System' of the Ottonian and Salian Rulers: A Reconsideration," *Journal of Ecclesiastical History* 33 (1982), 347–74, has ameliorated historians' overdependence on the concept, but belief in the existence of a *Reichskirchensystem* as a model for episcopal–monarchic relations stimulated much early research on *Bischofsherrschaft* and continues to have many adherents. See the important recent article of Hartmut Hoffmann, "Der König und seine Bischöfe in Frankreich und im Deutschen Reich, 936–1060," in *Bischof Burchard von Worms*, ed. Hartmann, pp. 79–127.

[30] Among earlier studies was that of the American Edgar Nathaniel Johnson, *The Secular Activities of the German Episcopate, 919–1024*, The University Studies of the University of Nebraska 30–31 (Lincoln, NE, 1932), which stressed (pp. 96–100) the economic and political interests of the state in promoting secular clergy to episcopal office. A raft of studies by German scholars expanded the field to encompass early medieval institutional, prosopographical, and urban contexts; for example, Friedrich Prinz, *Klerus und Krieg im früheren Mittelalter: Untersuchungen zur Rolle der Kirche beim Aufbau der Königsherrschaft*, Monographien zur Geschichte des Mittelalters 2 (Stuttgart, 1971); idem, "Die bischöfliche Stadtherrschaft im Frankenreich vom 5. bis zum 7. Jahrhundert," *Historische Zeitschrift* 217 (1973), 1–35; Martin Heinzelmann, *Bischofsherrschaft in Gallien: Zur Kontinuität römischer Führungsschichten vom 4. bis zum 7. Jahrhundert: Soziale, prosopographische und bildungsgeschichtliche Aspekte*, Beihefte der Francia 5 (Zurich, 1976); Georg Scheibelreiter, *Der Bischof in merowingischer Zeit*, Veröffentlichungen des Instituts für Österreichische Geschichtsforschung 27 (Vienna, 1983); Reinhold Kaiser, *Bischofsherrschaft zwischen Königtum und Fürstenmacht* (above, n. 28), at pp. 7–8; and, for a summation of research, Friedrich Prinz, "Herrschaftsformen der Kirche vom Ausgang der Spätantike bis zum Ende der Karolingerzeit," in *Herrschaft und Kirche: Beiträge zur Entstehung und Wirkungsweise episkopaler und monastischer Organisationsformen*, ed. Friedrich Prinz (Stuttgart, 1988), pp. 1–21, and that volume's essays by Martin Heinzelmann, Reinhold Kaiser, and Georg Jenal.

[31] Reuter, "'Imperial Church System,'" pp. 349, 369–70.

[32] C. Stephen Jaeger, "The Courtier Bishop in *Vitae* from the Tenth to the Twelfth Century," *Speculum* 58 (1983), 291–325; idem, *The Origins of Courtliness: Civilizing Trends and the*

Historiography on episcopal lordship and on episcopal involvement in lay power structures in this period has made important contributions to our understanding of bishops. This research has shown that bishops were among the elites of society: prosopographical studies of episcopal familial origins confirm this fact from Late Antiquity up through the twelfth century.[33] Studies of episcopal lordship have thus illuminated a crucial, indeed central, aspect of the medieval bishop's experience—his activities as warriors, lords, builders, diplomats, and administrators. Conversely, this focus on episcopal lordship has presented problems for our understanding of tenth-century bishops. First, the religious aspects of the episcopal office, if they were discussed at all, took second place to the political. Second, some of the work on episcopal involvement in worldly activities and power has been tinged with disapproval, stemming from one of two sources. On the one hand, early studies on bishops' institutional connections and political or territorial interests often implicitly bore the patina of Marxist philosophy and its criticism of religion as a mask for power and its material trappings.[34] On the other, the view of reformers who opined that bishops had no business in lay politics has been influential in shaping scholarly opinion of bishops in the central Middle Ages, and has obscured the fact that such a separation of the bishop's worldly and religious powers would have been alien to most prelates in this period.

Formation of Courtly Ideals, 939–1210 (Philadelphia, 1985). On episcopal *vitae* from tenth- through twelfth-century Germany, see the important new study by Stephanie Haarländer, *Vitae episcoporum: Eine Quellengattung zwischen Hagiographie und Historiographie, untersucht an Lebensbeschreibungen von Bischöfen des Regnum Teutonicum im Zeitalter der Ottonen und Salier*, Monographien zur Geschichte des Mittelalters 47 (Stuttgart, 2000).

[33]   These studies were undertaken almost precisely at the moment when German historians opened up the field of episcopal lordship. For Frankish bishops, see Jean Gaudemet, "Recherches sur l'épiscopat médiéval en France," in *Proceedings of the Second International Congress of Medieval Canon Law, Boston College, 12–16 August 1963*, ed. Stephan Kuttner and J. Joseph Ryan (Vatican City, 1965), pp. 139–54 (mostly covering the late twelfth and thirteenth centuries); Léopold Genicot, "Haut clergé, princes et nobles dans le diocèse de Liège du XIe au XVe siècle," in idem, *Études sur les principautés lotharingiennes*, Université de Louvain, Recueil de Travaux d'Histoire et de Philologie, 6th ser., fasc. 7 (Louvain, 1975), pp. 140–71 (which first appeared in Gerd Tellenbach, Josef Fleckenstein, and Karl Schmid, eds, *Adel und Kirche: Gerd Tellenbach zum 65. Geburtstag dargebracht von Freunden und Schülern* [Freiburg, 1968]); Bernard Guillemain, "Les origines des évêques en France aux XIe et XII siècles," in *Le istituzioni ecclesiastiche della 'societas christiana' dei secoli XI–XII: Papato, cardinalato ed episcopato. Atti della quinta Settimana internazionale di studio (Mendola, 26–31 agosto 1971)*, Miscellanea del Centro di studi medioevali 7 (Milan, 1974), pp. 374–402. For German bishops, see the survey of Carlrichard Brühl, "Die Sozialstruktur des deutschen Episkopats im 11. und 12. Jahrhundert," in *Le istituzioni ecclesiastiche della "societas christiana" dei secoli XI–XII: Diocesi, pievi e parrocchie. Atti della sesta Settimana internazionale di studio (Milano, 1–7 settembre 1974)*, Miscellanea del Centro di studi medioevali 8 (Milan, 1977), pp. 42–56; Herbert Zielinksi, *Der Reichsepiskopat in spätottonischer und salischer Zeit, 1002–1125* (Stuttgart, 1984); and A. Graf Finck von Finckenstein, *Bischof und Reich: Untersuchungen zum Integrationsprozess des ottonischen– frühsalischen Reiches (919–1056)* (Sigmaringen, 1989).

[34]   Discussed in Prinz, "Herrschaftsformen der Kirche," pp. 1–2.

In recent years, however, writing on episcopal lordship has moved in several profitable directions. First, the dual nature of the bishop's office, the close relations between bishops and lay authorities, and the temporal activities of the bishop have increasingly been studied without any hint of the criticism present in some earlier work. This has allowed historians to explore fully the complexity of the episcopal office and of the bishops' attitude towards their own role.[35] Indeed, scholars have begun to explore the evidence that the bishops' position at the junction of various networks of power gave them a very particular type of authority, which made them effective as judges and mediators.[36] Historians of diplomatics have begun to plumb the role of charters in the expression of episcopal authority and lordship in this period, as part of a growing emphasis on the role of literacy in the early and high Middle Ages.[37] Essays in this volume contribute to this trend in two ways. Anna Trumbore Jones's article (Chapter 2) refines our understanding of the relations between bishops and lay lords by investigating the case of the dukes of Aquitaine and the bishops of Poitiers, and showing that while the influence of the dukes over the see was important, it was neither as long-standing nor as all-encompassing as has been assumed. Other contributors expand our knowledge of the episcopate in this period by moving away from an exclusive focus on episcopal lordship. Renée R. Trilling (Chapter 4) demonstrates the complexity of relations (on both the theoretical and practical level) between religious and secular authorities in this period in her examination of the *Institutes of Polity* of Archbishop Wulfstan of York (1002–1023). In this text, Wulfstan, hoping to mitigate the political turmoil facing Anglo-Saxon England during his reign, lays out a plan for the administration of civil society by

---

[35] See, for example, the studies by Constance Brittain Bouchard, "The Bishop as Aristocrat: The Case of Hugh of Chalon," in *The Bishop*, ed. Gilsdorf (above, n. 2), pp. 37–49, and *Spirituality and Administration: The Role of the Bishop in Twelfth-Century Auxerre*, Speculum Anniversary Monographs 5 (Cambridge, MA, 1979); Bowman, "The Bishop Builds a Bridge," pp. 3–6; John Nightingale, "Bishop Gerard of Toul (963–94) and Attitudes to Episcopal Office," in *Warriors and Churchmen*, ed. Reuter (above, n. 8), pp. 41–62; Michel Parisse, "Princes laïques et/ou moines: Les évêques du Xe siècle," in *Il secolo di ferro: Mito e realtà del secolo X, 19–25 aprile 1990*, Settimane di studio del Centro italiano di studi sull'alto Medioevo 38 (Spoleto, 1991), pp. 449–516.

[36] Jeffrey Bowman, *Shifting Landmarks: Property, Proof and Dispute in Catalonia around the Year 1000* (Ithaca, NY, 2004), pp. 100–108; Sean Gilsdorf, "Bishops in the Middle: Mediatory Politics and the Episcopacy," in *The Bishop*, ed. Gilsdorf, pp. 51–73; Wilfried Hartmann, "L'évêque comme juge: La pratique du tribunal episcopal en France du Xe au XIIe siècle," in *Hiérarchies et services au Moyen Âge*, ed. Claude Carozzi and Huguette Taviani-Carozzi (Aix-en-Provence, 2001), pp. 71–92; Adam J. Kosto, "Oliba, Peacemaker," in *Actes del Congrés Internacional Gerbert d'Orlhac*, ed. Imma Ollich i Castanyer (Vic, 1999), pp. 135–49, which includes a survey of recent historiography.

[37] Hubert Flammarion, "Les textes diplomatiques langrois et le pouvoir des évêques aux IXe et Xe siècles," in *Les actes comme expression de pouvoir au Haut Moyen Âge: Actes de la Table Ronde de Nancy, 26–27 novembre 1999*, ed. Marie-José Gasse-Grandjean and Benoît-Michel Tock, Atelier de Recherches sur les Textes Médiévaux 5 (Turnhout, 2003), pp. 51–68; Joseph Avril, "La fonction épiscopale dans le vocabulaire des chartes (Xe–XIIe siècles)," in *Horizons marins, itinéraires spirituels (Ve–XVIIIe siècles)*, ed. Henri Dubois, Jean-Claude Hocquet, and André Vauchez, 2 vols (Paris, 1987), 1:125–33.

God through his representative, the king. Trilling's close reading, however, reveals the tensions within Wulfstan's text, as it is in fact the bishop, not the king, who takes center-stage in the government he envisions. Eric Palazzo and Evan Gatti (Chapters 5 and 6) analyze the evidence found in liturgical books and their decoration for contemporary understandings of the episcopal office. Palazzo surveys the correlative position of the bishop in his social and liturgical contexts from the early to late Middle Ages, while Gatti, in a detailed study of the Benedictional of Engilmar of Parenzo (modern Poreč, Croatia), suggests that the Benedictional's liturgical portrait of Engilmar offering a blessing presents a counterpoint to traditional episcopal "iconographies of secular power."

Episcopal Identity, Representation, and Ecclesiastical Reform

As we have already noted, scholarly debate about the role of the bishop in European society has been guided and greatly influenced by the emphasis on reform in the historiography of the medieval church.[38] Suspended against the ebb and flow of numerous and varied ecclesiastical reforms over the course of the Middle Ages, the eleventh and twelfth centuries have traditionally been considered an epoch of enormous, even revolutionary, consequence for Christian and European history. The pontificate of Gregory VII (1073–1085) and those of his immediate predecessors and successors continue to enjoy a central place in narratives treating ecclesiastical history.[39]

As the emphasis on Gregory and his colleagues suggests, church reform has often been viewed as a revolution initiated *par en haut*, to use the phrase of Jean-François Lemarignier, with the centralization of papal power and the popes' drumbeat stress on the hieratic nature of priestly authority slowly eroding local traditions of episcopal autonomy and administration.[40] More recently, scholars have modified this view. In addition to individual initiatives on the part of clergy and laity, calls to reform issued from orthodox and heterodox sects, institutions, and religious orders, the Peace and Truce of God movement, and civic or communal campaigns.[41]

---

[38]   See again Van Engen, "Future of Medieval Church History," pp. 492–97.

[39]   Jean-François Lemarignier, Jean Gaudemet, and Guillaume Mollat, *Histoire des institutions françaises au Moyen Age*, vol. 3, *Institutions ecclésiastiques* (Paris, 1962), p. 78: "On a pu dire qu'elle [the gregorian reform] avait été la première révolution européenne, et c'est sans doute à juste titre qu'on lui a donné le nom du pape Grégoire VII qui, avant et pendant son pontificat (1073–1085), en a été le principal artisan. . . ."

[40]   Jean-François Lemarignier, "Les institutions ecclésiastiques en France de la fin du Xe au milieu du XIIe siècle," in *Histoire des institutions françaises*, ed, Lemarignier et al., vol. 3, *Institutions ecclésiastiques*, p. 78. See also Werner Goez, *"Papa qui et episcopus*: Zum Selbstverständnis des Reformpapsttums im 11. Jahrhundert," *Archivum Historiae Pontificiae* 8 (1970), 27–59.

[41]   Giving voice to popular participation in the process of social and clerical reform has been a central preoccupation of historians for the past several decades. Scholarly efforts have generally centered attention on the Peace and Truce of God and on the kernels of social protest seemingly embedded in the heretical movements of the early eleventh and twelfth centuries. An early piece that stressed the laity's desire to put an end to conflict was Loren C. MacKinney,

The modern explication *par excellence* of papally-driven reform, and its resistance by bishops with vested interests in the status quo, was that of Augustin Fliche (1884–1951), professor at the Université de Montpellier. Fliche's seminal and pugilistically-titled *La réforme grégorienne et la reconquête chrétienne (1057–1123)* generally portrayed the episcopate and priesthood—*pace* those few prelates who sympathized with the initiatives of papal reform—as obdurate resisters to needed changes within the institutional church.[42] Steadily pressured by Rome, these simoniacs, fornicators, and old guard stonewallers slowly yielded place to canonically-elected, reform-minded bishops. A crucial wedge driven by papal reformers into the power base of Europe's bishops was their insistence on *obedientia*, clerical obedience to St Peter and his heirs. For instance, Rome claimed the power—usually in the face of vigorous episcopal protest—to adjudicate local disputes, long the province of archbishops and metropolitans. Viewed through the lenses of the reformist agenda, a bishop who recognized and ultimately acceded to papal authority in matters pertaining to clerical discipline and morality, monastic autonomy, and the removal of secular influence from the church's ministry bore the mark of a "reformer" or "Gregorian."[43] Those who did not—like the twenty-six bishops who assembled at Worms in early 1076 and renounced their obedience to Gregory VII—courted heresy.[44] Where reform succeeded, Fliche credited the impulse to remove the laity and their episcopal creatures from church governance.[45]

"The People and Public Opinion in the Eleventh-Century Peace Movement," *Speculum* 5 (1930), 181–206. See more recently R.I. Moore, "Family, Community and Cult on the Eve of the Gregorian Reform," *Transactions of the Royal Historical Society*, 5th ser., 30 (1980), 49–69; and the collected essays in *The Peace of God: Social Violence and Religious Response in France around the Year 1000*, ed. Thomas Head and Richard Landes (Ithaca, NY, 1992), especially the article there by Amy G. Remensnyder, "Pollution, Purity, and Peace: An Aspect of Social Reform between the Late Tenth Century and 1076," pp. 280–307. On urban or civic contexts for action, see below.

[42] Augustin Fliche, *La réforme grégorienne et la reconquête chrétienne (1057–1123)*, vol. 8 in *Histoire de l'Église depuis les origines jusqu'à nos jours* ([Paris], 1940), pp. 65, 73, 84–89, 100–101, and elsewhere. This, Fliche's contribution to the *Histoire de l'Église* series he co-edited with Victor Martin, followed upon his own earlier work, *La réforme grégorienne*, 3 vols (Louvain and Paris, 1924–1937), and the preceding volume in the same series by Amann and Dumas, *L'Église au pouvoir des laïques* (above, n. 23).

[43] Hierarchy of authority culminating in the pope was likewise stressed in legal collections assembled in papal circles in the late eleventh century. See I.S. Robinson, *Authority and Resistance in the Investiture Contest: The Polemical Literature of the Late Eleventh Century* (Manchester, 1978); Jean Gaudemet, *Le gouvernement de l'Église à l'époque classique*, part 2, *Le gouvernement local*, vol. 8/2 in *Histoire du droit et des institutions de l'Église en occident*, ed. Gabriel Le Bras and Jean Gaudemet (Paris, 1979), pp. 43–47; Gerd Tellenbach, *The Church in Western Europe from the Tenth to the Early Twelfth Century*, trans. Timothy Reuter (Cambridge, 1993), pp. 308–12 (the German original appeared as *Die westliche Kirche vom 10. bis zum frühen 12. Jahrhundert* [Göttingen, 1988]).

[44] I.S. Robinson, "'Periculosus Homo': Pope Gregory VII and Episcopal Authority," *Viator* 9 (1978), 103–31.

[45] Fliche, *La réforme grégorienne*, pp. 407–9.

Significantly, the core principles of moral and disciplinary reform as elucidated by Fliche and his disciples bore an aura of intellectual coherence, doctrinal orthodoxy, canonical precedent—and inexorable achievement. The transformation of the Latin church as recounted in *La réforme grégorienne* delineated an ascending arc, a telos, culminating in the papal monarchy.[46] Fliche and others stressed that the papal vision of world order eventually triumphed over the imperial. Its victorious standard was raised in 1215 at the Fourth Lateran Council, during the pontificate of Innocent III. Rome's ascendance would cement, in both medieval and modern historiography, "Gregorian" ideals as benchmarks for analyzing the words and deeds of medieval prelates before and after the phase of reform which concluded with the Concordat of Worms in 1122.

Since its appearance more than sixty-five years ago, Fliche's influential synthesis has been modified in numerous ways. Scholars have rehabilitated individual prelates in the post-Carolingian world from the imputation of incompetence, self-interest, or vice; they have explored regional initiatives of church reform before and after 1050; and they have placed episcopal notions of reform into local, legal, literary, and artistic contexts, furnishing a counterweight to Fliche's pronounced Romano-centric bias.[47] Still, we have not always avoided projecting the ideological norms born of papal reform into locales where Roman authority had at best a restrained influence, if any at all.[48] Although held with increasing regularity from the eleventh century onwards, transalpine councils presided over by papal legates or the pope himself had a relatively limited effect in modifying local religious customs and were infrequently convened outside Italy and France.[49] Certainly, papal legates adjudicated disputes between local monasteries and their prelates. They deposed,

---

[46]   See the comments of Cinzio Violante, "La réforme ecclésiastique du XIe siècle: Une synthèse progressive d'idées et de structures opposées," *Le Moyen Âge* 97 (1991), 355–65. Of course, the leading intellectuals of the papal reform held different perspectives on various issues, notably on the question of the validity of sacraments performed by simoniac priests, but these debates were contained within a relatively enclosed intellectual atmosphere.

[47]   A sampling of post-Flichian works includes: Bouchard, "The Bishop as Aristocrat" (above, n. 35); Sébastien Peigné, "Les évêques de Nantes et la réforme grégorienne (vers 1060–1140)," in *Église et société dans l'Ouest Atlantique du Moyen Âge au XXe siècle*, ed. Marcel Launay, Centre de Recherches sur l'Histoire du Monde Atlantique, Enquêtes et documents 27 (Nantes, 2000), pp. 11–26; Jean-Marie Mayeur, Charles and Luce Pietri, André Vauchez, and Marc Venard eds, *Histoire du Christianisme des origines à nos jours*, vol. 4, *Evêques, moines et empereurs (610–1054)* ([Paris], 1993), esp. chapter three; Werner Goez, "Riforma ecclesiastica—Riforma gregoriana," *Studi gregoriani* 13 (Rome, 1989), 167–78; John Howe, "The Nobility's Reform of the Medieval Church," *The American Historical Review* 93 (1988), 317–39, with extensive bibliography; Jacques Boussard, "Les évêques en Neustrie avant la réforme grégorienne (950–1050 environ)," *Journal des savants*, s.n. (1970), 161–96.

[48]   As Constance Brittain Bouchard, *Sword, Mitre, and Cloister: Nobility and the Church in Burgundy, 980–1198* (Ithaca, NY, 1987), pp. 100–101, has noted, and as Tellenbach, *Church in Western Europe*, p. 312 and passim, reminds us.

[49]   Amann and Dumas, *L'Église au pouvoir des laïques*, pp. 172–73; Fliche, *La réforme grégorienne*, pp. 34–38, 89–95; Lemarignier et al., *Histoire des institutions françaises*, vol. 3, *Institutions ecclésiastiques*, pp. 83–85. For the clergy's own initiatives at reform, see

excommunicated, and humbled bishops acting in violation of canon law.[50] But they had little practical power to instill unilateral changes in local clerical culture, and in some cases were obliged to soften or modify standing Roman synodal judgments in deference to prevailing political conditions.[51] In fact, beyond the Alps regional customs and cultures conditioned the meaning and perception of practices such as simony, clerical marriage, and lay involvement in church affairs. Any or all might be embraced not only as socially or culturally normative, but as critical for the proper functioning of an orderly society.[52] By favoring Roman experiences and expectations, we have either bypassed the ideologies and roles of prelates in local contexts altogether, awkwardly apologized for them, or forcibly made them conform to ideas and practices that were ideologically or culturally foreign to the bishops and the people they shepherded.[53]

Several of the chapters in this collection take up precisely this issue. Theo Riches, John S. Ott, and John Eldevik all demonstrate, in their chapters on the bishops of Mainz and Cambrai (Chapters 7, 8, and 9), that classifying prelates or episcopal ideologies as either essentially "Gregorian"—or, conversely, "imperial"—often obscures the more complex local identities that bishops and clergy cultivated. Even Archbishop Alfanus I of Salerno, a close friend of Gregory VII and frequent correspondent of Peter Damian, emerges from Valerie Ramseyer's close scrutiny (Chapter 10) as a more complex figure than traditional historiographical frameworks allow. Like some contemporary eleventh-century popes, Alfanus embraced direct military action as a means of combating his political adversaries.[54] His military endeavors, however, also laid the groundwork for pastoral care in his diocese. The

---

Johannes Laudage, *Priesterbild und Reformpapsttum im 11. Jahrhundert* (Cologne, 1984), pp. 90–122.

[50] Papal legate Peter Damian humiliated Drogo, the bishop of Mâcon, at the council of Chalon-sur-Saône, in 1063; see also the letter of Pope Alexander II to the archbishops of Francia (1063), PL 146:1295–96.

[51] As happened during the legatine councils of Stephen of Lorraine in France in 1060; see Lemarignier et al., *Histoire des institutions françaises*, vol. 3, *Institutions ecclésiastiques*, p. 84. Fliche, *La réforme grégorienne*, p. 103, argued that in general "dans l'ensemble [of European states] se dessine un progrès [of reform] qui se révèle plus ou moins accusé."

[52] An important example of a local clerical culture persisting in Rome's shadow, one which both absorbed some mandates of the reform agenda and maintained features particular to itself, is given by Maureen C. Miller, *The Formation of a Medieval Church: Ecclesiastical Change in Verona, 950–1150* (Ithaca, NY, 1993).

[53] When Fliche perceived that individual popes failed to adhere to the reform agenda, he offered apologies for their conduct, as, for example, Alexander II during the Cadalan schism of 1061–1064; *La réforme grégorienne*, p. 25. In some cases, including Boussard's study of the bishops of Neustria (above, n. 47), assertions of regional "backwardness," contrasted with more properly reformist sees, remain. Gerd Tellenbach appositely raises serious questions about the whole concept of "church reform" and its utility as a tool of historical analysis in his *Church in Western Europe*, for example at pp. 157–64, but does not fully pursue analysis of the issue in that work.

[54] Norman Housley, "Crusades against Christians: Their Origins and Early Development, c. 1000–1216," in *The Crusades: The Essential Readings*, ed. Thomas F. Madden (Oxford, 2002), pp. 71–97, at pp. 72–78.

archbishop did not see, as Gregorian reformers would have him see, the importance of divorcing a pastoral duty from his secular role as war-leader. Indeed, the two functions were complementary facets of the same agenda.

Fliche's emphasis on Rome's role was further recalibrated in subsequent decades by scholars' interest in the monastic contribution to ecclesiastical reform. Nearly half a century ago, Jean-François Lemarignier (1908–1980), an influential heir of Fliche, drew attention to the impetus for ecclesiastical and social reform nurtured in monastic circles in Burgundy, Francia, and Normandy from the early tenth century.[55] With the abbey of Cluny as standard-bearer, monks, Lemarignier argued, sought alliances with the papacy to win exemption from episcopal power and jurisdiction. Once monastic exemption was achieved, true reform, freed from the secular interests that bishops frequently represented, could occur.[56] Indeed, in the papal-monastic axis perceived by Lemarignier, bishops played the role of determined counter-resistance—"united, much feared, and well armed"—in the monks' struggle for liberty and exemption from episcopal oversight.[57] Such a division of the medieval religious into camps favoring and opposing monastic ambitions and the push for exemption is simplistic, as subsequent studies of Cluny's own relationship with bishops have shown.[58] A

---

[55]   Lemarignier's studies were by no means the first to stress a monastic contribution to church reform. In a study published in 1892–1894, Ernst Sackur had argued that Cluny and its abbots played a significant role in encouraging the moral reform of the laity and clergy, furnishing a template for later papal efforts along the same lines. See his *Die Cluniacenser in ihrer kirchlichen und allgemeingeschichtlichen Wirksamkeit bis zur Mitte des elften Jahrhunderts*, 2 vols (Halle an der Saale, 1892–1894; repr. Darmstadt, 1965), 2:302–26. Barbara H. Rosenwein, *Rhinoceros Bound: Cluny in the Tenth Century* (Philadelphia, 1982), pp. 3–10, summarizes Sackur's prominent place in earlier Cluniac studies.

[56]   Jean-François Lemarignier, "Political and Monastic Structures in France at the End of the Tenth and the Beginning of the Eleventh Century," in *Lordship and Community in Medieval Europe: Selected Readings*, ed. Fredric L. Cheyette (New York, 1968), pp. 100–27 (originally published as "Structures monastiques et structures politiques dans la France de la fin du Xe et des débuts du XIe siècle," in *Il monachesimo nell'alto Medioevo e la formazione della civiltà occidentale, 8–14 aprile 1956*, Settimane di studio del Centro italiano di studi sull'alto Medioevo 4 [Spoleto, 1957], pp. 357–400); and "L'exemption monastique et les origines de la réforme grégorienne," in idem, *Structures politiques et religieuses dans la France du haut Moyen Âge: Recueil d'articles rassemblés par ses disciples* (Rouen, 1995), pp. 285–337 (first published under the same title in *À Cluny: Congrès scientifique* [Dijon, 1950], pp. 288–340).

[57]   The quotation is from Lemarignier, "Political and Monastic Structures," p. 112. A much-cited example of a reform-minded abbot at odds with his bishop is that of Abbo of Fleury and Bishop Arnulf of Orléans. See Marco Mostert, "L'abbé, l'évêque et le pape: L'image de l'évêque idéal dans les oeuvres d'Abbon de Fleury," in *Religion et culture autour de l'an mil: Royaume capétien et Lotharingie. Actes du colloque Hugues Capet 987–1987: La France de l'an mil*, ed. Dominique Iogna-Prat and Jean-Charles Picard (Paris, 1990), pp. 39–45; Thomas Head, *Hagiography and the Cult of Saints: The Diocese of Orléans, 800–1200* (Cambridge, 1990), chapter six; Barbara H. Rosenwein, Thomas Head, and Sharon Farmer, "Monks and their Enemies: A Comparative Approach," *Speculum* 66 (1991), 764–96, at pp. 780–84.

[58]   Jörg Oberste, "*Contra prelatos qui gravant loca et personas ordinis*: Bischöfe und Cluniazenser im Zeitalter von Krisen und Reformen (12./13. Jahrhundert)," in *Die*

residual image of the bishop as a frequent antagonist of monks has nonetheless remained behind, despite massive evidence of the close bonds bishops and abbots often cultivated, especially in the twelfth and later centuries.[59]

Finally, modern historiography has frequently signaled opposition to episcopal authority and prestige from another quarter: the laity and lower orders of clergy. Certainly, laymen and women vented outrage at the excesses of some clerical conduct, above all incontinence and immorality, just as they did at the arbitrary violence of noblemen.[60] People in some communities feared that clergy polluted by sexual intercourse invalidated the sacraments they ministered and risked the collective well-being and individual souls; Milan furnishes perhaps the best-known example.[61] In order to short-circuit such fears, canon law had long provided that before ordination, would-be bishops and priests renounce their consorts and make assurances that existing children would not inherit control of church property.[62] Yet as late as 1100, the church hierarchy did not consistently insist upon celibacy as a necessary qualification for clerical or even episcopal office.[63] Even in dioceses under the control of celibate "reform" prelates like John of Warneton, bishop of Thérouanne (1099–1130), men in holy orders continued to keep wives and lovers.[64] We may wonder whether the depth of popular opposition to clerical marriage has

---

Cluniazenser in ihrem politisch–sozialen Umfeld, ed. Giles Constable et al., Vita regularis: Ordnungen und Deutungen religiosen Lebens im Mittelalter 7 (Münster, 1998), pp. 349–92; Joachim Mehne, "Cluniacenserbischöfe," *Frühmittelalterliche Studien* 11 (1977), 241–87, with earlier literature.

[59] Oberste, "*Contra prelatos*," pp. 349–51; Martha G. Newman, *The Boundaries of Charity: Cistercian Culture and Ecclesiastical Reform, 1098–1180* (Stanford, CA, 1996).

[60] Bisson, "The 'Feudal Revolution,'" pp. 14–21, 28–33.

[61] The calls for reform of the Pataria, which gripped the see of Ambrose for two long decades, has been surveyed by H.E.J. Cowdrey, "The Papacy, the Patarenes and the Church of Milan," *Transactions of the Royal Historical Society*, 5th ser., 18 (1968), 25–48; Helmut Gritsch, "Die Pataria von Mailand (1057–1075)," *Innsbrucker historische Studien* 3 (1980), 7–42. See also Fliche, *La réforme grégorienne*, pp. 132–33; Moore, "Family, Community and Cult."

[62] Fliche, *La réforme grégorienne*, pp. 28–32.

[63] A significant number of the bishops of Neustria ruling from about 950–1050 examined by Jacques Boussard had children and wives, as did priests; "Les évêques en Neustrie," pp. 186–87. In northern Francia Ansellus of Caix/Boves, an archdeacon of Amiens elected bishop of Beauvais in 1096, most certainly had children and was probably married, as a letter of Ivo of Chartres to the papal legate Hugh of Die suggests. These circumstances delayed, but did not halt, his eventual consecration in June 1099. For Ansellus's career and family, see Guyotjeannin, *Episcopus et comes*, p. 75 and 75 n. 39.

[64] Letter (*c.*1110–1115) of Paschal II to the clergy of Thérouanne: "Gravem valde rem ex partibus vestris audivimus, quia post tanta sancto sanctorum decreta pontificum, post interdicta conciliorum, clericalis ordinis viri, qui audent publice, qui non audent occulte, mulieribus sociantur. Super quibus, preter ceteros pie memorie predecessor noster Urbanus papa constituit, ut officiis simul et beneficiis ecclesie privarentur. Nos quoque ejusdem predecessoris nostri sententie consonantes per presentia scripta precipimus, ut quicumque inter vos clerici ab episcopo suo canonice ammoniti, ab ejusmodi nequitia cessare noluerint, tam officiorum quam beneficiorum privatione plectantur": PL 163:369.

been overstated, when even Rome could rule on the subject with latitude when necessary.

Our understanding of the episcopacy of the central Middle Ages has been broadened considerably by research that has illustrated how papal, monastic, and popular demands for clerical reform molded the episcopacy over the tenth through twelfth centuries. A case in point is found in Dorothy F. Glass's analysis of the sculptural program on the western portal of the cathedral of Piacenza (Chapter 12). After decades in which the city and its prelates were uncomfortably caught between imperial and papal ambitions and agendas, Bishop Arduin of Piacenza (1119–1146/47) commissioned a sculptural program for the cathedral in 1122 that demonstrated his awareness of new Roman artistic models and an emphatic identification with the twelfth-century reform papacy. As the experience of Piacenza shows, episcopal willingness to identify closely with Rome certainly existed. If there is a recurring theme sounded within the diverse body of scholarship that is contained in this volume, it is that bishops reacted to the process of ecclesiastical reform—and also understood reform—both in the terms and ideals set by others *and* through the tailored lens of local custom, tradition, and culture. The essays here collectively remind us that the reality faced by bishops during the arduous decades of reform, and their responses to it, was usually far more complicated than simple labels and prevailing ideologies reveal.

The Aims of this Collection

Before concluding with a description of the aims and objectives of the essays in this volume, it may be helpful to characterize what this collection is not. We have consciously positioned it as a reaction to, not a reaction *against*, the recent historiography of medieval religion, which has placed much-needed emphasis on the experiences of social and religious outsiders. Critics of the medieval institutional church have rightly noted the extent to which church authorities, especially bishops, were instrumental in suppressing minority voices in the Middle Ages—or in rendering them in simplistic hues as orthodox or heterodox, faithful Christian or deviant. But if it has been argued that authorities sought to refashion a complex world of religious and social diversity into two dimensions, composed of insiders and outsiders, the same tactic should not then be exercised upon the bishops themselves.

The essays in this volume strive to re-examine the complexity of the episcopal office and its holder. The contributors signal the bishop's overlapping roles as artistic and architectural patron, as liturgist, as warrior and pastor, as intellectual and lawyer, and, not least, as lord and reformer. Together, they emphasize that the bishop's duties and expectations were multifaceted and fundamentally interconnected—part of a single emotional, psychological, and social whole. Modern scholars—much like the Gregorian reformers and their allies a millennium ago—have often sought to disentangle the bishop's secular and religious roles.[65] To bishops of the central

---

[65]   Lemarignier et al., *Histoire des institutions françaises*, vol. 3, *Institutions ecclésiastiques*, pp. 92–93.

Middle Ages, even after the Concordat of Worms redefined episcopal obligations to secular authorities, such exercises would have seemed a curious example of selective envisioning of their office. The tempestuous ecclesiastical career and political travails of Rather of Verona (*c.* 887-974), which Thomas Head elucidates in his Postscript (Chapter 14), demonstrate the challenge to medieval prelates who sought to align their own experiences with even the very ideals of episcopal office expressed in their writings.

The contributors, perhaps more importantly, have also stressed the extent to which bishops and their activities decisively shaped, and were themselves shaped by, their immediate environments. Local and regional concerns molded episcopal identities and established administrative agendas to a far greater extent than they are often credited with. The debates and mandates of the royal or papal courts at this time were often perceived faintly, a muffled echo against a din of local voices. More pressing concerns of pastoral care, conflict with clergy or aristocratic families, administrative oversight of religious houses, parish churches, and cultic sites—to say nothing of the episcopal *demesne*—required the bishop's immediate attention in a way that distant secular or ecclesiastical overlords did not. As Greta Austin demonstrates in her essay (Chapter 3), such exigencies fueled episcopal appetites before 1050 for copies of canon law collections, which served as guidebooks for navigating the tricky and sometimes treacherous waters of legal precedence and acceptable lay and clerical conduct. In short, bishops had to learn to negotiate multiple and conflicting demands while already on the job. Pressure from the reforming papacy and secular courts added to an already considerable burden, but did not completely refocus episcopal priorities. Episcopal identities instead tended to enfold external demands into their local personae as pastors and administrators, not surrender those local identities entirely. Bruce Brasington's article on Bishop Ivo of Chartres's periodic airing of agitation and outright anger (Chapter 11) in his correspondence illuminates how close, contextualized reading of even official letters can peel back the layers of rhetorical convention to expose an individual temperament in the raw. And as Maureen Miller's contribution on the ritual entry processions of Florentine bishops shows (Chapter 13), local episcopal identities and representations could remain exceptionally stable and resistant to external and internal pressures, even centuries after the eleventh- and twelfth-century reforms and the rise of a centralized papacy. Her essay offers a fitting coda, and a reminder, that even long after the Fourth Lateran Council, regional diversity of episcopal experience was the rule.

As scholars of all disciplines begin to construct a new vision of the medieval religious world, it is crucial that they not do so at the bishop's expense. This means shining the light of critical inquiry on both the center as well as the periphery of society, and of removing the limits that traditional historiographical narratives have imposed on our understanding of the bishop and his many roles. The contributions of studies on episcopal lordship and on the coalescence of a truly international church culminating in Rome have surely deepened our understanding of the episcopate. Studies examining the experiences of male and female religious frequently darkened by the bishop's shadow have done no less. It is time, therefore, that we reform our understanding of the medieval bishop by re-locating him squarely within his diocese and province, his cathedral city, and his immediate social and cultural context—where he typically lived and moved, ruled and died, prayed and governed.

Chapter 2

Lay Magnates, Religious Houses, and the Role of the Bishop in Aquitaine (877–1050)

Anna Trumbore Jones
Lake Forest College

In the late summer of 1025, Bishop Isembert I of Poitiers composed a letter to his colleague Hubert of Angers, in which he expressed his regret that he would be unable to be present at the consecration of Hubert's new cathedral church. Isembert explained that other duties prevented him from enjoying the "great privilege" of attending the occasion, writing: "Our lord, Count William, having met with the Italians, has instructed my fellow bishops Islo [of Saintes] and Roho [of Angoulême] and myself to take care of some serious matters that we cannot postpone."[1] The man whose business kept Isembert away from Angers was William the Great, Count of Poitou and Duke of Aquitaine (995–1030), who had entered into negotiations to acquire the kingdom of Italy for one of his sons, and who apparently had called on several bishops from his realm to aid in the enterprise.[2] Isembert's short letter of apology suggests that the duke and bishops were allies, with the bishops entrusted

---

A version of this essay was presented at the Medieval Academy of America meeting in Miami Beach on 1 April 2005. I would like to thank the panelists and audience of that session for their comments, as well as John S. Ott, Leah DeVun, Mary Doyno, Anna Harrison, and Lawrence Jones for their helpful suggestions. Any errors that remain are my own.

[1]   This letter is preserved in the correspondence of Fulbert of Chartres. *The Letters and Poems of Fulbert of Chartres*, ed. and trans. Frederick Behrends (Oxford, 1976), no. 102, pp. 184–87: "Domnus noster Guillelmus comes, habito consilio cum Italis, precepit mihi et domnis meis Isloni atque Rohos coepiscopis sua quaedam seria procurare, quae nullatenus sunt nobis postponenda." On Hubert of Angers, see Steven Fanning, *A Bishop and his World before the Gregorian Reform: Hubert of Angers, 1006–1047*, Transactions of the American Philosophical Society 78 (Philadelphia, 1988).

[2]   On this venture by William, see *The Letters and Poems of Fulbert of Chartres*, ed. and trans. Behrends, introduction, pp. lxxxv–lxxxvi; nos 103–4 (pp. 186–89) and 111–13 (pp. 196–203). Some scholars, including Alfred Richard (*Histoire des comtes de Poitou, 778–1204*, 2 vols [Paris, 1903], 1:182–83), have suggested that the gathering described in a charter from the monastery of Nouaillé concerned this offer of the Italian throne (P. de Monsabert ed., *Chartes de l'abbaye de Nouaillé de 678 à 1200*, Archives historiques du Poitou 49 (1936) [hereafter *Nouaillé*], no. 104, pp. 172–74). Thomas Head has argued, however, that this gathering was a Peace council: "The Development of the Peace of God in Aquitaine (970–1005)," *Speculum* 74 (1999), 656–86, here at p. 684 n. 129. This council is not included in the

with important ducal family matters and putting off other obligations in order to help. This impression is reinforced by another letter in the same collection, this time from Isembert to Archbishop Arnulf of Tours, in which Isembert showed himself to be sufficiently familiar with the duke's schedule and commitments to refuse a request in the duke's name.[3] These texts provoke a number of questions about the bishops in Aquitaine and their relations with the powerful local lay rulers. Were all bishops in Aquitaine allied with the duke in this period? Did the bishops follow the dukes' wishes in religious as well as political matters? Did these associations influence the bishops' conception of their office and their performance of its duties?

The questions about Aquitanian bishops raised by Isembert's letters tie into the larger issue of the involvement of powerful laymen in various aspects of the European church from roughly 877 to 1050, a topic that was debated by contemporaries and has been much discussed by historians to the present day. A great deal of scholarly work has explored the influence that emperors, kings, and counts in this period had on the churches in their regions; the literature on bishops in the Ottonian and Salian realms is particularly extensive.[4] Concerning France in the years between the Carolingian era and eleventh-century papal reform, meanwhile, excellent work has been done on the growth of episcopal lordships, rivalries between episcopal and lay powers, and the ways in which lay magnates used church assets and offices to consolidate their positions as royal power weakened. Indeed, there has been a tendency, particularly in research on bishops in this period, to focus not on the entirety of their office— including their liturgical duties, their relations with religious houses, or their role as leaders of the cathedral community—but on their interactions with laymen and their development of lordships. These areas of concentration arise from the great scholarly interest in the reorganization of societal and political structures in France around the year 1000, and, perhaps, from long-standing assumptions about the nature of the church before the eleventh-century papal reforms as essentially worldly in its occupations.[5]

---

list of Peace councils given by Odette Pontal, *Les conciles de la France capétienne jusqu'en 1215* (Paris, 1995), pp. 120–32.

[3]   *The Letters and Poems of Fulbert of Chartres*, ed. and trans. Behrends, no. 110, pp. 196–97.

[4]   For a reassessment of the utility of *Reichskirche* as a concept, see Timothy Reuter, "The 'Imperial Church System' of the Ottonian and Salian Rulers: A Reconsideration," *Journal of Ecclesiastical History* 33 (1982), 347–74. For responses to Reuter, see Josef Fleckenstein, "Problematik und Gestalt der ottonisch-salischen Reichskirche," in *Reich und Kirche vor dem Investiturstreit: Vorträge beim wissenschaftlichen Kolloquium aus Anlaß des achtzigsten Geburtstags von Gerd Tellenbach*, ed. Karl Schmid (Sigmaringen, 1985), pp. 83–98, and Geneviève Bührer-Thierry, *Évêques et pouvoir dans le royaume de Germanie: Les églises de Bavière et de Souabe, 876–973* (Paris, 1997), pp. 11–13. For a discussion of the complexity of contemporary attitudes to the *Reichskirche*, see John Nightingale, "Bishop Gerard of Toul (963–94) and Attitudes to Episcopal Office," in *Warriors and Churchmen in the High Middle Ages: Essays Presented to Karl Leyser*, ed. Timothy Reuter (London, 1992), pp. 41–62.

[5]   The scholarship on the question of the "transformation of the year 1000," which in great part responds to the model presented by Georges Duby in his study of the Mâconnais (*La société aux XIe et XIIe siècles dans la region mâconnaise* [Paris, 1953]), is voluminous.

Recent scholarship on lay involvement in the church in Isembert I's region of Aquitaine has focused on the family of William the Great, who held the dual titles of count of Poitou and duke of Aquitaine in this period.[6] The count-dukes nominated bishops, held councils of the Peace of God, and founded monasteries; indeed, their influence in the church was one of the most important bases of their power, to the point that the institution has been labeled a "ducal church."[7] This assertion of the dukes' domination of the church has also shaped our image of Aquitanian bishops around the year 1000. While bishops performed a variety of functions and interacted with a number of influential laymen, including local counts and castellans, as well as their own families, scholarship has focused on the relations between the bishops and the dukes. Those scholars who asserted the existence of a "ducal church" have labeled its prelates "ducal bishops," implying that bishops such as Isembert were merely tools of the ducal will.[8]

The latest work by scholars such as Thomas Head and Cécile Treffort has however begun to complicate our understanding of the Aquitanian church in this

---

Duby's model is supported in Jean-Pierre Poly and Eric Bournazel, *La mutation féodale: Xe–XIIe siècle*, 2nd edn (Paris, 1991), which gives extensive bibliography. For the anti-transformation school, see Dominique Barthélemy, *La société dans le comté de Vendôme de l'an mil au XIVe siècle* (Paris, 1993) and *La mutation de l'an mil, a-t-elle eu lieu? Servage et chevalerie dans la France des Xe et XIe siècles* (Paris, 1997). For a recent debate on the issue, see Thomas N. Bisson, "The 'Feudal Revolution,'" *Past and Present* 142 (1994), 6–42, and responses by Dominique Barthélemy, Stephen D. White, Timothy Reuter, Chris Wickham, and Thomas Bisson, "Debate: The 'Feudal Revolution,'" *Past and Present* 152 (1996), 196–223, and 155 (1997), 177–225.

[6]   For the purposes of this paper, "Aquitaine" refers to the southwest of France—the dioceses of Angoulême, Bordeaux, Limoges, Périgueux, Poitiers, and Saintes. This is the area ruled by the dukes of Aquitaine beginning in the middle of the tenth century, when the ducal title passed from the Auvergne house of William I the Pious to the counts of Poitou.

[7]   On William the Great and the church, see Françoise Brisset, "Guillaume le Grand et l'église," *Bulletin de la Société des antiquaires de l'Ouest*, 4th ser., 12 (1972), 441–60; Daniel Callahan, "William the Great and the Monasteries of Aquitaine," *Studia Monastica* 19 (1977), 321–42. Bernard S. Bachrach questions William's capability as a war leader and investigates the idea that the basis of his power lay in the church in "'Potius Rex quam esse Dux putabatur': Some Observations concerning Adémar of Chabannes' Panegyric on Duke William the Great," *The Haskins Society Journal* 1 (1989), 11–21, and "Toward a Reappraisal of William the Great, Duke of Aquitaine," *Journal of Medieval History* 5 (1979), 11–21. A discussion of the role of the church, including the Peace of God, in William's authority, comes in the work of André Debord: *La société laïque dans les pays de la Charente, Xe–XIIe siècles* (Paris, 1984), pp. 104–7; idem, "The Castellan Revolution and the Peace of God in Aquitaine," in *The Peace of God: Social Violence and Religious Response in France around the Year 1000*, ed. Thomas Head and Richard Landes (Ithaca, NY, 1992), pp. 135–64. Debord's view of ducal power is echoed in Dominique Barthélemy, *L'an mil et la paix de Dieu: La France chrétienne et féodale, 980–1060* (Paris, 1999), pp. 281, 332–58.

[8]   Barthélemy, *L'an mil*, pp. 293–94, 304 on ducal bishops. Marcel Garaud labeled the tenth and early eleventh century as the era of "La mainmise des comtes de Poitou sur l'éveché et les abbayes poitevines." Garaud, "Observations sur les vicissitudes de la propriété ecclésiastique dans le diocèse de Poitiers du IXe au XIIIe siècle," *Bulletin de la Société des antiquaires de l'Ouest*, 4th ser., 5 (1960), 357–77, at pp. 364–69.

period. Head and Treffort reject a model of full ducal control of the church and
emphasize instead the changing nature of the dukes' involvement.[9] The dukes did not
direct all church movements such as the Peace of God at all times, Head and Treffort
argue, but rather participated selectively on the basis of a variety of considerations.
A similar reassessment of the "ducal bishops" in this period is needed. The sort
of control exercised by laymen over bishops that this term implies has long been
assumed to be one of the characteristics of the tenth-century church—the notorious
"church in the hands of the laity" posited by the series on church history edited by
Augustin Fliche and Victor Martin.[10] The papal reform, to follow this model, then
separated the church and its clergy from worldly influences and cares. Other essays
in this collection ably challenge that schema for the years after 1050 and increase our
understanding of the use of lay and spiritual power by the bishops in that era. I shall
focus here on the period before 1050, when there is much to modify in the Flichian
model as well. Rather than simply accepting—or rejecting—the idea of lay influence
on the bishops, I wish to ask (following Head and Treffort) whether that influence
existed, in what form, and with what results. I will do this by focusing here on a
particular case: the interactions between the counts of Poitou-dukes of Aquitaine
and the bishops of their capital city of Poitiers, and particularly the specific ways in
which those ties affected the bishops' relations to religious houses. I will first outline
the relationship between the count-dukes and the bishops of Poitiers, including a
major shift that occurred in that relationship in the late tenth century. I will then
consider three specific cases of the effects of ducal involvement on the activities of
the bishops of Poitiers from 975 to 1050.

Beginning in the mid-tenth century, but particularly around the year 1000,
the counts of Poitou and dukes of Aquitaine became deeply involved in selecting
bishops in several of the dioceses within their domain. Perhaps the best-known case
of ducal engagement in episcopal elections took place in Limoges, where the ducal
family was connected to the see from the mid-tenth century. In 944, they elevated
one of their own—Ebles, the brother of Count (later Duke) William Tow-Head—to
the episcopate. If this was an attempt by the Poitevins to begin an episcopal dynasty
in Limoges, it would be thwarted when Ebles's foster-son and chosen successor,
Benedict, was murdered before Ebles's own death.[11] Despite this setback, the
influence of the ducal family on the see of Limoges did not disappear, as the dukes
went on to name four successive bishops in that city, according to the *Chronicle*

---

[9]   Cécile Treffort, "Le comte de Poitiers, duc d'Aquitaine, et l'Église aux alentours de
l'an mil (970–1030)," *Cahiers de civilisation médiévale* 43 (2000), 395–445; Head, "The
Development of the Peace."

[10]   Émile Amann and Auguste Dumas, *L'Église au pouvoir des laïques (888–1057)*, vol.
7 in *Histoire de l'Église depuis les origines jusqu'à nos jours*, ed. Augustin Fliche and Victor
Martin ([Paris], 1940).

[11]   On Ebles of Limoges and Benedict, see Ademar of Chabannes, *Ademari Cabannensis
Chronicon* 3.25, ed. Pascale Bourgain, Richard Landes, and Georges Pon, CCCM 129
(Turnhout, 1999), pp. 146–47. For the date of his predecessor's death and his succession, see
Annales Lemovicenses, ed. Georg Pertz, MGH SS 2 (Hannover, 1829), p. 251. The date of
Ebles's own death is less clear, but most scholars place it in 976 or 977. On the circumstances
surrounding Benedict's murder, see Head, "The Development of the Peace," p. 663.

of Ademar of Chabannes.[12] Examples from other dioceses in Aquitaine are not as numerous: in one case, Archbishop Godfrey II of Bordeaux (1027/8–*c*.1043) was appointed in a joint decision by Duke William the Great of Aquitaine and Duke William Sancho of Gascony.[13] The dukes may also have influenced elections to the sees of Saintes and Périgueux, although the evidence in these cases is less explicit.[14] Given this tradition of intervention in episcopal elections throughout Aquitaine beginning in the late tenth century, it is hardly surprising that the dukes involved themselves in the selection of bishops in their home city of Poitiers.

A discussion of the relationship between the ruling family of Poitou and the bishops of Poitiers in this period revolves around the pivotal year 975. From 876 to 975, the count-dukes seem not to have influenced the appointment of the bishops of Poitiers, and the bishops, for their part, appeared rarely at the comital court. There are, moreover, indications of occasional conflict between the two powers. Bishop Frotier II (900–936/7), for example, was deposed by Count Ebles Manzer sometime between 926 and 934, although he would later be restored by Ebles's son William

---

[12]   For the dukes of Aquitaine and the bishops of Limoges, see François de Fontette, "Évêques de Limoges et Comtes de Poitou au XIe siècle," in *Études d'histoire du droit canonique dédiées à Gabriel Le Bras*, 2 vols (Paris, 1965), 1:553–58; Michel Aubrun, *L'ancien diocèse de Limoges des origines au milieu du XI siècle*, Institut d'études du Massif Central 21 (Clermont-Ferrand, 1981), pp. 134–41; Brisset, "Guillaume le Grand et l'église," pp. 444–47; Treffort, "Le comte de Poitiers," pp. 433–35. For the primary accounts, see Ademar of Chabannes, *Chronicon* 3.35, pp. 156–57; 3.49, p. 168; 3.57, pp. 178–79. For a recent example of an examination of the use of bishoprics to cement the power of aristocratic families, see Florian Mazel, *La noblesse et l'église en Provence, fin Xe–début XIVe siècle: L'exemple des familles d'Agoult-Simiane, de Baux et de Marseille* (Paris, 2002), pp. 66–83.

[13]   Ademar of Chabannes, *Chronicon* 3.69, p. 189.

[14]   Françoise Brisset ("Guillaume le Grand et l'église," p. 444) argues that the dukes controlled the choice of bishops in Angoulême, Saintes, and Périgueux. Reinhold Kaiser (*Bischofsherrschaft zwischen Königtum und Fürstenmacht: Studien zur bischöflichen Stadtherrschaft im westfränkisch-französischen Reich im frühen und hohen Mittelalter*, Pariser historische Studien 17 [Bonn, 1981], p. 202 n. 481, for example) asserts the right of the dukes to choose bishops in these cities as well as in Limoges, Poitiers, and Bordeaux, citing Alfred Richard (*Histoire des comtes*, 1:205). Richard claims that the dukes controlled the Angoulême appointments through their alliance with the comital family there, but conversely provides no evidence for his assertion that the dukes controlled the see of Saintes. Richard asserts that Arnald of Périgueux (1010/13–1036/7) must have been the duke's choice because he was consecrated at a monastery in Poitou. See also P. Imbart de la Tour, *Les élections épiscopales dans l'église de France du IXe au XIIe siècle (étude sur la décadence du principe électif) (814–1150)* (Paris, 1891), pp. 50–53. The primary sources are not clear on this topic, however. For the consecration of Arnald, see Ademar of Chabannes, *Chronicon* 3.48, p. 167, who does not mention the duke's involvement in this choice, although he does confirm that Arnald was consecrated at Nanteuil in Poitou. The consecrations of contemporary bishops of Saintes are not described in the primary sources. Jane Martindale best expresses the closeness of the dukes with the bishops of Poitiers and Limoges in this period, but also the uncertainty of their involvement in elections elsewhere: "Peace and War in Early Eleventh-Century Aquitaine," in *Medieval Knighthood 4: Papers from the Fifth Strawberry Hill Conference, 1990*, ed. Christopher Harper-Bill and Ruth Harvey (Woodbridge, 1992), pp. 147–76 (at pp. 160–61 and n. 39).

Tow-Head.[15] Later in the century, Bishop Peter of Poitiers (963/4–975) witnessed an arrangement between Count Geoffrey Grisegonelle of Anjou and Abbess Ermengarde of the convent of Sainte-Croix in the city of Poitiers.[16] Geoffrey became the lay protector of lands belonging to the convent, and he traveled to Poitiers in order to take part in an elaborate ceremony confirming his new role. Geoffrey's action was motivated in part by his desire to establish a sphere of influence in Aquitaine, the realm of his longtime foe, Duke William Iron-Arm.[17] Peter's presence at the ceremony confirming this act thus seems politically charged and may have been a sign of tension between the bishop and the duke. It seems clear that before 975, the influence of the count-dukes over the bishops of Poitiers was at best intermittent; there is evidence of a lack of cooperation between the two, and even some instances of strife.

Beginning with the reign of Bishop Gilbert (975–1023/4) and continuing with that of his nephew, Isembert I (1023/4–1047), the picture of relations between bishops and dukes changes markedly. First, Gilbert heralds the advent of a new family to the see: the Isemberts, as modern scholars know them, had power bases near Poitiers at Chauvigny, Châtellerault, and elsewhere, and were allies of the count-dukes. This family would provide three successive bishops to the see, with the support of the

---

[15]   Count Ebles and Bishop Frotier appeared together in a document from 926, which was part of the "pancarte noire" of Saint-Martin of Tours. The cartulary was destroyed in 1793, but the charter is printed in Jean Besly, *Histoire des comtes de Poictou et ducs de Guyenne contenant ce qui s'est passé de plus memorable en France depuis l'an 811 jusques au Roy Louis le Jeune* (Paris, 1647), pp. 218–20, and discussed in Émile Mabille, "La pancarte noire de Saint-Martin de Tours, brulée en 1793 et restituée d'après les textes imprimés et manuscrits," *Mémoires de la Société archéologique de Touraine* 17 (1865), 319–542 (at no. 116, pp. 446–47). Ebles Manzer died sometime between January 934, when he appeared in a document at Saint-Cyprien (Poitiers, Archives Départementales de la Vienne, pièces restaurées 16; printed in L. Rédet ed., *Cartulaire de l'abbaye de Saint-Cyprien de Poitiers, Archives historiques du Poitou* 3 (1874) [hereafter *Saint-Cyprien*], pp. 318–19, footnote) and December of the same year, when a restored Frotier appeared in a charter from Nouaillé (*Nouaillé* no. 46, pp. 81–82). The passage concerning William Tow-Head's restoration of Frotier is found in *Saint-Cyprien* no. 126, p. 90; see also Françoise Coutansais, "Les monastères du Poitou avant l'an mil," *Revue Mabillon* 53 (1963), 1–21, at p. 18, and Richard, *Histoire des comtes*, 1:72, 83–84.

[16]   P. de Monsabert ed., "Documents inédits pour servir à l'histoire de l'abbaye de Sainte-Croix de Poitiers," *Revue Mabillon* 9 (1913), no. 1, pp. 57–58; the original is in Poitiers, Archives Départementales de la Vienne, carton 1, dossier 12, no. 1. For a general history of Sainte-Croix, see Yvonne Labande-Mailfert et al. eds, *Histoire de l'abbaye Sainte-Croix de Poitiers: Quatorze siècles de vie monastique, Mémoires de la Société des antiquaires de l'Ouest*, 4th ser., 19 (1986–1987).

[17]   Bernard Bachrach, "Geoffrey Greymantle, Count of the Angevins, 960–987: A Study in French Politics," *Studies in Medieval and Renaissance History* 7 (1985), 3–67, at p. 19; idem, "A Study in Feudal Politics: Relations between Fulk Nerra and William the Great, 995–1030," *Viator* 7 (1976), 111–21, at p. 114 n. 11; Olivier Guillot, *Le comte d'Anjou et son entourage au XIe siècle*, 2 vols (Paris, 1972), 1:6; Head, "The Development of the Peace," p. 660; Labande-Mailfert et al. eds, *Histoire de l'abbaye Sainte-Croix*, pp. 89–90; Richard, *Histoire des comtes*, 1:115–17.

dukes.[18] Second, with the reigns of Gilbert and Isembert the quantity of surviving charters increases dramatically relative to their predecessors. Gilbert and Isembert I appeared as bishop in seventy-four and forty-nine charters, respectively, although in many of these documents—or in Gilbert's case, almost all—the bishops appeared only as witnesses, a name among others in a list.[19] The patterns of when, where, and in whose company Gilbert and Isembert witnessed charters prove telling and point to a third change in ducal-episcopal relations beginning in 975: unlike their predecessors, Gilbert and Isembert were extensively involved with the dukes,

---

[18]   See Treffort's discussion of the relations between the dukes and the bishops of Poitiers, "Le comte de Poitiers," pp. 431–33. On the family that controlled the episcopate, see Jacques Duguet, "La famille des Isembert, évêques de Poitiers, et ses relations (Xe–XIe siècles)," *Bulletin de la Société des antiquaires de l'Ouest*, 3d ser., 11 (1971), 163–86; L. Faye, "Recherches sur l'ancienne maison de Châtelaillon en Aunis," *Mémoires de la Société des antiquaires de l'Ouest* 13 (1846), 383–423; Guy DeVailly, "Les grandes familles et l'épiscopat dans l'ouest de la France et les Pays de la Loire," *Cahiers de civilisation médiévale* 27 (1984), 49–55; Kaiser, *Bischofsherrschaft*, p. 194. The end of this episcopal dynasty came with the death of Isembert II in *c.*1087: although Isembert II's nephew wished to succeed him in the bishopric, his appointment was opposed by the abbot of Saint-Cyprien, and the reformer Peter II was elected instead. Although he came from the same family, I will not consider Isembert II here because his reign extended into the late eleventh century, when the atmosphere surrounding lay–clerical relations had altered.

[19]   There are three charters in which Gilbert appeared while he was archdeacon (*Saint-Cyprien* no. 130, pp. 91–92; no. 132, pp. 92–93; no. 401, pp. 248–54). It is possible that another charter (*Saint-Cyprien* no. 193, p. 127) was witnessed by Bishop Gilbert but it is not entirely clear, as the signature is "s. Gisleberti clerici"—it is not included in the numbers here. Of the seventy-four charters in which he appeared as bishop, he appeared only as a witness in sixty-four of them; in the remaining ten, he was never the actor, but he took a more substantial role than simply a witness—he confirmed donations, added his voice to an excommunication, asked for donations to be given, gave advice on foundations, and so on. Isembert I appeared in three charters as archdeacon or before he became bishop: *Saint-Cyprien* no. 261, p. 169; no. 369, pp. 227–28; no. 384, pp. 236–37. There are two documents—*Saint-Cyprien* no. 475, pp. 291–92, and a Charroux charter (P. de Monsabert ed., *Chartes et documents pour servir à l'histoire de l'abbaye de Charroux*, Archives historiques du Poitou 39 (1910), pp. 27–28)—in which it is not clear whether the bishop in question is Isembert I or his successor Isembert II; these have not been included in the numbers here. Further, a letter from Bishop Jordan of Limoges, which purports to have been written with the consent and will of Isembert, among others, may in fact be a forgery by Ademar of Chabannes, and thus it is not included here (Jacques de Font-Réaulx ed., "Cartulaire de Saint-Étienne de Limoges," *Bulletin de la Société archéologique et historique du Limousin* 69 (1922), no. 77, pp. 89–91; Jean Becquet ed., *Actes des évêques de Limoges des origines à 1197*, Documents, études et répertoires publiés par l'Institut de recherche et d'histoire des textes 56 [Paris, 1999], no. 13, pp. 39–42). Excluding these, Isembert I appeared in forty-nine charters as bishop. In twenty-nine of them, he had some larger or different function than simply being a witness, ranging from as passive a role as having his reign used to date the charter, to being the actor of the charter in several cases. In twenty charters, Isembert appeared only as a witness; in eighteen of these he signed the charter with a duke.

especially William Iron-Arm and William the Great.[20] Of the sixty-four charters in which Gilbert appeared exclusively as a witness, he appeared with a duke in forty-eight of them and with William Iron-Arm's uncle, Bishop Ebles of Limoges, in two; he thus witnessed only fourteen charters without a duke or a prominent member of the ducal family. This pattern continued under Isembert: he appeared with the duke in eighteen of the twenty charters in which he acted as a witness. The fact that such a high proportion of the transactions witnessed by Gilbert and Isembert were also endorsed by the dukes suggests that the bishops often traveled with the dukes. Furthermore, Gilbert and Isembert often appeared in the ducal entourage with members of their own family, suggesting that the relationship between the bishop and the duke was but one aspect of the larger bond between the two families. Although Dominique Barthélemy is correct in warning us against the assumption that two people who appeared in a single charter together were necessarily on good terms, this dramatic change in the overall pattern of interactions between the bishops and dukes seems to indicate a shift in the relationship.[21]

After 975 and the advent of Gilbert to the see of Poitiers, therefore, the bishops and dukes seem to have worked more closely together. The dukes supported the Isembert family's control of the see and frequently traveled with the bishops in their entourage. This represents a reversal of the previous century, which had seen the dukes and bishops rarely in each other's company and occasionally at odds. Given that the dukes had frequent contact with and influence on the bishops after 975, what effects did they have on the bishops' policies? I will devote the rest of this essay to a consideration of three areas in which ducal influence affected episcopal action: the bishops' behavior toward religious houses in Poitou, the geographical range of the bishops' powers, and the bishops' relations with their fellow prelates.

Within the diocese of Poitiers, the religious communities at which Bishops Gilbert and Isembert I appeared in the charters can be divided into two main categories. The first group consists of houses—the collegial church of Saint-Hilaire, in the city of Poitiers itself, for example, as well as the monasteries of Maillezais and Saint-Maixent in the Poitou—where the ducal family exercised particularly strong influence. Saint-Hilaire and Saint-Maixent were both founded before the sixth century and were probably damaged during the Norman incursions in the mid-ninth century.[22] In the tenth century, Saint-Maixent was restored by Bishop Ebles of Limoges, while Saint-Hilaire was restored at the instigation of Ebles and his

---

[20]   On the charters of the dukes of Aquitaine and the nature of the witnesses to those documents, see Jan Prell, "La place des témoins par rapport à l'auteur et au bénéficiaire des actes: La situation en Poitou aux Xe et XIe siècles," in *Les actes comme expression du pouvoir au Haut Moyen Âge: Actes de la Table Ronde de Nancy, 26–27 novembre 1999*, ed. Marie-José Gasse-Grandjean and Benoît-Michel Tock, Atelier de Recherches sur les Textes Médiévaux 5 (Turnhout, 2003), pp. 203–14.

[21]   Barthélemy, *L'an mil et la paix de Dieu*, p. 342. On the wider political context for the transitional period of the 970s, see Head, "The Development of the Peace," pp. 659–61.

[22]   Both Saint-Hilaire and Saint-Maixent existed by the time of Clovis's campaigns in Aquitaine in 507: Gregory of Tours, *Historia Francorum*, ed. Bruno Krusch and Wilhelm Levison, MGH SS rer. Merov. 1/1 (Hannover, 1951), pp. 86–87. Coutansais, "Les monastères du Poitou," pp. 1–2; Georges Pon, "Le monachisme en Poitou avant l'époque

brother, Duke William Tow-Head. William became abbot of Saint-Hilaire, while Ebles served as abbot of Saint-Maixent and treasurer of Saint-Hilaire. From this time forward, the ducal family exercised a strong hold over these two houses: William Tow-Head's son and grandson would continue the tradition of serving as lay abbots of Saint-Hilaire, for example. Maillezais had an equally profound link to the ducal family, as it was founded by Duke William Iron-Arm and his wife, Emma.[23]

The bishops of Poitiers, meanwhile, had very limited involvement at these houses from the mid-tenth century to the end of our period, despite the fact that the houses fell within their diocesan jurisdiction. When the bishops appeared at these communities, they were always accompanied by the duke, duchess, or a prominent member of the ducal family. Thus, for example, Gilbert appeared in nine Saint-Hilaire charters, always with the duke or with Ebles of Limoges;[24] he appeared only once at Saint-Maixent, again in the duke's company.[25] At Maillezais, Gilbert played a more prominent role, but he did so at the request of Duchess Emma. In 989, after meeting together at the council of Charroux, Archbishop Gumbald of Bordeaux and some of his suffragans, including Gilbert, came to Maillezais *en masse* to consecrate the new monastery. When Duke William then led most of the bishops away to consecrate a small church nearby, Emma asked Gilbert to remain behind with her while she buried relics of saints in the left aisle of the monastery's church. Gilbert also witnessed a major gift from Emma to the monastery, and he later ratified several further charters for Maillezais during the reign of Emma's son, William the Great.[26] This first group of religious houses in the diocese of Poitiers, therefore, had the ducal family as their primary influence, and the bishops appeared only in supporting roles.

By contrast, the monasteries of the second group saw episcopal involvement without as much direction or influence from the dukes. The clearest example of this is the monastery of Saint-Cyprien, which lay on the outskirts of the city of Poitiers, on the far side of the river Clain. Bishop Frotier II (900–936/7) had rebuilt the monastery, which may have been damaged by the Normans, in the early tenth century.[27] Subsequent to these renovations, it seems that the bishops of Poitiers and

---

carolingienne," *Bulletin de la Société des antiquaires de l'Ouest*, 4th ser., 17 (1983), 91–130, at pp. 101–3.

[23]   Georges Pon and Yves Chauvin eds and trans, *La fondation de l'abbaye de Maillezais: Récit du moine Pierre* (La Roche-sur-Yon, 2001), pp. 108–11. On the building of Maillezais and the abbacy of Emma's relative, Gauzbert of Saint-Julien of Tours, see Guy-Marie Oury, "La reconstruction monastique dans l'Ouest: L'abbé Gauzbert de Saint-Julien de Tours (v.990–1007)," *Revue Mabillon* 54 (1964), 69–124, at pp. 77–84.

[24]   L. Rédet ed., *Documents pour l'histoire de l'église de Saint-Hilaire-de-Poitiers*, *Mémoires de la Société des antiquaires de l'Ouest* 14 (1847) (hereafter *Saint-Hilaire*), no. 42, pp. 48–49; no. 43, pp. 49–50; no. 44, pp. 51–52; no. 47, pp. 54–56; no. 49, pp. 57–58; no. 67, pp. 75–76; no. 68, pp. 76–77; no. 71, pp. 78–80; no. 72, pp. 80–82.

[25]   Alfred Richard ed., *Chartes et documents pour servir à l'histoire de Saint-Maixent*, *Archives historiques du Poitou* 16 (1886) (hereafter *Saint-Maixent*), no. 61, pp. 77–79.

[26]   Pon and Chauvin eds and trans, *La fondation de l'abbaye de Maillezais*, no. 1, pp. 199–206; no. 2, pp. 207–10; no. 4, pp. 215–20.

[27]   *Saint-Cyprien*, no. 1, pp. 1–2; no. 3, pp. 4–5; no. 4, pp. 5–7; no. 118, p. 87; no. 183, p. 117; no. 232, pp. 150–51.

Saint-Cyprien enjoyed a particularly close relationship, because the bishops acted more frequently and more extensively at Saint-Cyprien than they did elsewhere, with more independence from ducal interests. Even Bishop Gilbert, who in the vast majority of his charters appeared as a member of the ducal entourage, signed several charters at Saint-Cyprien without the duke present,[28] and he took the lead in winning a charter from the duke protecting the entire suburb of Saint-Cyprien from any exactions.[29]

Gilbert's nephew and successor, Isembert I, also appeared several times at Saint-Cyprien outside the duke's company. Isembert acted as a judge for one case brought by the monks and consented to two donations made by laymen to the monastery.[30] It was, furthermore, to Saint-Cyprien that Isembert handed over control of the church of Chauvigny, which he had built on his own family's estate and generously endowed with lands and other assets, including an aqueduct.[31] Saint-Cyprien serves, therefore, as a contrast to the communities described previously that had a strong ducal influence: at this and selected other houses, the bishops acted more independently of the dukes.

What can we conclude, then, about the influence of the dukes of Aquitaine over the policies of the bishops of Poitiers toward religious houses in their diocese? It is true that Gilbert and Isembert I appeared at certain communities where the ducal family was powerful primarily in order to confirm or reinforce ducal actions there. We cannot, however, generalize from these cases and assert that the dukes guided episcopal involvement at all religious communities. At other houses, particularly Saint-Cyprien, the bishops had a stronger influence and more autonomy in shaping their own policy and dictating the status of the house. This independence of action did not, of course, mean that the bishop or the house was therefore hostile to the power of the dukes, given the harmoniousness of their relationship in general. Nor can we claim to understand the entirety of the bishop's relationship with a given house by looking only at the number of times he appeared there, and with whom. Nonetheless, this material suggests a significant variation in the nature of episcopal involvement at different houses in Poitou, and this should begin to complicate our understanding of ducal influence over Aquitanian bishops.

---

[28]   *Saint-Cyprien* no. 73, p. 64; no. 103, pp. 80–81; no. 163, p. 108; no. 261, p. 169; no. 316, pp. 197–98; no. 364, p. 225; no. 365, pp. 225–26; no. 368, p. 227; no. 384, pp. 236–37; no. 425, p. 269; no. 427, p. 270.

[29]   *Saint-Cyprien* no. 17, p. 22.

[30]   Isembert's judgment is found in *Saint-Cyprien* no. 438, pp. 275–76; he also consented to a treaty between the abbot of Saint-Cyprien and the abbot's brother (no. 185, pp. 119–20). For other examples see *Saint-Cyprien* no. 207, p. 135; no. 433, pp. 273–74.

[31]   Three documents survive concerning Isembert's donation of the church of Chauvigny and surrounding lands: *Saint-Cyprien* nos 210–12, pp. 136–39. There were other familial aspects to Gilbert and Isembert's involvement at Saint-Cyprien: Bishop Isembert II recounted that his parents and other relatives were buried at the monastery in *Saint-Cyprien* no. 191, pp. 125–26. For gifts by this family to Saint-Cyprien in the tenth and eleventh century, see, for example, *Saint-Cyprien* no. 126, p. 90; no. 130, pp. 91–92; no. 201, pp. 131–32; no. 202, pp. 132–33; no. 206, p. 135; no. 217, p. 141; no. 228, p. 148; no. 341, p. 210. See also Duguet, "La famille des Isembert," pp. 167–71.

In contrast, the second aspect of ducal influence on bishops that I wish to address—the bishops' spheres of activity—shows more consistent influence of the dukes on episcopal policy. The political and familial power of the dukes of Aquitaine allowed the bishops to expand their area of action outside their own dioceses. An important example of this phenomenon is the activity of the bishops of Poitiers across the northern border of Aquitaine, in the Touraine and Anjou. As Geoffrey Grisegonelle's activities at Sainte-Croix in Poitiers illustrate, the dukes of Aquitaine and the counts of Anjou were often in conflict, and thus loyalty to the dukes might keep a bishop such as Gilbert or Isembert from appearing in the regions controlled by Anjou, or in the company of an Angevin count. On the other hand, the changing fortunes of the ducal family might draw the bishops northward into those same areas. Gilbert, for example, acted in Anjou at the request of Emma, wife of Duke William Iron-Arm and a native Angevin. Emma established the house of Bourgueil on her own land in Anjou in 990 and during the reign of Emma's son, Duke William the Great, Gilbert witnessed four charters there.[32] This appearance by Gilbert is notable, not only because of the hostility between Aquitaine and Anjou—William the Great and Count Fulk Nerra (d. 1040) were frequently at odds[33]—but because it was unusual before this date for the bishops of Poitiers to appear at monasteries outside their dioceses; when they did so, they usually traveled to houses within Aquitaine in the presence of the dukes. It seems likely, therefore, that it was the influence of Emma that brought Gilbert north into Anjou.

Gilbert's successor, Isembert I, is mentioned in seven charters from monasteries in Anjou and the Touraine. Two of these documents, from the houses of Saint-Florent of Saumur and Saint-Martin of Tours, date to the reign of William the Great.[34]

---

[32]   The foundation charter of Bourgueil dates from 990, when Emma was estranged from her husband, Duke William Iron-Arm. This may explain why the four charters witnessed by Bishop Gilbert at Bourgueil all date from the reign of Emma's son, William the Great: after Iron-Arm's death, Gilbert would not seem to have been taking sides in the conflict between the ducal couple by appearing at Emma's house. On the foundation of Bourgueil, see Pierre de Maillezais, in Pon and Chauvin eds and trans, *La fondation de l'abbaye de Maillezais*, pp. 112–15. Guy-Marie Oury has questioned Pierre de Maillezais's chronology of these events, and so the argument concerning Gilbert's desire to avoid conflict with William Iron-Arm must remain only a guess (Oury, "La reconstruction monastique," pp. 79–81). Certain Bourgueil charters can be found in Besly, *Histoire des comtes de Poictou*, pp. 267–68, 280–81, 290–91, and 355–56. See also Michel Dupont, *Monographie du cartulaire de Bourgueil des origines à la fin du Moyen Âge, Mémoires de la Société archéologique de Touraine* 56 (1962). On the region of the Gâtine, see George T. Beech, *A Rural Society in Medieval France: The Gâtine of Poitou in the Eleventh and Twelfth Centuries* (Baltimore, 1964).

[33]   On Fulk Nerra, see Bernard S. Bachrach, *Fulk Nerra, the Neo-Roman Consul, 987–1040: A Political Biography of the Angevin Count* (Berkeley, CA, 1993), pp. 66–69, 176–77, 204–206; idem, "A Study in Feudal Politics." Although William and Fulk were rarely engaged in open hostilities, they were rivals for power in the lands bordering their two realms. It would thus be surprising to find Gilbert or Isembert I of Poitiers, who were staunch allies of William, active in Fulk's realm.

[34]   One of these is extremely short and undated and is not considered here: it is a brief passage titled "Ex libro statutorum Ecclesiae S. Martini Turon," and it is found in Jean Besly, *Evesques de Poictiers avec les preuves* (Paris, 1647), p. 58.

Isembert's involvement in these two cases probably stemmed from the fact that each involved land that lay in his diocese.[35] We also find evidence of contact between Isembert and the Angevin realm in this period in the two letters from Isembert to the bishops of Angers and Tours mentioned above.[36] The letter to Hubert of Angers indicates that Isembert had intended to travel to Anjou for the cathedral dedication there before his plans were changed at the duke's will. Was this projected journey unusual, to be made in honor of the rare occasion of the construction of a major new church? Other documents from William the Great's reign do not show Isembert traveling often to Anjou, although contact with clerics further north may have been more common than actual appearances there. It is surely significant that, even in the case of the consecration, Isembert changed his plans in order to serve the duke.

After these documents there is a gap of some years before we find Isembert active in Anjou or the Touraine again. Both the gap and the resumption of activity can be explained by political considerations: in 1030, William the Great died, leaving four sons by three different wives.[37] He was succeeded as duke by his eldest son, William VI. Two years later, William the Great's widow, Agnes, married Geoffrey, count of the Vendôme and heir to the county of Anjou. Agnes wished to remove the sons of William the Great's first two marriages and place her own sons by William, Peter and Guy-Geoffrey, into power in Aquitaine.[38] Geoffrey of Anjou therefore began a campaign to undermine William VI's power in Aquitaine. During this conflict between Anjou and Aquitaine, Isembert seems to have served William VI faithfully,

---

[35]   The Saint-Florent of Saumur charter discusses the foundation of a canonry at the church of Loudun (in the region of Thouars in northern Poitou) and states that Count Fulk Nerra and others, including Isembert I of Poitiers, confirmed the establishment (P. Marchegay ed., "Chartes poitevines de l'abbaye de Saint-Florent près Saumur (de 833 à 1160 environ)," *Archives historiques du Poitou* 2 (1873), 1–148, at no. 7, pp. 16–18. This charter dates from *c.*1020). The charter from Saint-Martin of Tours is found in the "pancarte noire" of that house (Besly, *Evesques de Poictiers*, pp. 56–58; also discussed in Mabille, "La pancarte noire," no. 146, pp. 463–64). This document describes an agreement made between Isembert and the canons of Saint-Martin. Isembert and all his successors received a prebend of Martin and a house inside the cluster of residential buildings belonging to the canonical community of Saint-Martin. In exchange, all the altars held by Saint-Martin in the diocese of Poitiers were freed from all payments to the bishops, except for the dues levied in connection with synods or with the bishops' inspection tours of the diocese. After the details of the arrangement were laid out and the penalties for violation listed, the charter stated that Isembert signed the document to strengthen it, and that he ordered Count William to do the same, along with other lay and clerical authorities (Besly, *Evesques de Poictiers*, pp. 56–58). In both cases, Isembert's involvement seemed to stem from the fact that the lands in question, if not the motherhouse, lay within his diocese.

[36]   *The Letters and Poems of Fulbert of Chartres*, ed. and trans. Behrends, no. 102, pp. 184–87; no. 110, pp. 196–97.

[37]   William's oldest son, the future William VI the Fat, was the son of Almodis of the March. William's second son, Odo, was the son of his second wife, Prisca of Gascony. William's third wife, Agnes, who survived him, bore him two sons: Peter and Guy-Geoffrey.

[38]   Isabel Soulard Berger, "Agnès de Bourgogne, duchesse d'Aquitaine puis comtesse d'Anjou: Oeuvre politique et action religieuse (1019–v. 1068)," *Bulletin de la Société des antiquaires de l'Ouest*, 5th ser., 6 (1992), 45–56.

helping to ransom him when he was imprisoned by Geoffrey and acting as a counselor to William's wife as she governed the duchy in her husband's absence.[39] We have no record of Isembert appearing in regions controlled by Geoffrey of Anjou in this period, or of any involvement with religious houses from those lands.

After the dukedom passed to Agnes' son Peter in 1039, however, Isembert's activity in the Touraine and Anjou would have been acceptable again; as a result of Geoffrey of Anjou's influence over his stepson, Aquitaine and its northern neighbors became, for all practical purposes, one. Sure enough, we find Isembert appearing in these regions shortly thereafter: in 1040, for example, he attended the consecration of the monastery of La Trinité of Vendôme, founded by Geoffrey and Agnes.[40] The close political ties between Aquitaine and Anjou lasted past the end of Isembert's reign, until Geoffrey of Anjou repudiated Agnes in 1050, thus losing the loyalty of her sons and his influence over Aquitaine.[41]

Through their political actions, religious establishments and donations, and changing dynastic fortunes, the ducal family thus allowed or even required the bishops of Poitiers to work intermittently outside their own diocese and indeed outside their region, in Anjou and the Touraine. In this case, the bishops' relations with (and loyalty to) the dukes clearly influenced the geographical range of their activities. Moving to the final and related topic to be considered, we find that the dukes also shaped the interactions of the bishops of Poitiers with their fellow Aquitanian prelates. In the late tenth century, at the same time that the bishops of Poitiers began to appear more frequently with the dukes, they too for the first time began to gather regularly with their colleagues in the other sees of Aquitaine. What occasions prompted these meetings, and what role did the dukes play in bringing them about?

In most cases, the gatherings of the Aquitanian bishops did indeed occur at the duke's behest or at least under his influence. Most famously, the bishops appeared together at the assemblies of the Peace of God, beginning with the council at Charroux in 989, where—as mentioned above—Archbishop Gumbald of Bordeaux gathered with his suffragans from Angoulême, Limoges, Poitiers, Périgueux, and Saintes.[42]

---

[39]   Jean Verdon ed. and trans., *La chronique de Saint-Maixent, 751–1140*, Les classiques de l'histoire de France au moyen âge 33 (Paris, 1979), pp. 114–17; *Saint-Maixent* no. 93, pp. 113–14.

[40]   Charles Métais ed., *Cartulaire de l'abbaye cardinale de la Trinité de Vendôme*, 5 vols (Paris, 1893), no. 39, 1:85–89; no. 40, 1:90–93. On La Trinité, see Penelope Johnson, *Prayer, Patronage and Power: The Abbey of La Trinité, Vendôme (1032–1187)* (New York, 1981).

[41]   There are other incidents in which Isembert appeared in documents related to Agnes's family: he was mentioned in the dating clause of a 1043 charter in which William VII (Peter) confirmed a gift of land in Poitou for the monastery of Saint-Maur-sur-Loire (Besly, *Histoire des comtes*, pp. 417–18). Isembert also confirmed a gift given by Agnes of land she held from the convent of Sainte-Croix in the *pagus* of Poitiers (Marchegay ed., "Chartes poitevines de l'abbaye de Saint-Florent," no. 68, pp. 85–87).

[42]   Giovanni Domenico Mansi ed., *Sacrorum conciliorum nova et amplissima collectio*, 53 vols (Florence and Venice, 1759–1798; repr. Paris, 1899–1927; repr. Graz, 1961–), 19:89–90. On the council of Charroux, see Robert Favreau, "Le concile de Charroux de 989," *Bulletin de la Société des antiquaires de l'Ouest*, 5th ser., 3 (1989), 213–19 (in which

Although Duke William Iron-Arm did not call this council, the participants met with him immediately thereafter, presumably to discuss the proceedings of the assembly.[43] Later councils would include the tenants of the same sees but would often be called by the duke and held in his presence.[44] The nature of the Peace of God—whether it was essentially ecclesiastical (driven by bishops in opposition to lay encroachment on church land and rights) or political/ducal (orchestrated primarily by the dukes to control the behavior of lesser lords) in origin—has been much debated. Most scholars seem to have come to the conclusion that although the primary impetus behind each individual gathering might vary, both elements were crucial in the larger scheme, and that religious and secular authorities worked together to enforce measures against those who disturbed the peace.[45] In one area at least, it seems clear that political rather than ecclesiastical organization was determinate: the attendance lists of Aquitanian Peace councils and other gatherings of bishops. The bishop of Agen, a suffragan of Bordeaux whose diocese lay in the realm of the duke of Gascony, was always absent from these events, while the bishop of Limoges, a suffragan of

---

Favreau reproduces a fourth canon of Charroux, which he found in a 1666 printed edition and which he feels may have been original); Thomas Gergen, "Le concile de Charroux et la paix de Dieu: Un pas vers l'unification du droit pénal au Moyen Age?" *Bulletin de la Société des antiquaires de l'Ouest*, 5th ser., 12 (1998), 3–58; Head, "The Development of the Peace," pp. 666–73; idem, "Letaldus of Micy and the Hagiographic Traditions of the Abbey of Nouaillé: The Context of the *Delatio corporis S. Juniani*," *Analecta Bollandiana* 115 (1997), 253–67; Pontal, *Les conciles de la France capétienne*, pp. 120–21. A translation of canons of Charroux is found in *The Peace of God*, ed. Head and Landes, appendix A, pp. 327–28.

[43] Head, "The Development of the Peace," p. 670. During this gathering with the duke, the bishops also consecrated the new monastery of Maillezais, as discussed above.

[44] The Council of Limoges (994) is described in Ademar of Chabannes, *Chronicon* 3.35, p. 137, and in Ademar's sermons numbered 1–3: PL 141:115–24. On Ademar's sermons, see Daniel Callahan, "Adémar of Chabannes, Apocalypticism and the Peace Council of Limoges of 1031," *Revue bénédictine* 101 (1991), 32–49, at pp. 42–43; idem, "The Sermons of Adémar of Chabannes and the Cult of St. Martial of Limoges," *Revue bénédictine* 86 (1976), 251–95, at pp. 254–55. On the council, see Richard Landes, "Between Aristocracy and Heresy: Popular Participation in the Limousin Peace of God, 994–1033," in *The Peace of God*, ed. Head and Landes, pp. 184–218, at pp. 186–90. For other sources for Limoges 994, see Head, "The Development of the Peace," p. 674 n. 82. For the council of Poitiers in 1000, see Head, "The Development of the Peace," pp. 680–82. The canons of this council are found in Mansi ed., *Sacrorum conciliorum*, 19:265–68; for a translation, see *The Peace of God*, ed. Head and Landes, appendix A, no. 4, pp. 330–31. For the sources for later councils see Head, "The Development of the Peace," p. 684 n. 129.

[45] Head, "The Development of the Peace," p. 669. For a summary of historiography on the Peace of God, see Frederick S. Paxton, "History, Historians and the Peace of God," in *The Peace of God*, ed. Head and Landes, pp. 21–40. For a reevaluation of the Aquitanian councils that emphasizes their dual nature and the cooperation of lay and ecclesiastical lords in securing peace, see Jacques Paul, "Les conciles de paix aquitains antérieurs à l'an Mil," in *Année mil, an mil*, ed. Claude Carozzi and Huguette Taviani-Carozzi, Le temps de l'histoire (Aix-en-Provence, 2002), pp. 177–209.

Bourges, but in the realm of Aquitaine (and, as we saw earlier, selected by the dukes of Aquitaine), was present.

Beyond the Peace councils, a number of charters survive in which the Aquitanian bishops acted individually and collectively within Aquitaine but outside their own dioceses, witnessing donations or confirming acts in the duke's company. It was not unheard of for a bishop to appear outside his own diocese to witness an act, but in such cases the transaction usually concerned land or assets from within his diocese, as when Arnald of Périgueux oversaw the granting of the house of Tourtoirac, in the Périgord, to the Limousin house of Uzerche.[46] In other instances, however, the reason for the bishop's appearance in a document is less clear, as when, in 1004, Islo of Saintes approved a gift by William the Great to the monastery of Bourgueil that specifically concerned land in Poitou, rather than in the Saintonge,[47] or when Arnald of Périgueux approved another gift by William of land in the diocese of Saintes to Saint-Jean-d'Angély, a house in that same diocese.[48] In cases such as these, it is possible that a bishop witnessed these charters not because he had a special interest in the transaction, but simply because he was traveling in the ducal entourage at the time. From the late tenth century onwards, the dukes seem to have been more willing and able to call upon the bishops in their realm to witness their actions.[49] The bishops and dukes also appeared together as witnesses to gifts by others, reinforcing the argument that they moved in each other's company more frequently in this period.[50] This impression is bolstered by the letter of Isembert I with which we began; Isembert's mention of several Aquitanian bishops working together on behalf of the duke nicely epitomizes the sort of contact suggested in these other sources. It marks a major shift from the first part of our period, when charters rarely show the dukes interacting with the bishops of their realm.

In this same era we even find the bishops of Aquitaine meeting together more frequently when the dukes were not present. Sometimes these gatherings occurred

[46] Jean-Baptiste Champeval ed., *Cartulaire de l'abbaye d'Uzerche* (Paris and Tulle, 1901), no. 47, pp. 79–82.

[47] Bourgueil cartulary, Tours, Archives d'Indre et Loire, H990, pp. 55–56; printed in Besly, *Histoire des Comtes*, pp. 353–55.

[48] Georges Musset ed., *Cartulaire de Saint-Jean-d'Angély*, Archives historiques de la Saintonge et de l'Aunis 30 (1901) (hereafter *Saint-Jean*), no. 9, 1:29–30.

[49] For example, Gumbald of Bordeaux, Islo of Saintes, Gilbert of Poitiers, and (possibly) Hilduin of Limoges confirmed William the Great's donation to Maillezais in 1003 (Pon and Chauvin eds and trans, *La fondation de l'abbaye de Maillezais*, no. 1, pp. 199–206). Another case of bishops appearing to witness a ducal charter comes in *Saint-Jean* no. 181, 1:215–17, in 1038, when Islo of Saintes, Isembert of Poitiers, and Godfrey II of Bordeaux witnessed Duke William VII's confirmation of a gift.

[50] For example, *Saint-Hilaire* no. 76, pp. 84–85; *Saint-Jean* no. 42, 1:66–68; no. 197, 1:237–38; no. 339, 2:1–4. Godfrey II of Bordeaux, Isembert of Poitiers, Jordan of Limoges, Roho of Angoulême, Islo of Saintes, and Arnald of Périgueux appeared with the duke and others to consecrate the church of Limoges in 1028 (*Annales Lemovicenses*, MGH SS 2:251–52).

in order to carry out the dukes' instructions, but often they did not.[51] The bishops appeared together to witness dedications of churches, donation charters, and important events. In a typical example, Bishop Islo of Saintes, emphasizing that he acted in the presence and with the advice of his fellow Aquitanian bishops, issued a charter in 1029 granting privileges and protection to the new monastery of Bouteville.[52] In another such case, Radulf of Périgueux issued a privilege for the house of Saint-Astier, which was confirmed by Seguin of Bordeaux, Grimoard of Angoulême, and Islo of Saintes.[53] In this and other cases from the late tenth and eleventh centuries, we find the bishops of Aquitaine acting together, without the duke present, to confirm their own charters and those of other laymen.[54]

Thus we find that around 975, when the bishops of Poitiers began to work more closely with the dukes of Aquitaine, bishops from the other dioceses within Aquitaine began to appear more frequently in gatherings both with the dukes and with their episcopal colleagues from Aquitaine. What prompted this change? In some cases, the Aquitanian bishops may have been drawn into the ducal entourage if their own local lay power was a supporter of the duke, as may have been the case for the bishops of Angoulême in this period. This interpretation is, however, not plausible for all the dioceses. The bishops of Périgueux, for example, appeared frequently with the dukes and other Aquitanian bishops, while the counts of Périgueux had no recorded ties to the dukes in this period.[55] It has been suggested that the tenth century saw

---

[51]   The bishops acted together at the dukes' instructions to consecrate the bishops of Limoges, for example. On Hilduin of Limoges, see Ademar of Chabannes, *Chronicon* 3.35, pp. 156–57: he was consecrated at Angoulême by Archbishop Gumbald of Bordeaux, Frotier of Périgueux, Abbo of Saintes, and Hugh of Angoulême. Gerald (3.49, pp. 168–69) was consecrated by Archbishop Seguin of Bordeaux, Gilbert of Poitiers, Arnald of Périgueux, Islo of Saintes, and Grimoard of Angoulême. Jordan (3.57, pp. 178–79) was consecrated by Islo of Bordeaux, Roho of Angoulême, Arnald of Périgueux, and Isembert I of Poitiers.

[52]   François Marvaud ed., "Chartes relatives au prieuré de Bouteville et aux églises de Merpins et de Gimeaux," *Bulletin de la Société archéologique et historique de la Charente*, 4th ser., 3 (1865), no. 3, pp. 357–58.

[53]   Charter for Saint-Astier, in Paris, Bibliothèque nationale de France, Collection Périgord, vol. 12 (microfilm 14680), fols 206v–8r; vol. 34 (microfilm 16308), fols 188r–89r and 345v–46v; vol. 77 (microfilm 14683).

[54]   Other examples of this phenomenon include: Grimoard of Angoulême, Islo of Saintes, and Seguin of Bordeaux gathered to witness the donation by Auscenda to Saint-Silvain in the Périgord (Th. Grasilier ed., *Cartulaires inédits de la Saintonge*, vol. 2, *Cartulaire de l'abbaye royale de Notre-Dame de Saintes de l'ordre de Saint-Benoit* [Niort, 1871], no. 140, pp. 106–8). Ademar of Chabannes recounts that Seguin of Bordeaux, Grimoard of Angoulême, and Islo of Saintes consecrated the cathedral of Angoulême in 1014 (*Chronicon* 3.51, p. 171). Grimoard of Angoulême and Islo of Saintes were brothers, which would perhaps explain their appearance in several charters together. This cannot have been the only reason for the cooperation between the two sees, however, given that it continued after Grimoard's death; nor would family ties explain the other examples of this phenomenon.

[55]   On the counts of Périgord and the dukes, see Muriel Laharie, "Le pouvoir comtal en Périgord de la fin du IXe à la fin du XIIIe siècle: Traits généraux," *Bulletin de la Société historique et archéologique du Périgord* 106 (1979), 244–53, at p. 246. On the political situation in Saintes, where the bishops frequently cooperated with the duke and with other

the progressive weakening of the power of bishops within their own cities, causing them to turn to other bishops and to the dukes for support and to work in concert as a way of shoring up that power.[56] I would offer an additional interpretation of this new cooperation: that this period saw the development of an Aquitanian church, in that the bishops considered themselves part of a corps of bishops, brought together by their links to the duke but also—perhaps because of the familiarity engendered by those meetings—inclined to cooperate on their own, calling on each other to witness and reinforce their own actions.[57] The bishops saw a widening of their horizons from their dioceses to the whole of the duchy of Aquitaine, and even beyond.

In conclusion, I have tried to offer a more concrete picture of the interactions between the bishops of Poitiers and the dukes of Aquitaine, and the ramifications of that relationship on the bishops' sense of their position and on their actions. Were they "ducal bishops"? This was certainly not the case before 975, as the interactions between the dukes and bishops were rare and at times hostile. After 975, with the election of Gilbert, the relationship changed markedly and appears to have been more amicable. Even in this period, however, ducal influence on episcopal policy, like ducal involvement in the church more generally, varied. In the case of episcopal action at religious houses, for example, the dukes dictated the nature and extent of episcopal engagement at some houses, while at others, the bishop might act because of a tradition of episcopal involvement at that community, or because (as I did not explore here) the house was patronized by their family.

On the other hand, the dukes and their political ambitions did, it seems, often determine the regions in which the bishops of Poitiers might act. The dukes' varying relations with Anjou and the Touraine in this period, for example, helped to dictate whether or not the bishops appeared in those counties. Even more interesting, the extent of the dukes' political realm also determined which episcopal colleagues the bishop of Poitiers worked with: in consolidating their hold over Aquitaine, William Iron-Arm and William the Great frequently brought together bishops from that region, to the extent that an *esprit de corps* seems to have developed among those prelates, and they began to meet without the dukes present. Were the bishops of Poitiers, as prelates of the capital city of the duchy and the particularly close allies of the duke, seen as leaders of this group? There is no definitive evidence of this, but it is intriguing to find a charter from Cluny in which Isembert I of Poitiers was referred to as "Bishop of the Aquitanians"; it is possible that this indicated a strong identification between the bishop of Poitiers, his patron, and the entirety of his patron's realm.[58]

---

bishops in this period despite the fact that the region was dominated by the counts of Anjou, see Kaiser, *Bischofsherrschaft*, p. 198.

[56]   For a summary of this trend in Aquitaine, see Kaiser, *Bischofsherrschaft*, pp. 188–250.

[57]   Cécile Treffort refers to one of the goals or results of ducal policy in this period as "la constitution d'un corps épiscopal aquitain" (Treffort, "Le comte de Poitiers," p. 431); see also Barthélemy, *L'an mil et la paix de Dieu*, pp. 293–94.

[58]   Auguste Bernard and Alexandre Bruel eds, *Recueil des chartes de l'abbaye de Cluny*, vol. 4, *1027–1090* (Paris, 1888), no. 2816, pp. 19–21. The charter was given by Isembert at the request of a certain Viscount Cadelo and his son William, to confirm their gift of a church

I would suggest that two broader conclusions can be drawn from the evidence considered here. The first concerns the nature of the church in the tenth and early eleventh centuries. As Timothy Reuter and others have argued, labels that imply systematic control by lay lords over the church or its bishops in this period need to be used with care.[59] This is not to suggest that lay powers did not influence the tenth-century church; as we have seen, the dukes of Aquitaine shaped many aspects of episcopal behavior in their realm. That influence, however, was dependent on a variety of circumstances: the family to which a particular bishop belonged, the dukes' current political ambitions, or the individual religious house in question, for example. Work that nuances the idea of a tenth-century "church in the hands of laymen" thus brings us closer to the true complexity of the church before 1050 and challenges the outdated but persistent overtones of disapproval that creep into analyses of that institution.[60]

Second, the relations between the bishops of Poitiers and the counts of Poitou-dukes of Aquitaine shed light on political changes around the year 1000. As we have seen, in the late tenth and early eleventh centuries the count-dukes had closer relations with and more influence over the prelates of their realm than their predecessors. Striking parallels emerge when we turn to other regions in Aquitaine in this period: the counts of Angoulême and viscounts of Limoges, like the dukes of Aquitaine, appeared more often and seem to have enjoyed closer alliances with their local bishops beginning in the late tenth century.[61] This pattern deserves further

---

to Cluny. In the body of the document, Isembert refers to himself only with the title of bishop, but his signature reads "S. Isemberti, pontificis Aquitanorum." Duke William the Great was among the witnesses, as were the bishops of Angoulême and Limoges.

[59]   Reuter, "The 'Imperial Church System,'" pp. 373–74. Olivier Guyotjeannin argues against the simplistic dichotomy created by the term "royal bishop" with reference to the bishops of the Île de France in the reigns of the early Capetians in "Les évêques dans l'entourage royal sous les premiers Capétiens," in *Le roi de France et son royaume autour de l'an mil: Actes du colloque Hugues Capet 987–1987. La France de l'an mil*, ed. Michel Parisse and Xavier Barral i Altet (Paris, 1992), pp. 91–98, at pp. 96–98.

[60]   The classic formulation of this view is in Amann and Dumas, *L'Église au pouvoir des laïques*. For a call to understand the tenth-century church and its bishops on their own terms, see Karl Ferdinand Werner, "Observations sur le rôle des évêques dans le mouvement de paix aux Xe et XIe siècles," in *Mediaevalia christiana XIe–XIIIe siècles: Hommage à Raymonde Foreville de ses amis, ses collègues, et ses anciens élèves*, ed. Coloman Viola (Paris, 1989), pp. 155–95, at pp. 174–75.

[61]   In the case of Limoges, the bishops and viscounts came from the same family beginning in 977. On the viscounts, see François Marvaud, *Histoire des vicomtes et de la vicomté de Limoges*, vol. 1 (Paris, 1873). In Angoulême, we find a pattern that mirrors the situation in Poitiers: after acting independently from the counts of Angoulême from the late ninth to late tenth centuries, the advent of Count William IV Taillefer in 988 saw increased cooperation between bishops and counts. The transition in the relationship took place in the reign of Bishop Hugh (973/4–990): on Hugh's resistance to Count Arnald Manzer, see Jacques Boussard ed., *Historia pontificum et comitum Engolismensium* (Paris, 1957), c. 22, pp. 13–14; on Hugh's cooperation with Count William Taillefer, see André Debord ed., *Cartulaire de Saint-Amant-de-Boixe* (Poitiers, 1982), no. 4, pp. 95–96. On castellans in

study, but it is possible that the increased frequency of interactions between lay rulers and bishops throughout Aquitaine in this period was an attempt to establish a network of alliances in the face of the growing influence of castellans. Scholars who study these regions suggest that the years around 1000 saw challenges to ducal and comital authority from the burgeoning number of castles in private hands. The increased cooperation between the duke and the bishops of Poitiers from 975, which is mirrored in other regions of Aquitaine, may have been a measure to counter these problems.[62] Thus a careful study of the relations between bishops and lay lords illuminates not only the functioning of the church but also the political transformations taking place around the year 1000. These are, of course, two sides of the same coin, and the bishops, who were extensively involved in both political and religious life, are essential to a judicious assessment of both.

Poitou, see Marcel Garaud, *Les châtelains de Poitou et l'avènement du régime féodal, XIe et XIIe siècles, Mémoires de la Société des antiquaires de l'Ouest*, 4th ser., 8 (Poitiers, 1964); idem, "L'organisation administrative du comté de Poitou au Xe siècle et l'avènement des châtelains et des châtellanies," *Bulletin de la Société des antiquaires de l'Ouest*, 4th ser., 2 (1952–1954), 411–54. In Périgueux, Muriel Laharie's work indicates that the bishops had significant interactions with local lay lords from the late tenth century onwards, although they were not always amicable (Laharie, "Évêques et société en Périgord du Xe au milieu du XII siècle," *Annales du Midi* 94 (1982), 343–68, at pp. 351–55).

[62]   Debord analyzes the challenges to the power of the dukes of Poitiers and their allies, the counts of Angoulême, in *La société laïque dans les pays de la Charente*, pp. 104–51.

Chapter 3

Bishops and Religious Law, 900–1050

Greta Austin

University of Puget Sound

Europe in the tenth and early eleventh centuries was "a Europe of the bishops."[1] Put another way, "[t]he history of the church of Europe in the tenth and early eleventh centuries is essentially the history of many local churches, in which the dominant role in secular ecclesiastical and religious life was played by the bishops."[2] For a better understanding of the figure of the bishop, then, a better understanding is needed of the church as well as European society in these two crucial centuries of transition and transformation.

Relatively little work has been done to explore how tenth- and early eleventh-century bishops contributed to "the expansion and consolidation of Christianity in western Europe," as Rosamond McKitterick points out.[3] In the last decades, new attention has been paid to the roles and significance of bishops.[4] Still more remains to be done concerning both canon law and the entire period described by McKitterick.

This article examines the role of bishops in the development of canon law, or church law, between the years 900 and 1050. This period immediately preceded the papal reform movements of the late eleventh and early twelfth centuries. It has been

I am very grateful for the thoughtful and careful comments by Jörg Müller and by the editors, John Ott and Anna Trumbore Jones.

[1] Timothy Reuter, "Ein Europa der Bischöfe. Das Zeitalter Burchards von Worms," in *Bischof Burchard von Worms, 1000–1025*, ed. Wilfried Hartmann, Quellen und Abhandlungen zur mittelrheinischen Kirchengeschichte 100 (Mainz, 2000), pp. 1–28.

[2] Rosamond McKitterick, "The Church," in *The New Cambridge Medieval History*, vol. 3, *c. 900–c. 1024*, ed. Timothy Reuter (Cambridge, 1999), pp. 130–62, at p. 130.

[3] McKitterick also describes "how crucial the leadership of the bishops became in the course of the tenth century": "The Church," p. 162.

[4] See, for example, Stephanie Coué, *Hagiographie im Kontext: Schreibanlaß und Funktion von Bischofsviten aus dem 11. und vom Anfang des 12. Jahrhunderts*, Arbeiten zur Frühmittelalterforschung 24 (Berlin, 1997); eadem (as Stephanie Haarländer), "Die Vita Burchardi im Rahmen der Bischofsviten seiner Zeit," in *Bischof Burchard von Worms*, ed. Hartmann, pp. 129–60; and *Vitae episcoporum: Eine Quellengattung zwischen Hagiographie und Historiographie, untersucht an Lebensbeschreibungen von Bischöfen des Regnum Teutonicum im Zeitalter der Ottonen und Salier*, Monographien zur Geschichte des Mittelalters 47 (Stuttgart, 2000); *The Bishop: Power and Piety at the First Millennium*, ed. Sean Gilsdorf, Neue Aspekte der europäischen Mittelalterforschung 4 (Münster, 2004); and the growing bibliography listed at the *Episcopus* website: http://www.unc.edu/~egatti/episcopus/publications.htm (accessed 22 September 2005).

a commonplace of the scholarly literature that canon law grew dramatically during the period of Gregorian reform.[5] (This is at least true quantitatively: large numbers of texts were incorporated in books of church law for the first time during this period.[6]) According to an older school of thought, the reformers gave fresh energy to the study of canon law in their efforts to find legal support for their reforms. In this model, the papacy provided the impetus to the revival of canon law during the second half of the eleventh century.

Recent work has challenged the "top-down" model of a "Gregorian" reform on a number of fronts. Some, such as Maureen Miller, have pointed to "the work of local communities" as much as that "of popes and canonists."[7] Martin Brett, however, does not contrast canonists with "local communities." Instead, he attributes much of the growth of law prior to the mid-twelfth century to the crucial role of local communities *and* bishops (who were often, *de facto*, canonists).[8]

This paper investigates how bishops used and produced canon law during this period, particularly in Germany.[9] Bishops' interest in canon law can be identified in a number of ways: their requests for handbooks of law; their compilation of such handbooks; the laws they issued at councils; episcopal capitularies, or the codes of laws which individual bishops drew up for their dioceses; episcopal discussions of canon law in letters; and the clues about their judicial activities in *vitae*, or saints' lives. After first providing a brief introduction to the episcopacy during the period 900–1050, we will look next at the councils, at which bishops collectively issued new laws binding on their churches. The laws they enacted also provide a useful window onto the legal concerns of bishops. Third, we will examine the canonical collections, which were often made by bishops or for bishops. As handbooks designed for diocesan use, these collections often illuminate the particular legal needs of bishops. Fourth, we will examine some episcopal letters and *vitae* of bishops to find

---

[5]   The classic formulation of this position is Paul Fournier, "Un tournant de l'histoire du droit 1060–1140," *Nouvelle revue historique de droit français et étranger* 41 (1917), 129–80, reprinted in *Mélanges de droit canonique*, ed. Theo Kölzer, 2 vols (Aalen, 1983), 2:373–424. On church reform generally, see Uta-Renate Blumenthal, *The Investiture Controversy: Church and Monarchy from the Ninth to the Twelfth Century* (Philadelphia, 1988); Werner Goez, *Kirchenreform und Investiturstreit, 910–1122*, Kohlhammer Urban-Taschenbücher 462 (Stuttgart, 2000); and Wilfried Hartmann, *Der Investiturstreit*, Enzyklopädie deutscher Geschichte 21 (Munich, 1993).

[6]   Peter Landau has demonstrated quantitatively the increase in the number of canons available in the second half of the eleventh century: "Wandel und Kontinuität im kanonischen Recht bei Gratian," in *Sozialer Wandel im Mittelalter: Wahrnehmungsformen, Erklärungsmuster, Regelungsmechanismen*, ed. Jürgen Miethke and Klaus Schreiner (Sigmaringen, 1994), pp. 215–33.

[7]   Maureen C. Miller, "Masculinity, Reform, and Clerical Culture: Narratives of Episcopal Holiness in the Gregorian Era," *Church History* 72 (2003), 25–52, at pp. 26–27.

[8]   Martin Brett, "Canon Law and Litigation: The Century before Gratian," in *Medieval Ecclesiastical Studies in Honour of Dorothy M. Owen*, ed. M.J. Franklin and Christopher Harper-Bill, Studies in the History of Medieval Religion 7 (Woodbridge, 1995), pp. 21–40.

[9]   For studies of many individual dioceses, see Stefan Weinfurter ed., with Frank Martin Siefarth, *Die Salier und das Reich*, vol. 2, *Die Reichskirche in der Salierzeit* (Sigmaringen, 1991).

evidence of their canonical interests in this period. Finally, we will take a closer look at one early eleventh-century bishop whose legal interests may be indicative of "an episcopate avid for current legal doctrine," to borrow Brett's description of the bishops during this period.[10]

The Period 900–1050

As the Carolingian Empire crumbled, the position of bishops continued to change. With the breakdown of royal authority, and with very little oversight or intervention by the bishop of Rome, bishops often took on more responsibilities in their sees, acting as administrators, ecclesiastical judges, and sometimes even rulers. At the same time, regional lords and local rulers had also become increasingly important figures, and often encroached on the independence of the bishops.[11]

In the German *Reichskirchensystem*, or the "imperial church system,"[12] rulers and bishops enjoyed a symbiotic relationship. The rulers relied upon bishops for political advice and support. Aristocratic clerics advised the ruler as members of his *Hofkapelle*, the royal chapel,[13] and "future prelates were groomed at the court, under the scrutiny of the ruler, for another kind of service to the ruler as bishops."[14] Bishops, in turn, often depended upon these rulers for their appointments.

Archbishops and bishops served as ecclesiastical judges.[15] One important way in which they did so was to convene a court when they toured their diocese. During these

---

[10]   Brett, "Canon Law and Litigation," p. 36.

[11]   See, for example, the discussion of developments in the French church and episcopacy in the post-Carolingian period in Steven Fanning, *A Bishop and his World before the Gregorian Reform: Hubert of Angers, 1006–1047*, Transactions of the American Philosophical Society 78 (Philadelphia, 1988), pp. 7–15.

[12]   See Josef Fleckenstein, "Problematik und Gestalt der ottonisch-salischen Reichskirche," in *Reich und Kirche vor dem Investiturstreit: Vorträge beim wissenschaftlichen Kolloquium aus Anlaß des achtzigsten Geburtstags von Gerd Tellenbach*, ed. Karl Schmid (Sigmaringen, 1985), pp. 83–98; Hartmut Hoffmann, "Der König und seine Bischöfe in Frankreich und im Deutschen Reich, 936–1060," in *Bischof Burchard von Worms*, ed. Hartmann, pp. 79–127; Timothy Reuter, "The 'Imperial Church System' of the Ottonian and Salian Rulers: A Reconsideration," *Journal of Ecclesiastical History* 33 (1982), 347–74; and Rudolf Schieffer, *Der geschichtliche Ort der ottonisch-salischen Reichskirchenpolitik*, Nordrhein-Westfälische Akademie der Wissenschaften G 352 (Opladen, 1998).

[13]   See Rudolf Schieffer, "Burchard von Worms. Ein Reichsbischof und das Königtum," in *Bischof Burchard von Worms*, ed. Hartmann, pp. 29–49, at pp. 32–33. On the institution of the *Hofkapelle*, or royal chapel, see Josef Fleckenstein, *Die Hofkapelle der deutschen Könige*, MGH Schriften 16/1–2 (Stuttgart, 1959–1966).

[14]   C. Stephen Jaeger, "The Courtier Bishop in *Vitae* from the Tenth to the Twelfth Century," *Speculum* 58 (1983), 291–325, at p. 292.

[15]   On bishops as judges, see Wilfried Hartmann, "L'évêque comme juge: La pratique du tribunal épiscopal en France du Xe au XIIe siècle," in *Hiérarchies et services au Moyen Âge*, ed. Claude Carozzi and Huguette Taviani-Carozzi (Aix-en-Provence, 2001), pp. 71–92. For an earlier period, see idem, "Der Bischof als Richter nach den kirchenrechtlichen Quellen des 4. bis 7. Jahrhunderts," in *La giustizia nell'alto Medioevo (secoli V–VIII), 7–13 aprile*

annual visits, bishops investigated offenses of both the laity and clergy, instructed them as to proper Christian doctrine and practice, and assigned penances or sentences of excommunication.[16] According to Jean Gaudemet, bishops in Germany continued to serve as judges to the end of 1100, whereas those in France had ceased to do so by the end of the Carolingian period. This generalization, however, may be too broad. By investigating episcopal letters, including those of Ivo of Chartres (1090–1116), Wilfried Hartmann shows that some French bishops intervened in judicial disputes and carried out some judicial activities through the beginning of the twelfth century.[17] Hartmann concludes that bishops did act as judges up until the end of the twelfth century.[18] We should not overlook the obvious: that the regular duties of bishops demanded them to know canon law. As bishops came to fill some functions previously carried out by the Carolingian state, the demands upon them became even greater. The local demand for church law—a demand often spearheaded by bishops—bore fruit in a number of ways. Yet, at the outset, we should remember that not all bishops seem to have known much about canon law. Liudprand, the tenth-century bishop of Cremona, for instance, seems to have taken very little interest in canon law, even though he served as the head official of his city.[19] His disinterest should remind us that episcopal interest in church law must have varied from place to place, and from bishop to bishop. Further work remains to be done in order to understand the precise dynamics of the development of canon law.

Councils

Councils are essential to understanding episcopal concern with church law.[20] When bishops met in councils and synods, they addressed church business, issued new

---

1994, Settimane di studio del Centro italiano di studi sull'alto Medioevo 42 (Spoleto, 1995), pp. 805–42; and "Probleme des geistlichen Gerichts im 10. und 11. Jahrhundert: Bischöfe und Synoden als Richter im ostfränkisch-deutschen Reich," in *La giustizia nell'alto Medioevo (secoli IX–XI), 11–17 aprile 1996*, Settimane di studio del Centro italiano di studi sull'alto Medioevo 44 (Spoleto, 1997), pp. 631–72, and accompanying discussion at pp. 673–74.

[16]   On such visitations, see Walter Hellinger, "Die Pfarrvisitation nach Regino von Prüm," *Zeitschrift der Savigny-Stiftung für Rechtsgeschichte, Kanonistische Abteilung* 48 (1962), 1–116, and Andrew Leonard Slafkosky, *The Canonical Episcopal Visitation of the Diocese*, Catholic University of America Canon Law Studies 142 (Washington, DC, 1941).

[17]   See Hartmann, "L'évêque comme juge," pp. 77–88.

[18]   By the end of the twelfth century, Hartmann points out, papal legates or judges delegated by the pope took over most of the judicial functions of bishops; "L'évêque comme juge," p. 92 n. 74. On the papal judges delegate, see Charles Duggan, "Papal Judges Delegate and the Making of the 'New Law' in the Twelfth Century," in *Cultures of Power: Lordship, Status, and Process in Twelfth-Century Europe*, ed. Thomas N. Bisson (Philadelphia, 1995), pp. 172–99.

[19]   Jon N. Sutherland, *Liudprand of Cremona, Bishop, Diplomat, Historian: Studies of the Man and his Age*, Biblioteca degli 'Studi medievali' 14 (Spoleto, 1988), pp. 22, 109.

[20]   The Peace of God movement, which began in the late tenth century, provides one index of the importance of councils. On it see, for example, Thomas Head and Richard Landes eds, *The Peace of God: Social Violence and Religious Response around the Year 1000* (Ithaca,

laws (and, in doing so, reaffirmed existing laws), and sometimes functioned as courts which heard exceptional cases or disputes.[21] To see the bishops at councils is to understand how ecclesiastical business was carried out through legal means. The bishops also reaffirmed their judicial authority in the decrees they issued. In 922, for instance, the council of Koblenz saw fit to affirm "that judgments on ecclesiastical matters belong to the bishops alone."[22]

Councils could be held at the local or regional level; they might be imperial assemblies attended by bishops; or they might be ecumenical or general, although no such "universal" synods met in this period.[23] Their decrees thus varied in their authority. Whereas the decrees of a meeting held by a local bishop would be binding only upon his see, those issued by assemblies with papal legates and rulers in attendance would be considered to have a more general application. The tenth-century compiler Regino of Prüm made clear that not all conciliar decrees were created alike when he defended his choice to include the decrees of regional synods held in Gaul and Germany in his collection of canon law.[24]

The council of Hohenaltheim (916) provides a window onto the concerns of bishops and archbishops.[25] At this "general synod" (*generalis synodus*), the king Conrad I was present, as was the papal legate Peter, bishop of Orte.[26] The first canon reminded clergy of the need to defer to the interpretative tradition: those involved in ecclesiastical cases or judgments (*actionibus vel iudiciis ecclesiasticis*) should be guided by the decrees of the gospels and canons, and not by their own personal opinions. The same was true for those preaching on or explaining divine scriptures. The next four decrees discussed the scriptural roles which a bishop ought to fulfill, such as being the "light of the world" (Matt. 5.13–15). The council focused on the figure of the bishop and matters relating to him: accusations against bishops were then discussed in c. 13, and those who despoil bishops in c. 14. The council went on to issue decrees pertaining to excommunication (cc. 6–7, 27), the goods and rights of churches (cc. 10–11), and oaths and perjury (cc. 22–25). These topics

NY, 1992), and Thomas Gergen, *Pratique juridique de la paix et trêve de Dieu à partir du concile de Charroux (989–1250)/Juristische Praxis der Pax und Treuga Dei ausgehend vom Konzil von Charroux (989–1250)*, Rechtshistorische Reihe 285 (Frankfurt-am-Main, 2004).

[21] See, for example, James A. Brundage, *Medieval Canon Law* (London, 1995), p. 121.

[22] Canon 5: "Ut ecclesiasticarum rerum iudicia ad solos pertineant episcopos." See the edition in *Die Konzilien Deutschlands und Reichsitaliens, 916–1001*, ed. Ernst-Dieter Hehl, with Horst Fuhrmann, MGH Concilia 6/1 (Hannover, 1987), pp. 57–74, at p. 69.

[23] See the discussion by Robert Somerville, "Councils, Western (869–1179)," in *Dictionary of the Middle Ages*, ed. Joseph Strayer, 13 vols (New York, 1982–1989), 3:632–39, especially p. 633.

[24] Regino of Prüm, *Libri duo de synodalibus causis et disciplinis ecclesiasticis*, ed. F.G.A. Wasserschleben (Leipzig, 1840; repr. Graz, 1964), p. 2 (henceforward *Libri duo*); Robert Somerville and Bruce C. Brasington trans, *Prefaces to Canon Law Collections in Latin Christianity: Selected Translations, 500–1245* (New Haven, CT, 1998), p. 93.

[25] See, for example, Horst Fuhrmann, "Die Synode von Hohenaltheim (916)— quellenkundlich betrachtet," *Deutsches Archiv* 43 (1987), 440–68.

[26] All references here are to the edition by Hehl in MGH Concilia 6/1 (above, n. 22), pp. 1–40. For the description of the synod as "general," see p. 19.

would presumably have been of interest to bishops enforcing the canon law in their dioceses.

A century later, at the council of Seligenstadt in 1023, the German bishops continued to deal with topics of concern to the running of their sees: fasts (cc. 2–3, 15), the computation of consanguinity (c. 11),[27] accusations of adultery (c. 14), and the proper form of penance (cc. 18–20). Some canons underscore the authority of the bishop: no layperson may choose a priest without the bishop's permission (c. 13); no one may travel to Rome (presumably to appeal to the pope) without the bishop's permission (c. 16); and no priest may receive a penitent without his bishop's permission (c. 20). At the council of Seligenstadt in 1023, the attendees may have consulted a canon law collection, the *Decretum* made by Burchard, bishop of Worms (1000–1025), as they came up with decrees. Burchard himself was present, and some striking similarities exist between the *Decretum*'s texts and the conciliar edicts.[28]

Councils were also the sites, on occasion, of debates played out between powerful bishops. For instance, the archbishops of Mainz and Bernward, bishop of Hildesheim (993–1022), claimed jurisdiction over the convent of Gandersheim.[29] The "Gandersheim quarrel" was worked out at a series of councils, albeit with many setbacks, such as when Willigis of Mainz stormed out of the synod of Pöhlde in 1001.[30] In the process, at least one dossier of canonical texts was compiled, in part by taking canons from Burchard's *Decretum*. (This dossier was probably consulted again at the synod of Frankfurt in 1027.[31]) The Gandersheim controversy highlighted both the power of the bishops and their recourse to law as mediated by the council. At synods, bishops and papal legates used canon law to settle disputes, and canon law continued to develop and adapt to new historical circumstances, often at the behest of the bishops.

The Canonical Collections

The canonical collections are helpful in understanding the ways in which bishops might have used canon law in their dioceses. In some collections (although not all—others focus on monastic rights and the contemplative life), the laws already "on the

---

[27]   See Patrick Corbet, *Autour de Burchard de Worms: L'Église allemande et les interdits de parenté (IXème–XIIème siècle)*, Ius Commune Sonderhefte 142 (Frankfurt-am-Main, 2001).

[28]   Julius Harttung, "Die Synode von Seligenstadt und Burchards Decretum," *Forschungen zur deutschen Geschichte* 16 (1876), 587–93; see also the discussion in Hartmann, "Probleme," pp. 647–48.

[29]   Knut Görich, "Der Gandersheimer Streit zur Zeit Ottos III. Ein Konflikt um die Metropolitanrechte des Erzbischofs Willigis von Mainz," *Zeitschrift der Savigny-Stiftung für Rechtsgeschichte, Kanonistische Abteilung* 79 (1993), 56–94.

[30]   See the summary in Görich, "Der Gandersheimer Streit," pp. 63–64.

[31]   Wolfenbüttel, Herzog August Bibliothek, Helmst. 32. On it see Hartmut Hoffmann and Rudolf Pokorny, *Das Dekret des Bischofs Burchard von Worms: Textstufen—Frühe Verbreitung—Vorlagen*, MGH Hilfsmittel 12 (Munich, 1991), pp. 115–29, especially pp. 127–29; see also Hartmann, "Probleme," pp. 646–47.

books," which sometimes included recent decrees from councils, were gathered and arranged for use.

Bishops and archbishops evidently had a pressing need for books of canon law to help them administer and adjudicate disputes. Two important collections were made for bishops and archbishops soon before and just after the year 900: the *Collectio Anselmo dedicata*, or the *Collection Dedicated to Anselm*; and the *Libri duo de synodalibus causis et disciplinis ecclesiasticis*, or the *Two Books concerning Synodal Cases and Ecclesiastical Discipline*. These two collections were made in quite different places: the *Anselmo dedicata* was probably compiled in northern Italy, and Regino of Prüm made the *Libri duo* in southern Germany. Yet both compilers dedicated their works to archbishops. Furthermore, both collections appear to have been designed as handbooks for bishops. The creation of these two collections seems to reflect archbishops' and bishops' need for up-to-date, thorough, and topically-organized reference books of church law.

To see what archbishops might have found useful (or what a compiler imagined they would find useful), it is instructive to look briefly at the substantive law and topics of the two collections. The *Anselmo dedicata* is divided into twelve parts, each of which reflects issues of immediate concern to bishops and archbishops (as well as, presumably, priests and lower grades of the clergy).[32]

1. The Roman see and other primates (patriarchs, archbishops, and metropolitans)
2. Bishops and chorbishops
3. Synods and business done at synods, such as accusations and accusers, testimony and witnesses, judges and ecclesiastical business
4. Priests and deacons and the other ecclesiastical orders
5. The life of clerics
6. Monks and nuns
7. The laity
8. Norms of the Christian faith: what Christians must believe and do
9. Sacrament of baptism
10. Churches: worship and liturgy, oblations and tithes
11. The church year
12. Heretics, schismatics, Jews, and pagans

The collection provides a blueprint for Christian society by outlining the church's structure and function and delineating the roles and responsibilities of the clergy,

---

[32] See Lotte Kéry, *Canonical Collections of the Early Middle Ages (ca. 400–1140): A Bibliographical Guide to the Manuscripts and Literature*, History of Medieval Canon Law 1 (Washington, DC, 1999), pp. 124–28, for a comprehensive bibliography and list of manuscripts. There is also a useful overview of the *Anselmo dedicata* in Linda Fowler-Magerl, *Kanones: A Selection of Canon Law Collections compiled between 1000 and 1140. Access with Data Processing* (Piesenkofen, 2003), pp. 16–19. Frustratingly, there is no complete printed edition of the *Anselmo dedicata*. Book one of the *Anselmo dedicata* as it exists in one particular manuscript (Verdun) has been printed: Jean-Claude Besse, "Collectionis *Anselmo Dedicata* Liber Primus," *Revue de droit canonique* 9 (1959), 207–96 (but see Kéry, *Canonical Collections*, p. 124).

laity, and monks and nuns. An educated person like an archbishop or a bishop could understand the theoretical structure as well as the practical functions of the church. It was probably very difficult to find such general overviews of the church. We know that the anonymous compiler of the *Anselmo dedicata*, the "least little lamb of his flock" (as the compiler calls himself), had dedicated this work to Archbishop Anselm of Milan (882–896). Possibly, then, the archbishop had requested a handbook to be made for initiating and teaching new bishops. The *Anselmo dedicata*—of which almost twenty manuscripts (both fragmentary and complete) exist today[33]—seems to be a collection designed to map out the ideal Christian society.

By way of contrast, the collection of Regino of Prüm, the *Libri duo*, was oriented to the practical application of church law. It provided a handbook of canons for archbishops and bishops as they made their rounds in their dioceses.[34] (It must also have proven useful to priests in confession.) Regino divided the collection into two parts, one devoted to the clergy and one to the laity. Each part then addresses various individual topics, many of which pertain to morals and behavior, such as perjury or fornication. It is difficult to sum up the subjects of each book, because they are so sprawling in scope.

The *Libri duo* was clearly designed for diocesan visitation, and it provides a wealth of information about how bishops conducted such visits to the see. The bishop began by interrogating the clergy as to how they carried out their duties and ritual obligations, and by teaching them how to do so properly.[35] The *Libri duo* provides a list of questions which the bishop would pose to the clergy.[36] Next, the bishop would investigate the laity. Regino described this procedure in some detail at the beginning of book two of the *Libri duo*. The bishop convened the clergy and the laity in a synod.[37] After addressing the people, the bishop selected seven men as representatives.[38] These men then responded under oath[39] to a series of questions about public offenses, such as homicide, fornication, or perjury, committed in the parish.[40] It probably varied from place to place whether the bishop or a secular ruler then punished these offenses.

To carry out visitations properly, bishops had to be familiar with canon law. They needed to know the correct procedures and questions to ask, and to identify the canonical sanctions for these offenses. In fact, the *Libri duo* was created at the request of Archbishop Rathbod of Trier (883–915), and dedicated to Hatto, archbishop of

---

[33] Kéry, *Canonical Collections*, pp. 124–26.

[34] The *Libri duo* is divided into two parts. Part one concerns the clergy and part two the laity. Book one begins with a list of questions for priests. There are also questions for laity at 1.304 (ed. Wasserschleben, pp. 141–46) and a long list at 2.5 (ibid., pp. 208–16). On these questions for diocesan visitation, see Hellinger, "Pfarrvisitation."

[35] *Libri duo* 1.7, for instance, explains that bishops should travel through their dioceses, should interrogate and instruct their clergy, and then teach the laity and investigate any offenses.

[36] See the list that precedes *Libri duo* 1.1.

[37] *Libri duo* 2.1.

[38] *Libri duo* 2.2.

[39] *Libri duo* 2.2–3.

[40] *Libri duo* 2.5 gives a long list of questions to be asked.

Mainz (891–913). Regino wrote in the preface that he compiled the book because Hatto had to carry large volumes of conciliar decrees with him on his travels. Regino made this "handbook" for the archbishop of Mainz "as a guide when the abundance of your books is not at hand."[41]

The *Libri duo* also provides insight into the duties and legal knowledge of these archbishops. Regino depicted his archbishop as a legally sophisticated man of affairs, concerned with the welfare of his church as well as the state. In the preface, Regino wrote of the archbishop of Mainz that he "takes care of the whole province according to the sanctions of the holy canons," and that he worked "for the advantage of the whole kingdom."[42] He also described him as exceptionally wise and learned. In a "worn-out age," the archbishop provided a lone exemplar of "the skills of the philosophers about which learned Roman antiquity bragged."[43] Because the archbishop had the wisdom and ability to choose among canons, Regino included a wide variety of canons, some conflicting,[44] and left it up to the archbishop to select among them.[45] Thus, the *Libri duo* provides a window into the involvement of one German archbishop with canon law: he was a busy man of affairs, who owned books of conciliar decrees, and who could reason out legal answers from conflicting canons in order to administer justice as he visited his diocese. In other words, bishops continually needed new and improved books of law in order to carry out their duties to visit their diocese and administer law. The demand for law began, in very real ways, at the local level.

Bishops might have used the *Libri duo* in a number of ways, and not just as a reference book for diocesan visitation. For instance, it may have been consulted before and during the synod of Hohenaltheim in 916.[46] Regino's collection also influenced the *Capitula Helmstadtiensia*, which is an episcopal capitulary, or a collection of a bishop's directives for the see.[47] Finally, it was used in a number of

---

[41] ". . . ut plurima conciliorum volumina semper vobiscum longe lateque deferantur, idcirco hunc manualem codicillum vestrae dominationi direxi, ut illum pro enkyridion habeatis, si quando plenitudo librorum vestrorum in praesentiarum non est": *Libri duo*, Preface, pp. 1–2; Somerville and Brasington trans, *Prefaces*, p. 93.

[42] ". . . non solum iuxta sacrorum canonum sanctiones totius provinciae sollicitudinem gerere, verum etiam totius regni utilitatibus pervigili cura insudare": *Libri duo*, Preface, p. 1; Somerville and Brasington trans, *Prefaces*, p. 93.

[43] ". . . qui tantus in omni genere philosophiae estis, ut solus nobis repraesentetis hac decrepita aetate ingenia philosophorum, de quibus illa sollers latialis antiquitas gloriata est": *Libri duo*, Preface, p. 1; Somerville and Brasington trans, *Prefaces*, p. 93.

[44] This raises an important point: we cannot merely read the substantive law of a collection and assume that it reflects the compiler's legal viewpoint.

[45] *Libri duo*, Preface, p. 2; Somerville and Brasington trans, *Prefaces*, p. 94.

[46] Hartmann, "Probleme," p. 633; see also the discussion in Fuhrmann, "Die Synode von Hohenaltheim," pp. 444–46.

[47] *Capitula episcoporum: Dritter Teil*, ed. Rudolf Pokorny, MGH Capitula episcoporum 3 (Hannover, 1995), pp. 181–86. See also the discussion in Rudolf Pokorny, "Zwei unerkannte Bischofskapitularien des 10. Jahrhunderts," *Deutsches Archiv* 35 (1979), 503–13. On episcopal capitularies of this period, see generally Peter Brommer, *Capitula episcoporum: Die bischöflichen Kapitularien des 9. und 10. Jahrhunderts*, Typologie des sources du moyen âge occidental 43 (Turnhout, 1985).

canonical collections, including ones produced in Freising and Worms during the next century (to be discussed below).

The demands of administering law, especially by bishops and archbishops, seem to have spurred the creation of legal collections. We have examined two of the best-known books of canon law produced around the year 900. But there were many others. These two collections, which were fairly widely disseminated, did not satisfy the thirst of bishops and priests for satisfactory compilations of church law. There were, in fact, some sees whose bishops seem to have been remarkably devoted to seeking out and organizing the laws governing the church. In the later part of the tenth and early eleventh centuries, the scriptorium of the bishop of Freising was a center of canonical activity, spearheaded by three bishops: Abraham (957–993/4), Gottschalk (994–1005), and Egilbert (1005–1039).[48] Jörg Müller has suggested that Gottschalk led efforts to collect canons as raw materials for further collections.[49] The Freising scriptorium produced a number of canonical manuscripts, including four which have been recently dubbed the *Freising Collection of Canonical Materials*.[50] This "collection" consists of a *mélange* of materials. It contains, for instance, a collection within itself, the *Collectio canonum* attributed (incorrectly) to Remedius of Chur, which is a book of extracts from Pseudo-Isidore made between 880 and 895.[51] It also includes the decrees of the council of Tribur in 895 (what is called the "Vulgata" version), as well as extracts from the letters of Pope Nicholas I, and excerpts from conciliar decrees and some papal letters. Further study is needed to understand better this collection, and whether it was made as a collection in its own right or only as a preparatory step for other collections (since it provided material to

---

[48] Natalia Daniel has identified manuscripts from the Freising scriptorium during this period. Natalia Daniel, *Handschriften des zehnten Jahrhunderts aus der Freisinger Dombibliothek*, Münchener Beiträge zur Mediävistik und Renaissance-Forschung 11 (Munich, 1973). Jörg Müller subsequently demonstrated the use of these manuscripts in his *Untersuchungen zur Collectio duodecim partium*, Abhandlungen zur rechtswissenschaftlichen Grundlagenforschung 73 (Ebelsbach, 1989). He provides an overview of the Freising episcopal see and its library and scriptorium in his "Die Collectio Duodecim Partium und ihr Freisinger Umfeld," in *History of Medieval Canon Law*, ed. Wilfried Hartmann and Kenneth Pennington (Washington, DC, forthcoming), pp. 1–2 (draft numbering), on the Web at http://www.lrz-muenchen.de/~SKIMCL/CDP_10.pdf (accessed 23 August 2005).

[49] See Jörg Müller, "Collectio Duodecim Partium und Decretum Burchardi," *Proceedings of the Eighth International Congress of Medieval Canon Law, San Diego, University of California at La Jolla, 21–27 August 1988*, ed. Stanley Chodorow, Monumenta Iuris Canonici C/9 (Vatican City, 1992), pp. 63–75, at p. 73.

[50] Munich, Bayerische Staatsbibliothek, Clm 6245 and 6241; Vienna, Österreichische Nationalbibliothek, MS lat. 2198; and Bamberg, Staatsbibliothek, Can. 9. See Kéry, *Canonical Collections*, pp. 185–86. Another manuscript that resulted from their efforts is Munich, Bayerische Staatsbibliothek, Clm 27246, discussed below.

[51] This appears on fols. 106v–141r of Clm 6241. For bibliography and manuscripts on "Pseudo-Remedius," see Kéry, *Canonical Collections*, pp. 184–85; also Fowler-Magerl, *Selection of Canon Law Collections*, p. 15. For a description of the manuscripts and an analysis of the collection and its sources, as well as a critical edition, see Pseudo-Remedius, *Collectio canonum Remedio Curiensi episcopo perperam ascripta*, ed. Herwig John, Monumenta Iuris Canonici B/2 (Vatican City, 1976).

both the *Collectio duodecim partium* and to the *Decretum* of Burchard of Worms). But it attests to the considerable canonical activity, probably led by the bishop, of the Freising cathedral's scriptorium.

In another manuscript, Munich Bayerische Staatsbibliothek Clm 27246, the Freising compilers collected the legislation of tenth-century councils—Hohenaltheim (916), Koblenz (922), Duisburg (929), and Erfurt (932)—alongside decrees from Carolingian councils. "The compiler, possibly under the auspices of Bishop Abraham of Freising, presumably wished to make a point about the relationship of these two sets of decrees, a century apart in date but not in aspiration," McKitterick comments. "It is clear from the context in which many Carolingian conciliar decrees have survived, that individual tenth-century bishops made a direct connection between the preoccupations and concerns of the Carolingian synods and their own."[52] The Freising compilers loaned copies of the Freising Collection as well as Clm 27246 to the scriptorium at Worms. There, Bishop Burchard and his assistants used texts from these manuscripts to produce their influential collection, the *Decretum*, in the early eleventh century.[53]

Ultimately, the Freising compilers produced a monumental collection, the *Collection in Twelve Parts*, or the *Collectio duodecim partium*.[54] It begins, tellingly, with a book entitled "On bishops," *De episcopis*. Unlike the *Anselmo dedicata*, the *Twelve Parts* devotes entire books to topics which would presumably interest the bishop during episcopal visitation (and the priest when assigning penance), including homicide, marriage, excommunication (or perjury in another recension), and penance.[55] As Fowler-Magerl has pointed out, the collection emphasizes pastoral care and it includes many texts from Gregory the Great.[56] The *Collectio duodecim partium* includes a very large number of canons (almost 2,900 canons in its longer version), and it seems designed to serve as a comprehensive guide to the canonical literature for the clergy.

The many canonical collections produced in the tenth and early eleventh centuries attest to remarkable canonical activity, very often initiated or requested by the bishop, or carried out by him and/or his cathedral scriptorium. This demand continued to grow during the late eleventh century. Brett points to "a vast undergrowth of canonical interest, out of which the major collections of the late eleventh and early twelfth century rise less dramatically than they did for Fournier."[57] He also singles

---

[52]   McKitterick, "The Church," p. 154.

[53]   On the reception of these collections in the *Decretum*, see Hoffmann and Pokorny, *Das Dekret des Bischofs Burchard von Worms*, pp. 77–81.

[54]   For this see Kéry, *Canonical Collections*, pp. 155–57, and Fowler-Magerl, *Selection of Canon Law Collections*, pp. 33–35.

[55]   For a list of the topics, see for example Müller, "Die Collectio Duodecim Partium und ihr Freisinger Umfeld," pp. 9–10 (draft numbering), available on the Web at http://www.lrz-muenchen.de/~SKIMCL/CDP_10.pdf (accessed 23 August 2005).

[56]   Fowler-Magerl, *Selection of Canon Law Collections*, p. 33; see Jörg Müller, "Die Überlieferung der Briefe Papst Gregors I. im Rahmen der Collectio duodecim partium," *Licet preter solitum: Ludwig Falkenstein zum 65. Geburtstag*, ed. Lotte Kéry, Dietrich Lohrmann, and Harald Müller (Aachen, 1998), pp. 17–31.

[57]   Brett, "Canon Law and Litigation," p. 34.

out bishops as particularly important to the interest and development of canon law.[58] What this paper suggests is that "an episcopate avid for current legal doctrine"[59] preceded the Gregorian papacy, and that the bishops of the tenth and early eleventh centuries were also instrumental in the new interest in canon law. To study Lotte Kéry's bibliographical guide to early medieval canonical collections is to see this "vast undergrowth of canonical interest," particularly in the "collections of local importance" from the ninth to mid-eleventh centuries.[60]

"Local" collections from this period frequently reflect episcopal concerns or were made by or for bishops. For instance, we find in the Argrim Dossier, from the early tenth century, a set of canons discussing the installation of bishops.[61] Similarly, in the middle of the tenth century, Atto, bishop of Vercelli (924–*c.*963), made a collection of canons which drew texts from the *Anselmo dedicata*.[62] In fact, it appears that Atto ordered a copy of the *Anselmo dedicata* to be made for his cathedral library at Vercelli.[63] In his own collection of 100 canons, Atto tried to rectify the "ignorance and greed of the lower clergy."[64] The priests were reminded of their basic duties and responsibilities, such as knowledge of the Bible, the canons, and the Athanasian creed,[65] and of proper clerical behavior.[66] Atto provided guidelines for priests in baptizing (c. 18), excommunicating (c. 67), and marrying (c. 83).[67] As bishop, then, Atto drew upon canonical resources to create a handbook of basic guidelines for the parish priest.[68] This collection concludes with an affirmation of the authority of

---

[58] Ibid., p. 36.

[59] Ibid.

[60] Kéry, *Canonical Collections*, pp. 161–202; local collections are also identified for the period from Leo IX's papacy until Gratian (*c.*1050–1140), at pp. 276–94. For instance, the *Collectio 342 capitulorum* and the *Collectio 114 capitulorum* were produced during this period, probably in France (ibid., pp. 180–82). The *Collectio 77 capitulorum* was made after 922 in southern Germany, as a supplement to an existing collection, possibly to address local issues (p. 183). In the *Collectio 98 capitulorum*, Regino's *Libri duo* was excerpted, with other additions, after 922 in Germany (p. 187). We also see Regino's collection taken up and supplemented with blocks of texts in the *Collectio 4 librorum* in the tenth century (p. 189). Finally, in Italy, the *Collectio of Verona LXIII* may have provided a "handbook for the parish priests" (p. 191).

[61] See Kéry, *Canonical Collections*, p. 180.

[62] Ibid., pp. 191–92.

[63] Vercelli, Biblioteca Capitolare, MS XV. See Suzanne Fonay Wemple, *Atto of Vercelli: Church, State and Christian Society in Tenth-Century Italy*, Temi e testi a cura di Eugenio Massa 27 (Rome, 1979), pp. 12 and 204–6, and Fowler-Magerl, *Selection of Canon Law Collections*, p. 16.

[64] A recent printed edition of Atto's collection is found in *Capitula episcoporum*, ed. Pokorny, pp. 243–304. On it see Wemple, *Atto of Vercelli*, p. 112. On the manuscripts, editions, and bibliography of Atto's collection, see Kéry, *Canonical Collections*, pp. 191–93.

[65] Canons 3–4; *Capitula episcoporum*, ed. Pokorny, pp. 266–67.

[66] See, for example, cc. 36–37 (on relations with women) and cc. 42–51.

[67] Wemple, *Atto of Vercelli*, pp. 111–12.

[68] Modern scholars have categorized this work both as an episcopal capitulary (Brommer, *Capitula episcoporum*, pp. 47–48) and as a canonical collection (Kéry, *Canonical Collections*, pp. 191–93). Brommer points out that various terms were used to describe similar works (for

church law. As the rubric, or summary, of canon 98 reads, "No one should presume to refute these canons" (*ut haec canones nullus refutare praesumat*).[69]

In a broader sense, this work attests to Atto's reforming impulses, although his ideas differed in some important regards from those of later papal reformers. Unlike later reformers, Atto did not attack lay investiture or seek to consolidate papal leadership of the church.[70] Rather, the bishop sought "an autonomous church," "free from worldly entanglements, and a priesthood which not only led a model life but also had a high moral purpose."[71] In studying Atto's program of reform, Suzanne Wemple concludes that his ideas should be placed in a continuous canonical tradition with the Carolingians and the papal reformers of the eleventh century.

> Comparison of Atto's ideas on church government and clerical discipline with that of his predecessors and successors has revealed the existence of a canonical tradition running from the ninth to the eleventh century. A cluster of ideas—on clerical celibacy, the freedom of episcopal elections, the inalienability of church property and the immunity of clerks from secular jurisdiction—can be traced from the pronouncements of the synodists under the reign of Louis the Pious to the works of Atto, and to the writings of eleventh century churchmen. This supports Tellenbach's view that the Gregorian program did not originate in the monasteries. Rather, its roots go back to a movement of reform which started in the ninth century, was carried on sporadically in the tenth century, and gained momentum in the eleventh century. Although in its initial and final stages the movement became fused with monastic reform programs, its chief aim was the moral regeneration and autonomy of the secular clergy, and its chief source of inspiration was canon law.[72]

In Atto's case, the desire to reform the clergy was inspired by canon law, and this desire resulted in a new collection of church law.

Thus, local demand for canon law, much of it episcopal, and sometimes aimed at moral reform of the church, resulted in a steady production of canon law collections during the tenth century as well as the early eleventh century. There seem to be as many "local" canonical collections made between *c.*900–1025 as there were in the following 125 years. This suggests that the growth of canon law had deep roots in the tenth century. In many instances, such as the compilations made at Freising, the bishops seem to have initiated these new collections and enabled their production. Bishops were frequently the consumers as well as the producers of new collections of canon law.

---

example *capitulare, epistola, opusculum,* or *series capitulorum*). He proposes a definition of such texts as instructions produced by bishops for the clergy and people of a diocese, texts which tend not to be too bulky or large, which were sometimes compendiums and divided into sections, and which addressed church discipline and administration. See Brommer, *Capitula episcoporum,* pp. 10–11. On definitions of episcopal capitularies, see Pokorny, "Zwei unerkannte Bischofskapitularien," p. 489 n. 9.

[69]   *Capitula episcoporum,* ed. Pokorny, p. 301.
[70]   Wemple, *Atto of Vercelli,* pp. 142–43.
[71]   Ibid., p. 143.
[72]   Ibid., pp. 141–42.

Episcopal Letters and *Vitae*

That bishops were expected to know canon law can be seen in the letters of Rather, who served as bishop of Verona intermittently in the 930s and 940s and then briefly as bishop of Liège in the 950s. Asked a question about classical literature, he responded that he had "ceased working at it, thinking that this office required me to meditate on the law of God night and day."[73] In another letter, as part of a diatribe on episcopal authority and episcopal abuses, he summoned a variety of canons to support his point, even as he complained bitterly of the neglect of the canons, especially in Italy.[74]

Other letter collections attest to bishops' roles as judges and arbiters of ecclesiastical justice. For instance, over one-third of the letters of Fulbert, bishop of Chartres (1006–1028), treat a number of different cases he confronted or was asked to address.[75] These letters sometimes return to the same cases repeatedly. By contrast, however, only one of the 220 letters of Gerbert of Aurillac as archbishop of Reims (991–996) describes a judicial action.[76]

Other potential sources for the bishops' canonical and judicial activities of the tenth and eleventh centuries, particularly those of German bishops,[77] are their *vitae*, but these turn out to say frustratingly little about the bishops and church law.[78] Although a *vita* of St Ulrich, bishop of Augsburg, describes Ulrich visiting his diocese,[79] this passage is an exception, and not the rule. That there are few references to the legal activities of bishops makes sense, given the nature of the *vitae* themselves. As Haarländer has pointed out, the authors of these texts were not writing to provide logs of the daily life of individual bishops, but instead sought to establish the sanctity of their subjects.[80] Occasionally, however, the author of a *vita* has dropped a tantalizing tidbit. The biographer of Burchard, bishop of Worms, wrote, "He was always speaking about justice, or the judgments of the laws, or the

---

[73]   Letter 5. *Die Briefe des Bischofs Rather von Verona*, ed. Fritz Weigle, MGH Die Briefe der deutschen Kaiserzeit 1 (Weimar, 1949), p. 30; Rather of Verona, *The Complete Works of Rather of Verona*, ed. and trans. Peter L.D. Reid, Medieval and Renaissance Texts and Studies 76 (Binghamton, NY, 1991), p. 217.

[74]   Letter 28. See *Briefe*, ed. Weigle, pp. 71–106; *The Complete Works of Rather*, ed. and trans. Reid, pp. 352–80.

[75]   Forty-five of 131 letters address legal issues; Hartmann, "L'évêque comme juge," p. 78.

[76]   Ibid., pp. 77–78.

[77]   Hartmann points out the rarity of such *vitae* for French bishops; "L'évêque comme juge," p. 76.

[78]   Hartmann, "Probleme," p. 649, makes the same point. On these *vitae*, see the recent publications of Coué, *Hagiographie im Kontext*; Haarländer, "Die Vita Burchardi"; and eadem, *Vitae episcoporum*.

[79]   Gerhard of Augsburg, *Vita Sancti Uodalrici: Die älteste Lebensbeschreibung des heiligen Ulrich*, 1.6, ed. and trans. Walter Berschin and Angelika Häse, Editiones Heidelbergenses 24 (Heidelberg, 1993), pp. 143–47.

[80]   See Haarländer, *Vitae episcoporum*, pp. 17–26.

unremitting application of holy reading." (*Eius autem ori iusticia sive legum iudicia aut sacrae lectionis assiduitas numquam deerat.*)[81]

The Example of Burchard, Bishop of Worms

It is instructive to look more closely at Burchard as an exemplar of the judicially-minded bishop of the tenth and early eleventh centuries. Burchard judged ecclesiastical cases, as we learn in his *vita*, and participated in synods, such as that of Seligenstadt. In addition, he also actively engaged in systematizing and theorizing about law—both church law and secular law. He compiled a book of canon law, the *Decretum*, which was widely copied and studied through the twelfth century and even later.[82]

Burchard's book of canon law found practical application by bishops. In Constance, for instance, Bishop Eberhard (1034–1046) ordered a copy of the *Decretum* to be made.[83] Later, in some Italian manuscripts, an *ordo* for a diocesan synod was added. In other words, Italian bishops were using the *Decretum* as a reference tool and found it helpful to add instructions for running a synod.[84] In addition, as we have already seen, bishops found the collection useful in drawing up decrees at the synods of Seligenstadt and Frankfurt. In this way, a bishop not only compiled the *Decretum*, but the collection itself underlaid and informed later conciliar proceedings.

Burchard was apparently inspired by his own experience as bishop to make a book of canon law that could be used to teach priests and canons of the cathedral, and that could then be used as a handbook.[85] His motivations were both pastoral and

---

[81]   *Vita Burchardi episcopi*, c. 20, ed. Georg Waitz, MGH SS 4 (Hannover, 1841), p. 844. On Burchard's life see, for example, the entry by Reinhold Kaiser and Max Kerner in *Lexikon des Mittelalters*, 9 vols (Munich, 1983), 2:946–51, and Theo Kölzer, "Burchard I., Bischof von Worms (1000–1025)," in *Decretorum libri XX: Ex consiliis et orthodoxorum patrum decretis, tum etiam diversarum nationum synodis seu loci communes congesti*, ed. Gérard Fransen and Theo Kölzer (Cologne, 1548; repr. Aalen, 1992), pp. 7–23.

[82]   On the *Decretum*, see Kéry, *Canonical Collections*, pp. 134–44. Subsequent to Kéry's bibliography, the following studies and volumes of interest were published (in chronological order): Peter Landau, "Burchard de Worms et Gratien: À propos des sources immédiates de Gratien," in *Le Décret de Gratien revisité: Hommage à Rudolf Weigand, Revue de droit canonique* 48 (1998), 233–45; Gerold Bönnen and Irene Spille eds, *Bischof Burchard, 1000–1025: Tausend Jahre Romanik in Worms* (Worms, 2000); Thomas T. Müller et al. eds, *Bischof Burchard I. in seiner Zeit: Tagungsband zum biographische-landeskundlichen Kolloquium vom 13. bis 15. Oktober 2000 in Heilbad Heiligenstadt*, Beiträge aus den Archiven im Landkreis Eichsfeld 1 (Heiligenstadt, 2001); Corbet, *Autour de Burchard de Worms* (above, n. 27), and Greta Austin, "Jurisprudence in the Service of Pastoral Care: The *Decretum* of Burchard of Worms," *Speculum* 79 (2004), 929–59.

[83]   See Hoffmann and Pokorny, *Das Dekret des Bischofs Burchard von Worms*, p. 129.

[84]   Hartmann also concludes from this "daß in Italien auf Diözesansynoden Burchards Dekret als Handbuch für den Bischof präsent war": "Probleme," p. 637.

[85]   In the preface, Burchard wrote that he had made this book for "young boys for study, so that what our co-workers, today in their maturity, had neglected due to the ineptitude of our predecessors, is handed over to those now of tender age and to others willing to learn.

pragmatic. Yet, as this paper has argued, these very practical concerns inspired him to theorize about the nature of canon law, and to look for the underlying principles that gave it coherency.[86]

The practice of canon law inspired Burchard to investigate jurisprudence. Practice led to theory, and not vice versa. For instance, it seems likely that the canon law governing feuds in the *Decretum* was colored by Burchard's experience with how the *familia* of Worms had suffered from feuds.[87] Although Fournier proposed long ago that the claims of the papacy led to new interest in the law and resulted in new archival work, this may not, in fact, be a completely accurate summary of the situation. Perhaps what led to the dramatic increase of canons in the second half of the eleventh century was, in part, the curiosity of bishops like Burchard and other clergy who, in practicing canon law, found inadequacies or unanswered questions. As Brett has proposed, the rise of canon law seems to have been driven by local interest, often spearheaded by bishops. Tenth- and early eleventh-century bishops, such as Burchard, had also initiated and encouraged the development of canon law, and this process began before the so-called Gregorian reform.

In fact, Burchard did not restrict his interest in law to canon law. He acted both as bishop of Worms and as its lord, and thus was in charge of both secular and ecclesiastical justice. Burchard as bishop not only applied secular law, but he also codified it and had it written down. He initiated the creation of a book of secular law, the *Lex familiae*, for the dependents of the church of Worms, the *familia*.[88] In the *Lex familiae*, he ordered that the customary law of the *familia* be written down. He did this so that new laws could not be imposed arbitrarily upon the *familia*. From the *Lex familiae*, we can learn something about the administration of secular justice. Judges

---

Indeed let them first be made apt students, and afterward both teachers and leaders of the people, and let them learn in schools what some day they ought to say to those committed to themselves" (nunc demum pueris traderem addiscendum, ut quod nostri cooperatores in maturiore etate positi nostris diebus et antecessorum nostrorum tarditate neglexerant, modo aetate teneris et aliis discere uolentibus traderetur: siquidem ut prius fierent probi discipuli, post plebium et doctores et magistri, et ut perciperent in scolis quid quandoque dicere deberent sibi commissis): *Decretorum libri XX*, ed. Fransen and Kölzer, p. 46; translation from Somerville and Brasington, *Prefaces*, p. 100. It should also be noted that in the Preface, Burchard commented that his book should remain within the diocese "to be studied by our own" (nostris addiscendus): *Decretorum libri XX*, ed. Fransen and Kölzer, p. 48; Somerville and Brasington trans, *Prefaces*, p. 104.

[86]   Greta Austin, "Jurisprudence in the Service of Pastoral Care," and eadem, *Law, Theology and 'Forgery' around the Year 1000: The Decretum of Burchard of Worms* (Aldershot, 2007).

[87]   Greta Austin, "Vengeance and Law in Eleventh-Century Worms: Burchard and the Canon Law of Feuds," *Medieval Church Law and the Origins of the Western Legal Tradition: A Tribute to Kenneth Pennington*, ed. Wolfgang P. Müller and Mary E. Sommar (Washington, DC, 2006), pp. 104–21.

[88]   *Lex familiae Wormatiensis ecclesiae*, ed. Ludwig Weiland, MGH Constitutiones et acta publica imperatorum et regum 1 (Hannover, 1893), pp. 639–44. On it see Knut Schulz, "Das Wormser Hofrecht Bischof Burchards," in *Bischof Burchard von Worms*, ed. Hartmann, pp. 251–78, and accompanying bibliography, particularly Gerhard Theuerkauf, "Burchard von Worms und die Rechtskunde seiner Zeit," *Frühmittelalterliche Studien* 2 (1968), 144–61.

presided over a court for the *familia* of Worms,[89] and a *magister loci* made decisions about property damage.[90] Confessions were made before a *minister*.[91] There was also what we might call today a public defender, called an *advocatus*, who argued on behalf of an accused member of the *familia* before the count (and who also served as a judge).[92] This advocate seems to have served as a buffer between the local ruler and the *familia*. Burchard seems to have worked to limit the local count's power over the people of Worms. Only if a member of the *familia* were caught in the act of theft—a crime which the *Decretum* also considered to be particularly heinous—could the count imprison him.[93] The count could also get involved if the thief was found guilty by the *scabini*, the judges in the *mallus*, the public judicial assembly.[94] Otherwise, the count was not to interfere with legal proceedings. As bishop and lord, Burchard was involved in both the ecclesiastical and secular courts.

Burchard's practical experience with law as a bishop seems to have inspired him to theorize about law.[95] This theorizing resulted in two very useful books: a codification of secular law and a systematic compilation of ecclesiastical law. Burchard may be a representative, if outstanding, example of a bishop whose duties required him to be involved with canon law, and led him to think more deeply about the need for systematic and coherent books of laws that gave more rights to the poor. In short, the practice of canon law by a bishop led to his theorizing about it.

Conclusion

One significant source of reform before the mid-eleventh century seems to have been bishops, who often strived to make the behavior of their sees consistent with the norms of the canons, and to loosen the reins of secular rulers over the church. To do so, they consulted canon law collections in their visitations of sees, created new books, and issued decrees at councils.

During the tenth and early eleventh centuries, we see a continual and strong demand for canon law on the part of the episcopacy, particularly in Germany. To understand the dramatic expansion of canon law in the following centuries, we should look to the "Europe of the bishops." The growth of canon law had deep

---

[89]   We know that there was a court because the *Lex familiae* (c. 17, p. 642) dictates the proper conduct therein: the accused must not shout out, leave his seat in anger, or show up to court late. On judges, *Lex familiae*, c. 2, p. 640.

[90]   *Lex familiae*, c. 12, pp. 641–42.

[91]   *Lex familiae*, c. 24, p. 643.

[92]   Henry II decreed that anyone in the familia who committed a theft, an assault, or a crime should make restitution "into the bishop's hands to his advocate" (ad manus episcopi suo advocato componat). If anyone from the familia had a dispute with someone outside it, the advocatus represented him in front of the count. See *Die Urkunden Heinrichs II. und Arduins*, ed. Harry Bresslau, Hermann Bloch, and Robert Holtzmann, MGH Diplomata regum et imperatorum Germaniae 3 (Hannover, 1900–1903; repr. Munich, 2001), no. 319, p. 400.

[93]   Ibid.

[94]   Ibid.

[95]   See Austin, "Jurisprudence in the Service of Pastoral Care," and *Law, Theology and 'Forgery'*.

roots in the tenth and early eleventh centuries. The bishops' practical need for law to govern their sees probably underlay much of the "revival of jurisprudence." Much work, however, remains to be done in order to understand the growth of law and its deep connections to the bishops. This article merely serves as a starting point, and its suggestions will probably be refined and revised with more precise studies of this subject. All the same, it seems possible that bottom-up demand fueled the growth of jurisprudence, rather than a top-down policy of papal reform, and that this groundswell of new legal interest arose, at least in part, from the practical and pastoral concerns of the tenth- and eleventh-century episcopate.

Chapter 4

Sovereignty and Social Order: Archbishop Wulfstan and the *Institutes of Polity*

Renée R. Trilling
University of Illinois, Urbana-Champaign

In the famous *Sermo Lupi ad Anglos*, written in 1014, Archbishop Wulfstan of York (1002–1023) describes a country ravaged by more than three decades of continuous Viking attacks that had gradually transformed from seasonal raids into invasion and conquest and had met little or no effective resistance from the English leadership.[1] He portrays a land beset by economic and political turmoil, its resources exhausted by the repeated payment of exorbitant tributes. He addresses a people who had watched their king, Æthelred, go into exile and welcomed his conqueror, Swein, out of a desperate desire to put an end to the attacks. But, he warns, the current sufferings of the English are no more than they deserve:

> This nation, so it seems, has for a long time been made sinful through manifold sins and through many misdeeds: through murders and evil deeds, through avarice and through gluttony, through theft and through pillaging, through traffic in people and through heathen vices, through betrayals and through deceptions, through lawbreaking and through lawlessness, through attacks on relatives and through manslaughter, through attacks on

---

[1]   *Sermo Lupi ad Anglos*, in *The Homilies of Wulfstan*, ed. Dorothy Bethurum (Oxford, 1957), pp. 267–75 (hereafter *Sermo Lupi*). The date of 1014 comes from the rubric introducing the sermon in London, British Library MS Cotton Nero A. i: "SERMO LUPI AD ANGLOS QUANDO DANI MAXIME PERSECUTI SUNT EOS, QUOD FUIT ANNO MILLESIMO .XIIII. AB INCARNATIONE DOMINI NOSTRI IESU CRISTI." The precise dating of the *Sermo Lupi* and its three versions has been the subject of much debate; Jonathan Wilcox recently offered an extremely precise and quite convincing argument for dating the sermon to the consecration of Ælfwig as bishop of London, and the meeting of the *witenagemot* (governing council) he suggests accompanied it, in "Wulfstan's *Sermo Lupi ad Anglos* as Political Performance: 16 February 1014 and Beyond," in *Wulfstan, Archbishop of York: The Proceedings of the Second Alcuin Conference*, ed. Matthew Townend, Studies in the Early Middle Ages 10 (Turnhout, 2004), pp. 375–96. Malcolm Godden argues for an earlier date for the sermon; see "Apocalypse and Invasion in Late Anglo-Saxon England," in *From Anglo-Saxon to Early Middle English: Studies Presented to E.G. Stanley*, ed. Malcolm Godden, Douglas Gray, and Terry Hoad (Oxford, 1994), pp. 130–62. But scholars agree, following the Nero rubric, that the sermon is very much a response to the contemporary situation of Viking attacks and invasion, even if they disagree on the specifics of dating.

priests and through adulteries, through incests and through various fornications. And also many more than should be are lost and ravaged widely, as we said before, through oathbreaking and pledgebreaking and various lies . . . .[2]

The difference between the burning, raping, and pillaging of the Vikings and the lawbreaking, adultery, and human trafficking of the English is one of degree, not of kind, and the ravages of war are, in Wulfstan's view, a fitting punishment for a nation whose depravity has sunk even lower than that of the Romanized Britons.[3] The tribulations of the English in 1014 are a clear sign of God's justice, and the remedy for these punishments is equally clear: "And let us do what is needful for us, bow to right and in some part forgo injustice and make amends for that which we earlier broke. And let us love God and obey God's laws and very diligently fulfill that which we promised to undertake at baptism. . . . "[4] The law code issued by King Æthelred in 1014, which was also drafted by Wulfstan, echoes this conviction: "For it is only for that reason that things will improve at all in this land, that injustice be suppressed and righteousness be practiced before God and before the world [i.e., according to both religious and secular law]."[5]

Wulfstan speaks to his audience with the authority of a man of God and, more specifically, of the highest religious office in the kingdom. As archbishop, Wulfstan combined the religious authority of the bishop with the secular authority of the royal adviser, and he played an active role in the administration of both secular and ecclesiastical society; the homily and law codes cited above attest to considerable overlap in the archbishop's perception of his duties. Greatly influenced by the tenth-century Benedictine Reform, Wulfstan's life's work can be viewed as a single-

---

2   "[W]earð þes þeodscipe, swa hit þincan mæg, swyþe forsyngod þurh mænigfealde synna ᛝ þurh fela misdæda: þurh morðdæda ᛝ þurh mandæda, þurh gitsunga ᛝ þurh gifernessa, þurh stala ᛝ þurh strudunga, þurh mannsylena ᛝ þurh hæþene unsida, þurh swicdomas ᛝ þurh searacræftas, þurh lahbrycas ᛝ þurh æwswicas, þurh mægræsas ᛝ þurh manslyhtas, þurh hadbrycas ᛝ þurh æwbrycas, þurh siblegeru ᛝ þurh mistlice forligru. And eac syndan wide, swa we ær cwædan, þurh aðbricas ᛝ þurh wedbrycas ᛝ þurh mistlice leasunga forloren ᛝ forlogen ma þonne scolde": *Sermo Lupi*, lines 131–40. All translations are my own.

3   "ᛝ soþ is þæt ic secge, wyrsan dæda we witan mid Englum þonne we mid Bryttan ahwar gehyrdan [and it is true what I say, that we know of worse deeds among the English than we ever heard of among the Britons]": *Sermo Lupi*, lines 187–89. The Britons' loss of dominion is vividly recounted by the sixth-century historian Gildas, who attributes their defeat to the general depravity of the nation; see Gildas, *The Ruin of Britain and Other Works*, ed. and trans. Michael Winterbottom (London, 1978). Wulfstan is not the first to make this connection; Alcuin offered similar advice following the sack of Lindisfarne in 793 in both letters and in a poem. See Ernst Dümmler ed., MGH Epistolae 4 (Berlin, 1895), pp. 42–44; and Dümmler ed., MGH Poetae Latini Aevi Carolini 1 (Berlin, 1881), pp. 229–35.

4   "And utan don swa us þearf is, gebugan to rihte ᛝ be suman dæle unriht forlætan ᛝ betan swyþe georne þæt we ær bræcan. And utan God lufian ᛝ Godes lagum fylgean, ᛝ gelæstan swyþe georne þæt þæt we behetan þa we fulluht underfengan": *Sermo Lupi*, lines 190–94.

5   "Forþam þurh þæt hit sceal on earde godian to ahte, þe man unriht alecge ᛝ rihtwisnesse lufie for Gode ᛝ for worolde": V Æthelred 33.1, in *Die Gesetze der Angelsachsen*, ed. Felix Liebermann, 3 vols (Halle, 1903–1916), 1:244. Subsequent citations will use Liebermann's abbreviations for individual codes, i.e., V Atr 33.1.

handed attempt to bring the ecclesiastical reform begun in the monasteries to the people of the secular church—in direct contrast to the primarily monastic focus of both the original reformers and their other second generation successors, Ælfric and Byrhtferth.[6] Wulfstan's project finds its apotheosis in the *Institutes of Polity*, an idealized vision of harmony between law and religious belief and, surprisingly, one of Wulfstan's more obscure works. The *Sermo Lupi* and the law codes are well-studied texts, but in spite of Karl Jost's 1959 edition,[7] as well as a recent upsurge in Wulfstan studies,[8] *Polity* remains "one of the most regrettably under-researched items in the Old English canon."[9] While most work on Wulfstan makes reference to *Polity*, and the text is universally acknowledged to be the best-developed example of Wulfstan's thought on the conjunction of Christian and secular law, no full-length study of the text has yet appeared. In *Polity*, Wulfstan lays out a systematic plan for the administration of civil society, based on traditional notions of Christian kingship and rooted firmly in the belief that obedience to God and king are guarantors of salvation, both in this world and the next. He establishes a strict social hierarchy and defines the rights and responsibilities of each group according to rank. It is, *prima facie*, a thoroughly conventional statement of medieval political organization. Through a careful reading of the text, however, the figure of the bishop emerges at the center of this new world order. As this article will demonstrate, the bishop, rather than the king, becomes the architect of peace, unity, and justice in a Christian kingdom, revealing a fundamental contradiction at the heart of Wulfstan's *Polity*: the irreconcilability of divine and secular sovereignty in the administration of civil society. As I will argue, *Polity* radically rethinks the relationship between secular and divine power as it emerges in the dealings of kings and bishops in late Anglo-Saxon England. The ongoing tensions between the secular authority of the king and the religious authority of the bishop thus serve paradoxically as both the impetus for the project of reform embodied in *Polity* and the reason for its ultimate failure.

Wulfstan's Career and the Compilation of the *Institutes of Polity*

Wulfstan first appears in the historical record as bishop of London in 996.[10] He served as archbishop of York from 1002–1023, and he held that see in plurality with the see

---

[6]   See Joyce Hill, "Archbishop Wulfstan: Reformer?" in *Wulfstan*, ed. Townend, pp. 309–24.

[7]   *Die "Institutes of Polity, Civil and Ecclesiastical": Ein Werk Erzbischof Wulfstans von York*, ed. Karl Jost, Schweitzer anglistische Arbeiten/Swiss Studies in English 47 (Bern, 1959). All citations are taken from this edition.

[8]   As evidenced in part by the Second Alcuin Conference held at York in 2002, which commemorated the millennium of Wulfstan's elevation to the sees of York and Worcester; the proceedings are published as *Wulfstan*, ed. Townend.

[9]   Patrick Wormald, *The Making of English Law: King Alfred to the Twelfth Century*, vol. 1, *Legislation and its Limits* (Oxford, 1999), p. 458 n. 153.

[10]   The only information recorded under the year 996, in a stretch of annals that is otherwise quite detailed, is "Her was Wulstan gehadod to biscope into Lundonbyri [In this year, Wulfstan

of Worcester from 1002–1016.[11] His distinctive vernacular prose style has allowed scholars to attribute an enormous body of work to him, making him one of the most prolific authors of the Anglo-Saxon period.[12] While he is best known for the vitriolic and apocalyptic prose of homilies like the *Sermo Lupi*, he was also the author of numerous letters, two poems preserved in the Anglo-Saxon Chronicle, a series of important law codes, some Latin sermons, and various other pieces of writing whose ambivalent nature—are they legal treatises? homilies? notes for future reference?—makes them difficult to classify. Perhaps his most powerful role was that of legal adviser to two kings; Wulfstan was responsible for drafting several law codes for both the Anglo-Saxon King Æthelred and the Danish conqueror, Cnut, and these law codes mark a significant departure from previous legal discourse by incorporating the ideas and even the language of homiletic texts into decrees governing the behavior of English subjects.[13] While issued in the name of the king and therefore bearing his

was consecrated bishop in London]": *The Anglo-Saxon Chronicle: A Collaborative Edition. Volume 8: MS F*, ed. Peter S. Baker (Cambridge, 2000).

[11]   For the establishment of this chronology, see Dorothy Whitelock, "A Note on the Career of Wulfstan the Homilist," *English Historical Review* 52 (1937), 460–65.

[12]   See Jost, "Einige Wulfstantexte und ihre Quellen," *Anglia* 56 (1932), 265–315; Angus McIntosh, "Wulfstan's Prose," Sir Israel Gollancz Memorial Lecture, *Proceedings of the British Academy* 34 (1949), 109–42; and Bethurum ed., *Homilies*, pp. 24–49, 87–98. Wulfstan and Ælfric of Eynsham, the most prolific homilist of the Anglo-Saxon period, are primary figures in the explosion of vernacular literary production that was one side effect of the tenth-century reform. Through a vast body of vernacular texts, reform ideals were promulgated and disseminated to a wider population. The great poetic codices—the Exeter Book, the Junius Manuscript, the Nowell Codex, and the Vercelli Book—all date roughly from the period from 975 to 1025; see vols 1–4 of *The Anglo-Saxon Poetic Records: A Collective Edition*, ed. G.P. Krapp and E. van K. Dobbie, 6 vols (New York, 1931–1953). In addition to the poetic canon, hundreds of vernacular homilies were copied during this period, comprising the largest group of Old English texts extant today. Many of the homilies are anonymous texts, but more than half of them were authored by Wulfstan and Ælfric; see Bethurum ed., *Homilies*; *Ælfric's Catholic Homilies: The First Series*, ed. Peter Clemoes, EETS, s.s., 17 (London, 1997); *Ælfric's Catholic Homilies: The Second Series*, ed. Malcolm Godden, EETS, s.s., 5 (London, 1979); and *Ælfric's Lives of Saints*, ed. Walter W. Skeat, EETS, o.s., 76, 82, 94, and 114, vols 1–2 (London, 1881–1900; repr. 1966). On the impact of these two men on late Anglo-Saxon society, see Milton McC. Gatch, *Preaching and Theology in Anglo-Saxon England: Ælfric and Wulfstan* (Toronto, 1977); Eric John, "The World of Abbot Ælfric," in *Ideal and Reality in Frankish and Anglo-Saxon Society*, ed. Patrick Wormald (Oxford, 1983), pp. 300–16; and Joyce Hill, "The Benedictine Reform and Beyond," in *A Companion to Anglo-Saxon Literature*, ed. Phillip Pulsiano and Elaine Treharne (Oxford, 2001), pp. 151–69. Taken together, the various aspects of late Anglo-Saxon literary production constitute evidence of a major project of Christian edification for a broad secular audience, and they offer compelling testimony of a determined, "business as usual" attitude at the monasteries in spite of the ongoing Danish attacks.

[13]   For V–X Atr and I–II Cn, see Liebermann ed., *Gesetze*, 1:246–70, 278–371. For a quick but striking illustration of Wulfstan's influence, compare IV Atr (*c.*991–*c.*1002) and V Atr (1008) in Liebermann ed., *Gesetze*, 1:232–36, 236–47. IV Atr details the payments of tolls and the regulation of coinage; V Atr, on the other hand, is issued "In nomine Domini" and decrees rigid adherence to Christian practice in all aspects of life. Royal legislation of ecclesiastical

authority as lawgiver, the codes of Æthelred and Cnut also bear the unmistakable stamp of Wulfstan's rhetoric. Most of Wulfstan's law codes read like homilies; many of his homilies utilize legal diction; and some texts attributed to him, like *Polity*, occupy a literary no-man's-land between established genres.

The disintegration of genres is typical of Wulfstan's work, and it is due in great part to his larger project: the (re)integration of Christian principles into the governance of Christian society. During Wulfstan's long career, England was in an almost constant state of war, and the pastoral efforts of the archbishop focused on alleviating his flock's suffering by exhorting them to prayer, repentance, and almsgiving as a remedy for evils inflicted by an angry God. These exhortations are present in everything that Wulfstan wrote, whether homilies, where exhortation is a common rhetorical strategy, or law codes, where it is distinctly out of place. Patrick Wormald has commented that "Wulfstan becomes more than a preacher of genius who drafted laws too. He was the new English kingdom's main exponent of the Biblical ideal that God's People be ruled in accordance with His will: the pre-eminent ideal of Charlemagne's kingship."[14] Christopher A. Jones calls Wulfstan "one of relatively few early medieval figures . . . for whom the sources reveal the deep affinities between liturgy, law, and preaching as media to proclaim the ordinances of God."[15] Paradoxically, Dorothy Whitelock's famous formulation of Wulfstan as "homilist and statesman" obscures to a certain extent the complexity and scope of the archbishop's perceived objective.[16] For Wulfstan, his roles as homilist and statesman were merely two aspects of his pastoral calling; preaching and lawgiving were complementary means to a single end. Wulfstan's refusal, or inability, to distinguish between genres makes classifying his work difficult for modern scholars, but it serves as a compelling illustration of his own sense of a unified divine mission.

Complicating the question of genre is *Polity*'s manuscript context. The text does not exist in a complete copy; rather, it is a series of chapters scattered through five different manuscripts, none of which gives it a title, although many of the sections are rubricated. Nor do any of the manuscripts present the texts of *Polity* contiguously. Instead, the chapters are interspersed with a variety of other types of material: letters, homilies, law codes, biblical texts, extracts from commentaries, and canon law. The

---

issues is by no means unheard of in Anglo-Saxon England; the 695 law code of Kentish King Wihtræd focuses in great detail on the protection of churches and the regularization of marriage practices, and later codes follow its lead in taking up similar issues; see Liebermann ed., *Gesetze*, 1:12–14. In this respect, Wulfstan's work on the codes of Æthelred and Cnut revisits well-known territory; his incorporation of homiletic style, however, is something wholly new and links the legal texts explicitly with his other writings.

[14]   Wormald, *English Law*, 1:27.

[15]   Jones, "Wulfstan's Liturgical Interests," in *Wulfstan*, ed. Townend, pp. 325–52 at p. 350. With regard to *Polity* in particular, Raachel Jurovics writes, "Wulfstan's *Institutes of Polity*, a definition of all classes' social duties, is the only Old English work to deal with the limits of political power and the interrelationship of church and secular authority." See "*Sermo Lupi* and the Moral Purpose of Rhetoric," in *The Old English Homily and its Backgrounds*, ed. Paul E. Szarmach and Bernard F. Huppé (Albany, NY, 1978), pp. 203–20 at pp. 203–4.

[16]   Dorothy Whitelock, "Archbishop Wulfstan, Homilist and Statesman," *Transactions of the Royal Historical Society*, 4th ser., 24 (1942), 24–45.

five versions contain a good deal of overlapping material, but no two are identical.[17] Equally troubling is Wulfstan's frequent habit of citing himself, so that many passages in *Polity* are identical to passages in other extant law codes and homilies. As a result, *Polity* has proved difficult to collate, and sifting through the extracts to determine which belong together was a monumental task.[18] The first modern edition was published in 1959 by Karl Jost, who printed two versions of the text. One was a shorter version, copied in its entirety on pages 87–93 of Cambridge, Corpus Christi College MS 201; Jost calls this version *I Polity*. London, British Library MS Cotton Nero A. i represents an intermediate stage of the text; *I Polity* occupies folios 70r–76v, while additional material is scattered through later portions of the manuscript (fols 97r–98v, 102r–5v, 109r–v, 120r).[19] Oxford, Bodleian Library MS Junius 121 brings *I Polity* and the additional material in Nero A. i together; the resulting text has the final schema of the text Jost calls *II Polity* and offers a comprehensive overview of rank in a Christian society.[20] Even the Junius text is interrupted, however, by passages from other Wulfstaniana, such as the *Canons of Edgar* and the *Benedictine Office*.[21] These later additions, and their subsequent incorporation into what is

---

[17] Jost bases his edition on extracts found in Cambridge, Corpus Christi College (hereafter CCCC) MS 201 (D); London, British Library MS Cotton Nero A. i (G); London, British Library MS Cotton Tiberius A. iii (N); Cambridge University Library (hereafter CUL) Additional MS 3206 (Uc); and Oxford, Bodleian Library MS Junius 121 (X). No edition or translation before Jost collates all five manuscripts to generate a text of *Polity*; see Jost ed., *Polity*, pp. 15–16. The copy of *Polity* in Nero A. i is heavily annotated by Wulfstan himself; see N.R. Ker, "The Handwriting of Archbishop Wulfstan," in *England Before the Conquest: Studies in Primary Sources Presented to Dorothy Whitelock*, ed. Peter Clemoes and Kathleen Hughes (Cambridge, 1971), pp. 315–31. See also Henry R. Loyn ed., *A Wulfstan Manuscript Containing Institutes, Laws and Homilies: British Museum Cotton Nero A. i*, Early English Manuscripts in Facsimile 17 (Copenhagen, 1971).

[18] *Polity* was first printed by David Wilkins, under the title of *Liber Constitutionum*, in his *Leges Anglo-Saxonicae Ecclesiasticae et Civiles* (London, 1721). It was subsequently included by Benjamin Thorpe in *Ancient Laws and Institutes of England* (London, 1840), who titled it *Institutes of Polity, Civil and Ecclesiastical*. See Jost ed., *Polity*, pp. 15–16.

[19] But see Tadao Kubouchi, who argues that Nero A. i is actually the earliest MS of *Polity* in "Texts of 'Be Cynestole' in Wulfstan's *Institutes of Polity*," in *Arthurian and Other Studies Presented to Shunichi Noguchi*, ed. Takashi Suzuki and Tsuyoshi Mukai (Cambridge, 1993), pp. 211–17 at pp. 211–12.

[20] See below, Table 4.2.

[21] For the contents and dates of the various MSS, see N.R. Ker, *A Catalogue of Manuscripts Containing Anglo-Saxon* (Oxford, 1990), nos 11, 49, 163–64, 186, and 338; see also Jost ed., *Polity*, pp. 8–15. The *Canons of Edgar* is also found in CCCC MS 201, CUL Add. 3206, and Junius 121; see *Wulfstan's Canons of Edgar*, ed. Roger Fowler, EETS, o.s., 266 (London, 1972), and R.G. Fowler, "Archbishop Wulfstan's 'Commonplace-Book' and the *Canons of Edgar*," *Medium Ævum* 32 (1963), 1–10. *The Benedictine Office*, ed. James M. Ure (Edinburgh, 1957); Bernhard Fehr, "Das Benediktiner-Offizium und die Beziehungen zwischen Aelfric und Wulfstan," *Englische Studien* 46 (1913), 337–46; and Peter Clemoes, "The Old English Benedictine Office, CCCC MS 190, and the Relations between Ælfric and Wulfstan: A Reconsideration," *Anglia* 78 (1960), 265–83. J.E. Cross and Andrew Hamer

effectively a second edition of *Polity*,[22] indicate an ongoing interest on Wulfstan's part in the development of these ideas. It is still difficult, however, to talk of either version of *Polity* as a unitary text, since both the manuscript contexts and the extracts themselves indicate a collection of related ideas rather than a cohesive, planned composition. Whatever Wulfstan thought of his text, it seems clear that the scribes of these manuscripts could not have considered it a unified composition. Because of this, it seems reasonable to assume, as Jost does, that the text was not considered complete at Wulfstan's death in 1023.[23] This manuscript history is very much in keeping with Wulfstan's well-documented practice of compiling, or directing the compilation of, "commonplace books," or collections of extracted and excerpted material relating to specific subjects which were then used by the archbishop in preparing his own compositions.[24] These manuscripts, in particular Nero A. i (which is annotated in Wulfstan's own hand), are unified by both the themes of their contents and their utility as handbooks for pastoral administration. *Polity* is itself a handbook, and its manuscripts demonstrate its interconnectedness with Wulfstan's larger project of the revitalization of Christian society.[25] Moreover, its fragmentary form does not belie the strength of its organization; the individual sections of *Polity* may be split up, but they follow the same ordered sequence that defines Wulfstan's social hierarchy.[26]

If delimiting the text has been a complicated project, it is even more difficult to define, and what precisely *Polity* is remains an unanswered, and perhaps unanswerable, question. In form and organization, it is very similar to the law codes

---

identify Nero A. i as one of Wulfstan's collections of canon law; see *Wulfstan's Canon Law Collection*, ed. Cross and Hamer (Cambridge, 1999).

[22]   See also Wormald, *English Law* (above, n. 9), 1:199 and n. 152.

[23]   Jost ed., *Polity*, pp. 16–34.

[24]   Mary Bateson first identified the commonplace book as a collection of extracts of various kinds useful for an archbishop in both his administrative and pastoral tasks; see Bateson, "A Worcester Cathedral Book of Ecclesiastical Collections, Made c. 1000 A.D.," *English Historical Review* 10 (1895), 712–31. This particular commonplace book has since been identified as Wulfstan's, and several were produced during his lifetime. See Dorothy Bethurum, "Archbishop Wulfstan's Commonplace Book," *PMLA* 57 (1942), 916–29; Whitelock, "Homilist and Statesman"; Fowler, "Archbishop Wulfstan's 'Commonplace-Book'"; J.E. Cross, "Atto of Vercelli, *De Pressuris Ecclesiasticis*, Archbishop Wulfstan, and Wulfstan's 'Commonplace Book'," *Traditio* 48 (1993), 237–46; and Gareth Mann, "The Development of Wulfstan's Alcuin Manuscript," in *Wulfstan*, ed. Townend, pp. 235–78. On Wulfstan's use of elements from the commonplace book in his own compositions, including *Polity*, see Hans Sauer, "The Transmission and Structure of Archbishop Wulfstan's 'Commonplace Book'," in *Old English Prose: Basic Readings*, ed. Paul E. Szarmach, Basic Readings in Anglo-Saxon England 5 (New York, 2000), pp. 339–93 at pp. 368–70.

[25]   Mary Richards finds that manuscripts like Nero A. i and CCCC 201 clearly reveal the "close relationship between law and homily" in Anglo-Saxon England; see "The Manuscript Contexts of the Old English Laws: Tradition and Innovation," in *Studies in Earlier Old English Prose: Sixteen Original Contributions*, ed. Paul E. Szarmach (Albany, NY, 1986), pp. 171–92 at p. 178.

[26]   The sections are not copied contiguously, but they follow a consistent order in all manuscripts; see Ker, *Catalogue*, p. 86, and below, Table 4.2.

that Wulfstan drafted for Æthelred and Cnut. In content, it bears all the homiletic overtones and stylistic features so familiar from Wulfstan's well-studied sermons. Furthermore, there is absolutely no indication of what Wulfstan intended the text to be. Perhaps this is why *Polity* has failed to find an audience among modern scholars. Dividing Wulfstan's homilies from his legal writings has always been contentious, and *Polity* does not rightly fit into either category, although it has strong affinities with both. Yet, once the scattered pieces are picked up and fitted together, *Polity* presents readers with a truly magisterial formulation of social order. In both its form and its content, *Polity* clearly delineates temporal rank as a fixed structure set firmly in an ecclesiastical foundation (Table 4.1).[27] Each section lays out the responsibilities of the group concerned, followed by detailed descriptions in Wulfstan's characteristically hyperbolic style of the myriad ways in which those people fail to live up to the Christian standard (with the notable exception of the king, who escapes such censure).

Because of its unconventional form and ambiguous status, *Polity* is able to take up threads that run throughout Wulfstan's work and bring them together in one place, presenting an ordered and coherent meditation on the place of each individual within a Christian society. Part of *Polity*'s brilliance lies in its adaptation of current social structures to a new (or rather, a reinvigorated) ideal. Wulfstan does not propose to do away with contemporary polity; rather, he presents the status quo as simply a degraded version of an original, divinely-ordained ideal. His juxtaposition of class duties with their current abuses works to naturalize the current system while still insisting upon reform and renewal. The figure on whom the renewal turns is, of course, the bishop. As mediator between Christian and secular law, the bishop serves as the linchpin; he is the conduit through which the project of Christian education and political reform must take place. He is uniquely positioned to bring together the religious ideals of reform monasticism with the legislative force of secular authority. As such, the bishop becomes, in many ways, the most powerful player in Wulfstan's establishment; he is central to the *Institutes of Polity*, and the role, as Wulfstan performed it, became central to the development of Anglo-Saxon legal and political discourse in the first decades of the eleventh century.[28]

---

[27]   The schema depicted in Table 4.1 follows the order given in *II Polity*; *I Polity* differs only slightly, in placing a chapter rubricated "De Episcopis" ahead of "Be ðeodwitan." See Jost ed., *Polity*, p. 59, and below, pp. 71–73 and Table 4.2.

[28]   See Patrick Wormald, "Archbishop Wulfstan and the Holiness of Society," in *Anglo-Saxon History: Basic Readings*, ed. David A.E. Pelteret (New York, 2000), pp. 191–224; and "Archbishop Wulfstan: Eleventh-Century State-Builder," in *Wulfstan*, ed. Townend, pp. 9–27.

Table 4.1 Section Headings of *II Polity* in Jost, *Die "Institutes of Polity"*

Be heofonlicum cyninge	Concerning the heavenly king	3 chapters
Be eorðlicum cyninge	Concerning the earthly king	20 chapters
Be cynedome	Concerning the kingdom	8 chapters
Be cynestole	Concerning the throne	10 chapters
Be ðeodwitan	Concerning the nation's councillors	17 chapters
Item de episcopis	Likewise concerning bishops	27 chapters
Be eorlum	Concerning earls	9 chapters
Be Gerefan	Concerning reeves	8 chapters
Be sacerdum	Concerning priests	43 chapters
Be gehadedum mannum	Concerning consecrated men	25 chapters
Be aboddum	Concerning abbots	3 chapters
Be munecum	Concerning monks	12 chapters
Be mynecenan	Concerning cloistered nuns	1 chapter
By preostan and be nunnan	Concerning priests and secular nuns	1 chapter
Be læwedum mannum	Concerning laymen	11 chapters
Be wudewan	Concerning widows	5 chapters
Be cyrican	Concerning the church	20 chapters
Be eallum cristenum mannum	Concerning all Christian men	12 chapters

Between Church and State: Power, Sovereignty, and the Law

Lawgiving, in the Middle Ages as today, was a way of establishing a social contract between the people of a community. Subjects promised to obey the laws and ensure peace within the kingdom; rulers promised to uphold the laws by punishing lawbreakers. But there were some additional advantages for the king who issued laws. Law codes, especially in the early English period, designated the monarch as the recipient of the fines that were assessed for various crimes. They also connected the monarch's reign not only to the authority of the ancient traditions from which "common law" descended, but also to the power of the Roman and Old Testament models of lawgiving that underwrote early European states. A king who issued his own written code drew on the perceived power of law as a mark of civilization, as well as its resonances with biblical precedent.[29] Legislation enhanced the perception of a king as the highest power in the land, and by the late Anglo-Saxon period, when most of England had finally been united under the Cerdicings, the authority of Wessex was acknowledged in deed as well as in word.

From the beginning, Anglo-Saxon kings did not claim to make laws on their own, however. The seventh-century law codes of the Kentish kings represent law as the province of the king with his councillors; the prologue to Wihtræd's code indicates that "The blessed ones with the consent of all founded these judgments

---

[29]   Wormald, *English Law*, 1:29–30, 93–108.

and added them to the proper customs of the Kentish people."[30] Ine credits both his bishops and his father with advising him on the law code that became the foundation for West Saxon legislation.[31] The lengthy introduction to Alfred's laws similarly indicates reluctance on the part of the king to take sole responsibility for lawmaking, describing himself as having "gathered together" his code from previous sources with the advice of his councillors.[32] Alfred also explains that he has not written down many of his own laws, because he does not presume to know what will be acceptable to his successors. Athelstan's laws are similarly issued "with the counsel of Wulfhelm, the archbishop, and also my other bishops," and, like Alfred, Athelstan does not hesitate to issue decrees regarding the church, though both codes are primarily concerned with the punishment of and exaction of fines for secular legal matters.[33] This trend continues through the codes enacted by Edgar, Æthelred, and Cnut as well. The antiquity of laws—not quite in the sense of precedent, but rather of time-honored tradition—is a partial marker of their authenticity. But, as time went on, the king increasingly became the fount of legislative power; lawgiving is a clearly-established royal prerogative, and by the tenth century, the authority of a decree comes as much from the king who issued it as it does from the idea of law itself.[34] The prologues, which are almost universal in Anglo-Saxon written law, identify the subsequent decrees as the work of a specific king; the codes carry the force of law because they are issued in the name of the king, whose name is the mark of sovereignty:

These are the decrees that King Æthelberht set down . . .
These are the decrees that Hlothere and Eadric set down . . .
This is the decree of Wihtræd, king of Kent . . .
I, Ine, by the grace of God king of the West Saxons . . .
I, King Alfred . . . King Edward . . . I, King Athelstan . . . King Edmund . . .
King Edgar . . . King Æthelred . . . King Cnut.[35]

---

[30] Wi Prol. 3. "ða eadigan fundon mid ealra gemedum ðas domas ꞇ Cantwara rihtum þeawum æcton": Liebermann ed., *Gesetze*, 1:12.

[31] Ine Prol. Liebermann ed., *Gesetze*, 1:88.

[32] Af Introd. 49.9. "togædere gegaderode": Liebermann ed., *Gesetze*, 1:46.

[33] I As Prol. " . . . mid geþehte Wulfhelmes arcebiscopes ꞇ eac minra oþerra biscopa": Liebermann ed., *Gesetze*, 1:146.

[34] Thomas Edward Clemens finds that "As the legal authority of the Church grew, the laws reflected greater standardization of procedure, more reliance on the king's centralized authority, and the reduction of the power of the kinship system;" see *A Rhetoric of Early Anglo-Saxon Law: A Revisionary Interpretation of the Interrelationships among Rhetor, Audience, and Culture* (Ph.D. diss., Purdue University, 1996). Abstract in *Dissertation Abstracts International*, publ. no. AAT 9725529.

[35] Abt Inscr., Hl Inscr., Wi Inscr., Ine Prol., Af Introd. 49.9, I Ew Prol., I As Prol., I Em Prol., II Eg Prol., I Atr Prol., I Cn Prol. "Þis syndon þa domas, þe Æðelbirht cyning asette… Þis syndon þa domas, ðe Hloþhære ꞇ Eadric, Cantwara cyningas, asetton. Ðis synd Wihtrædes domas Cantwara cyninges. Ic Ine, mid Godes gife, Wesseaxna kyning . . . Ic . . . Ælfred cyning . . . Eadwerd cyning . . . Ic Æþelstan cyng . . . Eadmund cyngc . . . Eadgar cyngc . . . Æþelred cining . . . Cnut cyning": Liebermann ed., *Gesetze*, 1:3, 9, 12, 88, 46, 138, 146, 184, 194, 216,

Although the codes are compiled with the advice of councillors and bishops; although the codes may directly address ecclesiastical matters; although the codes may in some cases even be written by a bishop like Wulfstan; and although the king acknowledges that his power to rule comes from the grace of God, it is still the temporal power of royal sovereignty, embodied in the king and represented by his name, that underwrites the force of law.[36] In cases where decrees specifically address ecclesiastical concerns, such as the sanctuary of churches or the payment of tithes, royal authority lends its force to religious principle, but power remains clearly grounded in the secular realm. The union of church and state in royal legislation privileges secular power over divine power.

Medieval political theology, on the other hand, reverses that power dynamic and posits God as the ultimate source of temporal power. For Wulfstan, as for other contemporary political theorists, temporal authority is grounded in divine authority.[37] The power to rule comes from God, both in the sense of divine-right kingship and in the sense that every individual's rights and responsibilities are ultimately owed to God. In an ideology inherited from Charlemagne, Anglo-Saxon kings represented themselves as defenders of the faith as well as Germanic warrior-kings, and this impression was strengthened by Edgar's elaborate coronation at Bath in 973, where he was significantly "consecrated" ("gehalgod") as king.[38] As a rule, kings were not consecrated in the early Anglo-Saxon period; before Edgar, only Ecgferth is said to have been "gehalgod."[39] After Edgar, however, consecration became a regular part

---

and 278. In each of these cases, we are looking at the first written code attributed to each king; his name serves as a stamp of authority for the decrees that will follow.

[36] To what extent the king was actually able to enforce these laws, however, is debatable and another question entirely from their composition.

[37] According to Archbishop Hincmar of Rheims, whose work seems to have influenced Alfred's code (and consequently the rest of West Saxon legal writing), secular rulers should strive to ensure that their laws are in keeping with the dictates and principles of God's law; see Jean Devisse, *Hincmar, archevêque de Reims, 845–882*, 3 vols (Geneva, 1975–1976), pp. 671–723; and Janet L. Nelson, "Kingship, Law and Liturgy in the Political Thought of Hincmar of Rheims," *English Historical Review* 92 (1977), 241–79. Abbo of Fleury, one of the great Continental influences on the English Benedictine Reform, similarly makes the king subject to the Christian principle above all else; see Marco Mostert, *The Political Theology of Abbo of Fleury* (Hilversum, 1987), pp. 123–34. The idea of Christian kingship in Anglo-Saxon England goes back at least to Alfred, if not further; see E.G. Stanley, "The Administration of Law in Anglo-Saxon England: Ideals Formulated by the Bible, Einhard and Hincmar of Rheims—but No Formal Mirror of Princes," in *Germanic Texts and Latin Models: Medieval Reconstructions*, ed. K.E. Olsen, A. Harbus, and T. Hofstra (Leuven, 2001), pp. 53–71.

[38] *The Anglo-Saxon Chronicle: A Collaborative Edition. Volume 3: MS A*, ed. J.M. Bately (Cambridge, 1986). On the role of king as defender of the faith, see H.R. Loyn and J. Percival, *The Reign of Charlemagne*, Documents of Medieval History 2 (New York, 1976). On the political utility (and repercussions) of consecration, see Nelson, "National Synods, Kingship as Office, and Royal Anointing: An Early Medieval Syndrome," *Studies in Church History* 7 (1971), 41–59; J.M. Wallace-Hadrill, *Early Germanic Kingship in England and on the Continent* (Oxford, 1971); and Nelson, "Inauguration Rituals," in *Early Medieval Kingship*, ed. P.H. Sawyer and I.N. Wood (Leeds, 1977), pp. 50–71.

[39] S.a. 785 in all MSS of the Anglo-Saxon Chronicle.

of confirming royal succession. The act of consecration bestows the power of divine authority on the king, but it also makes him subject to God's law. As a consecrated king, the monarch becomes responsible for his people's salvation, and for ensuring that the church is protected—both its corporate body and its individual members—from temporal and spiritual harm. Wulfstan adheres strictly to this ideology and frequently reminds the king and the people alike that they owe allegiance to one another in the form of protection and loyalty, respectively. From its inception, however, this formulation of royal power suffers from a fundamental split between secular and divine authority. The monarch wields absolute temporal power at the same time that he is himself subject to divine law.[40] The tension between secular and divine authority at the center of royal sovereignty, although it never rose to the level of the Investiture Controversy in Anglo-Saxon England, presents certain difficulties for the theory and practice of lawgiving. Wulfstan's *Polity* engages directly with this paradox, but finds itself unable to contain its fundamental antinomy.

Polity begins clearly enough with the invocation of God as the foundational power behind the principles of justice that the text offers:

I. Concerning the heavenly king
1. In the name of the Lord. One is the eternal king, ruler and maker of all creation.
2. He is the rightful king and the glory of kings and the best of all kings that ever was or will be.
3. To him be ever praise and glory and eternal honor, always and forever. Amen.[41]

The text opens with a distinctly homiletic tone, and its rhythm and alliteration are characteristic of Wulfstan's work. By reiterating the most basic tenets of Christian belief as the foundation of his code, Wulfstan establishes both the stakes of his text and the legal force of its authority. The emphasis is on unity and oneness: the singularity of the one true God, the rectitude of his supremacy, and the duty and honor owed to him. These opening chapters echo the law codes issued "In nomine Domini," which emphasize, repeatedly, that "The first provision is that we all love and honour one God and zealously observe one Christian faith and wholly renounce all heathen practices."[42] Wulfstan clearly grounds the authority of his text, as his own authority is grounded, in a power beyond the human sphere. The second rubric in the text channels that power into the highest authority in the earthly realm:

II. Concerning the earthly king
4. It befits the Christian king of a Christian nation, that he be, as it is right, a comfort to

---

[40] Later ages would attempt to reconcile this problem with political doctrines such as the king's two bodies; see Ernst H. Kantorowicz, *The King's Two Bodies: A Study in Mediaeval Political Theology* (Princeton, NJ, 1957).

[41] "I. Be heofonlicum cyninge. 1. In nomine domini. An is ece cyning wealdend and wyrhta ealra gesceafta. 2. He is on riht cyning and cyninga wuldor and ealra cyninga betst, þe æfre gewurde oðð e geweorð e. 3. Him symble sy lof and wuldor and ece wyrð mynt a to worulde. Amen." All quotations from *Polity* are taken from *II Polity* and follow MS X unless otherwise noted.

[42] "Ðæt is þonne ærest, þæt we ealle ænne God lufian ꝥ weorð ian ꝥ aenne Cristendom georne healdan ꝥ ælcne hæð endom mid ealle aweorpan": V Atr 1. Liebermann ed., *Gesetze*, 1:236.

the people and a proper guardian of the Christian flock.

5. And it befits him, that he raise up Christendom with all his power and eagerly promote and defend God's church everywhere

6. and reconcile and bring together all Christian people with good laws, as he most earnestly might

6a. and through all things practice righteousness before God and before the world.[43]

Wulfstan goes on to stress that misfortune befalls nations as the result of bad governance, and *Polity* admonishes kings to be wise, just, prudent, moderate, patient, and righteous in the judgments they offer and in the decisions they make.[44] In these chapters, the king is responsible both for his people and for the church, and Wulfstan here indicates that the well-being of the Church and of the Christian community are inextricably linked; if one falls into depravity and degradation, the other will necessarily follow.

The Christian community must therefore fulfill its own duties as well. In 1009 and 1014, Æthelred issued two major codes (VII and VIII) that specifically addressed the Viking problem. Both were drafted by Wulfstan, and in them, royal authority backs the prescriptions of ecclesiastical discipline. VII Æthelred, issued at Bath in 1009, decrees a period of fasting and almsgiving "that we might earn God's mercy and his compassion and that we might withstand our enemies with his help."[45] The code emphasizes obedience to God's law, loyalty to the king, and defense of the nation as the foundational elements of England's salvation (both military and otherwise).[46] VIII Æthelred, issued in 1014 following the king's return from exile, emphasizes the protection of churches and the timely payment of tithes and dues to parishes and lords alike.[47] Together, the codes urge strict discipline for all people throughout England in both their religious and secular responsibilities. If tithes are rendered properly, dues paid to lords, and laws obeyed, then there will be peace in the realm. If prayers and alms are offered to God, then England will have God's help in military defense. Æthelred's law codes are Wulfstan's attempt to exercise the king's authority for the protection of his people and God's church in fulfillment of his royal duty, but they depend upon the actions of individual citizens—the Anglo-Saxons who are

---

[43]   "II. Be eorðlicum cyninge. 4. Cristenum cyninge gebyreð on cristenre þeode, þæt he sy, ealswa hit riht is, folces frofer and rihtwis hyrde ofer cristene heorde. 5. And him gebyreþ, þæt he eallum mægne cristendom rære and Godes cyrican æghwær georne fyrðrie and friðie 6. and eall cristen folc sibbie and sehte mid rihtre lage, swa he geornost mæge 6a. and ðurh ælc þing rihtwisnesse lufie for Gode and for worulde." It is interesting to note that the earlier version, *I Polity*, begins immediately with the section "Be cinincge [Concerning the king]"; the opening address to the heavenly king is added as part of the later revisions in *II Polity.* See Jost ed., *Polity*, p. 40.

[44]   *II Polity* 13–30.

[45]   " ... þæt we Godes miltse ⁊ his mildheortnesse habban moton ⁊ þæt we þurh his fultum magon feondum wiðstandan": VII Atr Prol. Liebermann ed., *Gesetze*, 1:262. On the dating of this code, see Whitelock ed., *English Historical Documents*, 2nd edn (London, 1979), 1:447; and Wormald, *English Law*, 1:331 n. 314.

[46]   In the Latin version of VII Atr 1 transmitted by *Quadripartitus*; see Liebermann ed., *Gesetze*, 1:260.

[47]   Liebermann ed., *Gesetze*, 1:263–68.

directed to say the prayers and provide the alms—for their efficacy. The people are thus implicated in social responsibility, and *Polity* likewise emphasizes that Christian rule is upheld by those who are ruled:

IV. Concerning the throne
31. Every rightful throne that stands perfectly upright stands on three pillars:
32. one is *Oratores*, and another is *Laboratores*, and a third is *Bellatores*.[48]

Each of the three orders is equally responsible to God's law, and the stability of the nation depends on their adherence to proper Christian practice. What precisely constitutes proper Christian practice is, in the wake of the monastic reform, a question of significant consequence, and the education of the laity is of paramount importance; hence the momentous project of vernacular literary production and the circulation of homily collections, all with the goal of disseminating a unified set of orthodox Christian values to a wide audience.[49] *Polity* works in conjunction with these other projects toward the larger goal of universal salvation.

In its first four sections, then, *Polity* offers an overview of the political structure of the kingdom: God at the very top, with a direct line of authority running to the monarch, whose throne is supported by the three orders of society. "Concerning the throne" closes with the injunction to "do what is necessary, put down injustice and raise up God's law; that may profit God and the world. Amen."[50] The "Amen" signals a decisive closing and reinforces Wulfstan's homiletic tone. At this point, *Polity* has outlined its basic argument. All of Christian society is accounted for in this brief sketch, and the rest of the text fleshes out the picture with detailed listings of the different ranks of life and their appurtenant duties. Each successive level of society has fewer responsibilities than the one before, although they are addressed to a much broader and more numerous cohort. Wulfstan addresses a mere eleven chapters to the behavior of laymen, with an additional five directed specifically toward widows. These are, significantly, the last two groups to be defined, placing the laity firmly at the bottom of the hierarchy—the foundation on which the other levels of society rest.

The fundamental outline of political authority is never questioned; God remains at the top of the diagram, with the king immediately below and the remaining segments of society in a clearly ranked hierarchy. But it becomes evident throughout *Polity* that the most concretely defined and, in Wulfstan's mind, most important duties fall to the English clergy—in particular to the bishop. Wulfstan argues that

---

[48] "IV. Be cynestole 31. Ælc riht cynestol stent on þrym stapelum, þe fullice ariht stent: 32. an is Oratores, and oðer is Laboratores, and ðridde is Bellatores." Wulfstan borrows this formulation of the three orders almost word-for-word from Ælfric's "Letter to Sigeweard," in *The Old English Version of the Heptateuch, Ælfric's Treatise on the Old and New Testament and his Preface to Genesis*, ed. S.J. Crawford, EETS, o.s., 160 (London, 1922), pp. 15–75 at p. 71. See also Timothy E. Powell, "The 'Three Orders' of Society in Anglo-Saxon England," *Anglo-Saxon England* 23 (1994), 103–32.

[49] See above, n. 12.

[50] " . . . do man, swa hit þearf is, alecge man unriht and rære up Godes riht; þæt mæg to þearfe for Gode and for worulde. Amen": *II Polity* 40.

the people responsible for enforcing the law are the councillors of the nation: "Kings and bishops, earls and generals, reeves and judges, scholars and lawyers."[51] It is hardly coincidental that the bishops lead off the list of the king's advisers,[52] and the section "Concerning the nation's councillors" in fact focuses almost exclusively on the responsibilities of the bishop, to the exclusion of the earls, reeves, generals, and judges.[53] "Concerning the nation's councillors" addresses seventeen chapters to these responsibilities, followed by another twenty-seven chapters headed "Item de episcopis" for a grand total of forty-four chapters on bishops. This is the largest number addressed to a single group, and it seems especially significant in comparison to the relatively small amount of text addressed to the other *þeodwitan*: twenty chapters for the king, nine for earls, and eight for reeves.[54]

Yet the placement of bishops in the hierarchy of councillors caused no small amount of difficulty for Wulfstan, as the codicological evidence for the development of *Polity* demonstrates (see Table 4.2). The text of *I Polity* occupies pages 87–93 of CCCC 201 and is written in a single hand. In this version, the chapters on bishops follow directly after the sections on king, kingdom, and throne. Earls follow bishops and are succeeded by a long list of ecclesiastical figures—abbots, monks, nuns, and priests—before laypeople make an appearance. Like all extant versions of *Polity*, the text in CCCC 201 ends with chapters addressed to the church and to all Christian people. If we accept Jost's dating of revisions to the text, then CCCC 201 represents a very early stage in *Polity*'s development. Nero A. i, on the other hand, represents an intermediate stage of revision. The manuscript contains a number of annotations, corrections, and additions in the archbishop's own hand, evidence of his personal interest in the production of the manuscript; one of those additions is the text of a chapter "On the earthly king" (fol. 120r).[55] In Nero, the organization of chapter headings offers some insight into Wulfstan's struggle with relative hierarchies of divine and secular authority. Folios 70r–76v contain a text of *Polity* roughly parallel to that found in CCCC 201, but with the chapters on bishops omitted entirely; the text moves directly from the throne to earls. The chapters on bishops are written in a different hand on folios 97r–98v. Additional material on bishops occupies folios 99r–102r, and chapters which would later become *II Polity* appear on folios 102r–9v and 120r. These include revised chapters on priests, abbots, and monks, new chapters dedicated specifically to reeves and councillors, and chapters that differentiate the

---

[51]   "Cyningan and bisceopan, eorlan and heretogan, gerefan and deman, larwitan and lahwitan": *II Polity* 41.

[52]   It is especially significant in light of Frank Barlow's observation that bishops and earls continually jostled for position throughout the early eleventh century; see *The English Church 1000–1066: A Constitutional History* (London, 1963), pp. 96–99.

[53]   The section is headed "Be ðeodwitan" and occurs only in *II Polity*; *I Polity* (in CCCC 201) launches directly into six chapters "De episcopis" without considering the larger group of councillors; sixteen chapters under the heading "Item" then follow. *II Polity* here represents a significant expansion of Wulfstan's original precepts on bishops. See Jost ed., *Polity*, pp. 59–62. The Nero MS, however, does not include the heading "De episcopis" at this point in its copy of *I Polity*; these sections occur later in the MS; see below, Table 4.2.

[54]   See above, Table 4.1.

[55]   Ker, *Catalogue*, pp. 211–12.

heavenly king from the earthly king. In the revisions represented by Nero A. i, Wulfstan removed bishops from the initial version of *I Polity*. Those sections return later under the heading "Be ðeodwitan." It appears from these changes that Wulfstan was initially uncomfortable with the prominent placement of bishops in *I Polity* and sought to mitigate that prominence in the Nero revisions.

The text of *Polity* in Junius 121 might, therefore, be considered the final draft of the text, incorporating the revisions from Nero A. i into the main body of the text. *II Polity* in Junius 121 begins with the new chapter "On the heavenly king" from the latter part of the Nero manuscript; following it are chapters "On the earthly king," "On the kingdom," and "On the throne." The next spot, which was filled by bishops in *I Polity* but which went to earls in the Nero version of the text, is dedicated to the chapters "On the nation's councillors"; as noted above, the list of councillors is headed by "kings and bishops," emphasizing the importance of the bishops' role, while the chapters themselves discuss bishops to the exclusion of the other councillors.[56] In addition, the section on councillors is immediately followed by five headings dealing specifically with bishops before moving on to earls. If indeed Wulfstan oversaw the composition of this version of *Polity* as well, then it seems clear that his thinking on the importance of bishops in national governance won out, in the end, against any hesitation he might have felt earlier on about giving church leaders so prominent a place in the civil hierarchy.

If the placement of bishops at the head of the organizational chart can be taken as an indication of their importance to Wulfstan's schema, then the range of duties and responsibilities that the text goes on to assign them is further evidence of such a claim. Wulfstan calls bishops "God's heralds" and places the ultimate responsibility for the salvation of a Christian society firmly on their shoulders:

VI. Likewise concerning bishops

42. And bishops are heralds and teachers of God's law, and they must proclaim justice and forbid injustice: and he who despises to listen to them, let him complain to God himself.

43. And if bishops are delinquent, so that they do not punish sins, nor forbid injustice nor make God's law known, but mumble with their jaws, when they should cry out, woe to them for their silence![57]

---

[56] See above, pp. 71–72.

[57] "VI. Item de episcopis 42. And bisceopas syndon bydelas and Godes lage lareowas, and hi sculan riht bodian and unriht forbeodan: and se þe oferhogige, þæt he heom hlyste, hæbbe him gemæne þæt wið God sylfne. 43. And gif bisceopas forgymað, þæt hi synna ne styrað ne unriht forbeodaþ ne Godes riht ne cyþað, ac clumiað mid ceaflum, þær hi sceoldan clypian, wa heom þære swigean!"

Table 4.2 Order of Chapters in Three MSS of Wulfstan's *Institutes of Polity*[58]

CCCC 201 (s. xi med.)		BL Cot. Nero A. i (s. xi in.)		Bod. Jun. 121 (s. xi. [3d quarter])	
I Polity	**page**	**I Polity**	**folio**	**II Polity**	**folio**
				Be heofenlicum cyninge	9r
Be cinincge	87	Be cynge	70r–v	Be eorðlicum cyninge	9r–10r
Be cinedome	87	Be cynedome	70v–71r	Be cynedome	10r–v
Be cynestole*	87, 88	Be cynestole	71r–v	Be cynestole	10v–11r
				Be ðeodwitan	11r–12v
De episcopis Paulus dicit	88				
Item: Biscopas sculon bocum	88, 89			Item de episcopis. Biscopas sculon bocum	12v–13v
				Item. Bisceope gebyreð ælc rihting	13v–15r
				Item. Bisceopes dægweorc	15r
				Item. A gerist bisceopum wisdom	15r–v
				Incipit de synodo	15v–17r
Be eorlum	89	Be eorlum	71v–72r	Be eorlum	17r–v
Be sacerdum	89	Be sacerdan	72r	Be gerefan	17v–18r
Be gehadedum mannum	89, 90	Be gehadedum mannum	72r–73r	Be abbodum	18r–v
Be abbodum	90	Be abbodum	73r	Be mynecenan	18v–19r
Be munecum	90	Be munecan	73r	Be preostan. ꝛ be nunnan	19v
Be minecenan	90	Be minecenan	73r–v	Be wudewan	19v
Be preostum ꝛ be nunnan	90	Be preostan and be nunnan	73v	Be Godes þeowum	20r–v

[58] Manuscript data collated from Jost ed., *Polity*, pp. 8–15; Ker, *Catalogue*, items 49, 164, and 338; and Loyn, *A Wulfstan Manuscript*.

CCCC 201 (s. xi med.)		BL Cot. Nero A. i (s. xi in.)		Bod. Jun. 121 (s. xi. [3d quarter])	
I Polity	**page**	**I Polity**	**folio**	**II Polity**	**folio**
Be læwedum mannum	90, 91	Be læwedum mannum	73v–74r	Be sacerdum	20v–23v
Be wudewan	91	Be wudewan	74r	Be læwedum mannum	31v–32r
				Be gehadedum mannum	32r–34r
				[homiletic and liturgical texts]	34r–57v
Be circan	91, 92	Be cyricean	74r–75v	Be cyrican	57v–59r
Be eallum cristenum mannum	92, 93	Be eallum cristenum mannum	75v–76v	Be eallum cristenum mannum	59r–59*r
		[various Wulfstan homilies and law codes]	76v–96v		
		Item de episcopis	97r–v		
		Item. Biscopas scylan bocum [=II Polity]	97v–98v		
		Incipit de sinodo	99r–100r		
		Biscpas scoldan symle...	100v–2r		
		Be sacerdan	102r–3v		
		Be abbodum	103v		
		Be munecum	103v–4v		
		Be gerefan	105r–v		
		Be ðeodwitan	109r–v		
		[2 Wulfstan sermons (incl. Sermo Lupi) and V Atr]	110r–19v		
		Be hefenlicum cyninge	120r		
		Be eorðlicum cyninge	120r		

* Without chapter heading; begins "Ælc cynestole stent."

Upholding the law is of paramount importance; the warfare of the early eleventh century is evidence enough for Wulfstan of what happens when a nation falls away from faithful observance. The bishops bear the primary responsibility for seeing that the law is upheld, and they are further enjoined to speak out when it is not.[59] *Polity* goes on to stress, repeatedly, that the work of a bishop consists in study, prayer, and the proclamation of God's law:

58. Bishops must pursue books and prayers and again and again, day and night, call out to Christ and intercede diligently for all Christian people.
59. And they must study and accurately teach and carefully scrutinize the deeds of the people.
60. And they must preach and eagerly set an example for the spiritual duty of a Christian nation.[60]

With the injunction to teach and to cry out against injustice, *Polity* reinforces the bishops' position at the head of the nation's councillors. They have the power, and indeed, the duty, to ensure that secular leaders know and follow Christian principles of justice. *Polity* thus reminds earls and reeves to uphold God's law by administering justice, aiding the poor, defending the church, and eschewing the abuses of power to which secular lords often fall prey.[61] "Justice" here carries a twofold definition: both the justice of the king's law, which the earl or reeve is bound to uphold, and also the justice of God's law, which ideally informs the king's law and should certainly inform any decisions that these powerful men make. In the context of *Polity*, both God's law and the king's law have been codified by Wulfstan, ensuring agreement between the two. Secular lords take instruction from the bishops in order to ensure that they make good judgments and fulfill the duties of their station in the eyes of both God and king. Bishops thus outrank secular lords in both the structural hierarchy of *Polity* and in the text's command to admonish the unjust, no matter what their rank.

If bishops outrank all secular lords because of their separate status as ordained men and because of their special duty to instruct the nation in the precepts of Christian justice, then *Polity* raises the very important question of the power relations between the bishop and the king. At no point does the text state that the bishop should or could have power over the monarch; the direct line of power from God to the king ensures that the king will remain at the top of the hierarchy. Yet several elements within the text suggest that even as Wulfstan reaffirms this hierarchy, he does not fully believe that bishops are subordinate to temporal authority. Rather, Wulfstan seems to indicate that a king, in order to rule properly, must follow the advice of bishops: "He must

---

[59]   On the responsibilities of bishops "to call out, not remain silent, act as God's messenger, and convey God's law," see Jonathan Wilcox, "The Wolf on Shepherds: Wulfstan, Bishops, and the Context of the *Sermo Lupi ad Anglos*," in *Old English Prose: Basic Readings*, ed. Szarmach (above, n. 24), pp. 395–418, at p. 412.

[60]   "58. Bisceopas sculon bocum and gebedum fyligean and dæges and nihtes oft and gelome clypian to Criste and for ealle cristen folc þingian georne. 59. And hi sceolan leornian and rihtlice læran and ymb folces dæda geornlice smeagan. 60. and hi scylan bodian and bysnian georne godcunde þearfe cristenre þeode."

[61]   *II Polity* 78–82.

obey the teachings of books most diligently and hold God's commandments eagerly and often seek out wisdom with the council, if he wishes to obey God properly."[62] The council, with the bishop at its head, thus takes on the role of co-ruler with the king; this impression is emphasized by the placement of "Kings and bishops" as paired terms in an appositive clause leading off the list of *þeodwitan*.[63] But the influence of the bishop goes beyond his role as councillor; the king must also "eagerly obey the divine teaching again and again, for his own good," for "he will be fortunate who obeys the divine teaching most often and holds it most eagerly."[64] For the king, as for everyone else, *Polity* prescribes obedience to divine teaching; and the source of divine teaching, as the text stresses again and again, is the clergy. In this stricture, the king becomes, however briefly, subordinate to the authority of the bishop. Not only is the bishop at the head of the king's councillors, to whom the king is enjoined to turn often in his search for wisdom and good judgment; the bishop also controls access to divine wisdom. In specifying these duties, *Polity* places the king under the bishop's divine authority; while the king may be responsible for ensuring that justice is carried out in his kingdom, the bishop is ultimately responsible for making sure that the king knows what justice is.

Finally, it is the very form of *Polity* that indicates its subtle subordination of royal to divine power. The text reiterates a great deal of material from royal law codes; it looks, in fact, much like those codes in its organization of material. Yet, unlike law codes, which are often transmitted with the dates and places they were issued, and which bear the name of the king who issued them, *Polity* is a free-standing work. It was compiled, revised, and polished over a long period of time, and while it is the work of a single man, it does not bear his name. In *Polity*, the power of lawgiving is abstracted from the specific context of a particular monarch proclaiming a particular code at a particular time and place. In lieu of that particularity, *Polity* offers the universality of a mode of governance independent of time, place, or monarch, based on the eternal authority of divine power and Christian teaching. The law is no longer dependent on the authority of the monarch for its force; rather, the law becomes its own authority, derived directly from God. *Polity* does not refer to men by their names, but by their ranks and stations; civil administration defines its subjects by what they do, rather than by who they are. In its abstraction, the system of government defined in *Polity* takes on the character of ideology: a set of ideas with no history and with significant power to impact the formation of individual subjects.[65] By its nature, ideology is transmitted as truth; its validity is not circumscribed by a particular historical moment or an individual monarch. While, on the surface, *Polity* seems to insist aggressively on the divine right and absolute power of the king, the text's

---

[62] "He sceal boclarum hlystan swyðe georne and Godes beboda geornlice healdan and gelome wið witan wisdom smeagan, gif he Gode wile rihtlice hyran": *II Polity* 16.

[63] See above, p. 72.

[64] " . . . godcunde lare georne gehyre oft and gelome him sylfum to þearfe;" " . . . se byð gesælig, þe godcunde lare oftost gehyreð and geornlicast healdeþ": *II Polity* 20, 22.

[65] See Karl Marx with Friedrich Engels, *The German Ideology* (Amherst, NY, 1998), pp. 41–43; and Louis Althusser, *Lenin and Philosophy and Other Essays*, trans. Ben Brewster (New York, 2001), pp. 106–20.

political unconscious chips away at that power by removing the authorizing name of the sovereign and by subjecting him to the educative power of the bishop.[66] In spite of himself, and quite possibly without intention, Wulfstan undercuts the position of the king in his hierarchical schema by focusing his textual efforts on the definition of what he views as true authority in a Christian kingdom: the religious, not secular, head of state.

To be sure, *Polity* does not offer any new ideas; its contents are mostly recycled passages from Wulfstan's earlier works and from many of his favorite sources, such as Sedulius Scottus, the *Capitula* of Theodulf of Orléans, the *Excerptiones* of Pseudo-Ecgbert, and the homilies and pastoral letters of his contemporary, Ælfric of Eynsham.[67] Yet setting down these institutes puts old ideas into a form that is uniquely Wulfstan's. *Polity* strives to be a reference manual for religiopolitical organization, a handbook for national governance, and a disciplinary discourse for the range of Christian subjects who comprise Anglo-Saxon England. In many ways, this is the realization of a bishop's dream for a Christian kingdom: a nation in which religious and secular authorities accord with one another, and in which the people as a whole accord with the rule of law. In the immediate historical context of the early eleventh century, such a plan is optimistic at best, and I would certainly not wish to argue that England or any part of it was ever actually governed in accordance with its institutes. But the document's very existence, and the evidence that Wulfstan worked on it over a period of several years, perhaps decades, allows us to see the developing ideas of one of early medieval Europe's great leaders as he struggled with the problem of how best to ensure the peace, prosperity, and salvation of his country.

Conclusions: *Polity* and History, Impetus and Influences

Given the historical moment of the generation of *Polity*, it is not surprising to see Wulfstan attempting to separate legal power from the power of the monarch. If, as Jost believes, *Polity* was begun as early as 1008, then the document becomes a harsh commentary on the debility of royal authority in the reign of Æthelred II. Certainly this is the historical picture sketched by the Anglo-Saxon Chronicle. Æthelred's reign is described as one of the darkest periods in medieval English history, and the monarch himself comes into question at the chronicler's hands. The annals tell a story of the progressive degradation and ultimate defeat of the English military at the hands of Viking raiders, whose attacks resumed after nearly a century's hiatus

---

[66]   The power of textuality to mask internal logical contradictions—and the subsequent task of the interpreter to uncover those contradictions—receives thorough treatment in Fredric Jameson, *The Political Unconscious: Narrative as Socially Symbolic Act* (Ithaca, NY, 1977), pp. 77–83 and 154–69.

[67]   On the important relationship between Ælfric and Wulfstan, see Gatch, *Preaching and Theology*; Malcolm Godden, "The Relations of Wulfstan and Ælfric: A Reassessment," in *Wulfstan*, ed. Townend, pp. 353–74; and E.G. Stanley, "Wulfstan and Ælfric: 'The True Difference between the Law and the Gospel,'" in *Wulfstan*, ed. Townend, pp. 429–41.

in 980, two years after Æthelred's accession.[68] These coastal attacks were repeated in the following years, and after the initial decade of incursions, the Chronicle records instance after instance of bad leadership and failed defense, often naming the shameful ealdormen who failed to protect the nation. For example, *sub anno* 992, MS C records that

> The king and all his councillors declared that all the ships that were of use should be gathered at London, and the king then entrusted the force to the leadership of Ealdorman Ælfric and Earl Thored and Bishop Ælfstan and Bishop Æscwig, and they were to try, if they could, to trap the Danish army anywhere at sea. Then Ealdorman Ælfric sent to warn the Danish army, and then on the night before the day on which they were to engage in battle, he fled by night from the army, to his own great shame, and then the Danish army escaped, except that one ship was slain; and then the Danish army met the ships from East Anglia and from London; and they slew a great many there. . . . [69]

This episode is an early indication of the disorganization that would plague the English forces in the decades to come, and it is easy to see how the rigid organization of a state hierarchy would appeal to a leader like Wulfstan.

The following annals are a more or less uninterrupted narrative of continuing defeat and increasing desperation, and over the years the Viking raiders transformed into an army of conquest with imperial ambitions. In the entry for the year 993, we learn that "A great army was gathered, and when they should have engaged in battle, the leaders first started the flight: they were Fræna, Godwine, and Frythegyst."[70] Similarly, under 998, 999, and 1001,[71] the chronicler records attempts at English defense where the warriors showed courage but lacked leadership and inevitably fled the field or were slaughtered. By 1009, the chronicler's disgust with the English leadership is clear:

> In this year the ships [commissioned by Æthelred in 1008] were ready, and there were so many of them as never before had been in England in the day of any king, from what books tell us, and they were all brought together at Sandwich and were to lie there and protect this country from every foreign army. But we still had not the good fortune or the

---

[68] " . . . wæs Suðhamtun forhergod fram scipherige ⁊ seo burhwaru mæst ofslegen ⁊ gehæft; ⁊ þy ilcan geare wæs Tenetland gehergod; ⁊ þy ilcan geare wæs Legeceasterscir gehergod fram norðscipherige [Southampton was ravaged by a naval force and most of the inhabitants slain or taken captive; and in the same year Thanet was harried; and the same year Cheshire was harried by a northern naval force]": *The Anglo-Saxon Chronicle: A Collaborative Edition. Volume 5: MS C*, ed. Katherine O'Brien O'Keeffe (Cambridge, 2001).

[69] "Þa gerædde se cyning ⁊ ealle his witan þæt man gegadrede ealle ða scipu þe ahtes wæron to Lundenbyrig, ⁊ se cyning þa betæhte þa fyrde to lædenne Ælfrice ealdormenn ⁊ Þorede eorle ⁊ Ælfstane bisceope ⁊ Æscwige bisceope, ⁊ sceoldon cunnian meahton hy þone here ahwær utan betreppan. Þa sende se ealdorman Ælfric ⁊ het warnian ðone here, ⁊ þa on ðære nihte þe hy on ðone dæig togædere fon sceoldon, þa sceoc he on niht fram þære fyrde him sylfum to myclum bysmore, ⁊ se here ða ætbærst, butan an scyp þær man ofsloh; ⁊ þa gemette se here ða scypu on Eastenglum ⁊ of Lundene; ⁊ hi ðær ofgeslogon micel wæl": MS C.

[70] "þa gegaderede man swiðe micle fyrde, ⁊ þa hi togædere gan sceoldon, þa onstealdan þa heretogan ærest þone fleam: þæt was Fræna ⁊ Godwine ⁊ Fryþegyst": MS C.

[71] MSS C, D, E; the entry s.a. 1001 is also found in MS A.

honor that the naval force might be of use to this country, any more than it often had been
before.[72]

The chronicler goes on to tell of more treachery, this time by Ealdorman Eadric and
his brother, Brihtric. By 1010, the English army is in shambles, and leadership is
a wreck; "Although something might be decided, it did not stand even a month; at
last there was no leader who would gather an army, but each fled as best he could,
and finally no shire would help the next."[73] In 1011, the chronicler proclaims that
"All these disasters happened to us because of bad counsel [*unrædas*],"[74] sealing
Æthelred's reputation and inspiring his unfortunate but enduring byname of Unræd,
or Unready. Finally, in 1014, England submitted to Swein, and Æthelred went into
exile in Normandy.[75] Swein subsequently died at midwinter, and Æthelred was
invited back on the condition that he govern more wisely.[76] For the next three years,
Swein's son Cnut waged a war of conquest on Æthelred and his successor, Edmund
Ironside, until in 1017 "King Cnut succeeded to all of the English kingdom."[77] The
Viking incursions came to an end, but the price was a Danish king on the English
throne.

Wulfstan reacted to these events forcefully and with great vigor in the *Sermo
Lupi*, Æthelred's and Cnut's law codes, and the successive drafts of *Polity*. Given
the failure of Æthelred to maintain peace in his kingdom, to the point where he
actually went into exile and saw his councillors welcome Swein as their king, the
history of the early eleventh century does little to inspire faith in the authority of
the monarch. In this context, work on a text like *Polity*, which establishes law as
its own power separate from the *lex regis* and directly connected to the *lex dei*, is
not only rational, but expedient. Placed on the level of ideological abstraction, law
returns from the domain of the monarch to the realm of tradition; it takes on its own
authority, separate from the authority of any individual lawgiver or enforcer, in the

---

[72] "Her on þissum geare wurdan þa scypu gearwe, ⁊ hiora wæs swa feala swa næfre ær
þæs, ðe us bec secgað, on Anglecynne ne gewurdon on nanes cyninges dæge, ⁊ hi man ða ealle
togædere ferode to Sandwic ⁊ ðær sceoldon licgan ⁊ þisne eard healdan wið ælcne uthere. Ac
we ða gyt næfdon þa gesælða ne þone wyrðscype þæt seo scypfyrd nyt wære þissum earde þe
ma ðe heo oftor ær wæs": MS C.

[73] "þeah mon þonne hwæt rædde þæt ne stod furðon ænne monað; æt nextan næs nan
heafodman þæt fyrde gaderian wolde, ac ælc fleah swa he mæst mihte, ne furðon nan scir
nolde oþre gelæstan æt nextan": MS C.

[74] "ealle þas ungesælða us gelumpon þuruh unrædas": MS C.

[75] MS C reports at 1013 that after Swein had harried throughout the country, "eal
þeodscype hine hæfde þa for fulne cyng, ⁊ seo buruhwaru æfter ðam in Lundene beah ⁊
gislude, forðon hi ondredon þæt he hi fordon wolde [the whole nation accepted him entirely
as king, and after that the citizens of London bowed and yielded, because they feared that he
would destroy them]".

[76] "Þa geræddon þa witan ealle þe on Engla lande wæron, gehadode ⁊ læwede, þæt man æfter
þam cyninge Æþelrede sende, ⁊ cwædon þæt him nan hlaford nære þonne hiora gecynda hlaford,
gif, he rihtlicor healdan wolde þonne he ær dyde [Then all the witan who were in England decided
that they should send for king Æthelred, and they said that no other lord was dearer to them than
their own lord, if he would govern them more properly than before]": MS C.

[77] "... feng Cnut kyning to eallon Angelcynnes ryce": MS C.

hope that the depravity of Æthelred's reign can be overcome by a law that draws power from a more solid and enduring source. What Wulfstan seeks is a return to the presumed unity between church and state that characterized Edgar's reign in the mid-tenth century: the age of the Benedictine Reform. *Polity* must therefore also be understood in the context of the monastic reform and the shadow it cast over the history of the late tenth and early eleventh centuries, because Wulfstan's proposed reform of English society is in many ways a continuation of the earlier monastic reform movement.

A necessarily brief summary of the Benedictine Reform oversimplifies a very complex and multifaceted process, and it can provide only the most basic outline of what was perhaps the largest joint effort by church and state in Anglo-Saxon England.[78] By the end of the ninth century, English monasticism had degenerated far enough to inspire King Alfred's famous lament in the Preface to his translation of Gregory the Great's *Regula pastoralis* that English men who could read and write English, let alone Latin, were few and far between.[79] Toward the middle of the tenth century, a movement to restore English monasticism to its former presumed glory got underway, inspired in part by current Continental developments. The reform began at Glastonbury in the 940s and 950s, where Abbot Dunstan and his colleague, Æthelwold, restored strict Benedictine observances and began to organize a comprehensive program to bring the rest of English monasticism into line with the Rule. After reforming Glastonbury and Abingdon, both men went on to episcopal sees: Dunstan as archbishop of Canterbury in 959 and Æthelwold as bishop of Winchester in 963. From these positions of power, it was possible for them to extend the reform to monasteries throughout the nation. They were joined in this task by Oswald, bishop of Worcester (961–992) and archbishop of York (971–992), who had trained as a monk, been ordained at Fleury, and brought the reform zeal of that house back to England with him.[80]

Like its Continental counterparts, ecclesiastical reform in England was helped considerably by royal patronage. King Edgar played a prominent role in the establishment of reformed monasticism, and his reign (959–975) consequently took

---

[78]   For a more detailed history and background of the English Benedictine Reform, see David Knowles, *The Monastic Order in England*, 2nd edn (Cambridge, 1966), pp. 31–82; and more recently Mechthild Gretsch, *The Intellectual Foundations of the English Benedictine Reform* (Cambridge, 1999). The English reform shared many influences with Contintental reform movements and had strong ties with Cluniac reform through Abbo of Fleury; see D.A. Bullough, "The Continental Background of the Reform," in *Tenth-Century Studies*, ed. David Parsons (London, 1975), pp. 20–36. Abbo's political thought also seems to be an influence on Wulfstan's; see Mostert, *Political Theology* (above, n. 37).

[79]   *King Alfred's West-Saxon Version of Gregory's Pastoral Care*, ed. Henry Sweet, EETS, o.s., 45, 50 (London, 1871–1872), pp. 2–3.

[80]   The last fifteen years have seen an explosion of work on, and consequently our understanding of, the three major figures of the Benedictine reform in England. See in particular the collections *Bishop Æthelwold: His Career and Influence*, ed. Barbara Yorke (Woodbridge, 1988); *St Dunstan: His Life, Times, and Cult*, ed. Nigel Ramsay, Margaret Sparks, and T. Tatton-Brown (Woodbridge, 1992); and *St. Oswald of Worcester*, ed. Nicholas Brooks and Catherine Cubitt (London, 1996); as well as Gretsch, *Intellectual Foundations*.

on the character of a Golden Age when referenced by later chroniclers, homilists, and lawgivers.[81] Æthelwold had served as Edgar's tutor when the king was a boy, and remained a close royal adviser. In 964, shortly after Æthelwold's confirmation as bishop of Winchester, the secular clerics were forcibly removed from both the Old Minster and the New Minster at Winchester and were replaced by monks from Abingdon. Æthelwold did not act alone in this controversial decision; rather, he had the king's help (and possibly also the king's troops) in accomplishing the task.[82] Unity of purpose between church and state—in the form of royal power, backing the bishop—effected significant changes in ecclesiastical governance and spread the reform beyond the monastic houses of Glastonbury and Abingdon. As a result, Edgar himself was considered in some respects to be as much a leader of the reform movement as Æthelwold or Dunstan. At the Council of Winchester in 973, the reform movement issued its customary, the *Regularis Concordia*, to prescribe uniform practices at all monasteries throughout England.[83] The preface to this text represents Edgar as the primary source, not just the patron, of the reform, and it casts his involvement in terms of his royal responsibility to protect and promote the proper worship of God within his kingdom. Underscoring (and perhaps exaggerating) this point is an eleventh-century copy of the *Regularis Concordia* which depicts Edgar enthroned, flanked by Dunstan and Æthelwold, holding between them a long scroll, presumably the document itself.[84] The significance of royal patronage, then, is not limited to its power to grant land and promote the interests of a group of reformers; rather, Edgar's role as patron of the reform is merely one facet of his larger role as protector and promoter of the faith. Royal and ecclesiastical power thus went hand in hand from the very beginnings of the reform movement, and these ties strengthened the impact of the reform. It is this image

---

[81]   In this, Edgar shares a great deal in common with Louis the Pious, on whom many of these representations are consciously modeled; see, for example, Wormald, "Æthelwold and his Continental Counterparts: Contact, Comparison, Contrast," in *Bishop Æthelwold*, ed. Yorke, pp. 13–42.

[82]   Contemporary sources are divided on the question of who was actually responsible for the expulsion of the secular clerics. MS A of the Anglo-Saxon Chronicle notes, for 964, that "Her dræfde Eadgar cyng þa preostas on Ceastre of Ealdanmynstre ⁊ of Niwanmynstre ⁊ of Ceortesige ⁊ of Middeltune ⁊ sette hy mid munecan [In this year, King Edgar drove out the priests in the city from the Old Minster and from the New Minster and from Chertsey and from Milton and replaced them with monks]." MS E of the Chronicle and the Latin *vitae* attribute the expulsion to Æthelwold; see *The Anglo-Saxon Chronicle: A Collaborative Edition. Volume 7: MS E*, ed. Susan Irvine (Cambridge, 2004); *Wulfstan of Winchester: The Life of St Æthelwold*, ed. and trans. Michael Lapidge and Michael Winterbottom (Oxford, 1991); and Ælfric, *Vita S. Æthelwoldi*, in *Three Lives of English Saints*, ed. Michael Winterbottom (Toronto, 1972), pp. 17–29.

[83]   *Regularis Concordia Anglicae Nationis*, ed. Thomas Symons and Sigrid Spath, in *Consuetudinum saeculi X/XI/XII monumenta non-Cluniacensia*, ed. Kassius Hallinger, Corpus Consuetudinum Monasticarum 7/3 (Siegburg, 1984), pp. 61–147. The *Regularis Concordia* is generally thought to have been written by none other than Bishop Æthelwold; see Michael Lapidge, "Æthelwold as Scholar and Teacher," in *Bishop Æthelwold*, ed. Yorke, pp. 89–117 at pp. 98–100; see also Lucia Kornexl, *Die "Regularis Concordia" und ihre altenglische Interlinearversion* (Munich, 1993), xxxi–l.

[84]   London, British Library MS Cotton Tiberius A. iii, fol. 2v.

of power unified in a single figure, the king, who represents both church and state that underwrites Wulfstan's efforts at civil reform in *Polity*.

For many contemporary historians, all of whom were monks, Edgar's death marked the end of a period of peace and prosperity for Anglo-Saxon England. His young son and successor, Edward, only survived his father by three years; he was murdered by political partisans in 978 in favor of his even younger brother, Æthelred. It was hard for the chroniclers to resist contrasting the political turmoil of Æthelred's reign with the peaceful era, now considered a Golden Age, of Edgar. A poem in the Anglo-Saxon Chronicle, written quite probably by Wulfstan himself, laments the death of Edgar and the evil days that followed:

> In his [Edward's] day, because of his youth,
> God's enemies broke God's law,
> Ealdorman Ælfere and many others,
> and disrupted the monastic rule, and destroyed churches,
> and drove out monks, and drove away the servants of God,
> whom Edgar had previously commanded
> the holy bishop Æthelwold to establish,
> and often and frequently deprived widows,
> and many wrongs and evil crimes rose up afterwards,
> and always after that it became much worse.[85]

In authoring a poem that finds its way into the Chronicle, Wulfstan becomes the mouthpiece for his people during a time of national crisis. Poet and people alike desire the restoration of peace and unity; as archbishop, Wulfstan became the architect of a grand design to end the nation's suffering by bringing England into a closer allegiance with God. But the unity of church and state in Edgar's reign was little more than historical fiction; while the power of the crown lent its force to the reform of English monasticism, secular and religious authorities remained separate. Wulfstan's attempts to (re)unify the two—in his letters and sermons as archbishop, in the law codes he helped to write, and in the *Institutes of Polity*—ultimately refuse to acknowledge the separate spheres of temporal and divine rule. The monastic reform stressed the unity of all monastic houses in obedience to one common rule; similarly, unity of one Christian people under one king in the worship of one God is the basis for Wulfstan's program of social reform. At the heart of this program is a theoretical, if not a practical, disjunction: the possibility of conflict between the supreme authorities of secular and

---

[85] "On his dagum, for his iugoðe, / Godes wiþersacan Godes lage bræcon / Ælfere ealdorman, ⁊ oþre manega, / ⁊ munucregol myrdon, ⁊ mynstra tostæncton, / ⁊ munecas todræfon, ⁊ Godes þeowas fesedon, / þe Eadgar kyning het ær þone halgan biscop / Aþælwo<l>d gestalian, ⁊ wydewan bestryptan / oft ⁊ gelome, ⁊ fela unrihta / ⁊ yfelra unlaga arysan up siððan, / ⁊ aa æfter þam hit yfelode swiðe": *The Anglo-Saxon Chronicle: A Collaborative Edition. Volume 6: MS D*, ed. G.P. Cubbin (Cambridge, 1996); Cubbin prints the text as prose. On the probability of Wulfstan's authorship, see Jost, "Wulfstan und die Angelsächsische Chronik," *Anglia* 47 (1923), 105–23; affirmed by McIntosh, "Wulfstan's Prose" (above, n. 12), p. 112; Dorothy Bethurum, "Wulfstan," in *Continuations and Beginnings: Studies in Old English Literature*, ed. E.G. Stanley (London, 1966), pp. 210–46 at p. 212; and Whitelock, *English Historical Documents*, pp. 225 n. 4 and 229 n. 2.

religious power. Wulfstan attempts to compensate for this disjunction in *Polity* by clarifying the descent of power from God to the king and onward down the social ladder. For all its formal rigor, however, *Polity*'s model does not resolve the tensions between the leaders of the secular and the religious realms. The text itself clearly privileges religious power, even in the temporal world, over the secular; by making the king subordinate to the bishop in taking Christian instruction, *Polity* disrupts its own hierarchy and affirms the bishop as the guarantor of unity and peace in a Christian kingdom. The bishop thus supplants the king as the *de facto* head of the Christian state, contravening the text's repeated insistence on the king's supremacy. *Polity*'s emphasis on the bishop as the bridge between secular and ecclesiastical authorities undercuts its attempts to create a strict and clearly-defined hierarchy, and the text itself plays out the very disjunction it wants to overcome. It reveals the limitations of medieval political theory in reform-era praxis; in working toward unity, Wulfstan's *Polity* paradoxically highlights the tensions between church and crown and belies its own intentions. In this respect, *Polity* is a utopian document, and its goals would not be realized. Kings and bishops would continue to struggle for control of the lives and souls of the English people, and *Polity*, like the ambitious program of Christian reform it embodies, would remain an unfinished opus at Wulfstan's death.

In spite of its attempt to create a universal and transhistorical mode of governance by dissociating law from the name of the king, *Polity* and the rest of Wulfstan's legislative rhetoric did not find its way into the legal discourse of medieval England. Post-Conquest rulers went to great (and, in the circumstances, surprising) lengths to incorporate established Anglo-Saxon institutions into their own governance of the nation. The laws of William I, issued in English as well as Latin and French, repeat and affirm the decrees of pre-Conquest kings.[86] The reign of Henry I saw the compilation of the great twelfth-century legal encyclopedia known as the *Quadripartitus*, which assembled and translated into Latin an enormous range of pre-Conquest legal material extending back to Ine's codes.[87] The author of *Quadripartitus* copied law codes from the reign of every king for whom written laws survive, but did not incorporate any excerpts from *Polity*. Even after Wulfstan's intervention, lawgiving continued to be the exclusive domain of the king, whose name was the primary guarantor of authority and testament of authenticity for legal discourse. Wulfstan's vision of a harmonious society governed by adherence to Christian principle was

---

[86]   William's laws note specifically that "iceles meimes que li reis Edward sun cusin tint devant lui [they are the same as King Edward his cousin observed before him]"; Liebermann ed., *Gesetze*, 1:492; in *The Laws of the Kings of England from Edmund to Henry I*, trans. A.J. Robertson (Cambridge, 1925), p. 253.

[87]   First printed by Liebermann ed., *Quadripartitus: Ein englisches Rechtsbuch von 1114* (Halle, 1892); see also Wormald, "*Quadripartitus*," in *Law and Government in Medieval England and Normandy: Essays in Honour of Sir James Holt*, ed. George Garnett and John Hudson (Cambridge, 1994), pp. 111–47; and Wormald, *English Law*, 1:236–44, 465–73.

never realized, but its traces remain throughout the body of work he left behind, and most completely in the *Institutes of Polity*.[88]

[88] I would like to thank a number of people for their generous intellectual contributions during the preparation of this essay: Jim Hansen, Rebecca L. Stephenson, and Charles D. Wright for reading and commenting on successive drafts; Matt Hart, Zack Lesser, and the Critical British Studies reading group at the Illinois Program for Research in the Humanities for illuminating discussions on sovereignty; and especially John S. Ott and Anna Trumbore Jones for their patient and thorough editorial comments.

Chapter 5

The Image of the Bishop in the Middle Ages

Eric Palazzo

Université de Poitiers; Centre d'Études Supérieures de Civilisation Médiévale

The bishop was a major figure in the Christian church, and, more generally, in the society of the European Middle Ages. Consequently, numerous medievalists—historians, art historians, archaeologists, scholars of liturgy—have applied themselves to retracing the principal stages of the construction of the episcopal image from the origins of Christianity until the end of the Middle Ages. The format of this brief contribution does not permit an overview of the different aspects of the history of the bishop, which the other authors in this collection have taken up in greater detail. A few years ago, I published a volume devoted to studying the varying facets of the bishop's image in the Middle Ages, principally through an exploration of the illustration of the bishop's liturgical book, the pontifical. The title of that work, *L'Évêque et son image*, sought to emphasize the idea that, in the Middle Ages, the bishop possessed an iconography designed to promote the main aspects of the political, ecclesiological, and ideological discourse of the episcopal image at the center of medieval Christian society.[1] In the following pages, I wish to make a rapid presentation of the multiple levels of reception of the bishop's image in the Middle Ages. Of course, this will briefly concern the visual image, based on material artifacts, such as the illustrations in pontificals or any other type of episcopal image painted or sculpted in media other than manuscripts. The better part of what follows, however, will be devoted to the different manifestations (liturgical, theological, ecclesiological, political) of the symbolic image. The image of the bishop that I propose to evoke here closely concerns the definition of the *imago* in the Middle Ages, which Jean-Claude Schmitt has explored in recent years.[2] The concept, as developed by Schmitt, rests upon the assertion that the medieval image not only illustrated a material reality, but also—and above all—functioned as a visual expression of ideas and mentalities.

This article was translated by John S. Ott and Anna Trumbore Jones.

[1]   Eric Palazzo, *L'Évêque et son image: L'illustration du Pontifical au Moyen Âge* (Turnhout, 1999).

[2]   Jean-Claude Schmitt, "Le Miroir du Canoniste: À propos d'un Manuscrit du *Decret de Gratien* de la Walters Art Gallery," *The Journal of the Walters Art Gallery* 49–50 (1991–1992), 67–82.

The Liturgical Construction of the Episcopal Image

From the earliest days of Christianity until the close of the medieval epoch, the bishop was a central figure in the organization of the first Christian communities and then of the institutional church. The first liturgico-canonical codifications from before the fifth century insist not only on the bishop's role in the life of these first communities, but also on the importance of his liturgical prerogatives. The codification of rituals, essential for the history of the Christian liturgy, would fix in substantial measure episcopal liturgical practices, thereby facilitating the solid anchoring of the bishop in social organization. In antiquity and at the beginning of the early Middle Ages, the bishop ruled over a diocese at the heart of which parishes, headed by priests, progressively took shape. The bishop's dominant position within his see, institutional by nature, was expressed notably by his hold over liturgical practices and his imprint on its spaces. For example, from the fifth century, the city of Rome saw a form of territorial organization essentially dominated by the search for the unity of the Christian community around the bishop's person. This model remained vital for several centuries in the Eternal City and exercised a considerable influence over a good number of episcopal sees in western Europe throughout the Middle Ages. Michelle Gaillard has recently called attention to the attempts of bishops in Late Antiquity and the early Middle Ages to reinforce the idea that the Christian community was centered on their person, with reference to four documents: the calendar of Perpetuus of Tours transmitted by Gregory of Tours; the liturgical guidelines of Bishops Aunarius and Tetricus of Auxerre; the famous list of stational celebrations of the churches of Metz; and the list of the churches of Clermont mentioning each one's altars and relics.[3]

From the Carolingian epoch, we witness an unprecedented development in episcopal liturgy. This development was conditioned and made possible above all by the bishop's ever-increasing role at this time at the center of political and ecclesiastical institutions. The Carolingian era marks a turning point in the history of western Christianity, which the bishop did not escape. The great religious and liturgical reforms carried out successively by Pippin the Short and Charlemagne facilitated the growth of monasteries on the one hand and the development of parish structures on the other. In this complex ensemble, the episcopacy remained rather on the margin of things, because, for the moment, it was principally monks who actively participated in the reorganization and who played a central role in the new directions taken by liturgical rituals. From the middle of the ninth century, however, bishops progressively found their place in the ecclesiastical system established by the temporal power. The number of episcopal capitularies created at this time testifies amply to the new social status acquired by the bishop, as well as to his growing role in the organization of liturgical practices and his control over their smooth functioning.[4]

---

[3] Michelle Gaillard, "La présence épiscopale dans la ville du haut Moyen Âge: Sanctuaires et processions," *Histoire urbaine* 10 (2004), 123–40.

[4] Eric Palazzo, "Arts somptuaires et liturgie: Le testament de l'évêque d'Elne, Riculf (915)," in *Retour aux sources: Textes, études et documents d'histoire médiévale offerts à*

The year 1000 saw the veritable birth of episcopal liturgy.[5] This is not to say that bishops had not previously celebrated services according to more or less distinct ritual forms, but rather that the millennium saw an important codification of episcopal liturgical usages across several genres of text, which favored the bishop's implantation at the heart of medieval society. In the second half of the tenth century, the Ottonian emperors moved toward a genuine "promotion" of the episcopate, which consequently became the pivot, at least in theory, of the Empire's religious organization. In order to favor this promotion, episcopal liturgy underwent an unprecedented official codification. The specific rites pertaining to the bishops were laid down in writing in their own liturgical book: the pontifical.

This book reflected the diversity of the bishop's liturgical activity at that time, which included solemn celebrations in the cathedral, pastoral liturgy in the parishes of his diocese, and official rites practiced while traveling, such as the dedication of churches and its corollary, the consecration of altars.[6] Preceded by a certain number of so-called "primitive pontificals," the first fully-fledged episcopal liturgical book was the Romano-Germanic Pontifical, created at Mainz in 962 in order to serve the political and ideological ambitions of the Ottonian rulers. The Romano-Germanic Pontifical enshrined an episcopal liturgy that was endowed with an official book with which the other books of the religious cult were aligned. The Romano-Germanic Pontifical likewise heralded a new period in the history of the liturgy and its books, for it was the first of the so-called "second generation" books (including most notably the breviary and the missal), which brought to an end the "first generation" of books (chiefly the sacramentary and ordinals) born of the Carolingian reform of the liturgy. Initially, the reception of the Romano-Germanic Pontifical was restrained, but the book's influence later in the Middle Ages was considerable owing to its appropriation by the popes and their liturgists in the papal curia from the twelfth, and above all the thirteenth, centuries. The Pontifical was adopted in order to serve the new ecclesiological ambitions of the papacy, which were principally aligned around the association between the liturgy of the papal chapel and the liturgy of the universal church. Alongside the essential role played by the pontifical in the construction of the episcopal liturgy around the year 1000, we must also mention the contemporary development of the conciliar *ordines*, which offer another testament to the growing power of the bishop in a new political and ecclesiological context.[7]

Michel Parisse, ed. Sylvain Gouguenheim et al. (Paris, 2004), pp. 711–17.

[5]   Eric Palazzo, "La liturgie de l'Occident médiéval autour de l'an mil: État de la question," *Cahiers de civilisation médiévale* 43 (2000), 371–94.

[6]   M. Klückener, "Das Pontifikale als liturgisches Buch: Geschichte, Aufbau und Inhalt. Bedeutung für die Gegenwart," in *Manifestatio Ecclesiae: Studien zu Pontifikale und bischöflicher Liturgie*, ed. Winfried Haunerland et al., Studien zur Pastoralliturgie 17 (Regensburg, 2004), pp. 79–127.

[7]   Herbert Schneider ed., *Die Konzilsordines des Früh- und Hochmittelalters*, MGH Ordines de celebrando concilio (Hannover, 1996).

The Multi-Dimensional Image of the Bishop

I have greatly enjoyed this comb. It is pleasing to me above all because of the interior relief of the beautiful symbol that it contains. One can compare tangles in the hairs to the disordered mores of the people, and I believe that your prudence, by this small gift, wished, by way of an admonition, to rouse my vigilance as I prepare to reform, by various kinds of exhortations, the chaotic habits of the people and to recall them, with moderation and discretion, to the order they ought to observe.

Thus did Bishop Ivo of Chartres express himself in the eleventh century concerning the intentions of a certain Gerard, who had given to him a liturgical comb on the occasion of his accession to the episcopate.[8] The bishop of Chartres's appreciation for the comb illustrates the commemorative dimension attached to certain liturgical objects, sometimes paired with value at once symbolic and of a theological or ecclesiological nature. In effect, during antiquity and throughout the Middle Ages, the bishop can be considered a veritable "artistic patron," whose commissions were often destined to fashion his personal remembrance and that of the cathedral and diocese he was called to lead.[9] During this time, abbots, bishops, and other clerical dignitaries endowed their monasteries, cathedrals, or churches with liturgical objects of every kind. These donative acts occurred normally at the beginning of one's abbacy or episcopacy, or more rarely at the end of life in the form of a final bequest. Apart from the strictly utilitarian motivations attached to these donations, their justification resided essentially in their memorial function, which contributed in its own way to the elaboration of the multi-dimensional image of the episcopal figure.

The multiple facets of the bishop's image in the Middle Ages appear also in iconographic discourse, which offers episcopal images charged with both a liturgical and ecclesiological viewpoint, and contributes strongly to the affirmation of the bishop's status in society. In this way, in the famous exultet rolls of southern Italy, created for the most part between the tenth and twelfth centuries, it was usual to represent the bishop in a number of situations.[10] He was portrayed frequently on his throne, in an image placed at the top of a roll. In such scenes, where he is shown at the head of members of the clergy and sometimes the faithful, emphasis was placed on the spiritual authority he represented, all the more because this painting generally preceded or followed another image showing the holders of temporal

---

[8] "Quod cum mihi placeat in suo genere quantum huiusmodi placere debent propter exteriorem pulchritudinem, vehementius tamen placet propter pulchri sacramenti interiorem celsitudinem. Nam cum in capillis inordinati mores, vel inordinati populi quadam comparatione possint intellegi, credo prudentiam tuam munusculo hoc quasi quodam monitorio vigilantiam meam excitare, ut studeam inordinatos populorum mores diversis exhortationum modis componere, atque habito discretionis moderamine ad debitum ordinem revocare": Ivo of Chartres, letter 6, PL 162:16.

[9] William North and Anthony Cutler, "Ivories, Inscriptions and Episcopal Self-Consciousness in the Ottonian Empire: Berthold of Toul and the Berlin Hodegetria," *Gesta* 42 (2003), 1–17.

[10] Thomas Forrest Kelly, *The Exultet in Southern Italy* (New York, 1996).

authority, with the sovereign at their head. Next to these official representations, the exultet rolls leave place for the demonstration of the liturgical power of the bishop during the Pascal vigil. In this way, the significance of the roll varies, depending on whether the image presents the bishop in an active liturgical role or rather as a passive celebrant. At times, the roll is inseparable from its function as symbol of the bishop's status. However, the production of exultet rolls under the direction of Abbot Didier of Monte Cassino progressively diminished the active role of the bishop in the Holy Saturday liturgy, to the benefit of the deacons. Between 969 and 982, Bishop Landulf of Benevento, aware of this danger, commissioned another roll destined for the celebration of rites of ecclesiastical ordination reserved exclusively for the bishop. Aside from his interest in comprehending the medieval conception of ecclesiastical orders, the iconography of this roll showed Landulf in one of his major liturgical roles. It is without doubt not an accident that the bishop of Benevento chose the form of a roll to emphasize his liturgical image, and at the same time his social and political status, in order to counteract the detrimental effects of certain images in the exultet rolls commissioned by the abbots.[11]

During the Middle Ages, the multi-dimensional image of the bishop was also the object of a more properly ecclesiological construction, which may be measured through certain theological texts, and which at the same time was addressed in canon law. This ecclesiological dimension of the bishops' image in the early Middle Ages is particularly striking in an unedited collection of canons compiled by Archbishop Hincmar of Reims between 857 and 858. Hincmar's "Collection on churches and chapels" gathers extracts from patristic works, but above all from conciliar canons and passages from papal letters defining the status and proper usage of buildings destined for cultic use. According to Michel Lauwers, this constitutes the first western text dealing specifically and explicitly with cultic sites and their definition.[12] In this collection, Hincmar attempts to define cultic sites and their typological variety as part of his strategy aimed at diminishing the power of the lay nobility over churches built on their lands. Drawing support from the affirmation of a necessary stability of sites of worship and their zones of influence, Hincmar inflected considerably the notion of the site of worship and its territorial anchorage, basing it on the ecclesiological affirmation of the bishop's power over the territory under his authority: the diocese.

---

[11] Beat Brenk, "Bischöfliche und monastische *committenza* in Süditalien am Beispiel der Exultetrollen," in *Committenti e produzione artistico-letteraria nell'alto medioevo occidentale, 4–10 aprile 1991*, Settimane di studio del Centro italiano di studi sull'alto Medioevo 39 (Spoleto, 1992), pp. 275–300.

[12] Michel Lauwers, *Naissance du cimetière: Lieux sacrés et terre des morts dans l'Occident médiéval* (Paris, 2005), pp. 32–40; see also Eric Palazzo, "La liturgie épiscopale au moyen âge: Réflexions sur sa signification théologique et politique," in *Bischofsstädte als Kultur- und Innovationszentren*, ed. Steffen Patzold, *Das Mittelalter: Perspektiven mediävistischer Forschung. Zeitschrift des Mediävistenverbandes* 7/1 (2002), 71–78.

Conclusion

By way of conclusion to this brief contribution to our knowledge of the multi-dimensional image of the medieval bishop, I wish simply to present a particular case of the liturgical and theological authority of the episcopal figure, found in an illuminated miniature taken from a late fifteenth-century book of hours. Completed in Austria for Johann Siebenhirter, MS A 225 of the Royal Library of Stockholm is a book of hours containing an iconographic cycle of nine paintings. Among them, on folio 158v, we find an image of an altogether exceptional nature relating to eucharistic liturgy. This painting illustrates the compline service of the office of Corpus Christi and represents symbolically the progression of the orthodox communion toward heresy. The animated ritual scene is purely fictive and in no way represents a codified moment in the liturgy. Rather, this imagined ritual is here destined to serve the discourse on the theology of the eucharist. Under the attentive gaze of a bishop, three priests give communion to three of the faithful. On the host administered to the first communicant, the figure of Christ appears; the second figure prepares to swallow a simple piece of bread; while the third sees a toad outlined on the host being offered him. The iconography of this image strives to show the three possible forms of communion. In the first, the faithful person believes in transubstantiation; in the second, doubt is present because the host has remained bread; and finally, in the third, denial of the sacrament leads the figure to heresy and toward a demonic transubstantiation. For the believer consulting his book of hours at the moment of prayer, the image gives a demonstration of the model faith that he ought to follow and apply to his life. Beyond its theological quality and its function in the devotion of the manuscript's recipient, the exceptional iconography of this image insists above all on the power of the bishop at the center of society. In effect, the three communions unfold before the authority of the bishop, who approves or condemns the liturgical gestures relative to the eucharist. In a certain sense, the miniature in this book of hours appears as a mirror of the bishop's liturgical and ecclesiological authority. In the same way, that authority is expressed in the illustration of the pontifical, or even in certain images accompanying the text of Gratian's *Decretum* from the twelfth century.

Chapter 6

Building the Body of the Church: A Bishop's Blessing in the Benedictional of Engilmar of Parenzo

Evan A. Gatti

Elon University

Visual images of the episcopate and especially portraits of historical bishops celebrate the place of the episcopacy between secular and spiritual politics. Medieval episcopal portraiture followed established iconographies of power, such as the bishop enthroned, suggestive of images of Christ in Majesty and secular ruler portraiture, or the bishop as donor, reflective of early Christian representations of the transmission of the law as well as royal donation imagery.[1] Around the turn of the millennium, however, a new iconography for episcopal portraiture emerged that depicted the bishop in liturgical postures, such as blessing a congregation, celebrating the eucharist, or dedicating an altar. These liturgical portraits highlight both the spiritual and social legitimacy of the episcopacy by referencing the ritual actions that made the bishop indispensable to the communities he served. In the following essay I will examine a portrait in the Benedictional of Engilmar of Parenzo as a case study of the episcopal liturgical portrait.[2] Drawing significance from the rituals they represent, liturgical portraits can

---

[1] The most famous example of the blending of the secular and spiritual connotations of the ruler enthroned image type can be found in Ernst Kantorowicz's reading of the frontispiece of the Aachen Gospels (Aachen, Domschatzkammer, MS 5594, fol. 16r). Ernst Kantorowicz, *The King's Two Bodies: A Study in Mediaeval Political Theology* (Princeton, NJ, 1957), pp. 61–78. Kantorowicz's reading of this miniature inspired subsequent research that resulted in a large bibliography dedicated to an "iconography of kingship," which highlights the medieval philosophy (or, following Kantorowicz, the "political theology") of the ruler as *rex et sacerdos*. Of special note for the history of art is Percy Ernst Schramm and Florentine Mütherich, *Denkmale der deutschen Könige und Kaiser*, vol. 1, *Ein Beitrag zur Herrschergeschichte von Karl dem Großen bis Friedrich II., 768–1250*, Veröffentlichungen des Zentralinstituts für Kunstgeschichte in München 2 (Munich, 1962). For scholarly investigations of the donor portrait see Elizabeth Lipsmeyer, "The Donor and his Church Model in Medieval Art from Early Christian Times to the Late Romanesque Period" (Ph.D. diss., Rutgers University, 1981). See also Joachim Prochno, *Das Schreiber- und Dedikationsbild in der deutschen Buchmalerei* (Leipzig, 1929).

[2] Los Angeles, J. Paul Getty Museum, MS Ludwig VII, 1, fol. 16r. For bibliography see Wilhelm Vöge, *Eine deutsche Malerschule um die Wende des ersten Jahrtausends: Kritische Studien zur Geschichte der Malerei in Deutschland im 10. und 11. Jahrhundert,*

be seen as part of an evolving episcopal iconography of sacerdotal privilege, which locates the power of the episcopacy within its partnership with *Ecclesia*.

A Case Study: The Benedictional of Engilmar of Parenzo

The liturgical portrait of Engilmar, included in the opening folios of an eleventh-century benedictional, depicts the bishop before an altar making a gesture of blessing toward his congregation (Fig. 6.1). A clear inscription, ENGILMARUS EPS, written in white uncial on gold ground, occupies two lines above the head of the bishop and identifies the celebrant as Engilmar, bishop of Parenzo (modern-day Poreč, Croatia) from 1028 to 1045.[3] Engilmar is portrayed as an older man with gray hair, tonsured and bearded, and dressed in mass vestments including the stola, chasuble, dalmatic, pallium, and episcopal buskins. The altar at the center of the miniature is equipped for the eucharist with a golden chalice and paten.[4] An open manuscript

Westdeutsche Zeitschrift für Geschichte und Kunst, Ergänzungsheft 7 (Trier, 1891); Ernst Friedrich Bange, *Eine bayerische Malerschule des 11. und 12. Jahrhunderts* (Munich, 1923); H. Köllner, "Eine wiedergefundene Handschrift aus Muri, Berlin MS. theol. lat. 4° 199," in *Studien zur Buchmalerei und Goldschmiedekunst des Mittelalters: Festschrift für Karl Hermann Usener zum 60. Geburtstag am 19. August 1965*, ed. Frieda Dettweiler et al. (Marburg, 1967), pp. 293–326; Georg Stadtmüller and Bonifaz Pfister, *Geschichte der Abtei Niederaltaich 741–1971* (Ottobeuren, 1972), pp. 129, 407, 412; Anton von Euw and Joachim M. Plotzek, *Die Handschriften der Sammlung Ludwig*, 4 vols (Cologne, 1979–1985), 1:293–96; Eckhard Freise, Dieter Geuenich, and Joachim Wollasch eds, *Das Martyrolog-Necrolog von St Emmeram zu Regensburg*, MGH Libri memoriales et necrologia, n.s., 3 (Hannover, 1986), p. 77; Rosemary Lee, "Das Benedictionale des Bischofs Engilmar inter besonderer Berücksichtigung der Ikonographie" (Master's thesis, Ludwig-Maximilians Universität, 1988); *Regensburger Buchmalerei: Von frühkarolingischer Zeit bis zum Ausgang des Mittelalters. Ausstellung der bayerischen Staatsbibliothek München und der Museen der Stadt Regensburg*, ed. Florentine Mütherich and Karl Dachs (Munich, 1987), no. 22, p. 36; *Masterpieces of the J. Paul Getty Museum: Illuminated Manuscripts*, ed. Thomas Kren (Los Angeles, 1997), no. 4, p. 17.

[3]   Wilhelm Vöge was the first scholar to link the miniature depicting a bishop blessing his congregation to Engilmar. Although Vöge was unsure of the exact dates of Engilmar's episcopate, he used this identification with Engilmar to date the manuscript to between 1028/1030 and 1040/1045: Vöge, *Eine deutsche Malerschule*, pp. 149–50. Subsequent research, however, has established 1028 to 1045 as the specific dates of Engilmar's episcopate in Parenzo. See Bernardo Benussi, "Privilegio eufrasiano," *Atti e Memorie della Società Istriana di Archeologia e Storia Patria* 8 (1892), 46–86, and Francesco Babudri, "I Vescovi di Parenzo e la loro cronologica," *Atti e Memorie della Società Istriana di Archeologia e Storia Patria* 25 (1909), 170–284, at pp. 171, 214–15. See also Gerhard Schwartz, *Die Besetzung der Bistümer Reichsitaliens unter den sächsichen und salischen Kaisern: Mit den Listen der Bischöfe 951–1122* (Leipzig, 1913), p. 38.

[4]   The blessings included in the benedictional are those pronounced by the bishop after the *Pater noster* but before *Pax domini vobiscum*. For a brief summary of scholarship concerning the evolution of the pre-communion blessing and the benedictional, see Andrew Prescott, "The Text of the Benedictional of St Æthelwold," in *Bishop Æthelwold: His Career and Influence,* ed. Barbara Yorke (Woodbridge, 1988), pp. 119–47, at pp. 121–28. See also

Fig. 6.1   Benedictional of Engilmar of Parenzo, Los Angeles, California, The J.
            Paul Getty Museum, MS Ludwig VII, folio 16r (photo: The J. Paul Getty
            Museum, Los Angeles)

Edmond E. Moeller, *Corpus benedictionum pontificalium*, CCSL 162, 4 vols (Turnhout,
1971–1979).

is included on the altar. To the left of the altar, a deacon is painted holding open the benedictional from which the bishop reads the blessing. At the far left of the miniature, six lay figures represent the congregation. The bearded figure at the front of the congregational group could be identified as a local nobleman. He is depicted in rich garments, including a short, embroidered tunic, calf-high boots, leggings, and a gold-trimmed cape. His right hand is shown in a reciprocal gesture to that of Engilmar, signaling the reception of the blessing made by the bishop. At the far right of the miniature, another ecclesiastic is depicted behind Engilmar holding a closed manuscript. The space of the miniature is rendered abstractly. The bishop, clerics, and congregation float before the background and the architectural elements of the miniature are sharply foreshortened.[5] The fortress-like walls of the cathedral, executed with a strong diagonal, appear rusticated and topped with crenellation, and the roof for the structure is articulated as terra-cotta tile.[6] A white triangular pediment caps the space enclosing the liturgical act and gold foil illuminates the background of the miniature. The golden background can be seen both at the center of the folio behind the altar and above the roof.

The figure of a bishop blessing is, of course, an apt opening for a benedictional, which includes the pre-communion blessings read by the bishop during the mass. But while the image may be deemed generally appropriate, the spiritual legitimacy and historical significance granted Engilmar as the specific figure depicted here should not be overlooked, especially as the portrait of Engilmar is an unusual addition to the benedictional's Christological program. As is common to liturgical manuscripts of this period, the Benedictional of Engilmar includes a series of miniatures illustrating the Nativity and Passion of Christ (Fig. 6.2).[7] The order of these miniatures follows the narrative of Christ's life as dictated by the liturgical calendar, with each miniature placed before its appropriate benediction. The style and iconography of all the miniatures exhibit hallmarks of Bavarian manuscript illumination attributed to the

---

[5]   These motifs, in particular, are typical of the Regensburg style. See Meyer Schapiro, *The Parma Ildefonsus: A Romanesque Illuminated Manuscript from Cluny and Related Works*, Monographs on Archaeology and Fine Arts 11 (New York, 1964), p. 22, fig. 61.

[6]   The square baldachin in the apse of the Euphrasian Basilica in Parenzo, which echoes the form of the architectural space of the miniature, is a thirteenth-century renovation. The form of the current baldachin, however, is said to have followed the original, which dates to the sixth century. See Otto Demus, "The Ciborium Mosaics of Parenzo," *The Burlington Magazine* 87 (1945), 238–45, and Milan Prelog, *The Basilica of Euphrasius in Poreč*, trans. Janko Paravić (Zagreb, 1986), pp. 26–28.

[7]   The Christological cycle includes: the Nativity of Christ (fol. 21r), the Adoration of the Magi (fol. 25v), the Presentation in the Temple (fol. 28r), Christ's Entry into Jerusalem (fol. 36r), the Last Supper (fol. 38r), the Three Marys at the Tomb (fol. 40v), the Ascension of Christ (fol. 45r), and finally the Pentecost (fol. 47v). For a summary of scholarship on the style of the manuscript, see Lee, "Das Benedictionale des Bischofs Engilmar," pp. 4–5. See also *Regensburger Buchmalerei*, ed. Mütherich and Dachs, no. 22, p. 36, and illustrations 15 and 102.

Fig. 6.2   Benedictional of Engilmar of Parenzo, Los Angeles, California, The J. Paul Getty Museum, MS Ludwig VII, folio 25v (photo: The J. Paul Getty Museum, Los Angeles)

Fig. 6.3   Benedictional of Æthelwold of Winchester, London, British Library, Add.
MS 49598, folio 118v (photo: British Library, London)

Regensburg school, yet in extant manuscripts attributed to Regensburg, there are no examples that could serve as a visual model for the Engilmar portrait.[8]

There are, however, a number of manuscripts dating to the latter half of the tenth and first half of the eleventh century that include miniatures of living bishops in liturgical postures. The most notable example can be found on folio 118v in the Benedictional of St Æthelwold (*c.*970), where Æthelwold (909–984) is depicted before an altar blessing his congregation (Fig. 6.3).[9]

This manuscript, dating to the end of the tenth century, is of Anglo-Saxon origin, and while it may have influenced Continental sacramental illumination, it does not provide a visual model for the Engilmar portrait.[10] Instead, the Æthelwold miniature and the Engilmar portrait should be considered among a group of dedicatory miniatures that depict the living bishop-patron of a manuscript celebrating a distinct liturgical ritual. Notable examples of this miniature style are folios 16v and 17r in the "Precious" Gospels of Bishop Bernward of Hildesheim (*c.*1015), which include a portrait of Bernward dedicating an altar to the Virgin Mary, and folio 9r in the Sacramentary of Bishop Sigebert of Minden (*c.*1022–1036), which depicts Sigebert receiving the eucharistic chalice from an allegorical figure of *Ecclesia* (Figs. 6.4–6.5).[11] These miniatures, which span almost forty years and a wide geographic range, have few if any stylistic or iconographic similarities and are not representative of a model-and-copy relationship. Instead, they define an iconography of episcopal authority dependent upon liturgical privilege.[12] As I will argue below, the episcopal liturgical portrait can be compared to similar examples in illustrated bishops' *vitae* where authority is defined through liturgical gesture; however, the specific meaning of each portrait must be determined by individual circumstances, including the liturgical act presented and its significance given the bishop's unique historical situation. It is only by reading the image as one would experience the liturgy—cognizant of both its synchronic and diachronic meanings—that the significance of the portrait of Engilmar can be revealed.

---

[8]   As will be noted below, a similar liturgical emphasis can be seen in the miniature of St Erhard performing the mass in the Uta Codex, also illuminated at the monastery of Saint Emmeram in Regensburg. These two miniatures share only general stylistic similarities and are completely dissimilar in iconography.

[9]   Benedictional of St Æthelwold of Winchester, London, British Library, Add. MS 49598. For bibliography see Robert Deshman, *The Benedictional of Æthelwold*, Studies in Manuscript Illumination 9 (Princeton, NJ, 1995), and Andrew Prescott, *The Benedictional of Saint Æthelwold: A Masterpiece of Anglo-Saxon Art* (London, 2002).

[10]   In particular, Robert Deshman argues that a sacramentary from the North Italian town of Ivrea may have been created from a model with Anglo-Saxon influence that can be traced back to the Benedictional of Aethelwold. See Deshman, "The Iconography of the Full-Page Miniatures of the Benedictional of Aethelwold" (Ph.D. diss., Princeton University, 1971), pp. 43–46, and idem, *The Benedictional of Æthelwold*, p. 194.

[11]   "Precious" Gospels of Bernward of Hildesheim, Hildesheim, Dom-Museum, MS 18 (*c.*1015); Sacramentary of Sigebert of Minden, Berlin, Staatsbibliothek, MS theol. lat. fol. 2 (*c.*1022–1036).

[12]   For a more detailed discussion of the relationship between ritual iconography and episcopal authority see Evan A. Gatti, "Developing an Iconography of the Episcopacy: Liturgical Portraiture and Episcopal Politics in Late Tenth- and Early Eleventh-Century Manuscripts" (Ph.D. diss., University of North Carolina at Chapel Hill, 2005). See also Eric Palazzo, *L'Évêque et son image: L'illustration du Pontifical au Moyen Âge* (Turnhout, 1999).

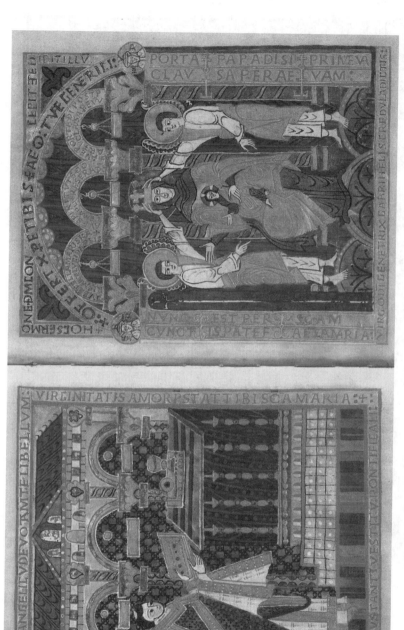

Fig. 6.4   "Precious" Gospels of Bernward of Hildesheim, Hildesheim, Dom-Museum, MS 18, fols 16v–17r (photo: M. Brandt, *Das Kostbare Evangeliar des Heiligen Bernward* [Munich, 1993])

Fig. 6.5 Sacramentary of Sigebert of Minden, Berlin, Staatsbibliothek, MS theol. lat. fol. 2, folio 9r (photo: Staatsbibliothek zu Berlin—Preussischer Kulturbesitz, Handschriftenabt)

Medieval Portraiture: Likeness and Representation

It must be emphasized that the miniature depicting Engilmar at the altar and the other liturgical miniatures noted above are *portraits* of historical bishops; most of them include an identifying inscription.[13] Despite the prominent role portraiture plays in art historical studies, it is still deemed curious to use the term in reference to medieval art. Arguably, medieval image-making favors more symbolic depictions over accurate physiognomic likeness, yet an investigation of the definition of portraiture suggests that because of its symbolic nature, examples of medieval portraiture can communicate complex notions of identity. Like the liturgy, medieval portraiture is experienced in the present, while at the same time it recollects something of the past; both are something temporal that has been re-presented.

A portrait has been defined as "a representation or delineation of a person, especially of the face . . . a likeness."[14] The term "likeness" has a specific connotation in the Middle Ages, especially because, according to Hans Belting, a medieval portrait belongs to the "era of images," rather than the "era of art."[15] In the era of images, a portrait, or an *imago*, refers to something "beyond itself" and thus has less to do with the presentation of a physically-defined individual and more to do with the historical or spiritual significance of that individual. Belting argues, following Gregory the Great, that the primary function of medieval art was to "recall to memory."[16] Seeing a medieval image, then, has a specific mnemonic function. As an act of memory, seeing an *imago* (or a portrait) was both retrospective and prospective; it reflected what had been, what existed, as well as what was promised, or what would be.[17] This multifaceted reaction to a medieval likeness signals the power of the medieval portrait. The medieval portrait, as an example of an *imago*, recognizes what has been, or a particular historical figure, while at the same time revealing what will be, which, in the case of a living medieval bishop, is the promise of commemoration or the possibility of sanctity.

Of central importance to the articulation of a medieval image as a likeness, or a portrait, is the recognition that the individual depicted is a named individual. As the medieval era was for the most part an era of anonymity, focus on a named individual implied a certain status for the person portrayed. In the case of the miniature in the Benedictional of Engilmar of Parenzo, the portrait is included in a manuscript made for and used by the individual it depicts. Additionally, the miniature mirrors the very gesture the celebrant-patron will enact when viewing the miniature. The function

---

[13]   As will be discussed below, the portrait miniature in the Benedictional of Æthelwold does not include an inscription; however, the manuscript does include a poem identifying Æthelwold as the patron of the manuscript.

[14]   Shearer West, *Portraiture* (Oxford, 2004), p. 2.

[15]   Hans Belting, *Likeness and Presence: A History of the Image before the Era of Art*, trans. Edmund Jephcott (Chicago, 1994), pp. 9–10.

[16]   Belting, *Likeness and Presence*, p. 10. See also Celia Chazelle, "Memory, Instruction, Worship: 'Gregory's' Influence on Early Medieval Doctrines of the Artistic Image," in *Gregory the Great: A Symposium*, ed. John C. Cavadini, Notre Dame Studies in Theology 2 (Notre Dame, IN, 1995), pp. 181–215.

[17]   Belting, *Likeness and Presence*, p. 10.

of a likeness that is not given away but instead received by the person it represents worked in the Middle Ages, as in the modern era, as a kind of self-fashioning.[18] As it is often assumed that the medieval patron had more say in posture, iconography, and, in some cases, the style of representation than the artist, the patron and maker of the manuscript became one, forcing a self-reflexive reading of the function of the portrait. Each episcopal portrait, then, presents a dynamic liturgical ritual that involves the viewer of the manuscript in the reconstruction of a series of synchronic events. In other words, they are active memories rather than still frames, and the reception of these liturgical portraits must have been very closely related to the literal experience of liturgical ceremony.

The active reading of these miniatures by the same bishops they depict is bolstered by the fact that examples of liturgical episcopal portraiture appear within illuminated manuscripts that can also be defined as liturgical, such as the sacramentary, benedictional, or pontifical.[19] During the late tenth and early eleventh centuries, the responsibilities of the bishop as celebrant were evolving according to the liturgies recorded in these manuscripts. The blessings included in the benedictional were originally included in the sacramentary, which contained all the prayers read by the celebrant during the mass. While often made for episcopal patrons, these manuscripts do not separate those parts of the mass read by a priest from those read by the bishop. The benedictional, on the other hand, contains only those blessings read during the mass by the bishop. At this same time, the episcopal duties of the altar were being culled from the sacramentary and brought together in the pontifical, which, under the sponsorship of the Ottonian emperors, would replace the sacramentary in defining the responsibilities and authorities of the bishop as celebrant.[20] It is at this same crucial point in the evolution of episcopal liturgical privilege—and the development of the bishop's public persona in terms of sacerdotal authority—that the liturgical miniature is singled out as a motif for episcopal dedication portraits.

What, then, did it mean to include an image of a historical bishop blessing his congregation in the opening folios of his benedictional? Let us begin with the structure of the manuscript itself. The codex containing the Benedictional of Engilmar measures 23.2 cm x 16 cm and is composed of 117 folios that can be broken down into four parts dating from the eleventh to the thirteenth centuries. The first two parts are attributed to the thirteenth century and include folios 1r–6r, comprised of miscellaneous blessings and a few blank folios, and folios 7r–15v, containing an opening rubric followed by blessings in liturgical order beginning with the first Sunday in Advent. The fourth part, folios 88r–117r, can also be dated

---

[18] For a discussion of the role of "self-fashioning" in portraiture as it relates to art of the modern era, see West, *Portraiture*, pp. 173–78.

[19] For a discussion of some of the problems associated with the term "liturgical books", see John Lowden, "Illuminated Books and the Liturgy: Some Observations," in *Objects, Images, and the Word: Art in the Service of the Liturgy*, ed. Colum Hourihane, Index of Christian Art Occasional Papers 6 (Princeton, NJ, 2003), pp. 17–53.

[20] See Eric Palazzo, *A History of Liturgical Books from the Beginning to the Thirteenth Century* (Collegeville, MN, 1998), p. 56, and idem, *Les sacramentaires de Fulda: Étude sur l'iconographie et la liturgie à l'époque ottonienne*, Liturgiewissenschaftliche Quellen und Forschungen 77 (Münster, 1994).

to the thirteenth century and includes an order of the mass.[21] The third and largest part of the manuscript, comprised of folios 16r–87v, contains the original eleventh-century benedictional.

The collation of these distinct parts into a single codex during the later Middle Ages has specific consequences for the liturgical portrait of Engilmar. First, the manuscript was intended to be used by a later bishop, as additional benedictions were included to facilitate its reuse within an expanded liturgical calendar.[22] Nonetheless, the portrait and inscription recognizing Engilmar's patronage of the manuscript remain intact. It is possible that the portrait of Engilmar was only kept within the text of the expanded benedictional to save the text on the verso of the folio, which includes the blessings for Christmas vigil. These same blessings, however, are repeated in the additions to the manuscript following the blessings for the first Sunday in Advent, an ordering common to later benedictionals.[23] So it seems that as part of the renovation of the benedictional, the portrait of Engilmar and its accompanying blessings were preserved, not as a mark of ownership of the manuscript or to preserve certain parts of the text, but instead as a remembrance of the legacy and legitimacy of the episcopate of Engilmar.

Second, in the original construction of the manuscript, the portrait of Engilmar (found today on folio 16r) would have been at or partnered with the opening text. A small stub before the Engilmar portrait suggests that the opening folio of the eleventh-century benedictional, which could have contained the manuscript's rubric and perhaps a dedicatory inscription, was removed when the thirteenth-century additions were made to the original codex. In fact, a rubric on folio 7r in the thirteenth-century benedictional reads, *Incipiunt benedictiones pontificales per totius anni circulum*, and may be an imitation of what was removed from the original manuscript.[24] In any case, the miniature would have either functioned as a kind of dedication portrait or have been part of a larger dedicatory program; the dedicatory nature of the miniature is preserved by the inscription ENGILMARUS EPS, which

---

[21] The collation of the manuscript, according to the microfilm published by the Getty Museum, is: 1^{8-1}, $2-3^8$, 4^{10}, $5-7^8$, 8^{8-1}, 9^{10-2}, preceded by a^1, b^4, c^{10}; and followed by $d-e^{10}$, f^8, g^2, totaling 117 leaves. Signatures a–g are additions, dating from the twelfth to the fifteenth centuries. See Von Euw, *Die Handschriften der Sammlung Ludwig,* 1:293; *Regensburger Buchmalerei*, ed. Mütherich and Dachs, no. 22, p. 36; and Lee, "Das Benedictionale des Bischofs Engilmar," p. 18.

[22] I would like to thank Elizabeth Teviotdale for sharing her knowledge of the Engilmar benedictional with me, and in particular for bringing to my attention some of the anomalies in the re-ordering of the episcopal blessings. There is much more to be done with regard to the text of the expanded benedictional that is beyond the scope of this essay. Ideally, liturgical imagery and liturgical texts would benefit from a truly multi-disciplinary discussion.

[23] The Engilmar benedictional includes the blessing for the Christmas Vigil on fol. 16v. The second addition to the manuscript begins with an opening rubric on fol. 7r followed by the blessings for the first Sunday in Advent, followed by the blessing for Christmas Vigil.

[24] As suggested to me by Elizabeth Teviotdale; however, during this period it was not unusual for the opening leaf of the first gathering to have been left blank, unlike later manuscripts that include flyleaves. For other interpretations, see Von Euw, *Die Handschriften der Sammlung Ludwig*, 1:293, and Lee, "Das Benedictionale des Bischofs Engilmar," p. 23 n. 47.

spans the width of the architectural space above the head of the bishop.[25] It is likely that the portrait of Engilmar was always intended to honor both the bishop's person and his position, especially as the placement of the miniature at the opening of the text suggests that the miniature was not included to illustrate a particular blessing from the benedictional. This placement, while relatively common to historical liturgical portraits, is not found in miniatures that can be described as liturgical illustrations or miniatures from illustrated *vitae*, which often include the bishop-celebrant at the altar as part of the narrative pictorial cycle. As a dedication portrait, the miniature both celebrates the general act of episcopal blessing and, as will be demonstrated below, establishes the political and spiritual legitimacy of Engilmar with specific reference to the episcopal see at Parenzo.

Engilmarus Episcopus: Monastic, Clerical, and Spiritual Statesman

The miniature of Engilmar has rarely been discussed as having specific relevance to Engilmar or his episcopate. This may be in part because little can be stated with certainty about the enigmatic Engilmar; there are no other artistic commissions or writings that can be associated with him, and as he was not beatified, no *vita* was written after his death. All that remains are a few notations of the name Engilmar in monastic records as well as two documents that survive from his tenure in Parenzo. Nevertheless, if the miniature of Engilmar is interpreted within the traditions of medieval portraiture and hagiographic illustration, even the modest information about Engilmar and Parenzo is enough to link the portrait of Engilmar to his most pressing responsibilities—defining and defending *Ecclesia*.

In 1006, a description of a gift from an Engilmar *archipresbyter* to the Benedictine monastery of Emmeram recognizes Engilmar as a generous man of wealthy means and a pious nature.[26] Additionally, the gift, which included costly liturgical

---

[25]   It should be noted that E.F. Bange believed the inscription was not contemporary with the miniature but instead dated it to *c.*1050, five to ten years after the episcopate of Engilmar. See Bange, *Eine bayersiche Malerschule* (above, n. 2), p. 55. In 1972, however, Romuald Bauerreiss argued that the inscription is from a similar time period as the rest of the text and that the later date proposed by Bange should not be a reason to separate the manuscript from the person of Engilmar. Bauerreiss cites the liturgy more specifically as a reason to continue to associate the manuscript with the bishop, since, as will be discussed below, special attention is given to feasts of particular importance to Parenzo. Romuald Bauerreiss, "Über den Mönch Engilmar von Niederharthausen (NDBY), später Bischof von Parenzo (XI. s.) und sein Benediktionale," *Zeitschrift für bayerische Landesgeschichte* 35 (1972), 31–39, at p. 32. In later publications, the date of the inscription and the attribution of the manuscript to Engilmar of Parenzo stand without question; see, for example, Von Euw, *Die Handschriften der Sammlung Ludwig*, pp. 293–96; *Regensburger Buchmalerei*, ed. Mütherich and Dachs, no. 22, p. 36; *Masterpieces of the J. Paul Getty Museum*, ed. Kren, no. 4, p. 17.

[26]   "Dedi etiam non vilis taxationis missale unum et antifonarium. . . . " For the full text, see Josef Widemann, *Die Traditionen des Hochstifts Regensburg und des Klosters S. Emmeram*, Quellen und Erörterungen zur bayerische Geschichte, 2nd edn (Aalen, 1988), no. 279, p. 226. See also Bauerreiss, "Über den Mönch Engilmar von Niederharthausen," p. 32. There is some debate as to whether or not this gift can be attributed to Engilmar: see Freise,

manuscripts, suggests a relationship with the Regensburg monastery of Emmeram that may help to explain the production of the Benedictional of Engilmar. No more is known of Engilmar before he took his post at Parenzo.

Episcopal documents from the tenure of Engilmar, as well as later episcopal histories and lists, place Engilmar in Parenzo between 1028 and 1045.[27] A document from Parenzo dated 7 August 1030 records the bishop's participation in the donation of land and products of the monastery of Saint Cassian to the monastic house of San Michele Arcangelo in Pola.[28] A second document dated 15 September 1040 records a conflict between the bishop and the abbot of San Michele di Leme for the privilege of tithing, a conflict that was to be decided by King Henry III.[29] While these documents suggest Engilmar's presence in Parenzo, the bishop is also known to have traveled back to his native Bavaria during his episcopacy in Istria.[30] According to the chronicle of Hermann of Altach, on 21 September 1037, Engilmar, together with the bishops of Passau and Eichstätt, was present at the re-consecration of Niederaltaich's monastic church, which had burned in 1033.[31] At about this same time, Engilmar is said to have visited Emmeram, where, as Arnold of Emmeram reports in his second book on the history of the house, he witnessed a miracle.[32]

Finally, an Engilmar is included in a necrology from the monastery of Emmeram in Regensburg covering the years between 1036 and 1045.[33] While there is no evidence to prove that Engilmar was ever a member of the community at Emmeram, his friendship with Arnold of Emmeram is well documented.[34] The relationship between Arnold and Engilmar, as well as Engilmar's visit to Emmeram as an

---

Geuenich, and Wollasch eds, *Das Martyrolog-Necrolog von St Emmeram zu Regensburg* (above, n. 2), pp. 77 and 174; and Lee, "Das Benedictionale des Bischofs Engilmar," p. 8.

[27]   See Babudri, "I Vescovi di Parenzo" (above, n. 3), pp. 214–15.

[28]   Pietro Kandler ed., *Codice Diplomatico Istriano*, 5 vols (Trieste, 1986), no. 91, 1:193.

[29]   Ibid., no. 99, 1:209.

[30]   It can be assumed that the first charter, dated 7 August 1030, was recorded in Parenzo, as the title, "Indizione XIII. Parenzo," suggests. The second document, which dates to 12 May 1040, is only entitled "Indizione X" and lists no city of origin.

[31]   For the chronicle of Hermann of Altach, see *De institutione monasterii Altahensis*, ed. Georg Pertz, MGH SS 17 (Hannover, 1861), pp. 369–73. Bauerreiss places Engilmar in Niederaltaich on 21 September 1037 ("Über den Mönch Engilmar von Niederharthausen," p. 35). See also Franz Heidingsfelder, *Die Regesten der Bischöfe von Eichstätt: Bis zum Ende der Regierung des Bischofs Marquard von Hagel 1324* (Erlangen, 1938), no. 168, p. 62, and Stadtmüller and Pfister, *Geschichte der Abtei* (above, n. 2), no. 108, p. 129.

[32]   Arnold of Emmeram, "Libris de S. Emmeramo," ed. Georg Waitz, in Georg Pertz ed., MGH SS 4 (Hannover, 1841), p. 570. As cited in Von Euw, *Die Handschriften der Sammlung Ludwig*, 1:294; see also Bernhard Bischoff, "Literarisches und künstlerisches Leben in St Emmeram (Regensburg) während des frühen und hohen Mittelalters," in Bischoff, *Mittelalterliche Studien: Ausgewählte Aufsätze zur Schriftkunde und Literaturgeschichte*, 3 vols (Stuttgart, 1966–1981), 2:77–115, at p. 84.

[33]   Augsburg, Universitätsbibliothek, Cod. I 22 8, fol. 30r. See the facsimile publication and commentary: Freise, Geuenich, and Wollasch eds, *Das Martyrolog-Necrolog von St Emmeram zu Regensburg*.

[34]   For a discussion of the friendship between Engilmar and Arnold, see Lee, "Das Benedictionale des Bischofs Engilmar," p. 8. See also MGH SS 4:570 and PL 141:1065.

"honored guest," have led scholars to suggest that the Benedictional of Engilmar was made at Emmeram, either as a gift for the bishop or perhaps commissioned by him sometime between 1030 and 1040.[35] It is here in particular that one laments the manuscript's lack of a dedicatory inscription.

As noted earlier, the origin and style of the miniatures reflect Engilmar's roots in Bavaria, but the text of the benedictional was written with Engilmar's position at Parenzo in mind. For example, the liturgical blessings contained within the

Fig. 6.6   Poreč, Basilica Euphrasiana, apse mosaic (photo: Conway Library, Courtauld Institute of Art)

benedictional include those for the feast day of the bishop-saint Maurus.[36] Maurus, whose image was included in the sixth-century apse mosaic of the cathedral at Parenzo, was recorded in legend as the church's first bishop and is believed to have been buried at the cathedral (Fig. 6.6).

When one notes that the Benedictional of Engilmar was commissioned for use at Parenzo, the pastoral act of blessing seen in the portrait of Engilmar seems particularly significant. Part of the Istrian Peninsula on the Adriatic Sea, today

---

[35]   *Masterpieces of the J. Paul Getty Museum*, ed. Kren, no. 4, p. 17.

[36]   For a transcription of the prayer see Bauerreiss, "Über den Mönch Engilmar von Niederharthausen," p. 36.

Parenzo is located in Croatia near the modern border with Slovenia. At the time of the miniature's creation, Parenzo was on the edge of the German Empire, bordering on the territories of Byzantium and the medieval kingdom of Croatia.[37] In the centuries before Engilmar's episcopate, Parenzo had shifted from the control of Byzantium to that of the German Empire, and it had seen instability caused by Slav, Lombard, Frankish, and Byzantine invasions.[38] Therefore, as bishop of Parenzo, Engilmar's most significant contribution may have been securing and defining this often-disputed territory as part of the social and religious fabric of the German Empire.[39]

Furthermore, the religious history of Istria is complicated by shifting political allegiances. At the time of Engilmar's episcopate, Parenzo's metropolitan see, Aquileia, was mired in conflict with the city of Grado over supremacy in the region.[40] From the tenth to the eleventh century, the metropolitan see alternated between these cities four times; Engilmar's episcopate, from 1028 to 1045, coincided with a particularly active period in the dispute, with the transfer of power from Grado

---

[37] It is important to note that Parenzo (modern-day Poreč) was not included within the borders of early medieval Croatia, but instead considered a part of the German Empire. See Tomislav Raukar, "Land and Society," in *Croatia in the Early Middle Ages: A Cultural Survey*, ed. Ivan Supicic, Croatia and Europe 1 (London, 1999), pp. 181–95, at pp. 183 and 193. There is little Germanic cultural influence that can be found in medieval Croatia, even in areas ruled by Germanic feudal lords. See also Ivo Goldstein, "Between Byzantium, the Adriatic and Central Europe," in *Croatia in the Early Middle Ages*, ed. Supicic, pp. 169–78, at p. 176.

[38] As German influence waned in Northern Italy, Istria was designated as a separate marquisate under Henry III and given in fief to Ulderich of Weimar (1040–1070). By the twelfth century Istria had begun to gain its independence from the German Empire. See Darko Darovec, *A Brief History of Istra (Pregled Zgodovine Istre)*, trans. Ilario Ermacora (Yanchep, Western Australia, 1998), p. 33.

[39] The idea that the nomination of bishops of German origin to episcopal posts throughout the Empire was part of an institutionalized relationship between the Ottonian Church and the Empire (known as the *Reichskirchensystem*), wherein Germanic bishops were elected to keep the local aristocracy at bay, has recently been called into question. See in particular Timothy Reuter, "The 'Imperial Church System' of the Ottonian and Salian Rulers: A Reconsideration," *Journal of Ecclesiastical History* 33 (1982), 347–74, and a rebuttal by Josef Fleckenstein, "Problematik und Gestalt der ottonisch-salischen Reichskirche," in *Reich und Kirche vor dem Investiturstreit: Vorträge beim wissenschaftlichen Kolloquium aus Anlaß des achtzigsten Geburtstags von Gerd Tellenbach*, ed. Karl Schmid (Sigmaringen, 1985), pp. 83–98. In the case of Engilmar and Parenzo, there is reason to assume that the bishop was closely allied with imperial desires for stability in the area. The charters associated with Engilmar mention a relationship with both Conrad and Henry III, who was ultimately called upon to solve a dispute concerning the rite to tithe. See Kandler ed., *Codice Diplomatico Istriano*, no. 91, 1:193; no. 99, 1:209. Beyond asserting a continued (Germanic) episcopal presence in Parenzo, there is no reason to assume that Engilmar's posting was intended to squelch the nobility, or that the local rulers were hostile to his imperial connections.

[40] Parenzo was a suffragan of Milan until 404, when the capital of the Empire was moved to Ravenna. In the first half of the fifth century, Parenzo became a suffragan of Aquileia until the modern era, when the episcopate was transferred to Görz. See Francesco Babudri, "Parenzo nella storia ecclesiastica," *Atti e Memorie della Società Istriana di Archeologia e Storia Patria* 26 (1910), 81–148, at p. 89.

to Aquileia in 1028, and the reversal of that privilege back to Grado in 1044. Englimar's reign overlaps with that of the Aquileian patriarch Poppo (1019–1042), also known as Wolfgang, who was appointed to office by Emperor Henry II.[41] During his tenure, Poppo secured the primacy of Aquileia over Grado.[42] To celebrate this victory, Patriarch Poppo began reconstruction on the cathedral in Aquileia, which was eventually consecrated on 12 July 1031.

A link between Parenzo and Aquileia is preserved in the apse decoration of the two cathedrals, as the early Christian mosaics in Parenzo's sixth-century Euphrasian Basilica may have served as a model for the eleventh-century program commissioned by Poppo for Aquileia.[43] The sixth-century apse mosaic in Parenzo (Fig. 6.6) depicts the Virgin and Child flanked by angels, local saints, and ecclesiastical figures, including: Parenzo's patron saint and legendary first bishop, Maurus; Bishop Euphrasius; Euphrasius's archdeacon (and later bishop), Claudius; and Claudius's son. At the center of the apse in Aquileia, the Virgin and Child are flanked by the apostle St Mark, the late Emperor Henry II, the bishop-saint Hilary, Archbishop Poppo, and the deacon-saint Tatian. To the left of the Virgin are Prince Henry III, the bishop-saint Hermagoras, Emperor Conrad II, the deacon-saint Fortunatus, the martyr-saint Euphemia, and finally, Empress Gisela.[44]

While Parenzo may have served as a visual model for Aquileia, it is the apse in Aquileia that suggests a better model for contemporary ecclesiastical politics in Parenzo. Particularly interesting for the case of Engilmar are the overt references in the Aquileian frescoes toward the local ecclesiastical hierarchy, as it is dependent upon apostolic succession, saints of local significance, and the patronage of the Salian emperors.[45] In particular, members of the imperial family are included in the sacred space of the apse, marking a close and dependent relationship between the church and the Empire.

---

[41] Dates are from Lee, "Das Benedictionale des Bischofs Engilmar," p. 10 n. 25; see also Baburdi, "Parenzo nella storia ecclesiastica," p. 106. For a discussion of the role of Poppo in the art and politics of Aquileia, see Thomas E.A. Dale, *Relics, Prayer, and Politics in Medieval Venetia: Romanesque Painting in the Crypt of Aquileia Cathedral* (Princeton, NJ, 1997), pp. 10, 14–15.

[42] Dale, *Relics, Prayer, and Politics*, p. 10 n. 29. The text cited by Dale refers to Pope John XIX's bull confirming Aquileia as metropolitan and condemning the "false appropriation" of that title by the Grado patriarch. It was also during this synod that Pope John XIX crowned Conrad as emperor. See also *Conradi II. Constitutiones*, ed. Ludwig Weiland, MGH Legum 4, Constitutiones et acta publica imperatorum et regum 1 (Hannover, 1893), no. 38, pp. 82–84.

[43] For Aquileia, see Maria Cristina Cavalieri, "L'affresco absidale della Basilica patriarcale di Aquileia," *Bollettino d'arte* 61 (1976), 1–11, at pp. 3–4. The cathedral may have been in some decline during this period; see Prelog, *Basilica of Euphrasius* (above, n. 6), p. 26.

[44] Dale argues that Euphemia may have been included in the apse program "to usurp from Grado the patron of its cathedral church" and thereby the history and authority of the city as a metropolitan; see Dale, *Relics, Prayer, and Politics*, p. 130 n. 66.

[45] Further, Maria Cristina Cavalieri has linked the frescoes from the apse at Aquileia to Ottonian-style frescoes, such as those in Friuli and the abbey church of Saint George, Oberzell-Reichenau, as well as contemporary manuscripts, such as the Psalter of Egbert of Trier. See Cavalieri, "L'affresco absidale," pp. 5–6.

There is no record of Engilmar's nomination to his post by the Salian emperors; however, the bishop, of Bavarian heritage, had connections to Benedictine and imperial traditions that suggest he was part of the larger cooperation between the emperors and the church. With specific relevance to the Benedictional of Engilmar, an imperial connection can be argued from the style of the Christological miniatures that decorate the manuscript. Beyond the portrait miniature of Engilmar, the Benedictional includes the standard series of Christological miniatures including the Nativity of Christ, the Adoration of the Magi (Fig. 6.2), the Presentation in the Temple, Christ's Entry into Jerusalem, the Last Supper, the Three Women at the Tomb, the Ascension of Christ, and Pentecost. What is significant about these miniatures, however, is that they are similar to examples of eleventh-century illuminations executed for imperial patrons.[46] In particular, as noted earlier, the style and iconography of the miniatures exhibit similarities to the Bavarian school of Regensburg, and specifically, the Benedictine house at Emmeram.[47] During the reign of Emperor Henry II, who was educated at Emmeram, the monastery was considered a principal house in ecclesiastical politics and reform as well as an artistic center.[48] Manuscripts produced at Emmeram, such as the Sacramentary of Henry II, express a reciprocal relationship between episcopacy and empire.[49] For example, the portrait of Henry II in the sacramentary depicts the emperor crowned by the hand of Christ and handed the symbols of his office, the sword and lance, by two angels. Flanking the emperor, as well as literally supporting him, are the bishop-saints Emmeram of Regensburg and Ulrich of Augsburg (Fig. 6.7).[50]

While there are no overt iconographic links to the imperial politics of Henry II or his successors in the Benedictional of Engilmar, the style and compositional conformity of the miniature cycle is similar to miniatures of the same themes in manuscripts made at the monastery of Emmeram for members of the imperial house.

---

[46] See Henry Mayr-Harting for a discussion of the development of the Ottonian Christological cycle and in particular the entry into Jerusalem, which may have connections to imperial perspectives even when they are not overtly depicted: *Ottonian Book Illumination: An Historical Study*, 2 vols (London, 1991), 1:119–25.

[47] For a summary of the state of the research on the style of the manuscript, see Lee, "Das Benedictionale des Bischofs Engilmar," pp. 4–5. See also *Regensburger Buchmalerei*, ed. Mütherich and Dachs, no. 22, p. 36.

[48] In particular, Henry and Regensburg are associated with the eleventh-century Gorze reform. See Mayr-Harting, *Ottonian Book Illumination*, 1:129

[49] Munich, Bayerische Staatsbibliothek, Clm. 4456.

[50] A miniature in the Pericopes of Henry II (Munich, Bayerische Staatsbibliothek, Clm. 4452), given to the cathedral at Bamberg by Henry around 1014, also depicts the emperor being crowned by Christ, this time supported by Saints Peter and Paul. Meyer Schapiro has argued that the three central figures in these two miniatures reflect an older image type depicting Moses flanked and supported by Aaron and Hur. See Meyer Schapiro, *Words, Script, and Pictures: Semiotics of Visual Language* (New York, 1996), p. 26. Schapiro also argues that the image group was adopted throughout the Middle Ages to represent a sense of cooperation between bishops and kings. In particular, the Exodus story was told in support of the military campaigns of Charlemagne, the wars of King Robert of France, and the preaching of the First Crusade (ibid., pp. 25–46). Finally, the image group may reflect the posture of the king and bishops upon entering the church on certain feast days and at the king's coronation (ibid., p. 41).

Fig. 6.7   Sacramentary of Henry II, Munich, Bayerische Staatsbibliothek, Clm. 4456, folio 11r (photo: Bayerische Staatsbibliothek)

The cycle of miniatures included in Engilmar's benedictional, therefore, refers to both imperial and Benedictine systems of patronage. The manuscript acts as a metaphor for Engilmar's position in Parenzo, securing the episcopal see as a part of both an imperial and an ecclesiastical system.[51]

Although there are established iconographies for episcopal portraiture that borrow the power of secular ruler imagery or the piety of the monastic donor type, the portrait of Engilmar presents the bishop as celebrant. We return, therefore, to the question of a model for the portrait of Engilmar, not to explain away the invention of a medieval artist, but to understand what it meant to represent the bishop as *sacerdos* rather than as Christ or as king. Remember, too, that the liturgical portrait of Engilmar and similar portraits in other manuscripts appeared during the latter half of the tenth and first half of the eleventh centuries, a time of rising competition between the papacy and the German Empire.[52] By emphasizing liturgical acts—the privileges of priestly ordination—the authority presented in these images is not only distinct from that of secular rulers but also makes it clear that the bishop is an instrument of the church and a reflection of the saints.

The Bishop's Two Bodies: Blessings and Boundaries

It has been argued by Elizabeth Lipsmeyer that the "donor with model" type of episcopal and papal portraiture allowed the donor to equate himself with the martyrs and saints, with whom he is often depicted, as well as to "lay claim to the same considerations for eternal salvation and reward."[53] As noted earlier, conventional examples of episcopal portraiture recognize living bishops as conduits, enthroned at the head of their episcopal sees, but also as donors, at the feet of their sainted counterparts. Both kinds of episcopal portraiture can be seen in a series of dedicatory portraits in the tenth-century Psalter of Archbishop Egbert of Trier (977–993).[54] On folio 16v, the scribe, identified through the inscription as Ruodpreht, offers the psalter to Archbishop Egbert, who is represented on the facing page enthroned and wearing the square halo of a blessed living figure.[55] On the following two pages, 17v and 18r, the square-haloed Archbishop Egbert offers the psalter to his patron, St Peter, who is seated on a throne across the gutter of the manuscript on folio 19r (Fig. 6.8). This

---

[51] Rosemary Lee refers to Engilmar as a "spiritual statesman" (geistlichen Staatsmannes): Lee, "Das Benedictionale des Bischofs Engilmar," p. 10.

[52] For a basic survey of the Investiture Controversy, see Uta-Renate Blumenthal, *The Investiture Controversy: Church and Monarchy from the Ninth to the Twelfth Century* (Philadelphia, 1991), and Karl F. Morrison, *The Investiture Controversy: Ideas, Ideals and Results* (New York, 1971).

[53] Elizabeth Lipsmeyer, "The Donor and his Church Model" (above, n. 1), p. 25.

[54] Cividale, Museo Archeologico Nazionale di Cividale, MS 136. For bibliography see *Psalterium Egberti: Facsimile del ms. CXXXVI del Museo Archeologico Nazionale di Cividale del Friuli*, ed. Claudio Barberi (Cividale, 2000).

[55] For a discussion of the square halo, see Gerhart B. Ladner, "The So-Called Square Nimbus," *Mediaeval Studies* 3 (1941), 15–45.

Fig. 6.8   Egbert Psalter, Cividale del Friuli, Museo Archeologico Nazionale, MS 136, fols 18v–19r (photo: Schaar and Dathe, Trier, as published in *Der Psalter Erzbischofs Egbert von Trier: Codex Gertrudianus in Cividale*, ed. H. Sauerland and A. Haseloff, 2 vols [Trier, 1901])

pair of dedication miniatures recognizes Egbert's patronage of the manuscript, but greater attention is focused on the authority of his saintly counterpart.

In establishing a connection with St Peter, Egbert assures an apostolic connection for Trier.[56] Examples of liturgical episcopal portraiture likewise celebrate the authority of the episcopacy as it is linked to sanctity; however, they focus one's attention on the bishop-celebrant and the act of the liturgy more than on the patron saint. The authority of these images is not derived from the relationship of the bishop to the body of a saint, but the replacement of the bishop-saint's body with that of his historical counterpart.

In separate studies, Cynthia Hahn and Barbara Abou-el-Haj have established that the miniatures decorating manuscripts of the lives of bishop-saints define sanctity and authority in terms of the historical person's good work as a bishop rather than through his miracles or martyrdom.[57] The sanctity of the bishop-saints is reflected through conformity to certain image types, such as miniatures of the bishop celebrating the liturgy, which Hahn argues can be seen as representative of the local ecclesiastical hierarchy.[58] Both the sanctity and the authority of a bishop-saint's *vita* are established through these liturgical acts or postures, and even the miracles attributed to these saints often involve liturgical ceremony.[59] While Hahn and Abou-el-Haj are focused on narrative cycles, the images of the bishop-celebrant are often detached from a pictorial cycle and reused as honorific portraits.[60] For example, while not an iconographic or stylistic model for the Engilmar portrait, a similar emphasis on a liturgical motif can be seen in the frontispiece depicting St Erhard celebrating mass in the Uta Codex, which may also be attributed to the Regensburg school.[61] Each of these images has individual interpretations based on its historical context and place in a pictorial cycle, but as earlier bishops borrowed the iconography of the enthroned and the donor types, so here the saint as celebrant can be appropriated for the contemporary historical bishop.

What specifically can we learn from illustrated saints' *vitae* about the significance of episcopal blessing? Among those deeds recorded in episcopal *vitae*, scenes of blessing and healing appear with particular frequency. Through the gesture of blessing in scenes of healing or damning, episcopal *vitae* commemorate the bishop's power to admit or readmit the saved into the church or community. Miraculous images of the bishop articulate the bishop's power as an instrument of the church, which, Hahn argues, is referenced by the gesture accompanying a blessing—the sign of the cross: "Bishops . . . use the sign actively, as a liturgical gesture that they wield by prerogative: as God's instruments—the limbs, the arms of the body of

---

56   Thomas Head, "Art and Artifice in Ottonian Trier," *Gesta* 36 (1997), 65–82.

57   Barbara Abou-el-Haj, *The Medieval Cult of Saints: Formations and Transformations* (Cambridge, 1997); Cynthia Hahn, *Portrayed on the Heart: Narrative Effect in Pictorial Lives of Saints from the Tenth through the Thirteenth Century* (Berkeley, CA, 2001).

58   Hahn, *Portrayed on the Heart*, p. 26, fig. 57.

59   Abou-el-Haj, *Medieval Cult of Saints*, pp. 37–38.

60   Ibid., p. 100.

61   Uta Codex, Munich, Bayerische Staatsbibliotek, Clm. 13601. See also Adam Cohen, *The Uta Codex: Art, Philosophy, and Reform in Eleventh-Century Germany* (University Park, PA, 2000), pp. 77–96.

the church—bishops transmit God's power."[62] Liturgical gestures demonstrate the power of the bishop as celebrant, even after death.

Additionally, miraculous events, such as healing through blessing, can be recognized as metaphors for the bishop's responsibility in defining the boundaries of the community. The type of miracle most often attributed to the living bishop-saint, for example, is healing the blind. As Cynthia Hahn argues, when sight is given or restored to the supplicant, it is as if the bishop "brings a sinner into the fold."[63] The miracle of healing the blind references the bishop's role in conversion through baptism, reconciliation, ordination, and anointing. Through his touch, or blessing, the bishop brings "sight" to the victim of "blindness" as well as "life," new or renewed, in the church. In admitting or readmitting the saved into the church or the Christian community, expelling the damned, or even defining a certain place or thing as holy, the bishop continues the pastoral function celebrated through images of preaching and baptism. With specific relevance to the portrait of Engilmar, illustrations of episcopal sanctity emphasized the bishop-saint's role in establishing the "unity of the Church" as dictated by Gregory of Tours.[64] Further, liturgical scenes in illustrated hagiography establish a geography of sanctity, especially in death, where, Hahn argues, "the bishop bequeaths a heritage of sanctified land and purified community."[65]

The portrait of Engilmar blessing his congregation is tied to the benedictions of the bishop-saints, who, through liturgical gestures, delineated spiritual boundaries for the supplicants and their see. While the miraculous blessings cited above are not liturgical pre-communion blessings, as pictured in the Benedictional of Engilmar, the significance of the episcopal blessing, as with most liturgical gestures, is intended to recall events beyond it. With the development of the pontifical, a more specific series of episcopal blessings will appear within the pictorial cycles of liturgical manuscripts. As outlined by Eric Palazzo, miniatures depicting the bishop's role in ordination, royal consecration, and church dedication are regularly included among the pontificals of the twelfth to the fifteenth centuries.[66] Even in the period before these manuscripts, however, the illustration of liturgical ritual has a specialized meaning, which for the portrait of Engilmar of Parenzo is intimately tied to the spiritual and social power of episcopal blessing.[67] The dedication image in Engilmar's benedictional represents the bishop's authority by recalling an iconography of episcopal sanctity. It reminds

---

[62]   Hahn, *Portrayed on the Heart*, p. 161.

[63]   Ibid., pp. 153–54.

[64]   Hahn, *Portrayed on the Heart*, p. 132. "Gregory of Tours's *Glory of the Confessors* contains an abundance of miracle stories that show a saint defending 'his' property, and the illustrated Lives are similarly replete with pictorial representations of saintly defense": Ibid, p. 131 n. 10.

[65]   Ibid., p. 131.

[66]   Palazzo, *L'Évêque et son image*, pp. 141–78.

[67]   See Palazzo's discussion of liturgical illustration before the pontifical and of the tenth- and eleventh-century development of the Romano-Germanic Pontifical: *L'Évêque et son image*, pp. 111–42, at p. 142.

Engilmar, for he is the primary audience for the miniature, that it is through the performance of his liturgical responsibilities that he best represents his office.[68]

There is no record of the bishops who may have served in Parenzo immediately before and after the tenure of Engilmar.[69] Even the few details of Engilmar's episcopacy, however, suggest he brought attention, and a certain degree of stability, to his see. This stability is perhaps best demonstrated through the recognition of Engilmar's donation of Saint Cassian to San Michele Arcangelo, which was reconfirmed by Engilmar's successors through 1146.[70] Further, in keeping with the tradition of episcopal authority as it was reflected in the *vitae* of bishop-saints, all of the documentation related to Engilmar focuses on the bishop's role in defining boundaries, both physical and spiritual. Both charters that mention Engilmar refer to the land or privileges of Parenzo's monasteries. Additionally, Engilmar's travel back to his native Bavaria, where he participated in the re-dedication of the altar at the monastery at Niederaltaich, can be seen as a moment of particular significance in defining, or in the case of Niederaltaich, redefining a spiritual place. All of these actions, like those of a bishop-saint, mark the bishop's role as a defender of spiritual spaces. Given the history of Parenzo as a political crossroads, such a defense may have been one of the key elements of Engilmar's position there, even if that defense was simply played out in the regular celebration of the liturgical rituals that took place in the cathedral. Remember that in the miniature the architecture surrounding Engilmar and his congregation was rusticated and topped with crenellation, resembling a city gate more than a cathedral interior. If the bishop's blessing can be seen as defining and defending a spiritual space, the defensive attributes of the space of the miniature give additional credence to such an interpretation.

A similar depiction of the liturgical space as a city gate or fortification can be seen in the portrait miniature in the Sacramentary of Sigebert of Minden (Fig. 6.5). The miniature depicts Sigebert, bishop of Minden, standing before a draped altar prepared for mass with a golden paten. The open space behind the figures, decorated with gold foil, is dominated by a rusticated triumphal arch or city gate complete with a crenellated roofline. Two barrel-vaulted aisles, sheathed in white marble and roofed with red terracotta tiles, further flank the arch. Each of these barrel-vaulted aisles rests on a red entablature supported by two thin marble columns. From the apex of the central arch hangs a golden votive crown. The martial aspects of the architecture are further emphasized by the personification of *Ecclesia* who offers the bishop the eucharistic chalice. As is traditional to her iconography in the Ottonian era, *Ecclesia* carries a standard surmounted by a cross and wears "helmet-like" headgear. Her military accoutrements are matched by her stern demeanor and steady gaze, which is directed at and met by the bishop. Behind *Ecclesia* stands a smaller female figure, often identified as the Virgin Mary, another symbol for the church.[71] Mary's hands

---

[68]   Ibid., p. 41.

[69]   See Babudri, "I Vescovi di Parenzo" (above, n. 3), pp. 214–15. Note the dates for Arpus, which may be used in some sources as the *terminus ante quem* for Engilmar.

[70]   Kandler ed., *Codice Diplomatico Istriano*, no. 91, 1:194.

[71]   Mayr-Harting, *Ottonian Book Illumination* (above, n. 46), 2:92.

are raised in an *orans* gesture of prayer or acceptance, and both Mary and the figure of *Ecclesia* are depicted with haloes.

Like the portrait of Engilmar, the miniature of Sigebert receiving the eucharistic chalice is a dedication or donor portrait. The inscription around the border of the image reads: "Take, Sigebert, the gifts of eternal life through which the mother of graces gently refreshes you."[72] The text acknowledges the ownership of the manuscript and the role of "the mother of graces," whom here we imagine to be both the Virgin Mary and the Mother Church, as a focus of the bishop's devotion. The action of this liturgical portrait is not a literal representation of the mass but instead an allegory for the eucharist centered upon the relationship between the bishop and his church or between the episcopacy and *Ecclesia*.

A description of the eucharistic mass from Benedict Steuart's *The Development of Christian Worship* provides one explanation for the inclusion of the figure of *Ecclesia* within the miniature.

> There are three chief elements in the Rite of the Holy Eucharistic—which are found in all liturgies, Eastern and Western. These are: (i) 'Taking' bread and wine—in order to set them apart for special use; (ii) 'Giving thanks' over the bread and wine; (iii) 'Communion'—that is, eating and drinking the 'eucharistised' (consecrated) bread and wine, and *so entering into communion with Christ and all the members of His Mystical Body, the Church.*[73]

Liturgical *formulae* prescribe that after the communion of the bishop, the remaining orders of the clergy would take the host and chalice in order of their rank, and lastly, the chalice and bread would be offered to the members of the congregation.[74] The action of the image represents the taking of the chalice by the bishop and, because of the presence of *Ecclesia*, a greater sense of the communion of the whole of the church.

The Sigebert miniature, which is included as the last within a series of canonical illuminations, recognizes the bishop as both a leader and a member of the ecclesiastical community. Sigebert's humble regalia and the celebration of the liturgy reinforce the reading of the miniature as a celebration of the power of the episcopacy as it is derived from its good service in the name of *Ecclesia*. *Ecclesia*'s presence in the miniature works as a unifying symbol, celebrating Christian communion as well as the anthropological idea of *communitas*.[75] First defined by Victor Turner, *communitas* is "A relational quality of full unmediated communication, even communion,

---

[72] "Hauri perpetuae Sigeberte charismata vitae: Hiis tua clementer reficit te gratia mater": Berlin, Staatsbibliothek, MS theol. lat. 2, fol. 9r. Translation taken from Joanne Michelle Pierce, "Sacerdotal Spirituality at Mass: Text and Study of the Prayerbook of Sigebert of Minden (1022–1036)," (Ph.D. diss., University of Notre Dame, 1988), p. 22.

[73] Emphasis mine. Benedict Steuart, *The Development of Christian Worship: An Outline of Liturgical History* (London, 1953), pp. 9–10 and p. 10 n.1.

[74] "It was a matter of importance in the Roman Church that the ritual of the Communion should contain a clear and striking expression of ecclesiastical unity": Louis Duchesne, *Christian Worship: Its Origins and Evolution. A Study of the Latin Liturgy up to the Time of Charlemagne*, trans. M.L. McClure, 5th edn (New York, 1949), p. 185.

[75] See also Hahn's use of the term *communitas* to designate the smaller communities within the universal church (Hahn, *Portrayed on the Heart*, p. 132).

between definite and determinate identities, which arise spontaneously in all kinds of groups, situations, and circumstances."[76] The miniature claims a public presence for the episcopacy, which is careful to reflect the significance of the bishop only as part of a larger whole. As recounted in saints' *vitae* as well as enacted in the liturgy of the church, the rituals celebrated by the bishop and bishop-saint mark the responsibility of the bishop as representative of the greater body of the church. The portrait miniature of Sigebert of Minden, like the blessing depicted in the Benedictional of Engilmar, recall the legacy of the bishop-saint who both protected and defined the spiritual community to which he had been assigned.

Returning to the portrait of Engilmar (Fig. 6.1), recall that it depicts liturgical blessing as it would have taken place in the apse of the cathedral at Parenzo. A connection, then, can be drawn between the donor portraits of bishop-saints Maurus and Euphrasius in the sixth-century apse mosaics at Parenzo (Fig. 6.6) and the liturgical portrait of Engilmar. As Engilmar looks at the portrait of himself blessing his congregation, he literally and figuratively stands at the feet of his episcopal predecessors. Engilmar's reception of his own likeness activates and collapses liturgical space and time. The act of seeing the image of himself at the altar, with the mosaics of his episcopal predecessors above his head, recalls the devotional posture of traditional episcopal dedication portraiture, such as the sequence of miniatures in the Psalter of Egbert of Trier (Fig. 6.8), which includes the bishop-donor at the feet of the saint.

The imagined relationship between Engilmar and the saints activated by the performance of the liturgy and the reception of Engilmar's own likeness would not have been far from the mindset of a medieval celebrant, as two contemporary examples illustrate. First, in book three of the *Praeloquium*, the tenth-century bishop Rather of Verona wrote:

> But if you charge that I ought not to apply what was written about the saints to us who are so far below their feet, I answer that in this world, just as we are partners to them in the ministry of the order, so also are we their partners both in dignity of the name and in the privilege of the honor. If we study to conform our lives to theirs, we will be sharers in their eternal glory.[77]

Rather, an avid supporter of the rights of bishops over those of local lords, allies the episcopacy with the bodies of the saints "both in dignity of the name and in the privilege of the honor."[78] While Rather of Verona had an exceptional episcopacy— he was imprisoned, exiled, and expelled from the episcopal see at Verona as well as Liège—his opinion of a bishop's relationship to the saints is representative of the

---

[76] Victor Turner and Edith L.B. Turner, *Image and Pilgrimage in Christian Culture: Anthropological Perspectives*, Lectures on the History of Religions, n.s., 11 (New York, 1978), p. 250.

[77] Rather of Verona, *The Complete Works of Rather of Verona*, ed. and trans. Peter L.D. Reid, Medieval and Renaissance Texts and Studies 76 (Binghamton, NY, 1991), p. 104.

[78] Here the term "dignity" could also be used to mean the liturgical responsibilities shared by the bishop and the saints as part of their ordination.

period.[79] A second example of this mindset literally pictures a devotional posture. Another episcopal liturgical portrait depicts Bishop Bernward of Hildesheim standing before an altar to be dedicated to the Virgin Mary (Fig. 6.4). The subject of his dedication, the Virgin and Child, are pictured on the folio across the gutter of the manuscript—as if the liturgical gesture itself brought the body of the blessed Virgin to the sanctuary of the church.[80]

When analyzed against the tradition of illustrated hagiography, the image of Engilmar blessing his congregation has a more pointed meaning. In adopting the iconography of the bishop-saint as celebrant, Engilmar secures the physical and spiritual boundaries of his see, and in so doing, he links his episcopate to that of the saintly Parentine bishops Euphrasius and Maurus.

Conclusion: Building a Spiritual Geography

To flesh out fully the partnership between *Ecclesia* and the episcopacy referenced in the Engilmar frontispiece, the miniature should be compared with one final liturgical portrait, folio 118v in the Anglo-Saxon Benedictional of Æthelwold (*c*.963–984). The miniature depicts Bishop Æthelwold of Winchester beneath a baldachin, reading from a benedictional and making a gesture of blessing toward a congregation composed of clerics, monks, and laypeople (Fig. 6.3).[81] An assistant helps to support the golden book from which the bishop reads. The pose of the bishop and his proximity to the congregation are similar to the portrait of Engilmar; however, the style of the miniature and state of the manuscript are different, as are the miniature's placement within the manuscript and function within the pictorial cycle. Instead of appearing at the beginning of the manuscript, the image of Æthelwold is included at the end of the manuscript's pictorial cycle. Its position before the prayers for the dedication of the church and its lack of identifying inscription have been used to suggest that the miniature of Æthelwold functions less as a dedication portrait and more as an illustration of the liturgical rite. This reading of the miniature as illuminating a liturgical text is bolstered by its unfinished state. Æthelwold, the baldachin, the book, and the altar, which is dressed with an altar cloth, chalice, and paten, are depicted in full color, in keeping with the style of the manuscript's many other elaborate full-folio illuminations. The outlines of the cathedral, the city, and the congregation

---

[79] On Rather's career, see *Complete Works of Rather*, ed. and trans. Reid, p. 3; Erich Auerbach, *Literary Language and its Public in Late Latin Antiquity and in the Middle Ages*, trans. Ralph Manheim (Princeton, NJ, 1993), pp. 151–52; and the essay by Thomas Head in this volume.

[80] Hildesheim, Dom- und Diözanmuseum Hildesheim, Inv. no. DS 18. For bibliography see Michael Brandt and Arne Eggebrecht eds, *Bernward von Hildesheim und das Zeitalter der Ottonen*: *Katalog der Ausstellung, Hildesheim, 1993*, 2 vols (Hildesheim, 1993), no. VIII–30, 2:570–76.

[81] There is some debate about this as there is no identifying inscription within the miniature. See Prescott, *The Benedictional of Saint Æthelwold* (above, n. 9), p. 19. A poem included on fols 4v–5r ties the commission to Bishop Æthelwold and identifies the manuscript's scribe, Godeman: Prescott, *The Benedictional of Saint Æthelwold*, p. 5.

who wait to receive the blessing are marked out simply with a red-tinted under-painting, however. The folio also lacks the ornate frame found throughout the rest of the manuscript. Finally, the last three lines of the benediction from the preceding page spill over onto the illuminated folio.[82]

Some scholars have argued that because the bishop's portrait is the last miniature in the manuscript, it may have simply remained unfinished at the time of the gift of the codex.[83] A closer look at the dedication ritual for the church as well as the ritual that precedes the image, however, led Robert Deshman to suggest that the miniature reinforces the role of the bishop in defining the church and building a congregation.[84] Deshman argues that the miniature was not left unfinished, nor was it a later addition to the manuscript.[85] Following Francis Wormald, Deshman argues that the "mixed technique" of the miniature was intentional and was used to signal the most important parts of the composition.[86] Ecclesiastical commentary had long drawn connections between the building and dedication of architectural monuments and the conversion and baptism of "a spiritual Ecclesia in the souls of believers. . . . "[87] The episcopal blessing takes place between the consecration of the eucharist and communion, and Deshman notes that the presence of the chalice and paten on the altar refers to the sacrament about to be performed as well as to the role of the bishop-celebrant during that liturgy. Placing the illumination before the text represents "not only the external appearance but also the inner spiritual meaning of the rite of episcopal benediction."[88]

Deshman's reading of the miniature pushes the symbolism of the bishop at the altar further, declaring that the figure of the bishop becomes the altar, as he is in

---

[82] Deshman, *The Benedictional of Æthelwold* (above, n. 9), p. 139.

[83] See George F. Warner and H.A. Wilson, *The Benedictional of Saint Æthelwold, Bishop of Winchester* (Oxford, 1910), pp. xxix–xxx.

[84] Deshman, *The Benedictional of Æthelwold*, pp. 139–41, and Prescott, *The Benedictional of Saint Æthelwold*, p. 19.

[85] Deshman, *The Benedictional of Æthelwold*, pp. 139–41. Deshman argues that the layout of the text at the top of the folio, which leaves space for, or is written around, the decoration, suggests that the miniature was always intended for this program. Second, the size of the miniature without the decorative frame is equal in size to those with it, and so a frame could never have been intended for this miniature. Further, Deshman suggests that the lack of a frame in this scene could denote the contemporary nature of this miniature versus the "sacred historical persons or events" from the other examples. Third, the state of the folio with the bishop fully painted before the background is inconsistent with the working methods of Anglo-Saxon painters. The artist would first complete the under-drawing for the entire folio, then lay out solid fields of color, and only then return to lay in the details of the figures, such as, "internal details of drapery folds, highlights and facial features." See Deshman, *The Benedictional of Æthelwold*, p. 139 n. 195. See also C. Reginald Dodwell, "Techniques of Manuscript Painting in Anglo-Saxon Manuscripts," in *Artigianato e tecnica nella società dell'alto medioevo occidentale, 2–8 aprile 1970*, Settimane di studio del Centro italiano di studi sull'alto Medioevo 18 (Spoleto, 1971), pp. 643–62.

[86] Francis Wormald, *The Benedictional of St Ethelwold* (London, 1959), p. 30, and Deshman, *The Benedictional of Æthelwold*, p. 140, nn. 196–97.

[87] Deshman, *The Benedictional of Æthelwold*, p. 142.

[88] Ibid., p. 142.

the position immediately beneath the altar canopy that is usually occupied by the altar. And so the bishop himself becomes the church: as the altar, dressed for the eucharist, the bishop recalls the "divine gift of God" and becomes the "temple of the Holy Spirit."[89] Finally, as the miniature does not include an elaborate frame around the main scene, and the towers of the church break into the prayers preceding it, Deshman sees these too as integral to a full reading of the closing miniature. The prayers preceding the miniature recall the wise virgins, who, having saved the oil in their lamps, were allowed entrance into the kingdom of heaven by their bridegroom, Christ. In recalling the wise virgins as the brides of Christ, we are reminded of another of Christ's brides, *Ecclesia*.[90]

In the Benedictional of Æthelwold, therefore, we find yet another example of liturgical portraiture, which, when combined with an understanding of the dynamic tradition of liturgical representation, exegesis, and hagiographic traditions, outlines an iconography for depicting the sacerdotal authority of the bishop. The liturgical dedication miniatures mentioned here—of Engilmar of Parenzo, Sigebert of Minden, Bernward of Hildesheim, and Æthelwold of Winchester—appear in diverse manuscripts, have no stylistic similarities, and are representative of four distinct episcopacies that cross both chronological and geographical boundaries. Yet, when placed within a history of liturgical miniatures and juxtaposed with traditional dedication portraits, each miniature highlights the sacerdotal nature of the episcopacy in such a way that the office appears almost monolithic.

If we see the portrait of Engilmar and the others like it as part of the longer tradition of episcopal portraiture, and within a better understanding of the function of liturgical miniatures in general, a counterpart to iconographies of secular power emerges. We can see in these liturgical portraits an iconography of the episcopacy that articulates the unique authority of the bishop in terms of both his sacred privileges and his secular responsibilities. By looking at images not as narrative scenes but as portraits of a liturgical action, we are able to see them with all the connotations that their bishop-patron might, both as portraits of sacerdotal responsibilities, or earthly authority, and as reflections of spiritual alliances, or episcopal sanctity. While each of these miniatures must be understood individually in the context of its own historical creation, when taken together as a group and situated within larger historical trends, they highlight the tensions defined by the capricious relationships between the emperors, the pope, local bishops, and nobles in the years leading up to the Investiture Controversy.

It is disappointing that more is not known of Engilmar and his artistic patronage. Unlike better-known episcopal art patrons, such as Archbishops Egbert of Trier or Bernward of Hildesheim, a group of manuscripts cannot be associated with Engilmar. Instead, it is only from this illuminated benedictional that notions of the bishop's sense of place and position can be inferred. What is telling about this example, however, is how well it seems to reflect the most significant aspect of Engilmar's situation: his liturgical responsibilities. Because of the portrait's liturgical nature, the iconography of the miniature highlights that aspect of Engilmar's responsibilities

---

[89]   Ibid.
[90]   Ibid., p. 143 and n. 212.

most necessary for a successful episcopate, the element that would make him most like his blessed predecessors. And indeed, the miniature and its accompanying inscription did preserve a legacy for the bishop, as his benedictional continued to be used and expanded into the fifteenth century.

Chapter 7

Bishop Gerard I of Cambrai-Arras, the Three Orders, and the Problem of Human Weakness

T.M. Riches
University of Birmingham

The history of the idea of dividing society into three orders—those who work, those who fight, and those who pray—is one of the longest-lasting conceptualizations of European society (alongside that of the "body politic"), providing the basis of many a justification of the status quo up to the French Revolution and beyond, even into the twentieth century.[1] One of its oldest expressions in Western society occurs in an early eleventh-century history of the bishops of Cambrai-Arras: the *Gesta episcoporum Cameracensium*, where it is included in a speech (*eloquium*) put in the mouth of Bishop Gerard I of Cambrai-Arras (1012–1051).[2] Another, near contemporary, formulation is to be found in Bishop Adalbero of Laon's (977–*c.*1035)[3] satirical poem *Carmen ad Rotbertum regem*.[4] The two texts formed the starting point of undoubtedly the most significant treatment of the Three Orders topos by a medieval historian, Georges Duby's *Les trois ordres ou l'imaginaire du féodalisme*.[5]

---

[1]   Georges Duby, *The Three Orders: Feudal Society Imagined*, trans. Arthur Goldhammer (Chicago, 1980), pp. 4–5. Originally published as *Les trois ordres ou l'imaginaire du féodalisme* (Paris, 1978).

[2]   *Gesta episcoporum Cameracensium*, ed. L.C. Bethmann, MGH SS 7 (Hannover, 1846), pp. 393–489 (hereafter referred to as *GEC* followed by the relevant book and chapter number).

[3]   Adalbero is last attested in 1030–1031, by which point he was roughly eighty years old, and his successor is first mentioned in 1043; Robert T. Coolidge, "Adalbero, Bishop of Laon," *Studies in Medieval and Renaissance History* 2 (1965), 1–114, at pp. 92–93.

[4]   Adalbero of Laon, *Poème au roi Robert*, ed. and trans. Claude Carozzi (Paris, 1979). Note that the scheme as such has since been noted in ninth-century Auxerre: Dominique Iogna-Prat, "Le 'baptême' du schéma des trois ordres fonctionnels: L'apport de l'école d'Auxerre dans la seconde moitié du IXe siècle," *Annales ESC* 41 (1986), 101–26. Nonetheless, it should be pointed out that Iogna-Prat sees this expression as "monastic" and "eschatological," to which Adalbero of Laon's and Gerard of Cambrai's formulations are the "episcopal" and anti-eschatological response; ibid., p. 126. Even at the time he wrote, Duby knew of the scheme's occurrence in Alfredian Wessex; see *The Three Orders*, pp. 99–102.

[5]   They dominate parts one and two of the book (pp. 13–119) and heavily inform part three (pp. 123–66).

In Duby's reading, Gerard and Adalbero were heirs of a Carolingian past conserved in the archiepiscopal school of Reims. Both Gerard and Adalbero were believed by Duby to have defended a dying public order against a societal crisis around the year 1000 brought on by the onset of feudalism and heralded by the Peace of God movement, against which Gerard delivered his Three Orders speech.[6] This was the same feudalism that would later be harnessed by the French monarchy to create the Ancien Régime and its Three Estates. Janus-like, Gerard (and Adalbero) look back to the Carolingian order of previous centuries and simultaneously prophesy the feudal monarchy of the later Capetians.

Duby was, in part, reacting to an article published in 1937 by Theodor Schieffer in the first number of the newly reconstituted house journal of the *Monumenta Germaniae Historica*.[7] There Schieffer argued that eleventh-century Lower Lotharingia, on the very western edge of which the city of Cambrai was located, suffered from the same lack of central authority which allegedly characterized West Francia at this time. In addition to the unruliness of the local aristocracy, the area also faced threats from the west—either from aristocrats to whom the indigenous counterparts would go for help against the monarchy, or from the expansionist ambitions of the counts of Flanders. In spiritual matters, Gerard was supposed to have been a reformer, but not one who allowed imperial rights to be corroded by the excessive religious zeal of the Peace of God movement—the Western Franks might have needed to construct a new legal framework to deal with the anarchy in their kingdom, but no such initiatives were welcome in the East. Gerard would have gained in authority through the Peace measures, but his loyalty to the emperor made him refuse an opportunity to usurp royal prerogatives.[8] Schieffer sees Gerard as a member of a specifically *imperial* church created by the Ottonians to counterbalance the centrifugal ambitions of the regional aristocracy. As such he was the representative of central, imperial power in the locality, stood up for state order (which Schieffer equated with a strong monarchy), and opposed the anarchic feudal principle.[9]

Taking their cue from Gerard's rather general statement about how society is divided, both Schieffer and Duby therefore interpret his speech in terms of their respective over-arching models: the former that of the bishop's role in the *Reichskirche* and the latter that of dramatic social change. Yet by seeing the speech in these terms—of an imperial bishop commenting on dangerous social change—two of its crucial aspects have been missed. First, the description of the Three Orders only occupies the introductory section of the speech. The oration as a whole is not interested in describing society, but in explaining the need for the existence of the perfect and the imperfect. Second, the account of the speech was written roughly

---

[6] See also Georges Duby,"Gérard de Cambrai, la paix et les trois fonctions sociales, 1024," *Comptes rendus des séances–Académie des Inscriptions et Belles-Lettres* 282 (1976), 136–46.

[7] Theodor Schieffer, "Ein deutscher Bischof des 11. Jahrhunderts: Gerhard I. von Cambrai (1012–1051)," *Deutsches Archiv für Geschichte des Mittelalters* 1 (1937), 323–60. See Duby, *The Three Orders*, p. 17.

[8] Schieffer, "Ein deutscher Bischof," p. 345.

[9] See ibid., p. 335, for the opposition between a strong monarchy and feudal anarchy, and p. 336 for that between the feudal principle and state order.

fifteen years after Gerard is alleged to have delivered it, shortly after his death and in trying times for his successor Lietbert's (1051–1076) relations with the German monarch. A corollary of both these points is that we may not be looking at a statement about social change or an expression of loyalty to an older, Carolingian-imperial ideal. By examining the speech in the context of ideas about human weakness and penance, and by demonstrating that its comments were equally applicable to the very different circumstances under which it was written down, I hope to show that it was in fact a restatement of the primacy of the bishop's right to determine the contours of the political community.

Unlike the *Carmen ad Rotbertum regem*, the circumstances of the composition of the *Gesta episcoporum Cameracensium* are relatively well known.[10] They were written in Cambrai by a canon of that cathedral, originally at the behest of Bishop Gerard I himself.[11] The diocese of Cambrai-Arras straddled the Franco-imperial border and was also within the area of influence of the counts of Flanders. By the eleventh century it was believed to have once been two dioceses, of Cambrai and Arras, that were united in the sixth century.[12] Arras therefore had its own cathedral, albeit one overshadowed in importance by the abbey of Saint-Vaast. Although the city of Cambrai was in the Empire and the bishopric was in the gift of the emperor, it was in the province of Reims. In addition to the emperors, the bishops therefore also had to deal with the kings of France, the archbishops of Reims, the dukes of Lower Lotharingia, the Flemish counts, and their own local aristocracy.

The *Gesta* themselves are divided into three books. The first and longest covers the history of the diocese from its earliest times to the death of Gerard's predecessor, Erluin (995–1012). The second and shortest is a descriptive catalogue of the religious communities of the diocese. The third and incomplete book recounts Gerard's career from his becoming bishop to the time of its writing, or rather *times* of writing. Erik Van Mingroot has convincingly demonstrated that those parts of the *Gesta* which cover the career of Gerard I were written in two phases, the first at the bishop's order in 1024–1025 and the second between 1051 and 1055, a short time after his death.[13] The speech attributed to him in which the Three Orders scheme appears is from the latter redaction of the text.[14] It will be necessary to examine the *Gesta* account step by step, since it is more complex than some historians have allowed.

At first glance, the trigger for Gerard's Three Orders speech seems to be the religious revival of the Peace of God movement and the threat that it is alleged to

---

[10]   There are outstanding editorial issues with the *Carmen*. It may even be that the poem as we have it is largely not the work of Adalbero of Laon, but an accumulation of Cluniac school exercises over the top of a now-fragmentary original work by him, and that it reflects internal debates within the Cluniac brotherhood. See Otto Gerhard Oexle, "Adalbero von Laon und sein *Carmen ad Rotbertum regem*: Bemerkungen zu einer neuen Edition," *Francia* 8 (1980), 629–38, at pp. 632–35.

[11]   See Bethmann's introduction, MGH SS 7:393.

[12]   There is, however, little evidence that this was the case; see Lotte Kéry, *Die Errichtung des Bistums Arras, 1093/1094*, Beihefte der Francia 33 (Sigmaringen, 1994), pp. 211–25.

[13]   Erik Van Mingroot, "Kritisch onderzoek omtrent de datering van de *Gesta episcoporum Cameracensium*," *Revue belge de philologie et d'histoire* 53 (1975), 281–332.

[14]   *Pace* Duby, "Gérard de Cambrai," passim.

have posed to the ecclesiastical authorities.[15] Thus, the *Gesta* describe an attempt at "innovation" by unnamed French bishops. One of them claimed to have received a letter from heaven ordering peace on earth. On its authority, he supposedly forbade violence and instituted fasting, which was to constitute full penance for all sins. Anyone who did not swear to obey this was to be excommunicated, left unattended when dying, and was not to be taken to be buried.[16]

In a wonderful piece of detective work, David C. Van Meter has demonstrated without doubt that this "innovation" refers to the peace of Amiens-Corbie described in the *Miracula sancti Adelardi*, and was able to date it to 1033–1034.[17] He is able to show that an outbreak of miracles at Corbie drew pilgrims away from Cambrai, thus grounding Gerard's and the *Gesta*'s hostility to the Peace. I would argue nonetheless that he goes on to make two errors of interpretation. First, in rightly criticizing Roger Bonnaud-Delamare's claim that the entire account of the *Miracula sancti Adelardi* is a late eleventh-century fiction by Gerard of Sauve-Majeure, he ignores other, useful aspects of Bonnaud-Delamare's work.[18] Namely, Bonnaud-Delamare was able to show how the *two* attempts at peace regulation described in the *Miracula*, one taking place apparently in Amiens and one at a spot between the two sites, in fact reflect struggles between the abbots of Corbie and Bishop Fulk II of Amiens over the abbey's immunity.[19] That Van Meter was able to date the *Miracula* instead to shortly after 1051 only supports Bonnaud-Delamare's interpretation, since this was when

---

[15]   This argument is most eloquently put by David C. Van Meter, "The Peace of Amiens-Corbie and Gerard of Cambrai's Oration on the Three Functional Orders: The Date, the Context, the Rhetoric," *Revue belge de philologie et d'histoire* 74 (1996), 633–57.

[16]   "Istiusmodi decretum a Franciae episcopis datum est servari subiectis sibi populis. Unus eorum celitus sibi delatas dixit esse literas, quae pacem monerent renovandam in terra. Quam rem mandavit ceteris, et haec tradenda dedit populis: Arma quisquam non ferret, direpta non repeteret; sui sanguinis vel cuiuslibet proximi, ultor minime existens percussoribus cogeretur indulgere; ieiunium in pane et aqua omni sexta feria observarent, et in sabbato a carne et pinguamine; soloque hoc contenti ieiunio in omnium peccatorum satisfactione, nullam se scirent ab eis aliam addicendam poenitentiam. Et haec sacramento se servare firmarent; quod qui nollet, christianitate privaretur, et exeuntem de saeculo nullus visitaret nec sepulturae traderet. Alia quoque inportabilia quam plurima dederunt mandata, quae oneri visa sunt replicare": *GEC* 3.52, p. 485. Note that this is the second description of a peace initiative in the *Gesta*. The first belongs to the initial redaction of the text and is described in very different terms. I hope to examine this elsewhere.

[17]   Van Meter, "Peace of Amiens-Corbie." Hartmut Hoffmann, *Gottesfriede und Treuga Dei*, Schriften der MGH 20 (Stuttgart, 1964), p. 64, refers to both peace promulgations in the context of the 1030s but does not notice that the two references are one and the same thing.

[18]   Roger Bonnaud-Delamare, "La paix d'Amiens et de Corbie au XIe siècle," *Revue du nord* 38 (1956), 167–78. Van Meter is following the East German historian Bernhard Töpfer here: Van Meter, "Peace of Amiens-Corbie," p. 636 n. 13; Bernhard Töpfer, "Die Anfänge der Treuga Dei in Nordfrankreich," *Zeitschrift für Geschichtswissenschaft* 9 (1961), 876–93, at p. 879 n. 9.

[19]   Bonnaud-Delamare, "La paix d'Amiens et de Corbie," pp. 168–75. See also Hoffmann's comments, *Gottesfriede*, pp. 64–65. For traces of Fulk II's claim to Corbie and the use of peace rhetoric found on Amiens coinage, see Reinhold Kaiser, *Bischofsherrschaft zwischen Königtum und Fürstenmacht: Studien zur bischöflichen Stadtherrschaft im westfränkisch-*

Corbie had at least temporarily won their case after the excommunication of Fulk II by Leo IX at the synod of Reims in 1049, and papal confirmation of the abbey's privileges in 1050.[20] Thus, the *Miracula* are certainly no objective description of popular fervor, nor even just an attempt to promote the cult (although that is, like all miracle collections, their primary purpose); they also record the abbey's version of conflicts of jurisdiction dating to the 1030s and only recently resolved in their favor.[21]

There is no sign of this background in the *Gesta*; indeed, there is no reason for there to be. Instead, the *Gesta* concentrate on the (unnamed) bishop's production of a letter from heaven and his announcement of universal penance. Van Meter seeks lexical similarities between the *Gesta*'s indirect report and a twelfth-century Corbie incarnation of the *carta dominica* in order to demonstrate apocalyptic fears. In particular he argues that such rhetoric reflects "radical egalitarianism," of which Gerard was afraid.[22] Yet the *Gesta* is our only source for the Corbie council which refers to a letter from heaven, and even if we can assume the account is not entirely fictional, we must allow for the fact that the competition over miracles gives the *Gesta* an a priori reason to be hostile and therefore to misrepresent the events at Corbie. Additionally, the provisions of the first Corbie peace provide for the strengthening of public power, in particular that of the bishop and the count, to whom the bishops of Amiens were closely related.[23] Given that the bishop of Cambrai was himself

---

französischen Reich im frühen und hohen Mittelalter, Pariser historische Studien 17 (Bonn, 1981), p. 604.

[20]   PL 143:641–42.

[21]   The *Miracula* themselves, of course, portray the first meeting as a triumph of Adalard's thaumaturgical powers, whereas the peace agreement is shown to be temporary. The telltale signs of the dispute are to be found in the fact that the peace was probably held and certainly to be renewed in Amiens, at the feast of St Firmin, the patron saint of Amiens, and in front of the count and bishop; *Miracula sancti Adelardi abbatis* in AASS Jan., vol. 1, p. 119.

[22]   Van Meter, "Peace of Amiens-Corbie," p. 657. Van Meter claims (p. 655), "The threat was posed by a dangerous if somewhat odd [!] current of institutionally-sponsored egalitarianism—conceived in imitation, no doubt, of the apostolic life—that emanated from a particularly millenarian manifestation of the peace movement." He is explicitly following Georges Duby, "Les laïcs et la paix de Dieu," in *I laici nella "societas christiana" dei secoli XI e XII: Atti della terza Settimane internazionale di studio, Mendolo, 21–27 agosto 1965*, Miscellanea del Centro di Studi Medioevali 5 (Milan, 1968), pp. 448–61.

[23]   The counts were able to place their family members on the episcopal throne for much of the eleventh century; see P. Feuchère, "Une tentative manquée de concentration territoriale entre Somme et Seine: La principauté d'Amiens-Valois au XIe siècle. Étude de géographie historique," *Le Moyen Âge* 60 (1954), 1–37. Fulk II was the brother of Count Drogo and uncle of Walter III (not son and brother as usually claimed by, for example, Feuchère); see David Bates, "Lord Sudeley's Ancestors: The Family of the Counts of Amiens, Valois and the Vexin in France and England during the Eleventh Century," in *The Sudeleys–Lords of Toddington* (Thetford, 1987), pp. 34–48, at pp. 37–38. Note that Van Meter himself cites a charter of Fulk from 1034, which uses eschatological rhetoric; Van Meter, "Peace of Amiens-Corbie," p. 643 and n. 34.

both bishop and count,[24] the reasons for the *Gesta*'s particular depiction of the Peace council must lie elsewhere than in anxiety that his authority would be eroded by millennial enthusiasm.

The Three Orders speech follows on immediately from the *Gesta*'s account of the Amiens-Corbie council. The precise setting of the speech is not given: we do not know whether it was given as a sermon in either Cambrai or Arras cathedral or was part of some episcopal meeting, or indeed whether it was actually delivered at all. Whatever it might have been, the speech begins with the description of the functional Three Orders, leading into a justification of the *pugnatores*, and of the right to take back what is stolen and to avenge wrongdoing. Gerard then denounces as uncanonical the ideas that fasting is sufficient penance,[25] and that people should be forced to swear the oath. He finishes by arguing that those who repent, even if they do so at the last moment, should be given full burial.[26]

"It was after this occasion," as the *Gesta* author puts it, that Gerard went to Douai. There a meeting of the people was taking place that was trying to set up a "false peace." Among those assembled was the castellan of Cambrai, Walter II, with whom Gerard had had repeated trouble, and with whose father his predecessors had struggled too. Walter spread the opinion among everyone "inside and out" that Gerard did not want to acquiesce to the peace. The specific terms being discussed, say the *Gesta*, were that no one should carry arms or demand back what was theirs. Walter II wanted this to be agreed on so that he could be freed from responsibility for his previous wrongdoing and be unhindered by anyone in the future. Gerard essentially gave in, "proving" his commitment to peace by forgiving Walter everything the castellan owed him.[27]

---

[24] He had held both titles since 1007. See François-Louis Ganshof, "Les origines de la Flandre Impériale: Contribution à l'histoire de l'ancien Brabant," *Annales de la Société Royale d'archéologie de Bruxelles: Mémoires, rapports et documents* 46 (1942–1943), 99–137, at pp. 109–12.

[25] Jean-Pierre Poly and Eric Bournazel are right that this would be a perfect way for Gerard's enemies to escape the threat of excommunication, but strictly speaking his long-time enemy, Cambrai's castellan Walter II, is connected not with this initiative but with the subsequent one at Douai. Poly and Bournazel have collapsed two incidents into one another, a mistake the *Gesta* author may have wished to promote; Jean-Pierre Poly and Eric Bournazel, *The Feudal Transformation: 900–1200*, trans. Caroline Higgitt (New York, 1991), pp. 166–67 (originally published as *La mutation féodale: Xe–XIIe siècles* [Paris, 1980]).

[26] The speech continues in the MGH edition, dealing with the question of having different rules for the perfect and the imperfect; *GEC* 3.52, p. 486. This is an emendation by the editor Bethmann based on later manuscripts, which is unlikely to be correct since, as Van Meter has pointed out, our earliest witness, Sigebert of Gembloux, ends his summary of the speech at the unemended place; Van Meter, "Peace of Amiens-Corbie," p. 645; Sigebert of Gembloux, *Chronicon*, ed. L.C. Bethmann, MGH SS 6 (Hannover, 1844), p. 357 (s.a. 1033). For our purposes, the latter part of the speech will therefore be assigned to where it appears in the earlier manuscripts—at the end of 3.54.

[27] "Causa post haec fuit, qua Duacum petiit. Ubi conventus populi vocibus de statuenda pace falsa, respondit pro tempore, quod perceperat ab eo qui est idem heri et hodie nec immutatur crastino tempore. Suggesserat in aures omnium Walterus, qui erant foris et intus, episcopum paci nolle adquiescere; non quia erat filius pacis, sed quia liberius quaerebat studere

The pressure is said to have continued, however, now from Baldwin IV of Flanders, to order that the peace be sworn on oath. Gerard responded that he would do nothing against the law and gospel (*lex et evangelium*), but caved in again, "conquered by weariness," and ordered relics to be gathered and brought to "a/the designated place . . . on the borders of Cambrai and Arras."[28] Again Walter was present, slandering Gerard "inside and outside" to the point where the people (*populus*) were almost ready to use violence. However, Gerard publicly denounced Walter, and then, after speaking on the health of the soul, made the people promise (there is no mention of an oath) that they would obey Christian law of their own free will. Should they deviate, they promised to return to penance—in other words, the author insists on Gerard's orthodoxy and again on his defense of church law. This apparently defused the situation.[29] There then follows in the manuscripts a speech about the different rules for the perfect and imperfect, which appears to be the words spoken "de salute animae."[30]

Those who characterize the Peace of God movement as millennial are therefore right to highlight the issue of the purity of the faithful and their penance before God. Indeed, peace legislation picks up on this topic explicitly, although not to create a perfect world before the coming of Christ but to regulate man's imperfections. Gerard's own peace legislation survives in the municipal library in Douai (Douai, Bibliothèque municipale, MS 856), in a twelfth-century manuscript from the abbey of Marchiennes, but it is not alone in its stipulations.[31] On the contrary, a close textual

---

artibus suae malignitatis. Collegerat duo superius dicta [3.52, pp. 485–86; the reference is to the Amiens-Corbie peace]: ne quis arma ferret, nec direpta repeteret; studebatque, ut preteritae vitae rapinis et caedibus, quibus pastus fuerat, silentium daretur, et ex tunc licentius, nullo ferente arma, assuetis malis frueretur. Quod praesciens episcopus, sedato populo calliditates illius exposuit, utque paci non esset contrarius, debita sua multiplicia illi indulsit, tantum ut in reliquum populus de eo pacem haberet. Tunc deinde turba coepit episcopum benedicere, qui iam cognoverat, eum omnium pacem in veritate quaerere, etiam cum dampno, si per hoc posset fieri, propriae substantiae, qui illi, ut dictum est, pro hoc universa relaxaverat debita": *GEC* 3.53, pp. 486–87.

28   The traditional term "Peace of Douai" seems therefore strictly to be a misnomer. Douai lay close to, but not on the border between, the two dioceses. Given that some passage of time is implied by the ablative absolute and by phrases such as "Baldwin began to urge him" and "conquered by weariness," we may postulate some negotiation about where the meeting was to take place. Given that Douai was a stronghold of the counts of Flanders, and Hugh, the castellan of Douai, had probably married Walter II of Cambrai's daughter, Adela, the result seems to be a compromise on "neutral ground," similar to the arrangements arrived at between Amiens and Corbie. See Félix Brassart, *Histoire du château et de la châtellenie de Douai, des fiefs, terres et seigneuries tenus du souverain de cette ville, depuis le Xe siècle jusqu'en 1789*, 2 vols (Douai, 1877), 1:50–62. It would also imply, however, that the agreement covered the whole of the double diocese, and not just the diocese of Arras, *pace* Brassart, *Histoire*, pp. 59–60.

29   *GEC* 3.54, p. 487.

30   *GEC* 3.52, p. 486. For the positioning of this speech, see above, n. 26.

31   Dominique Barthélemy has seriously questioned the attribution of this text to Gerard. He points out that there is no specific link between this text and Douai, other than that the (later) manuscript originates in the appropriate diocese. Dominique Barthélemy, *L'an mil*

relative is now in Laon.[32] The provisions are similar: from sundown on Wednesday to sunup on Monday (and every day from the beginning of Advent to the octave of Epiphany, from Septuagesima to the octave of Easter, and from Rogation Day to the octave of Pentecost), no man or woman was to attack, wound, or kill another man or woman, nor raid, take, or burn any castle, burg, or vill by stratagem, violence, or deception, nor were they to take another's lands, animals, money, clothes, or any other belongings.[33] The key difference lies in the sanctions. Both Gerard's peace and that of Laon prescribed excommunication and exile for any violator of the peace who did not accept thirty years' penance (for the major crimes) or seven years' (for the minor), and for anyone who knowingly had anything to do with them. Nevertheless, the Laon text stated that if violators died having accepted but not yet having completed the penance, then no Christian might visit them on their deathbed, take their body away, bury it (apparently at all), or take things from their belongings. The Marchiennes text was more moderate.[34] It allowed that if, on their deathbed, violators were moved to repentance, summoned a priest, and gave guarantors of their doing penance for the wrongs they had committed, then the priest should absolve them and provide a proper burial. If the violator died obdurate, the body might only be approached by the few who could take it to be buried in "a remote place."[35] Thus, even assuming there was any threat from an egalitarian Peace of God ethos, the Marchiennes and Laon legislation defuses any such threat by incorporating the

---

et la paix de Dieu: La France chrétienne et féodale, 980–1060 (Paris, 1999), pp. 547–48 n. 3. Barthélemy rightly rejects the idea that just because the text mentions heresy, we can necessarily associate it with Gerard, *pace* Heinrich Sproemberg, "Gerhard I., Bischof von Cambrai (1012–1061[sic])," in idem, *Mittelalter und demokratische Geschichtsschreibung: Ausgewählte Abhandlungen*, ed. Manfred Unger, Forschungen zur mittelalterlichen Geschichte 18 (Berlin, 1971), pp. 103–18 at p. 115. However, the monks of Marchiennes had good reason to be interested in Gerard, since it was by him, Leduin of Saint-Vaast, and Baldwin IV that the community was reformed in 1024; *GEC* 2.26, p. 461. I would also point out that Bonnaud-Delamare's original attribution was based on the text's "leniency" toward burial, which fit with details of the *Gesta*, more specifically the Three Orders declaration; see Roger Bonnaud-Delamare, "Les institutions de paix dans la province ecclésiastique de Reims au XIe siècle," *Bulletin philologique et historique (jusqu'à 1715) du Comité des travaux historiques et scientifiques (Années 1955 et 1956)* (Paris, 1957), 143–200, at pp. 184–85.

[32]   For the texts, see Bonnaud-Delamare, "Les institutions de paix," pp. 184–88.

[33]   Note that these crimes were all punishable by secular authority and that unarmed clerics, merchants, and the powerless were not specified. This differs greatly from the Burgundian peace declarations and places the text clearly in the context of ecclesiastical sanctions strengthening preexisting secular law; Hans-Werner Goetz, "Kirchenschutz, Rechtswahrung und Reform. Zu den Zielen und zum Wesen der frühen Gottesfriedensbewegung in Frankreich," *Francia* 11 (1983), 193–239, at pp. 220–37; Karl Ferdinand Werner, "Observations sur le rôle des évêques dans le mouvement de paix aux Xe et XIe siècles," in *Mediaevalia christiana XIe–XIIIe siècles: Hommage à Raymonde Foreville de ses amis, ses collègues, et ses anciens élèves*, ed. Coloman Étienne Viola (Paris, 1989), pp. 155–95, at p. 160. Note that women were envisaged as possible criminals.

[34]   In the case of the minor crimes, the body could not be buried or moved from the place of death until the family of the deceased made restitution to the injured party.

[35]   Bonnaud-Delamare, "Les institutions de paix," p. 184bis.

peace into standard penitential practices.[36] Not only are the bishops in question flexible with regard to peace legislation, as the account of Gerard's negotiations with his opponents claims, but the similarity of the two texts as well as their differences shows that authorities were in communication about such issues and could differ according to individual needs. None of this should be surprising, except that such a discourse is not envisaged in models that emphasize social revolution, imperial loyalty, or millennial enthusiasm.

There is, moreover, other evidence of Gerard's interest in issues surrounding penance and burial. Investigating the use of the *Regula pastoralis* in Cambrai, Bruno Judic describes two fragments in an eleventh-century manuscript, also from Marchiennes.[37] One is an extract from the *Sentences* of Taio of Saragossa, dealing with the necessity of stopping malefactors from uniting for a peace that would allow them to do more evil, a text very appropriate for Gerard's position.[38] The other fragment concerns the burial of Solomon, despite his having committed evil acts, because he secretly repented before his death.

This might not be considered significant except that Gerard mentions the Solomon case in a sermon to captured heretics in Arras, where he spells out his theology of burial in detail.[39] While the sermon is alleged to have been delivered in January 1025, it was almost certainly greatly expanded after being written up.[40] The purported context remains important for our purposes, however, since the heretics allegedly doubted the necessity of the Church and clerical hierarchy, and thus Gerard (or the author) frames his discussion of burial within a general theology of the Church, including of the church building (c. 3). Gerard argues that the people meet there for two reasons: out of "old tradition," i.e. the Old Testament, to acquire judgments on things and knowledge; and, from the New Testament, to eat the body of Christ. For everyone seeks judgment of good and bad acts, knowledge of God, and to eat the body of Christ.[41] A church is called a church because it contains the Church, i.e. the people (*populus*) called together by God.[42] The people are to leave behind trivial, worldly thoughts and speech, enter the church where God and his angels are, and there think on the dealings of the angels and the presence of the majesty of God, and

---

[36] Because this legislation protects certain periods as well as persons, it is normally described as a "truce" rather than "peace" of God. The term "treuga" is contemporary, while "pax dei" is later. The distinction at this stage between the two is one of modern scholarship. See Hoffmann, *Gottesfriede*, p. 4.

[37] Bruno Judic, "La diffusion de la *Regula pastoralis* de Grégoire le Grand dans l'Église de Cambrai, une première enquête," *Revue du nord* 76 (1994), 207–30, at pp. 219–21.

[38] Ibid., p. 221. Note that Judic also records a sister MS in Laon.

[39] *Acta synodi Atrebatensis in Manichaeos*, PL 142:1296.

[40] Erik Van Mingroot, "*Acta synodi Attrebatensis* (1025): Problèmes de critique et de provenance," in *Mélanges G. Fransen*, vol. 2, *Studia gratiana* 20 (1976), 201–29, at pp. 222–28. Although note that the author of our text specifically says the sun was setting by the time the bishop stopped speaking; *Acta synodi Atrebatensis*, PL 142:1311.

[41] Ibid., PL 142:1286.

[42] Ibid., PL 142:1287.

invoke his name with hymns and spiritual psalms.[43] Essentially, the church building replicates the Church in unifying the "people" in timelessness.[44] Later in the sermon (c. 7), Gerard deals directly with burial, which he says the heretics claim to be a moneymaking scam on the part of the priests.[45] Gerard asks,

> In fact since the Christian faithful lead their mortal lives together in the unity of the Holy Spirit within the mystery of the Catholic faith in this earthly Church, so that they can pass via it into Heaven, where, I ask, should their bodies be more fittingly buried after their death than in the bosom of the Mother Church? For if they have remained faithfully with the earthly Church during their mortal lives, they should then also rest in its bosom once they have met an earthly death, to await the day of the Resurrection and the glory of the immortal Church. For she is the mother of the believers, who brings to immortality those who were born to death, who protects her children's bodies soundly as they sleep through time, but raises them to undecaying glory at the universal Resurrection.[46]

The heretics should say from where they think the spirit of eternal life will come to them.[47] Thus, burial by the Church is necessary because it extends the community of Christians, created by separating the people from the tribulations of the world, beyond death to the Last Judgment. Additionally, it is burial by the Church that separates the worthy from the unworthy, the penitent from the impenitent.[48] It is at this point that Gerard refers to Solomon being buried with others although he had not done penance.

The implication here is that the risk of worldly corruption extends beyond death. The church building was necessary to create a community because in it worldly things could be left behind. Similarly, it was not fitting for Christians to be buried next to sinners, since that would disturb the boundaries between clean and unclean. This could be quite literal, as in what seems to have been one of Gerard's favorite

---

[43]   Ibid.

[44]   Henri Platelle, "La cathédrale et le diocèse: Un aspect religieux du rapport ville-campagne. L'exemple de Cambrai," in *Villes et campagnes au Moyen Âge: Mélanges Georges Despy*, ed. Jean-Marie Duvosquel and Alain Dierkens (Liège, 1991), pp. 625–41, at pp. 626–28. Platelle sets the theory propounded here against the practice of the ceremony of consecration of the new cathedral of Cambrai.

[45]   *Acta synodi Atrebatensis*, PL 142:1295. Such sentiments seem to have been common. In a letter to Abbot Leduin of Saint-Vaast written about five years after these events, Gerard mentions criticism of clerics for living off the sins of the people. Gerard admits there is a lot of truth to the accusations; *GEC* 3.32, pp. 478–79.

[46]   "Porro cum fideles Christiani temporalem vitam in unitate Spiritus sancti sub mysterio catholicae fidei in hac temporali Ecclesia communiter exigunt, ut per hanc ad coelestem perveniant, ubi, rogo, debent corpora eorum post resolutionem rectius quam in sinu matris Ecclesiae tumulari? Sicut enim temporali ecclesiae temporaliter vivendo per fidem adhaerent, ita et temporaliter moriendo in sinu ipsius requiescunt, diem videlicet resurrectionis et intemporalis Ecclesiae gloriam exspectantes. Haec est enim mater credentium quae natos ad mortem regenerat ad immortalitatem, quae filiorum corpora servat sane ad tempus sopita, in generali tamen resurrectione ad immarcessibilem gloriam suscitanda": PL 142:1295.

[47]   Ibid.

[48]   PL 142:1296.

anecdotes, picked up from Bishop Adalbold of Utrecht.[49] A chief man among the Frisians had persuaded the locals not to take the eucharist on the basis that they should rather drink a pitcher of beer. He then died shortly afterwards. He was buried in a churchyard because he was an important person in the locality, and even when Adalbold, who was with Henry II in Saxony at the time, ordered that he be disinterred, no one dared do so out of fear of his kin. Eventually, Adalbold had to come back personally and order the man dragged out of the grave by the feet, and although he had been buried almost fifty days before, within a mile[50] he vomited up his beer as if he had recently drunk it. This is clearly an example of horrendous stories designed to disgust the audience into holiness.[51] It is interesting here how bodily corruption communicates sin even after death. It is no wonder Adalbold is said to feel it was unworthy for an unfaithful man to be treated equally to a faithful one. Indeed, in a letter to the archdeacons of Liège, Gerard explains that it is impossible to absolve the dead, with reference to John 11.44, where the disciples unbind Lazarus after his resurrection, pointing out that if they had done so before the resurrection, they would have found not vigor (*virtus*) but foulness (*fetor*).[52]

This letter to the archdeacons of Liège, dated to 1018–1021,[53] demonstrates that Gerard's "leniency" was no general attitude but determined by the principle of his office. According to the author of the *Gesta*, the archdeacons, "led either by the love of money or for the sake of friends," allowed excommunicates "to be buried as equals among faithful Christians."[54] And indeed, Gerard argued precisely that to absolve those who had died unrepentant was an abuse of the priestly power of binding and loosing, and an offense against God's judgment.[55] Gerard has specific grievances, however. The archdeacons of Liège had buried people Gerard had excommunicated—specifically one Erlebold, who had slept with a nun and had perpetrated "many evils" in Gerard's diocese, and whom, at his co-bishop's instigation, Gerard had excommunicated, but whom that bishop had received

---

[49]   *GEC* 3.22, pp. 472–73. This anecdote is related in a section of the *Gesta* written during Gerard's lifetime, and the author claims to have heard it from Gerard himself.

[50]   The distance may be significant—he was seemingly being taken to be buried in "a remote place." See above, p. 129.

[51]   See also the subsequent story, *GEC* 3.23, p. 473. Here the sinner is burned by the eucharist placed in his mouth on his deathbed.

[52]   *GEC* 3.28, p. 475.

[53]   Van Mingroot, "Kritisch onderzoek," p. 303. However, the fact that the letter addresses the archdeacons directly, while referring generally to decisions by "your lord" and "our brother," suggests that the letter is taking advantage of a vacancy to complain about past practices. This would place it in either 1018 (between the episcopates of Balderich and Wolbold) or in 1021 (between those of Wolbold and Durand). The later date is suggested by Gerard singling out and thus seeming to ascribe importance to the archdeacon John, who only became archdeacon in 1018 and left to be provost of Saint-Lambert in 1021.

[54]   *GEC* 3.28, p. 474.

[55]   Gerard speaks of those who continued to do evil "right up to the very departure of life," but this is likely rhetorical exaggeration and cannot be taken to indicate theological "leniency"; *GEC* 3.28, p. 474.

back into communion without consulting Gerard.[56] Additionally, other, unnamed, malefactors from Gerard's diocese, excommunicated for burnings and plundering, received burial in the diocese of Liège, specifically in Nivelles.[57] Gerard insinuates that they bought absolution or burial by suggesting that the money or gifts be used to erect palaces or restore churches,[58] and he fears that the archdeacons—and here he singles out John (who between 1021 and 1025, as prior of Saint-Lambert, would be censured by the not-yet-bishop Wazo of Liège for trying to become dean as well[59])— might appeal to "authorities" to defend their action. Against a possible claim that they were free to absolve people in their own diocese, Gerard cites what he thinks is a canon of the council of Meaux, to the effect that:

> 'Regarding those who have a benefice or inheritance in a diocese and are parishioners of another bishop and, while travelling from one place to another, practice robbery and plundering: it pleases us that they be excommunicated and not leave the diocese until they have made satisfactory amends for what they have done.'[60]

Thus, what we see here is clearly a dispute over jurisdiction. Individuals, or, as Gerard calls them, *moderni seniores*, who could move back and forth between the dioceses of Liège and Cambrai, were playing one diocese against the other to raid and plunder not just with impunity, but, by extension, with legitimacy.[61]

This becomes clearer as we look at the history of relations between Gerard and his castellan Walter II. The allegation of the *Gesta* that Walter wanted a general ban on carrying arms so that he could act with impunity could simply be exaggeration, but it is hard to imagine how such a situation was supposed to work in practice,

---

[56]   *GEC* 3.28, p. 476.

[57]   Curiously, this is where Lambert of Louvain, on his way to the battle of Florennes in 1015, slept with another (the same?) nun, who gave him a relic which almost won him the battle; *GEC* 3.12, p. 469.

[58]   The line between this and pious benefaction is thin indeed! The only difference is whether, as Gerard says in relation to the *pugnatores*, there is sin in the conscience; *GEC* 3.52, p. 485.

[59]   Anselm of Liège, *Gesta episcoporum Leodiensium*, ed. Rudolf Köpke, MGH SS 7:211–15; for its dating see idem, p. 214 n. 73.

[60]   'De hiis qui infra parrochiam beneficium et habent, et alterius episcopi parrochiani sunt, et dum de loco ad locum iter faciunt, rapinas et depraedationes peragunt, placuit nobis, ut excommunicentur nec ante ex parrochia exeant, quam quae perpetrarunt digne emendent': *GEC* 3.28, p. 476. This is, in fact, a slightly modified extract from canon 6 of the Capitulary of Verneuil (884), in *Karolomanni Capitulare Vernense*, ed. Victor Krause, MGH Capitularia regum francorum 2 (Hannover, 1897), p. 373. Gerard had the extract in turn from canon 291 of Regino of Prüm's *Libri duo de synodalibus causis et disciplinis ecclesiasticis*, ed. F.G.A. Wasserschleben (Leipzig, 1840), p. 327, who falsely attributed it to Meaux. There is still a tenth-century copy of Regino's collection of canons in the municipal library of Arras, housed in the former abbey of Saint-Vaast, Bibliothèque municipale, MS 723 (675). For the connection between Verneuil and the peace legislation, see Werner, "Observations sur le rôle des évêques," pp. 167–68.

[61]   Note that these malefactors are coming from Liège, further inside the Empire, which fails to correspond to models featuring French feudal anarchy and imperial public order.

unless Walter was to be the authority enforcing the peace.[62] In his Three Orders speech Gerard assigns the role of peacekeepers to the *pugnatores*, but unlike an earlier disquisition of his on the roles of bishops and kings, it remains to be defined which *pugnatores* legitimately take on the role.[63] Presumably the absolute minimum qualification was membership in the Christian community, as represented by communion in church both in life and death. A universal oath would obliterate precisely this distinction, theoretically including everyone in communion, but in practice leaving them all outside it. The decision over the distinction—over whether there was "sin in the conscience" or not—had to be left in the hands of the bishops, and Gerard's insistence on being able to forgive deathbed penitents may reflect a desire to leave as much room for episcopal maneuver as possible. However, the bishops themselves were not united, as we have seen with reference to Liège. How this might work is quite plain in the circumstances of Walter's death in 1041. He was apparently killed by four enemies while praying before the doors of Cambrai cathedral, leaving a wife, Ermintrude, and a young son.[64] Gerard considered Walter excommunicate and ordered his burial away from Christians. At Ermintrude's order, and in alliance with John, advocate of Arras, "almost the whole region of Cambrai was consumed by fire and completely devastated." Under pressure from the archbishop of Reims and Count Baldwin V, Gerard relented.[65] French preponderance in the concentration of forces here is reflected in the former supporters of Walter listed elsewhere in the *Gesta*, including King Robert, Bishop Harduin of Noyon, and Odo of Blois, as well as Baldwin IV.[66] In the end Gerard was forced to grant absolution to Walter as having died penitent, although his attempts at satisfaction

---

[62]   *GEC* 3.53, p. 487. Even if it is rhetoric, it needs to be plausible.

[63]   *GEC* 3.52, pp. 485–86, and 3.27, p. 474.

[64]   *GEC* 4.2 (3.62), pp. 489–90; *Chronicon s. Andreae Castri Cameracesii*, 1.8, ed. L.C. Bethmann, MGH SS 7:532; *Annales Elnonenses*, in *Les annales de Saint-Pierre de Gand et de Saint-Amand*, ed. Philip Grierson (Brussels, 1937), p. 155 (s.a. 1041).

[65]   For Ermintrude's order to devastate Cambrai, the quotation, and the pressure from the archbishop and count to bury Walter properly, see *Annales Elnonenses*, p. 155 (s.a. 1041). For the involvement of John of Arras, see *GEC* 4.2 (3.62), p. 490. The *Chronicon s. Andreae* compares Ermintrude with Jezebel at 1.8, p. 532.

[66]   *GEC* 3.3, p. 467, and 3.42, pp. 481–82. The text of the oath in the latter seems to relate to the narrative in the former. On the occasion of Walter's burial at Saint-Amand, Ermintrude donated to the monastery, and the charter mentions Countess Adela and Bishops Fulk II of Amiens and Drogo of Thérouanne escorting the body. The two bishops as well as Abbot Leduin of Saint-Vaast are among the charter witnesses; Charles Duvivier ed., *Actes et documents anciens intéressant la Belgique* (Brussels, 1898), pp. 32–33 (my thanks to John Ott for drawing my attention to this). The occurrence of these names allows no straightforward reading. Both redactions of the *Gesta* describe Leduin with approval (*GEC* 3.16, p. 470; 3.59, p. 488), but there are traces of tension between the abbot and Gerard in its record of their opposing stances vis-à-vis the peace oath of Warin of Beauvais (*GEC* 3.27, p. 474). We have seen how Cambrai competed with Corbie for pilgrimage custom, but although there is evidence of tensions between Fulk II and Corbie, there is little to suggest any between the two bishops. Gerard had once intervened with Fulk II's predecessor Fulk I on Drogo of Thérouanne's behalf (*GEC* 3.34, p.479). In short, the people named in the charter seem not to have been Gerard's enemies. Instead, the names may indicate that Walter's burial at

had been rejected by Gerard himself as insufficient.[67] Successful or not, both here and in regard to the archdeacons of Liège, Gerard is seen to draw on his authority not as a representative of the Empire, let alone as the representative of an older, Carolingian tradition, but simply on his canonically-given episcopal power.

It has been argued that Gerard relied on such spiritual sanctions because he did not have the material means to successfully carry out his function as a representative of the emperor, and there is some truth to this claim.[68] Nonetheless, this still sees Gerard first and foremost as part of the *Reichskirche*. An examination of the behavior of his successor, Lietbert, faced with similar problems in different circumstances, will show that the interests of the diocese were foremost in any consideration of episcopal action. Troublesome aristocrats, both lesser and greater, were after all not unique to Gerard's episcopate. The issues were just as important, if not more so, in the 1050s, to which we should most likely date the section of the *Gesta* recording Gerard's speech as well as the first part of the continuation of the *Gesta*, the *Gesta Lietberti*.[69] There are, however, instructive differences between the political constellation of Gerard's time and that of Lietbert's initial period. In Lietbert's reign, no longer was the Flemish count necessarily on the castellan's side against the bishop, for example. The late 1040s had featured repeated conflicts between Godfrey "the Bearded" and Henry III over the former's claim to his father's duchy of Lower Lotharingia.[70] Count Baldwin V of Flanders used the opportunity provided by the political instability to extend his control to the south and east.[71] Part of that exercise involved aiding Lietbert in his struggle with John of Arras, in return for which the bishop named Walter II's young son Hugh as castellan in John's stead. Indeed, it was only with Baldwin's help that Lietbert was able to enter his city at all. When Baldwin's ambitions extended toward Liège, it was John of Arras who helped Henry III against the dangerous Flemish count, and he was given the castellany of Cambrai as a reward.[72] Cambrai had, then, become a political football between the emperor and the counts of Flanders, and at the time of the composition of this section of the *Gesta*, the emperor was not on the bishop's side. Thus, at a time when Lietbert was quite prepared to turn to the count of Flanders if that guaranteed his episcopal authority, he clearly considered Gerard's speech to be a fitting inclusion in the redaction of the *Gesta* written under his auspices. When Gerard had originally commissioned the work, an earlier speech about the roles of various orders had also been included, but rather than three orders, Gerard had allegedly spoken only of

---

Saint-Amand was a solution mediated by parties of good standing with both Gerard and Ermintrude.

[67]   *Annales Elnonenses*, p. 155 (s.a. 1041), although note that the *Annales* are pro-Walter in this matter.

[68]   Laurent Jégou, "L'évêque entre autorité sacrée et exercice du pouvoir. L'exemple de Gérard de Cambrai (1012–1051)," *Cahiers de civilisation médiévale* 47 (2004), 37–55.

[69]   Van Mingroot, "Kritisch onderzoek," p. 331.

[70]   Egon Boshof, "Lothringen, Frankreich und das Reich in der Regierungszeit Heinrichs III.," *Rheinische Vierteljahrsblätter* 42 (1978), 63–127.

[71]   Ganshof, "Les origines de la Flandre Impériale," pp. 124–34. For the conflict between Lietbert and John, see *GEC* 4.5–4.15 (3.64–3.71), pp. 492–94.

[72]   Boshof, "Lothringen," pp. 103–4.

kings and bishops.[73] By the time of the later composition, there was no more mention of any kings. Gerard's words on burial and Lietbert's unusual alliances are part of the same attitude—the priority of diocesan interests over and above other powers, whether castellanal or imperial.

Previous interpretations of the Three Orders speech have related it to Gerard's anti-feudalism and pro-imperialism. I hope to have shown that the proper context is one of the defense of episcopal rights as such, quite separate from historiographical concerns. As Timothy Reuter has argued elsewhere, it is a mistake to see bishops primarily in their relation to, for example, royal authority. Their interests were aligned with their dioceses, where they spent most of their time and from which they drew their resources and authority.[74] Gerard's speech and its recording are best understood in this context: as an effort to use episcopal rights and claims to manage the challenges posed by given political constellations at given moments, not in terms of his alleged Carolingian conservatism or loyalty to the *Reichskirche*. By insisting on his right to hold the keys to the Christian community, Gerard (or the *Gesta* author) is leaving the bishop the widest room for maneuver possible. In contrast perhaps to a later generation, neither Gerard nor Lietbert were engaged in epic ideological battles. They were the intelligent, pragmatic heads of an institution whose interests they were there to protect in even the most difficult political waters.

---

[73]   *GEC* 3.27, p. 474.

[74]   Timothy Reuter, "Ein Europa der Bischöfe. Das Zeitalter Burchards von Worms," in *Bischof Burchard von Worms, 1000–1025*, ed. Wilfried Hartmann, Quellen und Abhandlungen zur mittelrheinischen Kirchengeschichte 100 (Mainz, 2000), pp. 1–28. See also his seminal "The 'Imperial Church System' of the Ottonian and Salian Rulers: A Reconsideration," *Journal of Ecclesiastical History* 33 (1982), 347–74.

Chapter 8

'Both Mary and Martha': Bishop Lietbert of Cambrai and the Construction of Episcopal Sanctity in a Border Diocese around 1100

John S. Ott
Portland State University

The city of Cambrai enjoys one of the richest documentary troves in Europe to have survived from the central Middle Ages. The deeds of its bishops, from the see's founder Vedast down to the prelates of the late twelfth century, fill around 185 printed pages in two volumes of the *Monumenta Germaniae Historica*. The episcopal *gesta* are further supplemented by a generous collection of diplomatic and narrative sources, including annals, chronicles, and saints' lives.[1] Medieval Cambrai held a further distinction, one commented upon by historians since the nineteenth century: it was a *Grenzprovinz*, a border diocese.[2] The city's status as

This essay was conceived and written under the welcome auspices of a Mellon Post-Doctoral Fellowship at the Pontifical Institute of Mediaeval Studies, Toronto, Ontario, in 2004–2005. An abridged version of this article was first presented at the annual meeting of the Medieval Association of the Pacific in San Francisco, 10–12 March 2005. The author thanks the audience of that session, especially Jehangir Malegam, for their feedback, and above all John Eldevik, Brigitte Meijns, Diane Reilly, and Anna Trumbore Jones for their generous reading of this article. They are in no way responsible for any faults, errors, or omissions it may still contain.

[1]   The following texts detailing the lives and deeds of Cambrai's bishops are principally employed here; others are detailed in the notes below: *Gesta episcoporum Cameracensium*, ed. L.C. Bethmann, MGH SS 7 (Hannover, 1846), pp. 393–500 (henceforward *GEC*, followed by book and chapter number); *Gesta episcoporum Cameracensium continuata*, ed. Georg Waitz, MGH SS 14 (Hannover, 1883), pp. 183–248 (henceforward *GEC Cont.*); *Chronicon s. Andreae Castri Cameracesii*, ed. L.C. Bethmann, MGH SS 7:526–50 (henceforward *Chronicon*). The tradition of *gesta* writing for episcopal sees was well established in Lorraine in the tenth through twelfth centuries, with collections attested for, besides Cambrai, Reims, Metz, Toul, Trier, Liège, and Verdun. See Michel Sot, *Gesta episcoporum, gesta abbatum*, Typologie des sources du moyen âge occidental 37 (Turnhout, 1981), pp. 32–37.

[2]   A feature noted by: Alfred Cauchie, *La querelle des investitures dans les diocèses de Liège et de Cambrai*, 2 vols (Louvain, 1890–1891), 1:xxi–xxiii, xxxii–xxxiii; Wilhelm Reinecke, *Geschichte der Stadt Cambrai bis zur Erteilung der Lex Godefridi (1227)* (Marburg, 1896); Theodor Schieffer, "Ein deutscher Bischof des 11. Jahrhunderts: Gerhard

a "ville frontière" was primarily geo-political in nature. Its prelates obeyed the archbishop of Reims in spiritual matters. Politically, however, the city leaned eastward. The German monarch conferred to Cambrai's prelates comital authority over the city in the mid-tenth century, later extending their powers over the entire Cambrésis. The diocese was bounded by the German-leaning county of Hainaut and dukedom of Lower Lotharingia, and by the independent-minded and expansionistic county of Flanders, whose rulers successfully absorbed Hainaut from 1056–1071 and were later instrumental in fashioning a re-established diocese of Arras out of the westernmost part of Cambrai in 1093–1094.[3] The bishops of Cambrai were obliged to negotiate long-running political contests between the counts of Flanders, the German monarchs, the French kings, and, after 1071, the counts of Hainaut. Linguistically, the see was home to speakers of both Romance and, in its northern reaches, Flemish.[4] Cambrai's position at a political crossroads has led historians to perceive its economic, civic, and above all ecclesiastical and religious development as the highly particular product of a contested past.[5]

Of the bishops who ruled Cambrai from the tenth through the twelfth centuries, scholarly interest has traditionally favored Gerard I of Florennes (1012–1051).

I. von Cambrai (1012–1051)," *Deutsches Archiv für Geschichte des Mittelalters* 1 (1937), 323–60; Michel Rouche, "Cambrai, du comte mérovingien à l'évêque impérial," in *Histoire de Cambrai*, ed. Louis Trenard (Lille, 1982), pp. 23, 39; Lotte Kéry, *Die Errichtung des Bistums Arras, 1093/1094*, Beihefte der Francia 33 (Sigmaringen, 1994), and most recently by Laurent Jégou, "L'évêque entre autorité sacrée et exercice du pouvoir. L'exemple de Gérard de Cambrai (1012–1051)," *Cahiers de civilisation médiévale* 47 (2004), 37–55.

[3]   For an overview of the political situation, see Emanuel Hoeres, *Das Bistum Cambrai: Seine politischen und kirchlichen Beziehungen zu Deutschland, Frankreich und Flandern, und Entwicklung der Commune von Cambrai von 1092–1191* (Leipzig, 1882); Marinette Bruwier, "Le Hainaut, le Cambrésis, et l'Empire au XIIe siècle," *Annales du 36e congrès de la Fédération archéologique et historique de Belgique* (1955–1956), 207–26; and Egon Boshof, "Lothringen, Frankreich und das Reich in der Regierungszeit Heinrichs III.," *Rheinische Vierteljahrsblätter* 42 (1978), 63–127. On the bishops' interventions in Hainaut, and the region's frontier status, see Anne-Marie Helvétius, *Abbayes, évêques et laïques: Une politique du pouvoir en Hainaut au moyen âge (VIIe–XIe siècle)* (Brussels, 1994), esp. pp. 35–36, 284–90, and for the division of Arras and Cambrai, the superb study of Kéry, *Errichtung des Bistums Arras*.

[4]   On the linguistic division, which did not intersect French-speaking Cambrai or the Cambrésis proper, see Jan Dhondt, "Essai sur l'origine de la frontière linguistique," *L'antiquité classique* 16 (1947), 261–86, and David Nicholas, *Medieval Flanders* (London, 1992), pp. 8–11. The linguistic boundary between medieval French and *thiois* lay further north, in Brabant, as notes Erik Van Mingroot, "Gérard II de Lessines, évêque de Cambrai (†1092)," in *Dictionnaire d'histoire et de géographie ecclésiastiques*, vol. 20 (Paris, 1984), cols 751–55, at col. 751 (henceforward *DHGE*).

[5]   On its economic and especially civic development, Fernand Vercauteren, *Étude sur les civitates de la Belgique Seconde: Contribution à l'histoire urbaine du nord de la France de la fin du IIIe à la fin du XIe siècle*, Mémoires de l'Académie royale de Belgique, 2nd ser., 33 (Brussels, 1934), pp. 205–32; Rouche, "Cambrai"; Henri Platelle, "Les luttes communales et l'organisation municipale (1075–1313)" and "L'essor d'une cité (1075–1313)," all in *Histoire de Cambrai*, ed. Trenard (above, n. 2).

Gerard was a dynamic individual—a descendant of the dukes of Lower Lotharingia, a man of letters who commissioned the *gesta* of his see in 1024–1025, a reformer and founder of monasteries, a builder, and a confidant to three German monarchs.[6] For all these sterling attributes, however, it was Gerard's nephew and successor, the often overshadowed Lietbert of Lessines (1051–1076), who garnered a more transcendental distinction: he was the first bishop of Cambrai in approximately 400 years to be elevated to sainthood and endowed with a posthumous *vita*.[7]

Earlier French- and Flemish-speaking historians such as Alfred Cauchie and Milo Koyen sought to demonstrate the sympathies of Cambrai's eleventh-century "imperial" bishops, Gerard and Lietbert, for church reform. Episcopal reforms of the local church were seen as prefiguring the aims of the "Gregorian revolution," and were presumed to have been carried out in the same spirit. Similar assumptions about the ways in which the bishops of Cambrai perceived their office and its roles still color appraisals of their tenures.[8] Specifically, modern writers consistently view

---

[6]   Works on Gerard and Gerard's episcopacy abound. Essential biographical information, drawing heavily on the portrait in book three of the *GEC*, may be found in: Cauchie, *Querelle des investitures*, 1:xxiv–xxvi, xli–xlvi; Schieffer, "Ein deutscher Bischof"; Édouard de Moreau, *Histoire de l'Église en Belgique*, vol. 2, *La formation de l'Église médiévale*, 2nd edn (Brussels, 1945), pp. 16–21, 166–68, 412–13; Milo Hendrik Koyen, *De prae-gregoriaanse hervorming te Kamerijk (1012–1067* [sic: should read '1076']*)* (Tongerlo, 1953), pp. 11–22, 34–51, 68–85; Erik Van Mingroot, "Gérard Ier de Florennes, évêque de Cambrai (†1051)," in *DHGE*, vol. 20 (Paris, 1984), cols 742–51; Kéry, *Errichtung des Bistums Arras*, pp. 233–36, and additional references below. Gerard's role in the Peace of God movement has been much discussed. See Georges Duby, *The Three Orders: Feudal Society Imagined*, trans. Arthur Goldhammer (Chicago, 1980); David C. Van Meter, "The Peace of Amiens-Corbie and Gerard of Cambrai's Oration on the Three Functional Orders: The Date, the Context, the Rhetoric," *Revue belge de philologie et d'histoire* 74 (1996), 633–57, at pp. 644–57, and the essay by T.M. Riches in this volume. On the role of Gerard as reformer of monasteries and visionary of episcopal office, see the new study by Diane Reilly, *Art of Reform in Eleventh-Century Flanders: Gerard of Cambrai, Richard of Saint-Vanne and the Saint-Vaast Bible*, Studies in the History of Christian Traditions 128 (Leiden, 2006), whom I thank for permitting me to read her manuscript before its publication. A useful adjustment to the image of Gerard I as a reformer of monasteries in Hainaut is in Helvétius, *Abbayes*, pp. 286–90. In some cases, Gerard's "reform" of an abbey consisted only of replacing its abbot with the permission of the lay or ecclesiastical lord who exercised direct power over the house.

[7]   In addition to the works of Cauchie, de Moreau, and Milo Koyen (above, n. 6), brief biographical sketches of Lietbert's life and episcopacy have been compiled by Henri Platelle, "Liberto, vescovo di Cambrai," in *Bibliotheca Sanctorum*, vol. 8 (Rome, 1967), cols 28–29, and Rudolf Schieffer, "Lietbert, Bischof von Cambrai," in *Neue Deutsche Biographie*, vol. 14 (Berlin, 1985), p. 542.

[8]   The influence of Cauchie's *La querelle des investitures* has been enormous; his general line of argumentation was applied to the early eleventh century by Koyen, *De prae-gregoriaanse hervorming te Kamerijk*. For echoes of the warm welcome Gregorian reform supposedly enjoyed in Cambrai, see Jean-Marie Duvosquel, "Les chartes de donation d'autels émanant des évêques de Cambrai aux XIe–XIIe siècles éclairées par les obituaires. À propos d'un usage grégorien de la chancellerie épiscopale," in *Hommages à la Wallonie: Mélanges d'histoire, de littérature et de philologie wallonnes offerts à Maurice A. Arnould et Pierre Ruelle*, ed. Hervé Hasquin (Brussels, 1981), pp. 147–63, at p. 161.

Lietbert, whose rule overlapped with the first few years of Gregory VII's pontificate, as a *bona fide* proto-Gregorian reformer, and undeniably a Gregorian sympathizer in the last years of his life.[9]

At the same time, the *Vita Lietberti episcopi Cameracensis*, a text composed a quarter-century after its protagonist's death, bears literary and thematic features common to contemporary episcopal *vitae* composed elsewhere in the German *regnum*, and to the literary type of the imperial "courtier bishop" outlined by C. Stephen Jaeger.[10] This model, in light of Jaeger's analysis, was at base antithetical to the image of the good pastor developed in the writings of Pope Gregory I, especially in his *Rule of Pastoral Care*.[11] The recent work of Stephanie Haarländer has further augmented and nuanced our understanding of imperial bishops' representation in narrative texts. The *vita* of Lietbert exhibits an affinity, shared with the other German episcopal biographies analyzed in nearly exhaustive detail by Jaeger and Haarländer, for describing the bishop's engagement with the local nobility, his connection to the emperor and episcopal court of Cambrai, his dedication as *pater patriae* and defender of his city, and his education and character.[12] To summarize crudely

---

[9]   The roots of this latter characterization, largely based on the existence of three 1075 charters of Gregory VII for religious institutions in Cambrai, may be found in Cauchie, *La querelle des investitures*, 1:lxxxviii–lxxxix, and were further developed by Koyen, *De prae-gregoriaanse hervorming te Kamerijk*, especially pp. 86–94: "Op het einde van zijn leven schijnt Lietbert zuch nochtans te hebben aangesloten bij de hervormingspartij" (p. 94). Koyen clearly was influenced by the monumental work of Augustin Fliche, *La réforme grégorienne et la reconquête chrétienne (1057–1123)*, vol. 8 in *Histoire de l'Église depuis les origines jusqu'à nos jours*, ed. Augustin Fliche and Victor Martin ([Paris], 1950), although he does not always agree with Fliche's emphasis on the central role of Gregory VII in the reform process. For the charters in question, see below.

[10]   C. Stephen Jaeger, "The Courtier Bishop in *Vitae* from the Tenth to the Twelfth Century," *Speculum* 58 (1983), 291–325.

[11]   Jaeger followed the assessment of Heinz Hürten, "Gregor der Große und der mittelalterliche Episkopat," *Zeitschrift für Kirchengeschichte* 73 (1962), 16–41, at pp. 40–41, who contrasted the orthodox ideal of episcopal office formulated in the writings of Gregory the Great with the reality and the biographies of the German episcopate in the central Middle Ages. Jaeger (p. 295) acknowledges the presence of Gregory's pastoral ideals in the *vitae* of Brun of Cologne and Ulrich of Augsburg, and it is likewise found in the biography of Otto, bishop of Bamberg (d. 1139), analyzed recently by Marie-Luise Laudage: *Caritas und Memoria mittelalterlicher Bischöfe*, Münsterische Historische Forschungen 3 (Cologne, 1993), esp. pp. 262–88, 307–17. Hürten's conclusions must be further tempered owing to the favored place of Gregory I's writings, including the *Regula pastoralis*, in tenth- and eleventh-century *scriptoria* and libraries like those of Trier and Cologne, discussed by Henry Mayr-Harting, *Ottonian Book Illumination: An Historical Study*, 2 vols (London, 1991), 2:104–6, 116–23, 205–10. On Gregory VII's embrace of Gregory I's ideas, see I.S. Robinson, *Authority and Resistance in the Investiture Contest: The Polemical Literature of the Late Eleventh Century* (Manchester, 1978), pp. 22–24, 31–39, 139–42, to which should be compared Gerhart B. Ladner, "Gregory the Great and Gregory VII: A Comparison of their Concepts of Renewal," *Viator* 4 (1973), 1–31.

[12]   Stephanie Coué, *Hagiographie im Kontext: Schreibanlaß und Funktion von Bischofsviten aus dem 11. und vom Anfang des 12. Jahrhunderts*, Arbeiten zur

the two historiographical traditions, we might say that Lietbert was an evidently proto-Gregorian bishop whose literary portrait was rendered in an "imperializing" biographical style.

Or so we are led to conclude from the ways in which modern scholars have characterized the bishop, his biographer, and the themes of contemporary episcopal biography. Yet Lietbert's own associates, especially the author of his *vita*, did not perpetuate the same image of the bishop. The *vita* describes Lietbert as a conscientious pastor personally admired by the German emperors and French kings. It also portrays him as largely disconnected from the broader currents and controversies surrounding church reform and lay investiture of prelates, downplaying sharply his allegiances to the grander programs of secular and religious authorities. Precisely because Lietbert's *vita* and the other narrative accounts of his prelacy do not easily fit the interpretive molds modern historians have prepared for them, the construction of Lietbert's sanctity in the eleventh- and twelfth-century histories of his episcopacy are of paramount interest for discerning the ways in which the authors of these texts negotiated political and ideological borders between frequently antagonistic polities and between complex, often competing, religious and ecclesiastical agendas. As I hope to show in this article, the evidence of Lietbert's literary dossier also calls into question the applicability and utility of such categorical ascriptions as "reformist" and "imperial" to the bishops—and other religious figures—of German border or frontier regions during the eleventh and twelfth centuries.[13]

What of this literary tradition? The *vita*'s author was named Raoul.[14] He was a priest and monk of Saint-Sépulchre, an abbey founded by Lietbert outside the old Roman *castrum* of Cambrai in 1064.[15] Raoul's life is mostly a mystery to us.[16] It is clear that he personally knew Lietbert and several key figures in Lietbert's life; that he was well acquainted with the works of classical and Christian authors; and that

---

Frühmittelalterforschung 24 (Berlin, 1997); eadem (as Stephanie Haarländer), *Vitae episcoporum: Eine Quellengattung zwischen Hagiographie und Historiographie, untersucht an Lebensbeschreibungen von Bischöfen des Regnum Teutonicum im Zeitalter der Ottonen und Salier*, Monographien zur Geschichte des Mittelalters 47 (Stuttgart, 2000). Lietbert's *vita* is one of the fifty-five that Haarländer analyzes. The first historian to take up fully the image of the imperial bishop in Germany was Oskar Köhler, *Das Bild des geistlichen Fürsten in den Viten des 10., 11. und 12. Jahrhunderts* (Berlin, 1935), to whose work many of the above writers (nn. 11 and 12) responded.

[13] See also the contributions of T.M. Riches and John Eldevik in this volume.

[14] Raoul of Saint-Sépulchre, *Vita Lietberti episcopi Cameracensis*, ed. Adolf Hofmeister, MGH SS 30/2 (Leipzig, 1934), pp. 838–66 (henceforward *VL*, followed by chapter and page number). Hofmeister's edition of the *vita* is preferable to that of Godfrey Henschen in the AASS June, vol. 4, pp. 499–515.

[15] For a map of eleventh-century Cambrai, see Rouche, "Cambrai," in *Histoire de Cambrai*, ed. Trenard, p. 24; for Raoul's obituary, see Hofmeister ed., *VL*, p. 838 n. 2.

[16] He was undoubtedly a monk under Walter, abbot of Saint-Sépulchre, who ruled from 1064–1096 and was an ally of the bishop. That Raoul was also a *sacerdos* in close company with the bishop suggests he may have converted to a monastic profession after a career as a secular clerk.

he attended a central event in the bishop's life, his pilgrimage to Jerusalem.[17] Like Lietbert, Raoul is typically classified as a "Gregorian."[18] The *vita*'s chronological *termini* are 1094 and 1133, but scholarly consensus secures its composition sometime around 1100.[19] This date puts it squarely in the middle of the fifteen-year episcopal succession dispute which rocked Cambrai from 1093–1116, pitting imperial, papal, and French-leaning bishops, clerical factions, and townspeople against one another.[20] As we shall see, this political context is critical for understanding Raoul's narrative strategies.

The *vita*'s diffusion was limited to the dioceses of Cambrai and Arras. Three manuscript copies from the late twelfth or early thirteenth century have survived— one from Saint-Sépulchre, a second from Saint-Géry of Cambrai (a possession of the cathedral of Notre-Dame), and a third from the abbey of Anchin.[21] Veneration of Lietbert as a saint appears to have been restrained: beyond Raoul's biography, there is little evidence of a formal cult until the thirteenth century.[22] Luckily, we

---

[17]   On Raoul's learnedness and fondness for Cicero, see A. Hofmeister, "Cicero in der *Vita Lietberti*," *Neues Archiv* 30 (1948), 165–74.

[18]   By Koyen, *De prae-gregoriaanse hervorming te Kamerijk*, pp. xx, 25, who does note that Raoul is not a polemist for the Gregorian or imperial causes. Koyen is followed by Erik Van Mingroot, "Kritische onderzoek omtrent de datering van de *Gesta episcoporum Cameracensium*," *Revue belge de philologie et d'histoire* 53 (1975), 281–332, at p. 294, where the author refers to Raoul as "gregoriaans-gezinde." Raoul's "Gregorian" sympathies appear to lie in his re-writing of the account of Lietbert's elevation to the see by Emperor Henry III, first detailed in the *GEC* at 4.4 (3.64), p. 492. In the later *vita*, cc. 10–11, pp. 847–48, Raoul has Lietbert first elected canonically by the acclamation of the clergy and people of Cambrai, and only then chosen, or approved, by the emperor. As I will show, here as elsewhere Raoul is merely covering all bases by mentioning the people and clergy, since he leaves the emperor a primary role in the election process.

[19]   For the text's dating consult Hofmeister ed., *VL*, p. 838, and above all Koyen, *De prae-gregoriaanse hervorming te Kamerijk*, pp. xix–xx; they are followed by Kéry, *Errichtung des Bistums Arras*, p. 239 n. 101, and Haarländer, *Vitae episcoporum*, pp. 521–22. Raoul's focus on the pilgrimage, his frequent application of epithets such as *miles Christi* to Lietbert and his fellow pilgrims, and his reflective mention of the long life of Anselm of Ribemont, who died in spring 1099, suggest a date around 1099–1100.

[20]   The episcopal succession controversy at Cambrai following the death of Gerard II in August 1092 has been recounted many times. Detailed studies may be found in Hoeres, *Das Bistum Cambrai*, pp. 6–32; Cauchie, *La querelle des investitures*, 2:119–206; Reinecke, *Geschichte der Stadt Cambrai*, pp. 55–59; de Moreau, *Histoire de l'Église en Belgique*, 2:92–95, 100–101; and more recently Erik Van Mingroot, "Een decennium uit de geschiedenis van de stad Kamerijk (1092–1102/1103). De voornaamste acteurs," in *Villes et campagnes au Moyen Âge: Mélanges Georges Despy*, ed. Jean-Marie Duvosquel and Alain Dierkens (Liège, 1991), pp. 713–45; Kéry, *Errichtung des Bistums Arras*, pp. 297–306; and Irven M. Resnick, "Odo of Cambrai and the Investiture Crisis in the Early Twelfth Century," *Viator* 28 (1997), 83–98. No faction gained the upper hand until Burchard, an appointee from the imperial chapel, was finally consecrated in 1116.

[21]   These are detailed by Hofmeister in his introduction to the *VL*, pp. 839–40.

[22]   His relics were elevated in 1211 and again in 1271. An episcopal list written down during the episcopacy of Burchard (1116–1130) and attached to a manuscript copy of the early eleventh-century *Vita sancti Gaugerici episcopi confessoris*, in AASS August, vol. 2, new edn

are not wholly dependent on Raoul's *vita* for our image of the bishop. Two separate continuators to the *gesta* of the bishops of Cambrai composed, in the period from 1054 to 1076, an uneven narrative of Lietbert's episcopate. Later, an anonymous monk at Saint-André of Cateau-Cambrésis near Cambrai, drawing heavily on the pre-existing *vita* and *gesta*, detailed Lietbert's tenure in a chronicle written in 1133.[23]

As necessary prelude to assessing the literary image of the bishop in Raoul's *vita*, it is worth establishing Lietbert's actual political orbit. Generally speaking, Lietbert (and his predecessor, Gerard I) supported the German *Reichspolitik*. They participated in imperial campaigns in Flanders and Lorraine, and in turn depended heavily on imperial military support to counteract the power of the castellans of Cambrai and the increasingly eastward-looking Flemish counts.[24] Lietbert attended the German court on four or five occasions during his episcopacy: in 1051 (Cologne), 1054 (near Béthune), 1056 (Cologne), possibly 1066 (at Dortmund), and 1071 (Liège).[25] Three of the assemblies addressed the emperor's relationship with the count of Flanders, of paramount concern to Cambrai. In 1054, Lietbert was in Henry III's company during his campaign against Baldwin V of Flanders, probably acting in both an advisory and military capacity.[26] He also journeyed southeast to Reims on at least three occasions. According to Raoul, Lietbert was present for Henry I's nuptials with Anna of Kiev, which coincided with his own consecration in 1051, and there performed the queen's unction.[27] He attended the Capetian court twice more, in 1059 and 1066.[28] His presence on these two occasions coincided roughly with the

---

(Paris, 1869), p. 692, did not qualify him as "sanctus," nor did the author of the *Chronicon s. Andreae*.

[23]   Above, n. 1. Van Mingroot, "Kritisch onderzoek," pp. 289–99, postulates that the author of the first part of Lietbert's deeds may have accompanied the bishop on his pilgrimage in 1054, because the account breaks off at that point and resumes coverage only of the last years of the bishop's rule. In any case, Lietbert's *gesta* to 1054 were elided to the account of Gerard I's episcopacy, a convention likewise followed by Raoul in the *vita*.

[24]   Edgar Nathaniel Johnson, *The Secular Activities of the German Episcopate, 919–1024*, University Studies of the University of Nebraska 30–31 (Lincoln, NE, 1932), pp. 125–35; Koyen, *De prae-gregoriaanse hervorming te Kamerijk*; Boshof, "Lothringen, Frankreich und das Reich"; Kéry, *Errichtung des Bistums Arras*, pp. 242–54, among others.

[25]   *GEC* 4.4 (3.64), p. 492; 4.11 (3.68), p. 493; *VL*, cc. 11–13, pp. 847–48; c. 42, p. 858; Gerold Meyer von Knonau, *Jahrbücher des Deutschen Reiches unter Heinrich IV. und Heinrich V.*, 7 vols (Leipzig, 1890–1909; repr. Berlin, 1965), 2:46–59, at p. 47. Lietbert apparently issued the charter installing Benedictine monks at Saint-Autbert from Dortmund. It bears the signatures of Henry IV and the royal chancellors Sieghard and Siegbert, but is in some respects unusual; see *Die Urkunden der deutschen Könige und Kaiser*, vol. 6/1, *Die Urkunden Heinrichs IV*, ed. Dietrich von Gladiss, MGH DD 6/1 (Berlin, 1941; repr. Hannover, 1978), pp. 231–33.

[26]   Unlike Gerard I, who frequently attended the imperial court and took to the field on campaign between 1012 and 1040, Lietbert appears as an imperial counselor just this one time. For Gerard I's engagement with the German emperors, see Schieffer, "Ein deutscher Bischof," pp. 335–47.

[27]   *VL*, c. 19, p. 850.

[28]   On episcopal reunions with the French kings, see Olivier Guyotjeannin, "Les évêques dans l'entourage royal sous les premiers Capétiens," in *Le roi de France et son royaume*

minority of Henry IV in Germany and the growing power of the Count of Flanders in Hainaut, and Lietbert may have been seeking to secure French royal support against Flanders in light of diminished German ability to protect Cambrai.[29]

As to Lietbert's relationship with the papacy, it was limited to the final year of his life. In 1075, quite ill—Raoul reports that he suffered severely from gout—and at an advanced age, he requested papal confirmation and tutelage of the privileges and possessions of three abbeys: Saint-Sépulchre, Mont-Saint-Eloi, and Saint-Aubert.[30] Of the three papal bulls Gregory VII ostensibly issued in response, those for Saint-Aubert and Mont-Saint-Eloi appear suspect.[31] Assuming them to be authentic for argument's sake, the bulls place the institutions and their possessions under perpetual papal protection against lay or clerical usurpation. Such bulls, commonly issued in the eleventh century for monasteries and canonries across Europe, added papal anathema to episcopal injunctions against violators of the abbeys' liberties. In Saint-Sépulchre's case, the bull also upheld episcopal prerogative in the consecration of churches and ordination of monks and clergy belonging to the abbey, provided the

---

autour de l'an Mil: Actes du colloque Hugues Capet 987–1987. La France de l'an Mil, Paris-Senlis, 22–23 juin 1987, ed. Michel Parisse and Xavier Barral i Altet (Paris, 1992), pp. 91–99, who does not include the 1066 date in his overview; the diplomatic evidence and discussion of Anna's consecration is furnished by Maurice Prou ed., *Recueil des actes de Philippe Ier, roi de France (1059–1108)* (Paris, 1908), pp. xix–xxiii; no. 22, pp. 60–61 (1065 after 4 August); no. 26, p. 79 (28 September 1066). Lietbert was also involved with Baldwin V in the reform of Saint-Pierre of Hasnon in 1065, in Hainaut. The charter was confirmed by Philip I at Baldwin's request that year.

[29]   Henry IV attained his majority in 1065. Hainaut's absorption by Baldwin V was recognized by Agnes and Henry IV in 1056. See I.S. Robinson, *Henry IV of Germany, 1056–1106* (Cambridge, 1999), pp. 24, 31, 51–52.

[30]   The charters in question are reproduced in Julius von Pflugk-Harttung ed., *Acta pontificum Romanorum inedita*, vol. 1 (Tübingen, 1881), nos. 49–50, pp. 47–49 (Saint-Sépulchre and Saint-Aubert); and Charles Duvivier ed., *Actes et documents anciens intéressant la Belgique* (Brussels, 1898), pp. 148–49 (Mont-Saint-Eloi).

[31]   The grounds are these. The wording (and issue date, 1 November 1076) of the bulls for Mont-Saint-Eloi and Saint-Aubert is virtually identical, and closely mirrors both a papal bull of 7 March 1075 for Saint-Pierre of Lille (Pflugk-Harttung ed., *Acta pontificum Romanorum inedita*, no. 48, pp. 46–47) and the papal bull of 18 April 1075 for Saint-Sépulchre. Only the names of the recipients, dates of issue, and pontifical regnal dates differ, although Saint-Sépulchre's bull contains a full enumeration of its possessions. Bulls conferring papal protection of ecclesiastical liberties employed similar language at this time, but as only the original bull for Saint-Pierre of Lille survives, there remains a good chance that those for Saint-Autbert and Mont-Saint-Eloi (both preserved in copies at Paris, Bibliothèque nationale de France, Collection Moreau 31, fol. 134r) were modeled on it. More suspicious still is that by 1 November 1076, the date of issue for the bulls of Saint-Aubert and Mont-Saint-Eloi, Lietbert had been dead for more than four months. Note that Philipp Jaffé and Wilhelm Wattenbach eds., *Regesta pontificum Romanorum, ab condita ecclesia ad annum post Christum natum 1198*, 2nd rev. edn, 2 vols (Leipzig, 1885–1888), no. 5009, 1:619, considered the bull for Saint-Aubert authentic, but on the (faulty) grounds that they believed Lietbert had died on 28 September 1076 rather than 23 June.

bishop was canonically elected.[32] Thus, Lietbert's apparent Gregorian sympathies—an assertion based on what may be a single, authentic papal act—look less like an engagement with the pope's reform agenda than an indication of his belief that papal anathema provided an added disincentive to those who would infringe monastic liberties, and a further layer of protection to the legacy of the institution(s) he had reformed and endowed in the years between 1064 and 1068. The bulls' issuance at the end of Lietbert's reign also conforms to the bishop's own pattern of drawing up charters; fifteen of his twenty known charters were issued between 1070 and 1076.[33] For his part, Raoul makes no mention of any papal bulls or of papal involvement in Cambrai during Lietbert's episcopacy.[34]

According to the historiographical conventions that have guided scholarly appraisals of Lietbert's episcopacy, the literary image of the bishop in Raoul's *vita* seems at first glance a rather unorthodox amalgamation of disparate themes and ideas. Evidence of his adaptation of, and also his clear departure from, prevailing traits in German episcopal *gesta* and *vitae* appears throughout Raoul's biography. In general, German episcopal biographies stressed the bishop's education, the elegance of his *mores* (essentially meaning his refined conduct and behavior), his superior administrative capacities and service to the German emperors, his reform of religious communities, his resources as a builder and patron, and his exemplary personal qualities such as patience, eloquence, and *gravitas*—often furnished in service of the court.[35] Raoul's Lietbert is generally of a feather with this flock of virtues, especially in his education. The young novice was, Raoul says, "led running with a thirsting spirit to the font of philosophy, and there drinking from the seven rivers of threefold

---

[32]   Pflugk-Harttung ed., *Acta pontificum Romanorum inedita*, no. 49, p. 48. Such provisions distinguish this bull from those granting full abbatial exemption from episcopal prerogatives, outlined by Jean-François Lemarignier in two studies, "Political and Monastic Structures in France at the End of the Tenth and the Beginning of the Eleventh Century," in *Lordship and Community in Medieval Europe: Selected Readings*, ed. Fredric L. Cheyette (New York, 1968), pp. 100–27, and especially "L'exemption monastique et les origines de la réforme grégorienne," in idem, *Recueil d'articles rassemblés par ses disciples: Structures politiques et religieuses dans la France du haut moyen âge* (Rouen, 1995), pp. 285–337.

[33]   Erik Van Mingroot, "Liste provisoire des actes des évêques de Cambrai de 1031 à 1130," in *Serta devota in memoriam Guillelmi Lourdaux*, pars posterior, *Cultura mediaevalis*, ed. Werner Verbeke et al. (Louvain, 1995), pp. 13–55. I was unable to consult fully the same author's new edition of the episcopal *acta* for Cambrai before this article went to press (below, n. 102).

[34]   There is also no evidence that Lietbert supported Henry III or Henry IV in opposing papal initiatives. He did not attend the January 1076 Council of Worms, at which Henry IV demanded that Gregory abdicate the throne, but this probably was owing to his illness rather than from sympathy for the papal cause. On the synod see Robinson, *Henry IV*, pp. 143–47.

[35]   For examples, see above all Jaeger, "The Courtier Bishop"; idem, *The Envy of Angels: Cathedral Schools and Social Ideals in Medieval Europe, 950–1200* (Philadelphia, 1994); John Nightingale, "Bishop Gerard of Toul (963–94) and Attitudes to Episcopal Office," in *Warriors and Churchmen in the High Middle Ages: Essays Presented to Karl Leyser*, ed. Timothy Reuter (London, 1992), pp. 41–62, at pp. 41–43; and Haarländer, *Vitae episcoporum*.

wisdom," he studied logic, medicine, and ethics.[36] Trained in the episcopal school under the careful eye of his predecessor Gerard, the young clerk's masters soon noted with pleasure his industry, *sollicitudo, scientia, mores,* and *religio munda et immaculata.*[37] These were qualities conducive to his rapid professional ascent, first to the dignity of *archiscolus,* then to provost and archdeacon of the cathedral chapter. In the *gesta* account of Lietbert's election by Henry III, written about 1054, the emperor agrees on his suitability for office on the grounds that Lietbert had at one time been his chaplain and had proven his fidelity on many occasions, and Raoul follows this account nearly verbatim.[38] Raoul also noted his accomplishments in the service of local church reform. Copying and slightly augmenting passages from the earlier *gesta* of Lietbert, Raoul detailed the bishop's rehabilitation of the city's churches and the reform of their communities, and above all his building campaigns—including, most importantly for Raoul, the foundation of Saint-Sépulchre and the extension of the city's walls around it.[39]

If the literary Lietbert shared in some of the personal and professional qualities esteemed of a *Reichsbischof,* Raoul nevertheless limits his description of the bishop's attendance at the imperial court and his involvement in the affairs of the empire to just two occasions.[40] He is far more effusive, and contributes all new material to the pre-existing account of Lietbert's deeds, when talking about the prelate's involvement with the French king and the bishops of the archiepiscopal province of Reims. Not only does the bishop of Cambrai preside at the unction of Queen Anna in 1051, but, according to Raoul, so great is his reputation that King Henry I is said to have requested the queen's coronation ceremony be carried out in conjunction with Lietbert's own episcopal consecration.[41] Henry I's esteem of the bishop is shared by Lietbert's fellow suffragans, including two archbishops of Reims, Gui (1033–1055) and Gervais (1055–1067). Raoul heaps praise on Gui and Gervais, describing the latter as "conspicuous in all goodness."[42] So beloved was Lietbert to Gervais that he "revered and honored him above all the bishops of his archdiocese," and even

---

[36]   "Ducitur sitibundo pectore currens ad fontem philosophiae, et saporis tripertiti septem rivos ebibens modo studet logicae, nunc insudat phisicae, sic intendens vacat ethicae": *VL,* c. 3, p. 844.

[37]   *VL,* cc. 3–4, pp. 844–45. Compare with James 1.27: "religio munda et immaculata apud Deum et patrem."

[38]   *GEC* 4.3 (3.63), p. 491; *VL,* c. 11, p. 847.

[39]   *VL,* cc. 48–50, 57, pp. 859–61, 862. These tropes are commonly part of episcopal *vitae*; see Haarländer, *Vitae episcoporum,* p. 187.

[40]   Raoul omits altogether any mention of the bishop's presence during Henry III's military campaign against Count Baldwin V of Flanders in 1054—which the *gesta* of Lietbert and the *Chronicon s. Andreae Cameracesii,* cc. 16–21, pp. 532–34, describe in detail—and for which Lietbert would almost certainly have been obliged to furnish troops. When Raoul later recounts the bishop's presence at the imperial court in Cologne in 1056, on his return from a two-year pilgrimage, it is to remark on the bishop's excellent relationship with Baldwin V of Flanders, whose union of Hainaut to Flanders the Empress Agnes and the child-king Henry IV formally recognized at the council.

[41]   *VL,* c. 19, p. 850.

[42]   *VL,* cc. 16–17, 51, pp. 848–49, 861.

once requested him to perform the Easter mass at Reims cathedral.[43] As Lietbert proceeded to Châlons for his ordination into the priesthood and then to Reims for his consecration, the towns and prelates along the way welcomed him triumphantly.[44] His consecration was the very picture of social and religious concord, and Raoul's Lietbert was drawn into the liturgical and social bosom of the archdiocese.[45]

As the bishop appears to have been in his lifetime, so the saint Lietbert is politically amphibious, equally at ease amid his French brother-bishops or the bustling throngs of the German court. Of greater significance for Raoul than his ability to mingle with different crowds, however, is Lietbert's transcendence of the borders which separated one nation from another, *regnum* from *sacerdotium*, active life from the contemplative, earthly pilgrim from the celestial. While Raoul relied heavily on the *gesta* of Lietbert and Gerard I and drew inspiration from them, this thematic and literary emphasis is strictly his own. Lietbert's presence in Cologne and Reims and his familiarity with his fellow bishops and the two monarchs occur within specific, essentially liturgical, contexts—Easter celebrations and royal coronations. For Raoul, these moments reflect the ideal bond that should prevail between prelates, monarchs, and people, and express his own understanding of the proper relationship between *regnum* and *sacerdotium*.

Thus, to describe Raoul's viewpoint as "Gregorian" (or even "imperialist"), assuming this term could be satisfactorily defined, is misleading. Raoul accepted the superiority of clergy and canon law over secular dignity and tradition,[46] but stressed their essential complementarity. He set the tone in the opening chapters of the *vita*, waxing eloquent—even nostalgic—about the harmony of *regnum* and *sacerdotium* that prevailed during the reigns of Otto III and Henry II. This time, he wrote, "marked a solstice of peace and tranquility, when kingship and priesthood were in harmony," and when, "sustained by the arm of a peace-loving king, mother church delighted in the concordant justice of the saints."[47] In this happy age, Lietbert was born. By implication, in Raoul's own day a century later, such harmony was a fond but distant memory. His retelling of Lietbert's election confirmed how the

---

[43]   *VL*, c. 52, p. 861. At c. 16, p. 848, Raoul exalts Gui as "an utterly distinguished man, renowned in all things among his compatriots" (vir sane conspicuus interque suos compatriotas per omnia clarus).

[44]   *VL*, cc. 16–18, pp. 848–50.

[45]   "Infulis redimitus procedit metropolita, consequuntur pontifices populorum stipante caterva. . . . Sistitur Deo, presentatur pontifici, recitatur electio, testificatur a cunctis. Fit concursus populorum, fit strepitus gaudiorum": *VL*, c. 18, p. 849.

[46]   As, for example, when he compares Henry I's marriage to Anna of Kiev with Lietbert's espousal to his church: "Regi Francorum coniungitur carnalis sponsa, domno Lietberto Cameracensium pontifici, regio et sacerdotali cubiculario, sancta committitur ecclesia. Sed haec copula quanto sanctior, tanto melior": *VL*, c. 20, p. 850.

[47]   "Tripudiabat christianus orbis pacifici regis sustentatus brachio; gaudebat mater ecclesia sanctorum concordi iustitia, de virtute in virtutem gradientibus cunctis. . . . In hoc ergo pacis tranquillitatisque solstitio bene sibi consentientibus regno cum sacerdotio, preclui decoris iubar effulsit . . . nobilis infans nobili prosapia": *VL*, c. 3, p. 844. See the comments of David A. Warner, "Saints and Politics in Ottonian Germany," in *Medieval Germany: Associations and Delineations*, ed. Nancy Van Deusen (Ottowa, 2000), pp. 7–28, at p. 11.

prerogatives of clergy, people, and emperor, when left to operate together, yielded a consensus candidate.

According to Raoul, Lietbert arrived at court on Good Friday 1051 with other legates from Cambrai to announce Gerard I's death and Lietbert's election by the joint consent of the clergy and people. Henry III put off confirming the election until Easter Sunday, when, following the mass, he gathered his magnates and weighed the people and clergy's decision.[48] Rather than describing the imperial deliberation as a rubber-stamp process, Raoul first insisted that Henry III confirmed the popular choice: "mother church celebrated . . . [and] applauded the election of the celebrated lord Lietbert, above all at the prerogative of imperial election."[49] Then, when another candidate for the bishopric objected to Lietbert's election, it was Henry—citing the case of Martin of Tours, whose own election had been contested by a faction of clergy—who pronounced in favor of the bishop-elect's virtues.[50] It is true, as scholars have repeatedly noted, that Raoul whitewashed the more believable account of Lietbert's election contained in the *Gesta episcoporum Cameracensium*. The *Gesta*'s author attributed his elevation solely to the emperor's will and openly asserted that Lietbert had pledged faith to Henry III before returning to his city.[51] Raoul by contrast carefully noted that Lietbert received from the emperor's hands the city of Cambrai *cum suis appenditiis omnibus*, not his church. But Henry's own decision with the counsel of his magnates, and his defense of Lietbert were, for Raoul, critical to the legitimacy of the bishop's candidacy. Raoul was clearly staking out a middle ground between imperial precedent and canonical procedure at a time when the subject of lay investiture and the pledging of faith were very much in a state of flux and inconsistently enforced.

This leitmotif of equilibrium also seeps into Raoul's description of the bishop's words and actions. In an encomium celebrating Lietbert's virtues as pastor, Raoul includes the following passage adapted from Augustine's *De ordine*:

> The bishop lived as a student of divine law and as an example to his people. . . . He did nothing weakly, and nothing audaciously. With respect to the sins of his people, he either cast out all anger or so restrained it that it was like anger dismissed. He observed

---

48   *VL*, c. 10, pp. 846–47.

49   "Sollempnizabat mater ecclesia . . . plaudebat domni Lietberti celebri electione, presertim ad prerogativam electionis imperatoriae": *VL*, c. 13, p. 848.

50   *VL*, c. 12, p. 848; Sulpicius Severus, *Vie de Saint Martin*, 9.3–7, ed. and trans. Jacques Fontaine, Sources chrétiennes 133–35, 3 vols (Paris, 1967–1969), 1:270–73.

51   "Pontifex, facta fidelitate imperatori, et omnibus competentibus adimpletis, satagebat ad civitatem suam reverti": *GEC* 4.3–4 (3.63–64), pp. 491–92. The performance of homage by churchmen to secular rulers was explicitly banned at the Council of Clermont in 1095 ("Ne episcopus vel sacerdos regi vel alicui laico in manibus ligiam fidelitatem faciat."), and lay investiture (again) prohibited; numerous clergy from Cambrai attended the council owing to the then-raging succession dispute in the diocese. For the quote see Stefan Beulertz, *Das Verbot der Laieninvestitur im Investiturstreit*, Monumenta Germaniae Historica Studien und Texte 2 (Hannover, 1991), pp. 11, 41–42, 75; and Koyen, *De prae-gregoriaanse hervorming te Kamerijk*, pp. 22–26. Robinson, *Henry IV*, pp. 278–79, notes that Henry IV seems to have had no idea he was involved in an investiture "controversy," since not only does he not mention it, but there are no imperial polemics addressing lay investiture from 1086–1103.

as closely as possible that when he took vengeance he was not excessive, and not stingy in forgiving. He punished nothing that was not the better for it; he indulged nothing that might become worse."[52]

The broader context of this description in the *De ordine* has Augustine explaining to several interlocutors that there is a branch of learning (*disciplina*) that yields metaphysical knowledge of God and his order. This knowledge is revealed to those wise men who both contemplate it with their understanding and adhere to it in their manner of living. Thus, knowledge of God means regulating one's life and directing one's mind to its study—it results neither from contemplation nor action alone, but a balance or proportion between the two.[53] By his personal example, Lietbert demonstrated to his parishioners the best means for accessing knowledge of God. Here, as elsewhere in the *vita*, harmony between word and action, between interior and exterior dispositions, is the pastoral ideal.[54] This is confirmed early in the *vita*'s seventh chapter, where Raoul allows that "you would see in [Lietbert] Mary and Martha, now going about the business of the ministry, now humbly laying at Jesus's feet . . . with tears and attentive prayers."[55] For Raoul (taking his cues from Augustine and, as we shall see, Gregory the Great), Mary and Martha represented complementary ideals of action and contemplation, rather than mutually exclusive models.[56]

Another feature of the good pastor central to Raoul's depiction of episcopal sanctity is one who withstands tyranny and protects his flock from danger. This model is grounded in biblical tradition, drawing especially on passages from Ezekiel and John. In depicting Lietbert's conflicts with the castellan of Cambrai and the count of Flanders, Raoul had ample opportunity to put this ideal on display. In one memorable encounter, the aged Lietbert, ailing from gout, was transported by carriage into the siege tents of Robert, count of Flanders, arrayed outside Cambrai (in 1076?).[57] From his seat, he ordered the count to cease and desist, only to have Robert laugh him off. Lietbert then struggled to sit up, stood on his own feet, and

---

[52]   "Studiosus divinae legis pontifex exemplumque suis ita vivebat. . . . Nichil faciebat enerviter, nichil audacter. In peccatis autem suorum vel pellebat omnino iram vel ita frenabat, ut esset pulsae similis. Magnopere observabat, cum vindicabat, ne nimium; cum ignoscebat, ne parum. Nichil puniebat, quod non valeret ad melius; nichil indulgebat, quod verteretur in peius": *VL*, c. 25, pp. 851–52 (my translation). Augustine of Hippo, *De ordine libri duo*, 2.8.25, PL 32:1006–7; English translation with facing Latin text in *Divine Providence and the Problem of Evil: A Translation of St. Augustine's De ordine*, trans. Robert P. Russell (New York, 1942), pp. 118–19.

[53]   *De ordine*, 2.8.25.

[54]   Compare, for example, *VL*, c. 17, p. 849, at his ordination into the priesthood; c. 24, p. 851, with his sermon on the parable of the man given two bags of money.

[55]   *VL*, c. 7, p. 845.

[56]   See Giles Constable, *Three Studies in Medieval Religious and Social Thought* (Cambridge, 1995), pp. 19–22, 30–31, 40–41, and the contribution of Thomas Head in this volume. This evocation of the bishop as both Mary and Martha is often found in the *vitae* and *gesta* of eleventh-century bishops, including Wazo of Liège.

[57]   *VL*, c. 60, pp. 863–64.

taking crozier in hand excommunicated the tyrant *pontificaliter*. Robert, "in awe of the bishop's authority," quit the siege and left the scene.

To frame and contextualize Lietbert's pastoral sollicitude in this encounter, Raoul excerpted heavily from the fourteenth *Homily* of Gregory the Great, the sermon "Ego pastor bonus sum," I am the Good Shepherd.[58] General arguments from the fourteenth *Homily* are also found in the fourth chapter of the second book of Gregory's *Regula pastoralis* (*Rule of Pastoral Care*), written at precisely the same time (September 590–February 591). Together, this sermon and the *Rule* represent some of Gregory's earliest reflections on the obligations of pastoral care. Both Gregory's Gospel homilies and the *Regula pastoralis* enjoyed demonstrably wide usage in and around Cambrai in the eleventh century. Indeed, locally written episcopal *gesta* and *vitae* were saturated with allusions and excerpts from these texts. Bishop Gerard I himself, and subsequently the author of Gerard's *gesta*, employed Gregory's Homilies 17 and 26, as well as the *Regula*, in their writings.[59] Raoul availed himself of Gerard's *gesta*, a debt he explicitly acknowledges, and also appears to have been inspired by the *Vita sancti Gaugerici episcopi*'s use of Ezekiel 13.5, a passage commented on in Gregory's fourteenth homily and the *Regula pastoralis*.[60] In the homily, commenting on the passage, "He rises up in opposition, standing like a wall of the house of Israel,

---

[58]   From John 10.11–12. Gregory the Great, *Homiliae in Evangelia*, ed. Raymond Étaix, CCSL 141 (Turnhout, 1999), 14.1–6, pp. 96–102, here at 14.3, p. 98 ("I am the Good Shepherd."/Ego sum pastor bonus.); *Règle pastorale*, ed. and trans. Bruno Judic, Floribert Rommel, and Charles Morel, Sources chrétiennes 381–82, 2 vols (Paris, 1992) (henceforward *RP*), 2.4, 1:188–89. David Hurst has translated the homilies into English as Gregory the Great, *Forty Gospel Homilies* (Kalamazoo, MI, 1990), pp. 107–12, designating it Homily 15, not 14. Étaix, pp. lxi and lxx, proposes that Homily 14 was originally composed for the second anniversary of Pope Pelagius's death, thus 6 February 591. The editors of the *Pastoral Rule*, 1:21–22, place the composition of the first two books between September 590 and February 591. In the *RP*, Gregory's commentary on the passage from Ezekiel concerns pastors who keep silent when they should not, and speak when they should be silent: fearing to lose the favor of men, they do not speak freely when it is good and necessary, and in that respect are like the mercenary who flees when the wolf approaches the flock. However, Gregory's commentary on the passage *Non ascendistis ex adverso* is essentially the same in Homily 14 and the *RP*, even if the Homily is concerned less with the pastor's speech and more with general issues of pastoral responsibility.

[59]   Eleventh-century manuscripts containing the *vitae* of bishop-saints Remigius and Gaugericus, which borrowed directly from the *Regula pastoralis*, were copied and kept at Notre-Dame of Cambrai and Saint-Sépulchre itself. Passages in the *GEC* which employ Gregory's texts include 1.106, p. 446; 3.28, p. 475; 3.32, p. 479. Cambrai, Bibliothèque municipale, MSS 864 (eleventh century, Saint-Sépulchre) and 865 (eleventh century, cathedral of Notre-Dame), contain the *vitae* of Remigius and Gaugericus. For Gregorian influences in the latter text, the third recension of which was composed in the early eleventh century, see *Vita sancti Gaugerici episcopi confessoris*, in AASS August, vol. 2, new edn (Paris, 1869), 2.2.43–46, pp. 684–85. For a thorough consideration of the transmission of the Gregorian corpus locally, see in the first place Bruno Judic, "La diffusion de la *Regula pastoralis* de Grégoire le Grand dans l'Église de Cambrai, une première enquête," *Revue du nord* 76 (1994), 207–30, especially pp. 213–19.

[60]   *VL*, c. 60, p. 863; *RP* 2.4, 1:188–89; *Homiliae*, ed. Étaix, pp. 98–99.

so that he might stand in combat in the day of the Lord," Gregory states that to rise up in opposition is to constrain with a free voice of reason any powers acting with depraved reason, while "To stand in combat for the house of Israel in the day of the Lord and to raise up like a wall," is to vindicate innocent believers with the authority of justice against the injustice of perverse men. Raoul incorporates both Ezekiel 13.5 and Gregory's commentary wholesale into the *Vita Lietberti episcopi*, using Count Robert's "tyranny" as the bishop's foil. Lietbert is thus a bishop who acts *viriliter*, embodying John's ideal of the good pastor who lays down his life for his sheep.[61]

Raoul did not find Gregory the Great's pastoral model antithetical to his image of Lietbert. In fact, it is central to it, from the bishop of Cambrai's initial refusal to ascend the episcopal throne—an episode drawn from Gregory's own experience—to the very words he preached. Familiar ideas from Pope Gregory's writing on pontifical office are here: the bishop's attention to the consistency between the hortatory word and personal example, his utility as an exemplar of mores and good Christian conduct, his humble but determined defense of his flock, his power as a preacher, and his willingness to improve by correction (also an Augustinian theme). He blends these with contemporary episcopal virtues celebrating Lietbert's nobility, education, and statesmanship to create a bishop-saint not only capable of navigating the sometimes treacherous waters between *regnum* and *sacerdotium*, but also harmonizing them in action.

For all his concern with the bishop's pastoral sollicitude, the central event of Raoul's *vita*—and perhaps Lietbert's life—was the bishop's withdrawal from Cambrai and his two-year pilgrimage to the Levant. For Raoul, Lietbert's motivation to endure the trials of pilgrimage was best summarized as a profound desire "to embrace and kiss the pathways trod by Jesus's feet."[62] The reality is undoubtedly more complicated. It is probably no coincidence that the bishop's departure followed soon on the heels of a serious political setback in Cambrai. Despite Lietbert's strenuous attempts to keep the castellany of Cambrai out of the hands of John, the advocate of Arras—a layman who, in short order, had usurped the honor from the legitimate heir, blockaded the city to prevent Lietbert's ceremonial first entry as bishop, despoiled the cathedral's treasury, and bedded down with his wife in the episcopal palace—John had scandalously renounced his faith to Count Baldwin V of Flanders and led Henry III's army into the county during the summer of 1054.[63] In exchange for his loyalty and military leadership, Henry restored John as castellan, displacing Lietbert's favored candidate, Hugh d'Oisy, nephew of the legitimate castellan. "Humiliated and distraught," Lietbert resisted. The emperor had him

---

[61] John 10.11; *VL*, c. 60, p. 863: "Libertate nobilis animi sese viriliter ingessit hostibus, auctoritate pontificali redarguit tirannorum rabiem. . . ." Cf. Psalm 31.25.

[62] *VL*, c. 27, p. 853. Little scholarly attention has been turned on Lietbert's pilgrimage; brief mention is given in de Moreau, *Histoire de l'Église en Belgique*, 2:437–38.

[63] The events are recounted in the *GEC* 4.2–14 (3.62–71), pp. 490–94; *VL*, c. 8, p. 846; cc. 14–15, p. 848; c. 28, p. 853 (borrowing largely from the *GEC*), and summarized by Koyen, *De prae-gregoriaanse hervorming te Kamerijk*, pp. 51–57; Kéry, *Errichtung des Bistums Arras*, pp. 237–38.

seized and threatened him with violent expulsion from his see.[64] On the advice of his fellow bishops, Lietbert relented and was freed, but the political damage and personal dishonor had been done. A few months later, as autumn approached, the bishop turned his feet to Jerusalem.

Raoul's report of the events leading to the pilgrimage mentioned nothing of Henry's deal with John, noting only that John went over to the emperor's camp and had nefarious dealings with him.[65] Hinting at the threat of unrest, he described the people's fears about their bishop's departure, painting in vivid color how weeping townsfolk followed the episcopal party a full three miles from town.[66] From there, Raoul's account strikes chords similar to other pilgrimage stories. He detailed the trials of the road, the suspicions of the lords through whose lands they passed, the threat posed by Bulgarian bandits, dream-visions and saintly interventions, and visits to holy shrines. Raoul favored epic prose descriptions of the journey over gritty details, but in all it is a remarkable account, one of the best from the eleventh century.[67] As the companions left behind familiar cities and provinces, Raoul's narrative focused on increasingly alien landscapes and people. The crossing of frontiers—the *extremos fines* and *fines limitaneos* of Hungary and Bulgaria—marked the descent from cultivated to uncultivated lands, from cities to nomadic settlements, from peoples bounded by laws and religious cult to lawless and areligious tribes, animal-like in their behavior and appearance.[68]

---

[64] "Humiliatus igitur et conturbatus episcopus usquequaque, vivificationem petebat a divina miseratione, volens donum suum legitime perfectum inviolabiliter permanere": *GEC* 4.12 (3.69), p. 494.

[65] *VL*, c. 28, p. 853. Raoul then adds: "Cuius rei seriem, quoniam in gestis pontificalibus plenius describitur, omittimus et ad exequendum pontificis iter stilum dirigimus."

[66] *VL*, c. 29 and c. 31, pp. 853–54.

[67] There was nothing particularly novel in the bishop's pilgrimage, although it prefigured by a decade the massive German pilgrimage of 1064, which was led by the bishops of Mainz, Regensburg, Bamberg, and Utrecht; for this pilgrimage, see Einar Joranson, "The Great German Pilgrimage of 1064–1065," in *The Crusades and Other Historical Essays presented to Dana C. Munro by his Former Students*, ed. Louis J. Paetow (New York, 1928), pp. 3–43, and the new study by Hans-Henning Kortüm, "Der Pilgerzug von 1064/65 ins Heilige Land. Eine Studie über Orientalismuskonstruktionen im 11. Jahrhundert," *Historische Zeitschrift* 277 (2003), 561–92. Others who departed for the holy land about this time include Abbot Thierry of Saint-Hubert-en-Ardennes, Bishop Werner of Straßburg, and Benno of Osnabrück; for a summary and sources see Steven Runciman, "The Pilgrimages to Palestine before 1095," in *A History of the Crusades*, vol. 1, *The First Hundred Years*, ed. Marshall W. Baldwin (Madison, WI, 1969), pp. 68–78; Jonathan Riley-Smith, *The First Crusaders, 1095–1131* (Cambridge, 1997), pp. 25–39; Haarländer, *Vitae episcoporum*, p. 276. Bishop Hélinand of Laon, already in the eastern Mediterranean, accompanied Lietbert back to northern France; *VL*, c. 41, p. 858.

[68] "Pretergressus Pannoniorum fines limitaneos ingreditur solitudines saltuosas, quas deserta Bulgariae nominant quasque latrunculi Sciticae gentis inhabitant. Hi degentes more ferarum nullis cohercentur legibus, nullis continentur urbibus. Sub divo manent, quas nox coegerit, sedes habent, pretereuntes obsident, obvios interficiunt, ceteros depredantur. Gregatim vadunt, omnia sua secum portantes cum tota suppellectile, parvulis et uxoribus.

For Raoul, this journey into a decentered world lacking law or religion laid bare Lietbert's virtues. As Lietbert and his party crossed through the "deadly wastes" (*mortiferas solitudines*) of Bulgaria, they encountered wandering bands of "thieving Scythians" and frightened refugees from "barbarian" attacks.[69] His fellow travelers contemplated fleeing with the refugees, but Lietbert calmly plucked words of wisdom from the Bible (which he had been contemplating as he walked) and offered them to his companions. Citing Luke 9.62, he counseled that "no one who puts his hand to the plough and looks back is fit for the kingdom of God."[70] Cheerfully awaiting martyrdom at the brigands' hands, the bishop continued the voyage until he reached Latakia. There, the hardship of overland travel gave way to the monotony of delay. Three months passed while the travelers waited for the political situation to ease and the road to Jerusalem to re-open. The company of pilgrims, save for the bishop and his closest companions, dispersed.[71]

Determined to make the passage by sea, Lietbert finally boarded a vessel and disembarked at Cyprus. There he was delayed another two months, only to have another sailing crew fraudulently return him to Latakia. Dispirited, he at last agreed to return home, almost two years after his departure. Instead of making his devotional offering at Jerusalem, Lietbert made it to St Andrew at the abbey of Cateau-Cambrésis, on the return journey to Cambrai. Although the immediate objective of the bishop's pilgrimage had not been achieved, for Raoul the marvels of the journey and the pilgrims' perseverence furnished evidence of Lietbert's transcendant virtues: his assiduousness in prayer; his devotion to the saints and to Mary; his serene fearlessness in the face of death. As a pilgrim, the bishop was fulfilling the commands of Augustine's *On the true religion*, whose words Raoul put into Lietbert's mouth on the occasion of his first sermon to the people of Cambrai. "Love not the world," the prelate said, "because all around us is the concupiscence of the flesh . . . and worldly ambition. Those who love to depart rather than return shall be sent into more distant places, because they are flesh, a spirit moving and never returning. However, whoever makes good use of the five senses of the body to believe in and preach God's works and cultivate his love (*ad credenda et praedicanda opera dei et nutriendam caritatem ipsius*) . . . in order to pacify his nature and know God, shall enter his Lord's house in joy."[72] As Lietbert traversed frontiers he did not, with Luke's ploughman, look back. But following Augustine's exhortation, he

---

Nullius heresis nominata secta, nullius religionis divino cultu tenentur": *VL*, c. 32 and c. 33, p. 854.

[69]   *VL*, c. 33, p. 854. The pilgrims' meeting of refugees on the road is also a feature of the Annalist of Niederaltaich's account of the German pilgrimage. See Joranson, "Great German Pilgrimage," p. 19.

[70]   *VL*, c. 33, p. 855.

[71]   *VL*, c. 35, p. 855.

[72]   "Non diligamus mundum, quoniam omnia sunt concupiscentia carnis et concupiscentia oculorum et ambitio seculi. Qui enim magis amant ire quam redire, in longinquiora mittendi sunt, quoniam caro sunt et spiritus ambulans and non rediens. Qui vero bene utitur vel ipsis quinque sensibus corporis ad credenda et predicanda opera Dei et nutriendam caritatem ipsius vel actione vel cognitione ad pacificandam naturam suam et cognoscendum Deum, intrat in gaudium domini sui": *VL*, c. 24, p. 851. Compare with Augustine of Hippo, *De vera*

returned and put himself to the task of supporting the city's religious institutions and leading its flock.

Much has been made of pilgrimage as a marker of liminal space and time. On the road, the pilgrim is said to leave behind everyday social and religious structures and enter a physical and mental place where he embraces a more profound and idealized understanding of religious ideas and symbols—he leaves behind the "church" and society, and encounters the symbols of Christian religion and its founder face-to-face.[73] It is doubtful that Raoul quite understood Lietbert's pilgrimage in these terms. True enough, for Raoul the pilgrimage was an event where mundane socio-political preoccupations ceased to exist. Within the narrative framework of the *vita*, the pilgrimage is recounted in strict isolation from political events in Cambrai or the German Empire.[74] But the bishop's passage to the east intensified his already present religious and saintly qualities; it did not create them. The pilgrimage, set off from the other events of the *vita*, showed how Lietbert was at once of the world but fixated beyond it—a good pastor who left his city a pilgrim but returned to lead his people to God. Its inclusion in the *vita* established a thematic counterweight to Raoul's emphasis elsewhere on the ways in which Lietbert balanced the opposing demands and impulses of episcopal administration. The "solstitial harmony" prevailing in Lietbert's life is a harmony born, in part, of refusal: refusal of political ambition, refusal of favoritism, refusal ultimately, as pilgrim, of the world itself.

So far, we have barely touched on the circumstances of the *Vita Lietberti*'s composition, yet Raoul's depiction of the bishop and any interpretation of the text must be weighed in light of the fact that, when he wrote, Cambrai was in the midst of a pitched controversy over the episcopal succession to the see. The death of Bishop Gerard II (1076–1092), Lietbert's successor, brought momentous strife and change to the diocese. As different factions in the town threw their support behind rival candidates, the cathedral chapter of Arras, with comital and papal support, split from the diocese of Cambrai in 1094. Arras took with it two of Cambrai's archdeaconries and spiritual oversight of a number of important religious houses, including Anchin, Arrouaise, Mont-Saint-Eloi, and Saint-Vaast.[75] In the disputed election at Cambrai, Manasses, a canon of Soissons, was nominated in 1093 but rejected by Henry IV. Favored (though not always consistently) by Urban II, he acted as bishop until 1103. His claim was countered by the long-time archdeacon of Brabant, Gaucher, who was elected after Henry's refusal of Manasses. He received the emperor's blessing, and

---

religione liber unus, ed. K.-D. Daur, CCSL 32 (Turnhout, 1962), 54.105–6, p. 255; trans. J.H.S. Burleigh, *Of True Religion* (Chicago, 1959).

[73]   Victor Turner and Edith L.B. Turner, *Image and Pilgrimage in Christian Culture: Anthropological Perspectives*, Lectures on the History of Religions, n.s., 11 (New York, 1978), chapter one.

[74]   *VL*, c. 28, p. 853; c. 42, p. 858; c. 44, p. 859. At some point after summer 1054, Henry III restored the castellany to Hugh d'Oisy and his descendents. Soon after re-entering his see, raw political controversy with the castellan of Cambrai confronted the bishop. Although the exact chronological sequence of the affair is hazy, in Lietbert's absence Hugh had imprisoned the bishop's chamberlain and made off with his goods.

[75]   For this and what follows, see the thorough account by Kéry, *Errichtung des Bistums Arras*, pp. 353–412.

was finally consecrated in 1095. Gaucher exercised episcopal functions intermittently in the diocese from 1095 until 1107, despite his deposition and excommunication in 1095 and again in 1106. In support of their candidates, two archbishops of Reims, Popes Urban II and Paschal II, Count Robert II of Flanders, and two German emperors waged campaigns of propaganda, spiritual warfare, and military aggression. The city of Cambrai was caught in the middle, and the devastation there was particularly severe between late 1101 and 1103, when Robert II and Henry IV launched a series of military expeditions across the region. Seeking to broker their own deals and treaties with the parties in conflict, the citizens of Cambrai established an autonomous commune which played all sides of the dispute—now treating with Gaucher, now the emperor, now the Count of Flanders—until it was suppressed by Henry V in 1107.[76] The succession dispute was largely concluded in 1109, after Henry V had enfeoffed Robert II with the castellany of Cambrai and Gaucher had renounced his claim to the see, but full resolution remained elusive for many years.[77] Seen against this background, the Lietbert of Raoul's *vita* glows with an aura of mass appeal: as a man loved by two monarchs and the archbishop of Reims, as a doting shepherd to his flock, a pacifier of tyrants, and as a builder of the city.

Because we know so little about Raoul, the early development of his abbey of Saint-Sépulchre, or the immediate reception of the *vita* of Lietbert, however, determining Raoul's intention for the biography beyond general surmises is tenuous. The written memory of Lietbert in the *gesta* and *vita* certainly would have held appeal for urban commercial elites. The *gesta* acclaim the prelate for restoring peace to the city after the military campaigns and sedition of 1054, and describe in some detail how Lietbert excommunicated the castellan Hugh d'Oisy for unjustly afflicting the "better and wealthier" residents of the city with imprisonment and injuries.[78] As bishop, Lietbert led the people of Cambrai against one of Hugh's castles, a collaborative endeavor in the mutual interest of townspeople and bishop that was echoed by similar ventures at various times in the later eleventh and twelfth centuries.[79] More broadly, however, Raoul of Saint-Sépulchre extols Lietbert as a defender of liberty. As we have seen,

---

[76]   Full accounts in Hoeres, *Das Bistum Cambrai*, pp. 20–25; Cauchie, *La querelle des investitures*, 2:122–205; Reinecke, *Geschichte der Stadt Cambrai*, pp. 110–18; Kéry, *Errichtung des Bistums Arras*, pp. 301–6.

[77]   Bruwier, "Le Hainaut," p. 214; Kéry, *Errichtung des Bistums Arras*, pp. 413–17; Resnick, "Odo of Cambrai," pp. 93–96.

[78]   "Cives namque meliores et ditiores contumelia et iniuriis afficiebat, alios indempnatos et iniudicatos in cippo vilissimo concludens, et inter dedecora plurima barbam aliis evellens": *GEC* 4.15 (3.71), p. 494, and 4.18 (3.72), p. 495.

[79]   "Quod [devastation] etiam episcopus moleste accepit, copiosamque armatorum multitudinem ad locum illum deduxit; fuissetque continuo municipium illud solotenus subversum, nisi Rotbertus de Perrona cum suis dolo obstitisset, qui venerat in pontificis auxilium. His ita incassum decursis, Cameracenses infecto negotio ad civitatem suam sunt reversi": *GEC* 4.19 (3.73), p. 495. Bishop Burchard (1116–1130) and the *cives* of Cambrai joined forces to attack Hugh II d'Oisy, and Bishop Nicholas of Mons (1136–1167) teamed with the townspeople to combat the castellan again in 1153. For these episodes, see *GEC Cont.*, p. 214, and the *Annales Cameracenses* of Lambert of Waterloo, ed. Georg Pertz, MGH SS 16 (Leipzig, 1925), pp. 526–29; Platelle, "Les luttes communales," pp. 49–50.

he elaborated in some detail on Lietbert's confrontation with Robert I of Flanders and his seige army, which decamped outside the city, perhaps in 1076. In a typical play on words with the bishop's name and his protection of the city's *libertas*, Raoul writes: "those who had come armed in the fury of war, departed chastened by divine fear. The city, thus liberated (*ita liberata civitas*) from the terror of siege by the striving of its bishop, gave thanks to God and to his glorious mother."[80] Elsewhere, the bishop is *libertas patriae, libertas publica, libertas reipublicae.*[81] Even his images, Raoul says, were inscribed with the motto "Lietbertus publica libertas." For Raoul, "liberty" embodied a double meaning. Materially, it meant freedom from oppression by outsiders like the counts of Flanders. Spiritually—here, the monk of Saint-Sépulchre turned for inspiration to Augustine's *De vera religione*—liberty meant freedom from the love of mutable things.[82]

Raoul's use of such epithets and the themes of harmony, mass appeal, and worldly transcendance evoked throughout the *Vita Lietberti* furnish an image of a bishop revered not for his embrace of any one political or religious agenda, but for his embodiment of a particularly Cambrésien socio-political and religious identity—an identity both favorable to engagement (on its own terms) with outside ideas and political forces and contemptuous of them. In a city at the intersection of various cultural, political, and linguistic borders, suspicion of interference from external agents is commonly found in its eleventh- and twelfth-century histories. For example, Bishop Gerard I's well-known refusal to extend the Peace of God within his diocese stemmed from the incommensurability of the new practices and philosophy of a bishop-led peace—which was first propagated in northern France by bishops of Franco-Burgundian origin—with the imperial overlordship of the diocese of Cambrai.[83] In continuations of the episcopal *gesta*, Cambrésian bishops originating from outside the region are also often the subject of derision or slurs. The Saxon descent of Bishop Berengar (956–958) contributed to the later characterization in the *Gesta episcoporum Cameracensium* that he "seemed to his people to be a barbarian in his speech, descent, and mores," while Tetdo (972–978), also a Saxon, was forced from the city by vassals hostile to him who villified his origin.[84] Local scorn for the

---

[80]   "[Q]ui venerant armati furore bellico, recedebant gratificati timore divino. Ita liberata civitas ab obsidionis terrore studio sui pontificis laudes refert Deo suaeque gloriosae genitrici": *VL*, c. 59, p. 863.

[81]   *VL*, c. 3, p. 844; c. 9, p. 846; c. 22, p. 850; c. 60, pp. 863–64.

[82]   *VL*, c. 25, p. 852, quoting from Augustine, *De vera religione liber unus*, ed. Daur, 48.93: "Et quoniam delectabat libertas, quam nomine et opere praeferebat, ab amore mutabilium rerum liber esse appetebat."

[83]   *GEC* 3.27, p. 474. On the diffusion of the Peace of God in northern France, see Egied I. Strubbe, "La paix de Dieu dans le nord de la France," *Recueils de la Société Jean Bodin pour l'histoire comparative des institutions* 14/1 (1961), 489–501, at p. 497, and above all Hans-Werner Goetz, "La paix de Dieu en France autour de l'an Mil: Fondements et objectifs, diffusion et participants," in *Le roi de France et son royaume*, ed. Parisse and Barral i Altet, pp. 131–45, at pp. 137, 140.

[84]   On Berengar, see *GEC* 1.80, p. 431: "Hic etiam tantae feritatis extitisse dicitur, ut non modo lingua et natione, sed etiam moribus populo suo barbarus esse videretur." On mockery of Tetdo's ignorance of French by his men, see *GEC* 1.99, p. 441.

imperial bishop Lietard (1131–1135) drips from the continuation of his deeds, written following his suspension and deposition in 1135. He is denounced for having "loved foreigners like sons; / Germans were his intimates, / beardless youths and smooth young boys."[85] Conversely, two pro-imperial, twelfth-century accounts describing the election of Manasses of Soissons to the see in 1093 qualify him disparagingly as "francigena."[86] Not surprisingly, hostility toward invading powers, especially, as we have seen, the Flemish counts, is recurrent in the same texts.

A local identity predicated on disdain for the involvement by powerful outsiders in regional affairs often inheres in regions that constitute political borders.[87] Clergy and bishops from Gaucher to Burchard (1116–1130), for example, reacted angrily to the reconstitution of an independent diocese of Arras from Cambrai's diocesan territories.[88] Yet this hostility did not preclude an openness to alliances with external powers who had a stake in the city and diocese. There was no fortified or absolute line separating Flanders, the German Empire, or France in the early twelfth century; the Cambrésis and surrounding regions constituted a zone of interaction among polities and cultures, rather than exclusion. Consequently, the townspeople, clergy, and bishops coupled and uncoupled with secular powers as they negotiated changing political winds—this is immediately obvious from a reading of the continuations of the *gesta* composed in the wake of the succession dispute of 1093–1107.[89] If common Cambrésiens embraced a particular orthodoxy, it was that of political self-

---

[85] "Quos enim debebat amare oderat, / suum servitium pati non poterat; / expellit proximos, fugat domesticos / atque extraneos amat ut filios; / suique privati sunt Teutonici, / imberbes iuvenes et lenes pueri": *GEC Cont.*, strophes 16–18, p. 224.

[86] "Quidam tandem francigena, / cui Manasses onoma, / electus est per iurgia, / non per iura canonica": *GEC Cont.*, strophe 32, p. 187. The hostile *Gesta Manassis et Walcheri*, ed. L.C. Bethmann, MGH SS 7 (Hannover, 1846), p. 500, composed in 1180, and the 1191 *Gesta pontificum abbreviata per canonicum Cameracensem*, in idem, p. 504, show the persistence of this characterization. While Cauchie, *La querelle des investitures*, 2:119 n. 2, 123, 123 n. 3, seeks to downplay usage of this adjective by contemporary authors, favoring a view of the hostilities around 1093 as pitting Gregorian against anti-Gregorian camps, there is no question that *francigena* was used to identify Manasses by his own regional and kin-based affiliations and power bases.

[87] For recent treatment of the particularity of border regions and their inhabitants' identities, see Peter Sahlins, *Boundaries: The Making of France and Spain in the Pyrenees* (Berkeley, CA, 1989), pp. 103–23; Daniel Power and Naomi Standen, "Introduction," in *Frontiers in Question: Eurasian Borderlands, 700–1700*, ed. Daniel Power and Naomi Standen (New York, 1999), pp. 11–12, 21–22, and, in the same volume, Daniel Power, "French and Norman Frontiers in the Central Middle Ages," pp. 105–27, esp. at pp. 106–9. More recently, the issue has been revisited in the essays in David Abulafia and Nora Berend eds, *Medieval Frontiers: Concepts and Practices* (Aldershot, 2002); see the Preface, p. xi. Léopold Genicot, "Ligne et zone: La frontière des principautés médiévales," in idem, *Études sur les principautés lotharingiennes*, Université de Louvain, Recueil de Travaux d'Histoire et de Philologie, 6th ser., fasc. 7 (Louvain, 1975), pp. 172–85, is also useful.

[88] Burchard was still lobbying for the repatriation of Arras at the Lateran Council in 1123; *Chronicon* 3.34, p. 547.

[89] *GEC Cont.*, passim. See also Hoeres, *Das Bistum Cambrai*; Reinecke, *Geschichte der Stadt Cambrai*, pp. 118–32.

determination. The precocious erection of a commune in 1077, the first in either Francia or Flanders, furnishes evidence of this.[90] To an extent, this sentiment was shared by the secular and regular clergy of the region. In addition to the various legations dispatched to Reims and Rome to lobby against the dissolution of Arras from Cambrai and in favor of Gaucher in 1093 and 1095, local writers were at the very least ambivalent about, if not openly hostile to, the intervention of papal authority in local affairs and any imbalance in the carefully calibrated relationship of *regnum* and *sacerdotium*.

Of this ambivalence, the author of the *Chronicon sancti Andreae Cameracesii* furnishes a prime example. The abbey of Saint-André of Cateau-Cambrésis was an episcopal foundation, closely attached to the memories and largesse of bishops Gerard I and Lietbert.[91] The *Chronicon*'s anonymous author had also accompanied Gaucher to Clermont to defend his succession to the see.[92] As he was writing his chronicle in 1133, he frequently looked back with regret on the years of discord which the decisions of Gregory VII and Urban II had introduced in the region. Referring to Gregory VII by his birth name, Hildebrand—an obvious indication of his scorn—he dutifully listed the pope's programs to end clerical incontinence and lay investiture of clerical dignities.[93] These initiatives, he said, not only sparked a *grandis contentio* between the pope and German emperor, but pitched the church into a serious scandal everywhere in the world.[94] Of that "wisest of men" Odo, the future Urban II, the author of the *Chronicon* had more generous things to say, though as pope he followed in his predecessor's footsteps.[95] The author remarks with resignation that it would be "useless" and "superfluous" to describe how, after Urban deposed Gaucher at Clermont and overturned his lawful election, "the homeland (*patria*) of Cambrai was utterly devastated and the city left nearly desolate."[96] Such was the unfair outcome

---

[90]   The commune is said by the continuator of the deeds of Gerard II to have been "diu desideratam." It may be a testament to the friendly relations between Lietbert and the townspeople that a commune was not essayed earlier. For (hostile) accounts of the commune's foundation, see the *Gesta Gerardi II episcopi*, c. 2, p. 498, in the *GEC*, and *Chronicon* 3.2, p. 540. A general summary is furnished by Albert Vermeesch, *Essai sur les origines et la signification de la commune dans le nord de la France (XIe et XIIe siècles)* (Heule, 1966), pp. 88–98. For reasons too detailed to explain here, I do not consider the sworn conspiracy of Le Mans in 1070 to have been a commune.

[91]   *Chronicon* 1.19–20, p. 530; 2.31, p. 537; 2.34, pp. 538–39.

[92]   *Chronicon* 3.19, p. 544.

[93]   The author qualifies him as *Hildebrandus papa Romanae sedi*; *Chronicon* 2.36, p. 539, and 3.11, p. 542.

[94]   "Qua de re non solum inter eum et imperatorem grandis exorta est contentio, verum etiam per orbem exinde grave scandalum sancta pertulit ecclesia. Quae controversia usque ad tempora Calixti papae post eum quarti permansit": *Chronicon* 2.36, p. 539. Compare with 3.27, p. 545, referring to affairs between Calixtus II and Henry V: "Quid seditionis, quid perturbationis, quae divisio regni ac sacerdotii tunc fuerit Romae, quod nemo potest, non est nostrum explicare."

[95]   "Odo, qui et Urbanus, in Romana sede successit, vir sapientissimus": *Chronicon* 3.11, p. 542.

[96]   "Multa de ipso concilio, plura quae de ipsis postea contigerunt, et quomodo eorum Cameracensis patria omnino devastata et civitas pene fuerit desolata, quamvis sint stupenda,

for Gaucher, who as bishop had "brought justice to those seeking it and pacified the entire province from the doings of its enemies." Much harsher anti-Urban sentiments were still being aired at Cambrai a half-century later.[97]

In light of this, it is unsurprising that, despite devoting much of the second book of his *Chronicon* to Lietbert's episcopacy, to which he added all new material on Lietbert's patronage of his abbey, the chronicler of Saint-André establishes no connection between the bishop and Gregory VII.[98] He does narrate, following the main lines of Raoul's *vita*, Lietbert's election *pari consensu* of the people and clergy of Cambrai, his elevation by Henry III and his consecration by the archbishop of Reims.[99] He omits any hint of controversy surrounding Lietbert's election or investiture, saying obliquely: "he [the emperor] gave the gift [of the bishopric? of the city?] to the bishop."[100] Beyond a fleeting suggestion that Lietbert attended Henry III's war campaign into Flanders in 1054, the chronicler makes no further mention of the bishop's involvement with the German emperors.[101] Indeed, he devotes the majority of his description of Lietbert's episcopacy to the pilgrimage, which was of special interest owing to the visions of St Andrew experienced by one of the bishop's companions, and his subsequent monastic foundations and reforms. Such was the image of the bishop deemed worth perpetuating in 1133.

Thus to the anonymous chroniclers of his episcopal *gesta*, to the monk of Saint-André, and to Raoul of Saint-Sépulchre, Lietbert was ideologically neither an "imperial" bishop nor a "Gregorian." Similarly, Raoul's *vita* does not neatly conform to the generic literary category of imperial episcopal biography. While such descriptive categories are essential to the work of modern historians still engaged in the task of assessing and classifying a wide range of texts and sources, it is clear from the example of Lietbert that they are of limited applicability or utility for understanding the political, ideological, and cultural dynamics of a *Grenzprovinz* such as Cambrai. Indeed, we should question their usefulness at all outside the narrow intellectual circles surrounding the pope and emperor.

---

preterimus, qui iam amplius haec rememorari superfluum esse et inutile ducimus": *Chronicon* 3.19, p. 544. Note that the Chronicon's use of *patria* to describe the diocese of Cambrai bears a strong affinity with the word's frequent usage in the *Vita Lietberti episcopi*. The author further laments that after Gerard II's death in 1092, the world seemed to devolve from a silver age to an age of iron ("sub quo iam ad argentea, et post eius obitum ad ferrea saecula nos devolutos esse graviter sentimus"): prologue to book three, p. 539.

97   ". . . iustitiam quaerentibus faciens, omnem provinciam subactis hostibus pacificavit": *Chronicon* 3.18, p. 544. The author of the 1180 continuation of the *Gesta Manassis et Walcheri* is withering in his criticism of Manasses of Soissons, whom he accuses of openly bribing Urban II, and of Urban himself: cc. 7–9, pp. 502–3.

98   *Chronicon* 2.13–16, pp. 533–34; 2.21–31, pp. 535–37; 2.34–35, pp. 538–39; and 2.37, p. 539. His notice of Gregory's election is followed by the obituaries of Gervais of Reims and Lietbert, but their proximity within the text is not used to show any further affinity between the pope and the bishop of Cambrai.

99   *Chronicon* 2.13, p. 533.

100   *Chronicon* 2.13, p. 533: "donum episcopii largitus est." He thus charts a vague middle ground between the accounts of the *gesta* and the *vita*.

101   *Chronicon* 2.21, p. 535.

Of course, like his predecessors generations before, Bishop Lietbert owed service to the German emperors, and attended their courts. He routinely dated his charters by imperial regnal years and occasionally by comital years (but never employed papal regnal years).[102] He also attended the French court and mingled, at least twice, with his fellow bishops of the archdiocese of Reims. He founded or reformed the religious houses of Mont-Saint-Eloi, Sainte-Croix, Saint-Sépulchre, and Saint-Aubert of Cambrai. He collaborated with Baldwin VI of Flanders to reform the abbey of Saint-Pierre of Hasnon.[103] He resisted the ambitious designs of John of Arras, Hugh I d'Oisy, and Count Robert I of Flanders. In sum, Lietbert, like his predecessors, negotiated the competing and frequently antagonistic political and religious forces that swirled about his border diocese.

Raoul would transform these political necessities, made patently obvious by the succession dispute of 1093–1107, into saintly virtues. With Lietbert, Raoul developed an image of episcopal sanctity in which the bishop, because of his mass appeal to secular and religious authorities, remained insulated from the political agendas of the day. He was foremost a pastor who would "rise up in opposition, standing like a wall of the house of Israel, which is the church committed to him," to lead his flock by word and deed.[104] A saint Lietbert, who embodied the complementary traits of action and contemplation found in Mary and Martha, held out the hope of a return to the solstitial harmony between *regnum* and *sacerdotium* of days long past. This was an ideal that even in 1133, a decade after the Concordat of Worms, remained elusive.

---

[102]   As Erik Van Mingroot's new edition of the episcopal charters for Cambrai, *Les chartes de Gérard Ier, Liébert et Gérard II, évêques de Cambrai et d'Arras, comtes du Cambrésis (1012–1092/93)* (Louvain, 2005), appeared too late for me to make full use of it, I have come to this conclusion by relying upon existing editions of Lietbert's charters in M. Gysseling and A.C.F. Koch eds, *Diplomata Belgica ante annum millesimum centesimum scripta*, vol. 1 (Brussels, 1950); Duvivier ed., *Actes et documents anciens intéressant la Belgique* (above, n. 30); the notices in Alphonse Wauters ed., *Table chronologique des chartes et diplômes imprimés concernant l'histoire de la Belgique*, vol. 1, *275–1100* (Brussels, 1866); and charters from Cambrésien cartularies (though cartulary copies are not always reliable about furnishing regnal dates). Using the catalogue of Erik Van Mingroot, "Liste provisoire des actes des évêques de Cambrai," pp. 17–19, I have confirmed the dating style for fifteen of Lietbert's twenty extant *acta*. Dating of charters by papal regnal years only begins to appear under Bishop Gerard II (1076–1092), and then only sporadically.

[103]   Prou ed., *Recueil des actes de Philippe Ier*, no. 22, pp. 59–63 (1065 after 4 August).

[104]   "Ascendit ex adverso, opponens se murum pro domo Israel, hoc est ecclesia sibi commissa, ut posset stare in prelio in die Domini": *VL*, c. 60, p. 854. See Ezekiel 13.5 (above, nn. 58–59).

Chapter 9

Driving the Chariot of the Lord: Siegfried I of Mainz (1060–1084) and Episcopal Identity in an Age of Transition

John Eldevik
Pomona College

Although his episcopacy is well documented in a number of sources, Siegfried I of Mainz (1060–1084) remains one of the more enigmatic figures in German politics in the latter half of the eleventh century. His career has been assessed variously as a mixture of traditional episcopal conservatism, ambitious reformism, striking ineptitude, calculated partisanship, and deep, if quirky, piety.[1] A former abbot of Fulda, he rose to the episcopacy in 1060 during the regency of Henry IV under the Empress Agnes, joined the ill-fated pilgrimage of the German bishops to Jerusalem in 1064, attempted on at least one occasion to abdicate and enter the monastery of Cluny, supported Henry IV in calling for the resignation of Gregory VII at Worms in 1076, but then threw his support the following year behind Rudolf of Swabia and the anti-Henrician insurgency. While doing all this, he also promoted monastic and clerical reform, fought to recoup diocesan tithes in Thuringia and from the monks of Fulda and Hersfeld, and engaged in a bitter dispute with Gregory VII over his rights as a metropolitan to decide a dispute between two Bohemian bishops. This essay will examine three key aspects of his tenure as archbishop and their conceptual

---

[1] Some of the more recent treatments of Siegfried's episcopacy, generally without clear consensus about his qualities or legacy, include: Franz Staab, "Reform und Reformgruppen im Erzbistum Mainz. Vom 'Libellus de Willigisi consuetudinibus' zur 'Vita domnae Juttae inclusae,'" in *Reformidee und Reformpolitik im spätsalisch-frühstaufischen Reich: Vorträge der Tagung der Gesellschaft für Mittelrheinische Kirchengeschichte vom 11. bis 13. September 1991 in Trier*, ed. Stefan Weinfurter (Mainz, 1992), pp. 119–87; idem, "Die Mainzer Kirche. Konzeption und Verwirklichung in der Bonifatius- und Theonesttradition," in *Die Salier und das Reich*, ed. Stefan Weinfurter, 3 vols (Sigmaringen, 1992), 2:31–63; Rainer Rudolph, "Erzbischof Siegfried von Mainz (1060–1084). Ein Beitrag zur Geschichte der Mainzer Erzbischöfe im Investiturstreit" (Ph.D. diss., Erlangen, 1973); Heinz Thomas, "Erzbischof Siegfried von Mainz und die Tradition seiner Kirche: Ein Beitrag zur Wahl Rudolfs von Rheinfelden," *Deutsches Archiv* 26 (1970), 368–99; Heinrich Büttner, "Das Erzstift Mainz und die Klosterreform im 11. Jahrhundert," *Archiv für mittelrheinische Kirchengeschichte* 1 (1949), 30–64.

interrelationship: his reform of monasteries and churches in the diocese of Mainz; his attempt to restore diocesan tithes in Thuringia; and his patronage of historiographical projects. In doing so, I hope to bring some of the complexities of "ecclesiastical reform" during this period into sharper relief and contrast local and episcopal visions of reform with that of the Roman papacy in the mid-eleventh century.

Scholars have generally evaluated the role of German bishops during the Investiture Controversy, and within the Gregorian reform movement more broadly, by plotting a particular prelate's position along a continuum of either papal or imperial partisanship. This approach has underscored the fact that most bishops, even those strongly allied with one side or another (like Adalbero of Würzburg, a prominent papal ally), often occupied a political middle ground between the papacy and the king.[2] Stories about bishops like Benno II of Osnabrück, who, according to his biographer, secreted himself inside an altar at the Synod of Brixen in 1080 to avoid appearing disloyal to either the pope or the emperor, are well known, but are really only one part of a more complex dynamic.[3] Even Wibert of Ravenna, appointed by Henry IV to replace Gregory VII at that same synod, is now seen as having forged his own identity and agenda within the anti-Gregorian movement.[4] If a particular bishop can be said to have maneuvered "between" the papacy and the empire in some way, or created a sphere of political independence, what does this really mean? I suggest that we can construe the intermediary position negotiated by many bishops as more than just strategic triangulation. This position constituted a coherent vision of episcopal power that deserves closer examination and elaboration. At the same time, it also points toward a different way of conceptualizing the conflicts and debates about ecclesiastical and clerical reform in the eleventh century. The career of Siegfried of Mainz can serve as a case study for examining these issues, and understanding in particular the way in which a German prelate in the later eleventh century attempted to negotiate his power in a world where those traditional notions of episcopal identity, and the episcopal church overall, were coming under increased scrutiny from both the papacy and the German monarchy.

---

[2]   Giuseppi Albertoni, "*In loco horrido et asperrimo*: La sede vescovile de Bressanone tra Papa e Impero," in *Stadt und Hochstift: Brixen, Bruneck und Klausen bis zur Säkularisation 1803/Città e principato: Bressanone, Brunico e Chiusa fino alla secolarizzazione 1803*, ed. Helmut Flachenecker, Hans Heiss, and Hannes Obermair, Veröffentlichungen des Südtiroler Landesarchivs 12 (Bozen, 2000), pp. 115–29; Werner Goez, "Rainald von Como (1061–1084): Ein Bischof des elften Jahrhunderts zwischen Kurie und Krone," in *Historische Forschungen für Walter Schlesinger*, ed. Helmut Beumann (Cologne, 1974), pp. 462–95; Alfred Wendehorst, "Bischof Adalbero von Würzburg (1045–1090) zwischen Papst und Kaiser," *Studi gregoriani* 6 (Rome, 1959–1961), 147–64.

[3]   "Videns enim in utraque parte plurima magis odio quam ratione tractari et regi semper fidelis, nunquam autem papae inobediens esse desiderans, sed et, quem tanta res finem habitura esset, ignorans, diligentissime intendere coepit, quonam rationis exitu fieri posset, ut salva honestatis pristinae integritate neutra in parte posset iure culpari": Norbert of Iburg, *Vita Bennonis II. episcopi Osnabrugensis*, ed. Harry Bresslau, MGH SS rer. Germ. 56 (Hannover, 1902), c. 18, p. 24.

[4]   Jürgen Ziese, *Wibert von Ravenna, der Gegenpapst Clemens III (1084–1100)*, Päpste und Papsttum 20 (Stuttgart, 1982).

One problem with the traditional triangulation model is that it directs our gaze mainly toward the bishop's high-level political relationships, which, while obviously important, were only one part of the picture. Another is that it rests on a conceptual binary—papal reformers versus imperial anti-reformers—which appears less and less viable as historians since the 1980s have problematized, or even abandoned, the old model of the imperial church system as well as that of a single, unified reform movement directed from Rome in the eleventh century.[5] In situating themselves within complex interleaving and overlapping registers of authority and power, bishops occupied a position in medieval society which combined command over land and people with the pastoral prerogatives and spiritual dignity of their office. This did not necessarily mean a kind of "middle-of-the-road" strategy as implied by the triangulation view noted above, but a sense of preserving justice and defending certain ethical, moral, and political prerogatives that were different from those of secular rulers, as well as the cloistered religious. Sean Gilsdorf has recently shown how this conception of episcopal authority is reflected in the mediatory and intercessory functions performed by early medieval bishops.[6] Within an episcopal church regime, bishops constituted important poles and conduits of influence and power, and, as Gilsdorf demonstrates, were uniquely imbued with the authority to serve as go-betweens and facilitators of conflict resolution and mediation. Burchard of Worms, for example, not only produced an exhaustive compendium of canon law for the pastoral administration of his diocese—the *Decretum*—but also issued detailed regulations for the management of the episcopal *familia*, or network of dependents under his lordship.[7] C. Stephen Jaeger's work has also reminded us how bishops were mediators of culture, taste, and manners in aristocratic society, critiquing and admonishing royal behavior as well as producing literature and interpretive texts

---

[5] The classic critique of the traditional model of the imperial church is Timothy Reuter, "The 'Imperial Church System' of the Ottonian and Salian Rulers: A Reconsideration," *Journal of Ecclesiastical History* 33 (1982), 347–74, but see as well Giuseppi Sergi, "Poteri temporali del vescovo: Il problema storiografico," in *Vescovo e città nell'alto medioevo: Quadri generali e realtà Toscane. Convegno internazionale di studi, Pistoia, 16–17 maggio 1998*, ed. Giampaolo Francesconi (Pistoia, 2001), pp. 1–16; Harald Zimmerman, "Die 'gregorianische Reform' in deutschen Landen," *Studi gregoriani* 13 (Rome, 1989), 263–79; Hans Hubert Anton, "Frühe Stufen der Kirchenreform: Tendenzen und Wertungen," in *Sant'Anselmo, Mantova e la lotta per le investiture: Atti del Convegno internazionale di studi (Mantova, 23–24–25 maggio 1986)*, ed. Paolo Golinelli (Bologna, 1987), pp. 241–68; Gerd Tellenbach, "'Gregorianische Reform': Kritische Besinnungen," in *Reich und Kirche vor dem Investiturstreit: Vorträge beim wissenschaftlichen Kolloquium aus Anlaß des achtzigsten Geburtstags von Gerd Tellenbach*, ed. Karl Schmid (Sigmaringen, 1985), pp. 99–113; Ovidio Capitani, "Esiste un' 'età gregoriana'? Considerazione sulle tendenze di una storiografia medievistica," *Rivista di storia e letteratura religiosa* 1 (1965), 454–81.

[6] Sean Gilsdorf, "Bishops in the Middle: Mediatory Politics and the Episcopacy," in *The Bishop: Power and Piety at the First Millennium*, ed. Sean Gilsdorf, Neue Aspekte der europäischen Mittelalterforschung 4 (Münster, 2004), pp. 51–73.

[7] Gerhard Theuerkauf, "Burchard von Worms und die Rechtskunde seiner Zeit," *Frühmittelalterliche Studien* 2 (1968), 144–61. See, too, now Greta Austin, "Jurisprudence in the Service of Pastoral Care: The *Decretum* of Burchard of Worms," *Speculum* 79 (2004), 929–59, and her article in this volume.

that reflected on principles of order and justice in royal rule.[8] The recent work of Ernst-Dieter Hehl echoes a similar theme. In a seminal article on "the stubborn bishop," Hehl pointed out that many bishops viewed themselves as counterbalances to imperial power, rather than simply part of it, and, even as imperial appointees, eagerly defended narrower diocesan interests against the crown.[9]

These observations make pigeonholing a prelate like Siegfried a complicated task, particularly in the context of the issues which typically frame the study of the Investiture Controversy and the ecclesiastical reform movements of the eleventh century. In the historiographical din created by the clash of *regnum* and *sacerdotium*, we have tended to miss the less explicit strategies employed by German bishops like Siegfried to negotiate the dispute not as a concrete partisan of one side or another, but as a regional lord and bishop determined to define and assert the integrity of his office and diocese. From an episcopal perspective, this included not only the restructuring of clerical and pastoral institutions in order to have them conform to an ordered system more amenable to episcopal control, but also a reorientation of legal and historical consciousness that attempted to produce—or reproduce, as the case may be—a coherent sense of community centered on the bishop, the diocesan church, and its prerogatives. This required the bishop to find ways to direct both clergy and public toward proper ways of remembering and understanding episcopal power.[10] Ecclesiastical reform fits into this broader pattern of re-imagining the present in terms of an idealized past, though less attention has been paid to bishops

---

[8]   In addition to C. Stephen Jaeger, *The Envy of Angels: Cathedral Schools and Social Ideals in Medieval Europe, 950–1200* (Philadelphia, 1994), esp. chapter three, see, too, his earlier article on episcopal "manners" and emerging ideas of courtliness in the eleventh century, "The Courtier Bishop in *Vitae* from the Tenth to the Twelfth Century," *Speculum* 58 (1983), 291–325.

[9]   Ernst-Dieter Hehl, "Der widerspenstige Bischof: Bischöfliche Zustimmung und bischöflicher Protest in der ottonischen Reichskirche," in *Herrschaftsrepräsentation im ottonischen Sachsen*, ed. Gerd Althoff and Ernst Schubert, Vorträge und Forschungen 46 (Sigmaringen, 1998), pp. 295–344.

[10]   As Stephanie Coué demonstrated in her survey of episcopal hagiography in the Salian period, this most often took the form of publishing biographies of certain previous bishops whose past deeds and achievements anchored new claims in the present; see her *Hagiographie im Kontext: Schreibanlaß und Funktion von Bischofsviten aus dem 11. und vom Anfang des 12. Jahrhunderts*, Arbeiten zur Frühmittelalterforschung 24 (Berlin, 1997). But it could also be expressed in the creation of new liturgical and memorial spaces within a town that articulated revised understandings of power and status, as Jean-Charles Picard shows in *Le souvenir des évêques: Sépultures, listes épiscopales et culte des évêques en Italie du Nord des origines au Xe siècle*, Bibliothèque des Écoles françaises d'Athènes et de Rome 268 (Rome, 1988), along with John S. Ott, "Urban Space, Memory, and Episcopal Authority: The Bishops of Amiens in Peace and Conflict, 1073–1164," *Viator* 31 (2000), 43–77, and especially Maureen C. Miller, *The Bishop's Palace: Architecture and Authority in Medieval Italy* (Ithaca, NY, 2000). Patrick Geary's work has underscored how individuals and institutions in the eleventh century were particularly concerned with re-remembering the past, searching for strategies of imbuing the past with new meanings in order to legitimate themselves in the midst of rapid social and political change. See his *Phantoms of Remembrance: Memory and Oblivion at the End of the First Millennium* (Princeton, NJ, 1994), esp. pp. 7–9.

and local institutions in this regard than to the papacy and the *Streitschriften* of the Investiture Controversy.[11] The episcopacy and its public functions and powers all served as sites of memory and history which bishops could use to frame political and social ideals. Siegfried made ample use of historical tradition, but also of public forums like regional church synods, to shape the meaning of episcopal authority.

Sources: Problems and Possibilities

A main focal point for the study of episcopal memory and historical consciousness has traditionally been the episcopal *vita* or *gesta*. Stephanie Haarländer noted in her recent analysis of episcopal *vitae*, however, that only six percent of all prelates in the German kingdom between the tenth and twelfth centuries became the subject of a biography or *vita*.[12] Siegfried of Mainz belongs to those remaining ninety-four percent for whom no narrative account dedicated uniquely to him survives. Often hagiographic or biographic material sheds critical light on how either contemporaries or some successor wished to portray a particular bishop and shape his legacy. In Siegfried's case, historians are fortunate in that while a convenient *vita* for his episcopacy has not survived, we do have access to a number of his own writings preserved in the *Codex Udalrici*, a letter collection compiled by the eponymous canon of the cathedral of Bamberg in the mid-twelfth century and intended for use as a kind of formulary, or set of exemplary stylistic pieces, for the famous school there.[13] Udalrich evidently had access to the archive of the Mainz bishops, as well as those of several other dioceses and courts, and made thorough use of many of

---

[11]   See especially Jürgen Ziese, *Historische Beweisführung in Streitschriften des Investiturstreites*, Münchener Beiträge zur Mediävistik und Renaissanceforschung 8 (Munich, 1972), as well as Gerhard Dilcher, "Zeitbewusstsein und Geschichtlichkeit im Bereich hochmittelalterlicher Rechtsgewohnheit," in *Hochmittelalterliches Geschichtsbewußtsein im Spiegel nichthistoriographischer Quellen*, ed. Hans-Werner Goetz (Berlin, 1998), pp. 331–54; Hans-Werner Goetz, "Tradition und Geschichte im Denken Gregors VII," in *Historiographia mediaevalis: Studien zur Geschichtsschreibung und Quellenkunde des Mittelalters. Festschrift für Franz-Josef Schmale zum 65. Geburtstag*, ed. Dieter Berg and Hans-Werner Goetz (Darmstadt, 1988), pp. 138–48; Ovidio Capitani, "Storiografia e riforma della chiesa in Italia," in *La storiografia altomedievale, 10–16 aprile 1969*, Settimane di studio del Centro italiano di studi sull'alto Medioevo 17 (Spoleto, 1970), pp. 557–629.

[12]   Stephanie Haarländer, *Vitae episcoporum: Eine Quellengattung zwischen Hagiographie und Historiographie, untersucht an Lebensbeschreibungen von Bischöfen des Regnum Teutonicum im Zeitalter der Ottonen und Salier*, Monographien zur Geschichte des Mittelalters 47 (Stuttgart, 2000), pp. 18–19.

[13]   Wilhelm Wattenbach and Robert Holtzmann, *Deutschlands Geschichtsquellen im Mittelalter*, vol. 2, *Das Zeitalter des Investiturstreits, 1050–1125*, ed. Franz-Josef Schmale (Darmstadt, 1967), pp. 439–42. The most authoritative work on the *Codex* was done by Carl Erdmann, "Die Bamberger Domschulen im Investiturstreit," *Zeitschrift für bayerische Landesgeschichte* 9 (1936), 1–46. A new critical edition is planned by the MGH, but its progress remains unclear. The best available edition currently is still in Philipp Jaffé ed., *Monumenta Bambergensia*, Bibliotheca Rerum Germanicarum 5 (Berlin, 1869; repr. Aalen, 1964), pp. 1–469.

Siegfried's communications with his colleagues and especially the popes. Their inclusion in the codex makes perfect sense if one sees the collection in pedagogical terms: Siegfried had a flair for style in his writing and his letters display all the characteristics of good Latin *ars dictamini* of the eleventh century. But, like many of the other letters selected by Udalrich, they also deal with the sensitive issues of church and state of interest to a significant episcopal see such as Bamberg. Siegfried's letters reveal something of his self-perception as an archbishop, and in particular his testy relationship with reformist popes like Alexander II and Gregory VII.

The second most significant source for Siegfried's episcopacy is certainly Lampert of Hersfeld's *Annals*.[14] While a number of other contemporary historiographers, such as Frutolf of Michelsburg, or the Merseburg canon Bruno in his *Book of the Saxon War*, mention Siegfried with some regularity in their accounts, Lampert's interest in the archbishop is a bit more personal. His extensive chronicle represents the most significant account of German and imperial history in the eleventh century, though it was until recently viewed with something of a jaundiced critical eye.[15] Like those of Siegfried himself, however, Lampert's agendas and biases are not as transparent as they might first appear. Lampert is concerned with Siegfried particularly in the context of the famous Thuringian tithe dispute of 1073–1074,[16] and scathingly criticizes the archbishop's attempts to reclaim parish tithe rights from Lampert's own monastery, Hersfeld, as well as its sister abbey of Fulda. Yet he clearly supported the anti-Henrician nobility and, we might assume, Siegfried's decision to abandon Henry and support the Saxon and Swabian-led resistance in 1077. Furthermore, it appears that Lampert later served as abbot at Hasungen, a Hessian monastery reformed by Siegfried in 1081.[17] It is unclear whether or not this signaled a late reversal in Lampert's opinion about the bishop, or perhaps that his criticism of Siegfried's policies did not necessarily imply implacable opposition.[18]

---

[14]   *Lamperti monachi Hersfeldensis Opera*, ed. Oswald Holder-Egger, MGH SS rer. Germ. 38 (Hannover, 1898), pp. 1–304.

[15]   Nineteenth-century German scholars found Lampert to be a singularly untrustworthy historiographer. Some key critical treatments are: Oswald Holder-Egger, "Studien zu Lampert von Hersfeld," *Neues Archiv* 19 (1894), part one, 141–213; part two, 369–430; part three, 507–74; Leopold von Ranke, "Die Annalen des Lambertus von Hersfeld," in *Leopold von Rankes sämmtliche Werke*, vol. 51/3 (Leipzig, 1888), pp. 131–49. For a more current assessment of Lampert and a reconsideration of his work, compare Tilmann Struve, "Lampert von Hersfeld, Teil A," *Hessisches Jahrbuch für Landesgeschichte* 19 (1969), 1–123; and "Teil B," *Hessisches Jahrbuch für Landesgeschichte* 20 (1970), 32–142.

[16]   The classic treatment of this episode is Eduard Ausfeld, *Lampert von Hersfeld und der Zehntstreit zwischen Mainz, Hersfeld und Thüringen* (Marburg, 1880), but see, too, John Eldevik, "Ecclesiastical Lordship and the Politics of Submitting Tithes in Medieval Germany: The Thuringian Tithe Dispute in Social Context," *Viator* 34 (2003), 40–56.

[17]   Edmund E. Stengel, "Lampert von Hersfeld, der erste Abt von Hasungen," in *Aus Verfassungs- und Landesgeschichte: Festschrift zum 70. Geburtstag von Theodor Mayer, dargebracht von seinen Freunden und Schülern*, ed. Heinrich Büttner, vol. 2 (Constance, 1955), pp. 245–58.

[18]   Struve, "Lampert von Hersfeld, Teil A," p. 86; Stengel, "Lampert von Hersfeld," pp. 252–53.

Lampert's views, as complex as they are, nonetheless shed light on how Siegfried's policies were perceived among the Saxon-Thuringian elites and the sort of rhetoric in which they couched their responses. At the same time, Lampert's career and writings remind us not to assume that a work of medieval historiography has a single, transparent agenda, or that it cannot contain dissonant perspectives on the subjects it treats. It is, perhaps, to precisely such works that we should turn in order to begin understanding the political and social complexities and contradictions of a particular period or region.

The archival sources from the cathedral of Mainz and the region's other ecclesiastical foundations (especially Hersfeld, Fulda, and the collegiate churches of Mainz) reveal yet other sides of Siegfried's legacy—that of a skillful administrator, ambitious reformer, and defender of diocesan interests.[19] Like their more prominent royal counterparts, private charters and charter collections offer many clues about the ways their producers wished to articulate the bases of their authority and legitimacy.[20] As with his letters, Siegfried's privileges and grants to individuals and institutions throughout the diocese are witnesses to the social networks of patronage and alliance which bishops used to exert or display their authority. As Paul Hyams reminds us, medieval charters represent the end product of social processes of conflict, agreement, and accommodation among various parties.[21] They are, therefore, not merely witnesses to legal forms and modes of conveyance or immunity, but to relationships among people.[22]

---

[19]   *Mainzer Urkundenbuch*, vol. 1, *Die Urkunden bis zum Tode Erzbischof Adalberts I. (1137)*, ed. Manfred Stimming (Darmstadt, 1932; repr. Darmstadt, 1972) (henceforward cited as *MUB*). On the complex history of the documents of the church of Mainz, see Peter Acht, "Die erste Ordnung der Urkunden des Mainzer Erzstifts und Domkapitels," *Zeitschrift für bayerische Landesgeschichte* 33 (1970), 22–84.

[20]   Key technical surveys of so-called "private" documents (i.e., those not produced in royal, imperial, or papal chancelleries) in the medieval Empire include: Oswald Redlich, "Die Privaturkunden des Mittelalters," in *Urkundenlehre*, ed. Wilhelm Erben, L. Schmitz-Kallenberg, and Oswald Redlich, Handbuch der mittelalterlichen und neueren Geschichte 4/1, Hilfswissenschaften und Altertümer (Munich, 1909), part three; Harry Bresslau, *Handbuch des Urkundenwesens*, 4th edn (Berlin, 1969), pp. 179–85; Heinrich Fichtenau, *Das Urkundenwesen in Österreich vom 8. bis zum frühen 13. Jahrhundert*, Mitteilungen des Instituts für Österreichische Geschichtsforschung 23 (Vienna, 1971). There is an exceptional amount of more recent literature on this topic focusing on various regions, periods, and interpretive problems. A good sense of the newer approaches and scholarship on ecclesiastical, monastic, and lay documentary practices and literacy can be gleaned from the contributions in *Charters and the Use of the Written Word in Medieval Society*, ed. Karl Heidecker, Utrecht Studies in Medieval Literacy 5 (Turnhout, 2000), and in Adam J. Kosto and Anders Winroth eds, *Charters, Cartularies, and Archives: The Preservation and Transmission of Documents in the Medieval West*, Proceedings of a Colloquium of the Commission Internationale de Diplomatique (Princeton and New York, 16–18 September 1999), Papers in Mediaeval Studies 17 (Toronto, 2002).

[21]   Paul Hyams, "The Charter as a Source for the Early Common Law," *Journal of Legal History* 12 (1991), 173–89.

[22]   One must also mention in this context the foundational contributions of Stephen D. White, *Custom, Kinship, and Gifts to the Saints: The Laudatio Parentum in Western France,*

Finally, we must also consider texts such as the *Passio sancti Albani* by the renowned Mainz schoolmaster Gozwin, which he dedicated to Archbishop Siegfried.[23] The *Passio*, as Heinz Thomas observed some years ago, is an important witness to Siegfried's attempt to construct a privileged identity for the see of Mainz in a time of uncertainty and political competition with the other archiepiscopal sees of Germany.[24] In it, Gozwin describes the deeds and martyrdom of the missionary Theonast and his companion Alban, who preached against the Arian heresy in Germany. Alban suffered martyrdom at the hands of his enemies in Mainz, but—in a manner clearly reminiscent of St Dionysius of Paris—does not die before his corpse miraculously ambles to the spot in the city of Mainz where he finally lies down to be buried. The deeds and miracles of Theonast and Alban are not as important as the details about the history and importance of the see of Mainz, particularly those lifted from the *Life of Boniface*, that Gozwin uses to weave his account together and support the contention that Mainz was the oldest and most prominent episcopal see in German lands.

It would certainly have been useful and convenient had one of Siegfried's contemporaries, or even a later author, found the opportunity to craft a narrative *vita* or *gesta* of Siegfried's episcopacy, or the see of Mainz, in the way others did for his colleague Anno of Cologne, or the canon Adam did for the bishops of Bremen. Yet the absence of a single, dominant source of this type also allows us to approach Siegfried's life and career without some of the distortion of the hagiographer's gaze. Lampert's history might even be viewed as a type of narrative counterbalance, opposing the bishop's ambitious reshaping of historical precedent and memory by excavating its contexts and revealing them to be illegitimate. The letters and charters that survive from Siegfried's episcopacy, however, offer a picture of the prelate in his own words and on his own terms. This does not mean, of course, that we should uncritically privilege them as less tendentious or less problematic than other types of texts, but they do offer us a unique opportunity to deconstruct Siegfried's own image of himself—something few bishops of the period have left us the possibility of doing.

The See of Mainz and its Authority in the Eleventh Century

Siegfried's achievements—or failures, depending on one's perspective—need to be understood in the context of the foundations laid by his predecessors. The

---

1050–1150 (Chapel Hill, NC, 1988), and especially Barbara Rosenwein, *To Be the Neighbor of St. Peter: The Social Meaning of Cluny's Property, 949–1049* (Ithaca, NY, 1989).

[23]   This text is not available in a modern critical edition. The dedicatory preface to Siegfried and the abbot of St. Albans, Bardo, has been edited by Oswald Holder-Egger, MGH SS 15/2 (Leipzig, 1925), pp. 984–90. For the main text, see Heinrich Canisius, *Thesaurus monumentorum ecclesiasticorum et historicorum*, ed. Jacques Basnage, vol. 4 (Amsterdam, 1725), pp. 157–66. See, too, Max Manitius, *Geschichte der lateinischen Literatur des Mittelalters*, vol. 2, *Von der Mitte des zehnten Jahrhunderts bis zum Ausbruch des Kampfes zwischen Kirche und Staat* (Munich, 1923), pp. 471–73.

[24]   Thomas, "Erzbischof Siegfried von Mainz," esp. pp. 384–88.

diocese of Mainz in the second third of the eleventh century was an ecclesiastical province in dire need of re-imagining and redefining itself.[25] Following its heyday in the Ottonian period under bishops like Willigis (975–1011), Mainz's status as the primary ecclesiastical see in Germany suffered a number of setbacks. These included losing an ugly, multi-year dispute with the bishops of Hildesheim over the jurisdiction of the nunnery of Gandersheim, as well as Conrad II's decision to withhold Mainz's traditional coronation privilege for the young Henry III in 1028.[26] The appointment of the monk Bardo as archbishop in 1031 appeared to underscore a slow but inevitable decline in the diocese's political fortunes.[27] The fact that neither Archbishop Bardo nor his successor Liutpold appear as intervenients in royal charters suggests that the bishops of Mainz were indeed less active in royal affairs during the reign of Henry III.[28] This is only one measure of significance, however, that should not prejudice our overall assessment of a particular bishop's career.

Bardo had been a monk of Fulda and later abbot of Werden and Hersfeld before receiving his appointment to Mainz. He likely owed his promotion to the Empress Gisela, Conrad II's wife, to whom some sources report he was related.[29] He received the archiepiscopal pallium from Pope John XIX in 1032, although the privilege did not include the title of papal vicar in Germany, last granted to archbishop Frederick (937–939) during the reign of Otto I.[30] Bardo supervised the completion and dedication of a new cathedral in Mainz in 1036 and consolidated the diocese's

---

[25]   On Mainz generally in this period, see Ludwig Falck, *Mainz im frühen und hohen Mittelalter (Mitte 5. Jahrhundert bis 1244)*, Geschichte der Stadt Mainz 2 (Düsseldorf, 1972); Karl Heinemeyer, "Erzbischof Liutpold von Mainz—*Pontifex antiquę disciplinę*, 1051–1059," in *Geschichte und ihre Quellen: Festschrift für Friedrich Hausmann zum 70. Geburtstag*, ed. Reinhard Härtel (Graz, 1987), pp. 59–76. See, too, the contribution by Ernst-Dieter Hehl, "Zwischen Anspruch und Verlust (1011–1060)," in *Handbuch der Mainzer Kirchengeschichte*, ed. Friedhelm Jürgensmeier, vol. 1/1 (Mainz, 2000), pp. 257–80.

[26]   Ernst-Dieter Hehl, "Willigis von Mainz. Päpstlicher Vikar, Metropolit und Reichspolitiker," in *Bischof Burchard von Worms, 1000–1025*, ed. Wilfried Hartmann, Quellen und Abhandlungen zur mittelrheinischen Kirchengeschichte 100 (Mainz, 2000), pp. 51–77; Herwig Wolfram, *Konrad II, 990–1039: König zweier Reiche* (Munich, 2000), pp. 108–13, 273–76.

[27]   I remain unconvinced that the decision made during the reign of Henry III no longer to name the archbishop of Mainz as imperial archchaplain was intended primarily as a snub against the see of Mainz. The bishops of Mainz still retained the distinction of archchancellor of the German kingdom and the change probably had more to do with the desire by Henry III to reform the court and centralize its activities at the new royal palace at Goslar. Compare Josef Fleckenstein, *Die Hofkapelle der deutschen Könige*, Schriften der MGH 16/2 (Stuttgart, 1966), pp. 240–41.

[28]   Wolfram, *Konrad II*, p. 278.

[29]   Johann Friedrich Böhmer and Cornelius Will eds, *Regesta archiepiscoporum Maguntinensium: Regesten zur Geschichte der Mainzer Erzbischöfe von Bonifatius bis Uriel von Gemmingen, 742?–1514* (Innsbruck, 1877), p. 165 (henceforward cited as *Regesten Mainz*).

[30]   Harald Zimmermann ed., *Papsturkunden, 896–1046*, vol. 2 (Vienna, 1985), no. 595, pp. 1121–22. See, too, *Regesten Mainz*, p. 167.

control over its tithe rights in the province of Hesse.[31] Finally, he was able to win back a small but significant concession for Mainz within the imperial church in 1043: he crowned Henry III's new wife, the Poitevin princess Agnes, in his new cathedral despite the fact that Conrad II had made it a point to shift many of Mainz's previous honors and obligations to Cologne.[32] The *Annalista Saxo* even reports that in the early 1040s, Bardo participated directly in military campaigns along the Bohemian frontier, leading an army contingent alongside the Thuringian margrave Ekkehard of Meissen.[33] To be sure, these are not the activities of an introverted and ineffectual monk. As Josef Semmler has pointed out, the dedication of a new cathedral was itself a significant turn, bringing the cathedral clergy once again under a single roof, expanding the cathedral school, and attracting further donations for the church.[34]

Bardo's successor, Liutpold (1051–1059), built upon his predecessor's achievements and further asserted the archbishop's position within his own diocese. The consolidation of episcopal rights within the diocese is particularly significant, even if such details typically fall beneath the radar screen in larger surveys. Small-scale collegiate church reforms, building dedications, confirmation of aristocratic donations and tithe agreements are perhaps humdrum details of routine episcopal administration, but the documents that record these events are witnesses to the bishop's interaction with local communities of clergy and the laity. They are often equally important indications of the direction and character of episcopal policy and self-perception as royal and papal immunities or other more impressive sources.

Liutpold came from the ranks of the secular clergy; prior to his elevation, he was the provost of the cathedral at Bamberg, the leading cathedral school and intellectual center in Germany in the mid-eleventh century.[35] Like Bardo, he received the archiepiscopal pallium from Leo IX shortly after his elevation.[36] Liutpold used

---

[31]   *MUB*, no. 282, pp. 177–78. See also Josef Semmler, "Askese und Aussenwirkung," in *Handbuch der Mainzer Kirchengeschichte*, ed. Jürgensmeier, vol. 1/2, p. 610, and Staab, "Mainzer Kirche," p. 52.

[32]   Wolfram, *Konrad II*, pp. 276–78.

[33]   *Annalista Saxo*, ed. Georg Waitz, MGH SS 6 (Hannover, 1844), p. 684; Ernst Steindorff, *Jahrbücher des deutschen Reiches unter Heinrich III*, 2 vols (Darmstadt, 1963), 1:91–92. The agreement over the tithes of Kaufungen, above, which Henry witnessed along with a number of high nobles and churchmen, appears to have been undertaken in the process of gathering support, men, and arms for the Bohemian campaign.

[34]   See Semmler, "Askese und Aussenwirkung," p. 610, with references to the pertinent sources. The reconstruction of the cathedral also signaled the reestablishment of a communal life for the cathedral clergy. See Staab, "Reform and Reformgruppen," p. 137.

[35]   Ferdinand Geldner, "Das Hochstift Bamberg in der Reichspolitik von Kaiser Heinrich II. bis Kaiser Friedrich Barbarossa," *Historisches Jahrbuch* 83 (1963), 28–42; Marie Luise Bulst-Thiele, *Kaiserin Agnes* (Hildesheim, 1933), pp. 45–47; Claudia Märtl, "Die Bamberger Schulen—ein Bildungszentrum des Salierreichs," in *Die Salier und das Reich*, ed. Weinfurter, 3:327–45.

[36]   *MUB*, no. 293, pp. 183–85, noted at Philipp Jaffé and Wilhelm Wattenbach eds, *Regesta pontificum Romanorum, ab condita ecclesia ad annum post Christum natum 1198*, 2nd rev. edn, vol. 1 (Leipzig, 1885; repr. Graz, 1956), no. 4281, p. 543. The privilege restores the function of papal legate to the Mainz bishop, but only in circumstances where the arrival of a legate from Rome was expected or "as required by necessity" (tanta necessitas urget).

diocesan resources to found several churches and establish a stronger presence for the church in Hesse and Thuringia. In 1055 he founded a collegiate church at Nörten, near Hannover, dedicated to Mary and the apostle Peter.[37] He richly endowed it with revenues, tithes, and properties in the region from the episcopal *mensa*, or the bishop's personal endowment. Liutpold's other foundations include the eponymous convent of Lippoldsberg near Fritzlar, as well as the church of St. Jakob just outside the city walls of Mainz, for which Henry IV also provided a substantial endowment.[38] Lampert of Hersfeld even called this church a "monimentum" to the late bishop for using his own funds to establish the monastery.[39] As Lampert's remark suggests, foundations such as these were not merely acts of individual piety, but attempts to create a legacy and site of memory centered on the person of the bishop. While founding new churches was always an attribute of a good bishop, the eleventh century saw a marked increase not only in the building of new churches and cathedrals, particularly in Germany and Italy, but also in the attention paid to such activity in hagiographical literature.[40] To be sure, this is a kind of reform, but a reform of historical consciousness as much as of ecclesiastical institutions.[41]

Liutpold also continued the policy, initiated under Bardo, of reclaiming tithes in the diocese which had passed out of the bishop's control over time and into the hands of private individuals or institutions, or which were no longer being paid in their full amount. The bishops of Mainz faced a serious quandary in this area, however. Large tracts of property, particularly in Hesse and Thuringia, as well as many of the local churches within the diocese which collected tithes from the farmers and landowners, belonged to the abbeys of Hersfeld and Fulda and were thus excluded from episcopal jurisdiction on the basis of their papal and royal immunity privileges.[42] As late as 1049, Adalbero of Würzburg's attempt to challenge Fulda's control of its churches within his diocese was rebuffed by Pope Leo IX and Henry III.[43] Liutpold, however,

---

[37]   *MUB*, no. 296, pp. 185–87; Heinemeyer, "Liutpold von Mainz," p. 74.

[38]   *Die Urkunden der Deutschen Könige und Kaiser*, vol. 6/1, *Die Urkunden Heinrichs IV.*, ed. Dietrich von Gladiss, MGH DD 6/1 (Berlin, 1941; repr. Hannover, 1978), no. 121, p. 160.

[39]   Lampert, *Annales*, p. 77 (s.a. 1059).

[40]   Tilmann Struve, "Die Wende des 11. Jahrhunderts. Symptome eines Epochenwandels im Spiegel der Geschichtsschreibung," *Historisches Jahrbuch* 112 (1992), 324–65.

[41]   A later charter from the pontificate of Siegfried notes that shortly before his death, Liutpold transferred the church of St. Nikomedes, one of Mainz's oldest foundations, to the monastery of St. Jakob. In this way, Liutpold linked the present with the past, joining a new monastery to one of Mainz's foundational Christian institutions: see *MUB*, no. 327, pp. 217–18. The charter establishes the rights of peasants in several villages owned by St. Nikomedes, now under St. Jakob's control, vis-à-vis the church's advocates, who were alleged to have abused their power.

[42]   Erica Widera, "Der Kirchenzehnt in Deutschland zur Zeit der sächsischen Herrscher," *Archiv für katholisches Kirchenrecht* 110 (1930), 33–110; Erwin Hölk, *Zehnten und Zehntkämpfe der Reichsabtei Hersfeld* (Marburg, 1933); Konrad Lübeck, "Zehntrechte und Zehntkämpfe des Klosters Fulda," *Archiv für katholisches Kirchenrecht* 118 (1938), 116–64; Eldevik, "Ecclesiastical Lordship," pp. 48–50.

[43]   Alfred Wendehorst, "Fulda und Würzburg: Tausend Jahre Konfrontation," in *Fulda im Alten Reich*, ed. Berthold Jäger, Veröffentlichung des Fuldaer Geschichtsvereins 59 (Fulda,

remained undeterred and actively challenged both monasteries over their possession of certain tithes in Thuringia.[44] Despite the abbots' claim that their properties in Thuringia were exempted from such taxation, the matter was settled through an exchange of property that served to compensate the bishop for the lost revenue.[45] In a similar fashion, following an inquest (*inquisitio*) on the matter sometime before Henry III's death in 1056, Liutpold prevailed upon the king to compensate the diocese for tithes owed from royal domains in Thuringia. The final terms of the agreement were evidently not fulfilled, however, and in 1059 Liutpold received a reimbursement from Henry IV in the form of 120 estates in Hesse, Thuringia, and Franconia.[46] As Karl Heinemeyer noted, some thirty of the listed properties were close to either Lippoldsburg or Nörten, supporting Liutpold's earlier consolidation of episcopal interests in northern Hesse.[47]

As will become clearer when we examine the continuation of this effort under Siegfried, the reclamation of tithe rights had simultaneous financial, political, and pastoral aims. The right to receive and administer the ecclesiastical tithe ranked among the most important duties of a medieval bishop. According to Rather of Verona, writing in the latter part of the tenth century, keeping account of diocesan tithes was one of the most critical prerogatives of any bishop.[48] Thus, making an "inquiry"—as

---

1996), pp. 153–68.

[44]   Details of Liutpold's tithe campaign are related chiefly in remnants of a now-lost historical brief by Lampert of Hersfeld called the *Libellus de institutione Hersfeldensis*. Portions relating to the tithe dispute were excerpted in the fifteenth-century German chronicle of Wigand of Gerstenberg and reproduced by Holder-Egger in his edition of Lampert's *Opera*; see *Lamperti monachi Hersfeldensis Opera*, p. 352, in the apparatus.

[45]   Ibid. It is possible that a charter preserved in Hersfeld and dated to 1057 was part of this agreement, although it deals with churches and properties outside Thuringia: *Urkundenbuch der Reichsabtei Hersfeld*, ed. Hans Weirich, vol. 1 (Marburg, 1936), no. 102, pp. 183–86. In it, Liutpold agrees to accept compensation in return for withdrawing his claims to the tithes of four churches held by Hersfeld near the Main River, in addition to other unspecified tithes *in regione Francorum*, that is, in Franconia. For further details, see Hölk, *Zehnten und Zehntkämpfe*, pp. 39–45.

[46]   *MUB*, nos 301–2, pp. 192–94. The original agreement with Henry III does not survive, but the background story is related in the two later confirmations of it dating to the regency of Henry IV in 1059. See, too, Heinemeyer, "Liutpold von Mainz," p. 75. One additional interesting stipulation is that those under the king's authority (homines nostri iuris) will continue to pay the bishop "that which they had previously been accustomed to pay as the tithe" (ita tamen ut nostri iuris homines id ipsum pro decima solvant, quod et ante Magunt. Ecclesie pro decima persolvere soliti erant), suggesting that the episcopal inquest raised the fact that tithes from royal domains had become a fixed customary payment and probably reflected only a fraction of the income that would normally be due the bishop. As part of the agreement, however, the bishop allowed this practice to continue if he were compensated with property in other areas.

[47]   Heinemeyer, "Liutpold von Mainz," p. 75.

[48]   "Et cum de oblationibus et decimis fidelium vivere tabernaculi custodies debeant Domini, hoc est ecclesie clerici, si nescit episcopus, quot decimiani, quot mansi, quot modia tritici, quot congia vini tantis vel tantis sufficient clericis ad victum utique et tegumentum, none convincitur aut non esse pastor aut certe insipiens existere pastor, qui nesciat utique ubi

the sources often put it—about tithes was not simply a matter of rooting around for extra revenue, but fundamentally part of the obligations of pastoral care and a claim staked to episcopal authority in a region. Viewed over time, it becomes clear that the inquest for tithes was not a one-time event, but an ongoing process—during a bishop's own tenure and from bishop to bishop—of negotiating the bishop's power among local communities and institutions. Tithes were technically an economic resource and a possession, but like property more generally, their possession was also part of an infrastructure of memory, continuity, and authority. At a time when the see of Mainz needed to create new and more permanent markers of its centrality in the German realm, recouping diocesan tithes, or even receiving properties in compensation for recognized rights, served to enhance and enlarge the episcopal patrimony while also serving as a visible reminder throughout the diocese of the overlordship of the bishop.

Liutpold's agreement not only focused attention on the Mainz bishops' rights to tithes in Thuringia, but also strengthened the diocese's position around the bishop's new churches. The bishops of Mainz, it should be noted, were not the only ones interested in asserting their rights in this regard at that time. Lampert of Hersfeld also recalled how Bishop Burchard I of Halberstadt attempted to revive his diocese's old claims to Hersfeld's tithes in the Hochseegau area of lower Saxony around 1056, but was unsuccessful thanks to divine intervention on behalf of the monks.[49] Benno II of Osnabrück, his biographer tells us, likewise vigorously pursued the monasteries of Corvey and Herford over diocesan tithe rights despite the ongoing wars and disasters plaguing the empire in the 1070s.[50] This was in fact a rewriting and reassertion of history as reform—quite literally in the case of Benno, whose chancellery produced a spectacular series of forged royal and papal privileges in support of the bishop's case that constituted nothing more than the complete re-imagining of the history of the diocese of Osnabrück.[51] Like church buildings and hagiographical traditions, tithe rights were sites of memory and power that could be erected, changed, enlarged, and manipulated in the service of episcopal interest.

While Liutpold did not engage in the kind of creative reworking of the past as Benno of Osnabrück later would, he nonetheless understood the importance of framing the kinds of ambitious reforms he pursued in the correct contexts of liturgical and sacred memory. At some point during his episcopacy, Liutpold commissioned the canon Vulculd to write a biography of his late predecessor Bardo.[52] Vulculd chose an idiosyncratic format for his work, aligning details of Bardo's life and career to principles of the Beatitudes preached by Christ in the Sermon on the Mount. On

---

illa sint pascua, ubi pecora conducere debeat suae previsioni commissa?'': Rather of Verona, *De contemptu canonum*, in *Die Briefe des Bischofs Rather von Verona*, ed. Fritz Weigle, MGH Briefe der deutschen Kaiserzeit 1 (Weimar, 1949; repr. Munich, 1981), p. 76.

[49]   Hölk, *Zehnten und Zehntkämpfe*, pp. 79–81.

[50]   *Vita Bennonis II. episcopi Osnabrugensis* (above, n. 3), cc. 16–17, pp. 19–23.

[51]   These forgeries have been the subject of an intensive and lengthy formal study, in two parts, by Kurt-Ulrich Jäschke, "Zu Quellen und Geschichte des Osnabrücker Zehntstreits," *Archiv für Diplomatik* 9–10 (1963–1964), 112–285; and 11–12 (1965–1966), 280–402.

[52]   Vulculd, *Vita Bardonis archiepiscopi Moguntini*, ed. Wilhelm Wattenbach, MGH SS 11 (Hannover, 1854), pp. 318–21; Coué, *Hagiographie im Kontext*, pp. 100–9.

the surface, Vulculd's narrative would seem to confirm the impression of Bardo as someone whose pious disposition was fundamentally unsuited to the demands of the highly politicized world he inhabited. Indeed, it is a relatively brief account, but in styling Bardo as a saint in his humility, Vulculd, and his patron Liutpold, situate his legacy within the inversion of values expressed in the Beatitudes: truth and power lie with the meek and righteous, not those who vainly seek worldly glories. Such efforts often appear to modern scholars as a fairly transparent attempt to use hagiographic conventions to redeem an otherwise weak and ineffectual prelate in light of present challenges to Mainz's position.[53] We have to be mindful, however, of medieval attitudes toward humility and a medieval audience's appreciation for the inversion of values that define the qualities of a saint.[54] Understood in this light, the appeal to humility and Bardo's notably unsophisticated and un-aristocratic character in the *vita* served as a sort of backdrop for Liutpold's own episcopacy: Bardo had laid the foundations of piety and humility for the city and its diocese. His successors would enjoy the inheritance.

Siegfried's Background and Early Career

We know next to nothing about Siegfried's own educational or career background prior to his appearance in the sources as the new abbot of Fulda.[55] We do know, however, that he was a scion of the comital family who controlled the region north of Mainz, known as the Königssundergau, and whose descendants were known as the counts of Eppstein, after a fortress they later built in that same area.[56] This was a prominent family and one well connected in the city of Mainz and its environs. Siegfried's older brother, Udalrich, succeeded their father, also named Siegfried, as count of Königssundergau, and served as advocate of the diocesan church of Mainz between 1052 and 1074. Another brother, Reginhard, was *comes civitatis*—the chief military and judicial officer—of Mainz in the 1060s, and may have also served as Fulda's advocate earlier in the 1050s during his brother's abbacy. Another relative, Hartwin, appears as provost of the important church of St.Viktor, just outside the walls of Mainz, in the early 1070s.[57] The family's leading position in the city, and their prominence in the surrounding region, probably had more to do with Siegfried's appointment than any purported favor with Empress Agnes, although this may certainly have played a role as well. The family of the counts of Eppstein continued to dominate the Mainz episcopacy well into the thirteenth century.

---

[53]   Coué, *Hagiographie im Kontext*, pp. 102–3.

[54]   Some other examples of the "humble" bishop are in C. Stephen Jaeger, *The Origins of Courtliness: Civilizing Trends and the Formation of Courtly Ideals, 939–1210* (Philadelphia, 1985), pp. 35–36.

[55]   Mechthild Sandmann, "Die Folge der Äbte," in *Die Klostergemeinschaft von Fulda im früheren Mittelalter*, ed. Karl Schmid, Münstersche Mittelalter-Schriften 8/1 (Munich, 1978), pp. 178–204, at p. 198.

[56]   Heinz F. Friederichs, "Zur Herkunft der Herren von Eppstein," *Hessische Familienkunde* 8 (1966), 1–16.

[57]   *MUB*, no. 334, pp. 229–30, at p. 229.

According to the *Annals of Ottobeuron*, Siegfried left Fulda on Christmas Day in 1059 and was invested at a royal assembly in Mainz on Epiphany, 6 January 1060. Those present included Pope Nicholas II and his legate, Bishop Anselm of Lucca, who would soon become Pope Alexander II in a bitterly contested papal election.[58] Unlike most of his predecessors, Siegfried did not step into his position merely as a beneficiary of imperial patronage, or even as a powerful ex-abbot, but as a member of the local elite whose siblings already occupied key positions of power in and around the city of Mainz. To be sure, this did not give Siegfried the power of a major noble like Bishop Meinwerk of Paderborn (*c.*970–1036), whose massive personal wealth and lands provided unprecedented opportunities for both his pastoral and lordly activities,[59] but they did provide the bishop with a broad sphere of political support in the city itself and around the Main-Rhine region.[60] As we shall see, however, this background proved less useful when it came to projecting influence in other parts of his diocese, particularly Thuringia, where both the nobility and regional monasteries expected to enjoy a certain degree of independence from diocesan interference.

Siegfried faced several major issues as soon as he stepped into his new position. The first was the question of Henry IV's regency and the continued dominance of the archbishop of Cologne in imperial affairs. The second was the increasingly chilly relationship between the papacy and independent-minded metropolitan sees like that of Mainz. Although politically secure in Mainz and the Main-Rhine region, Siegfried remained something of an outsider in imperial politics of the 1060s, particularly during the contentious regency of young Henry IV.[61] Empress Agnes had served as co-ruler with her son since Henry III's death in 1056, but in 1062, Anno of Cologne seized the regency in the famous coup of Kaiserswerth and Agnes was obliged to cede power to the archbishop.[62] Although the details are sketchy, it appears that Siegfried had been part of a conspiracy of sorts in 1062 to relieve Anno of the regency and reassert Mainz's position as the primate church in Germany. A letter in the *Codex Udalrici* survives wherein Gunther of Bamberg congratulates Anno on having defused the plot to sideline him, and suggests that those behind it were none other than Siegfried and the Saxon margrave Dedi of Lausitz, a relative of King Henry.[63] Tuomas Heikkilä suspects that Siegfried may have been hoping

---

[58]   *Annales Ottenburani*, ed. Georg Pertz, MGH SS 5 (Hannover, 1844), p. 6 (s.a. 1060).

[59]   Timothy Reuter, "Property Transactions and Social Relations between Rulers, Bishops, and Nobles in early Eleventh-Century Saxony: The Evidence of the *Vita Meinwerci*," in *Property and Power in the Early Middle Ages*, ed. Wendy Davies and Paul Fouracre (Cambridge, 1995), pp. 165–99.

[60]   Alois Gerlich, "Der Aufbau der Mainzer Herrschaft im Rheingau im Hochmittelalter," *Nassauische Annalen* 96 (1985), 9–28.

[61]   On the regency, see I.S. Robinson, *Henry IV of Germany, 1056–1106* (Cambridge, 1999), pp. 20–62.

[62]   *Die Regesten des Kaiserreiches unter Heinrich IV. (1056[1050]–1106)*, vol. 3/3, *Salisches Haus: 1024–1125*, ed. Johann Friedrich Böhmer (Graz, 1951), no. 252, pp. 103–4.

[63]   "Et nostro et totius regni nomine gratulor vobis, quod, perditis emulorum consiliis tam mature vos occurrisse, tam prudenter ea dissipasse, ex litteris vestris cognovi. Verumtamen, dum singula mecum etiam atque etiam retracto, solidum sincerumque gaudium vix audeo

to stage some sort of coup at the royal Pentecost celebrations in Goslar in 1063, along with his successor at Fulda, Widerad, whom Lampert of Hersfeld notes was also relative of Siegfried.[64] Far from recognizing Siegfried as the first primate in Germany, the festival dissolved into a bitter brawl between Widerad's knights and those of the Hildesheim bishop Hezilo, a close ally of Anno. The damage and deaths that followed resulted in a legal judgment against Fulda that dealt a crushing blow to the monastery's wealth and prestige.[65]

Siegfried's complicity in the disaster may explain many of the difficulties he encountered over the course of his pontificate. Chastened by the disaster at Goslar, Siegfried attempted to be more of a "team player" from 1063 onwards, compliantly supporting Anno's regency and later urging the ouster of Adalbert of Bremen as Henry's counselor in 1066.[66] In 1064, Siegfried notified Alexander II that he intended to join Gunther of Bamberg and a number of other German and Lothringian bishops on a major pilgrimage to Jerusalem.[67] In the letter, he writes that he wished to undertake the journey *pro remedio delictorum et desiderio supernorum sanctam adire Ierosolimam.* This may be pious rhetoric, but it might well refer to Siegfried's attempt to reconcile with Gunther, Anno, and his circle of allies, and make some recompense for the aborted coup.

Reform Movement on the Local Level: Collegiate Churches and Monasteries

Because Siegfried eventually joined the opposition to Henry IV, he is usually included in the column of pro-Gregorian bishops during the Investiture Controversy. Siegfried, like Liutpold before him, had embarked on a restructuring of church discipline and administration in his diocese long before the papal reform edicts of the 1070s and 1080s reached their stride. The difference was that Siegfried's reforms, like Liutpold's, tied the churches and parishes within the diocese more closely to the bishop. Siegfried's attempts to regulate disputes among his suffragan bishops, this time in his authority as metropolitan, likewise strengthened his own position at the expense of the papacy, which very much wanted to place itself at the top of an ecclesiastical hierarchy and had grown deeply suspicious of the German episcopacy's independent streak.

In uncertain times, heroic monks and canons served as anchors of reassuring stability whose holiness shed its benefits on surrounding communities and especially

---

concipere. Suspectum quippe mihi est, quod de marchione D. et de archiepiscopo Moguntino, qui se velut caput coniurationis effert, nichil scripsistis": *Udalrici Babenbergensis Codex*, in *Monumenta Bambergensia*, ed. Jaffé (above, n. 13), no. 23, p. 47.

[64]   Tuomas Heikkilä, *Das Kloster Fulda und der Goslarer Rangstreit*, Annales Academiae Scientiarum Fennicae, Ser. Humaniora 298 (Helsinki, 1998), pp. 138–44.

[65]   Heikkilä, *Das Kloster Fulda*, pp. 156–63.

[66]   Robinson, *Henry IV*, pp. 59–60.

[67]   *Udalrici Babenbergensis Codex*, ed. Jaffé, no. 28, pp. 54–56. On the ill-fated 1064–1065 pilgrimage to Jerusalem, see *Die Regesten der Bischöfe und des Domkapitels von Bamberg*, ed. Erich von Guttenberg, Veröffentlichungen der Gesellschaft für frankische Geschichte 6 (Würzburg, 1963), no. 361, pp. 178–79.

their patrons. Establishing reformed monastic houses and collegiate churches not only sent a signal to the public in the diocese that their bishops were serious about creating communities of collective righteousness that benefited all Christians, but it also allowed landed and human resources to be organized in a way favorable to episcopal administration. Shortly after his appointment, Siegfried reorganized the church of St. Peter in Erfurt as a monastery.[68] His attention to Erfurt in this case is not surprising; the town was a critically important center of Mainz's economic and spiritual jurisdiction in remote Thuringia.[69] It had long been a major market town and served as the site of an important mint operating under the authority of the archbishops of Mainz.[70] Turning the local church of St. Peter into a monastery placed a congregation of monks loyal to the bishop in a politically and economically critical area. In other places, he supported monasteries established by his predecessors, providing them with new buildings or enlarging their patrimonies with land and tithes. A later, twelfth-century chronicle from the convent of Lippoldsberg also notes in a brief *encomium* for Siegfried, for example, that he replaced the small wooden church left by Bishop Liutpold with a larger stone building and guaranteed the nuns additional properties and tithe rights in the area.[71]

Siegfried also helped introduce a unique brand of reformed monasticism in Thuringia when he joined Anno of Cologne in converting the canonry at Saalfeld into a Benedictine monastery in 1071 under the patronage of Peter and Paul.[72] Anno settled monks from his own reform monastery of Siegburg in Saalfeld, where, Lampert of Hersfeld reports, they quickly gained a formidable reputation throughout the region for the strictness and holiness of their lifestyle. Unfortunately, when Lampert himself paid a visit to both Siegburg and Saalfeld, he claims to have been decidedly unimpressed by the routine he witnessed in both houses.[73] Although Siegburg's monks came originally from the Cluniac abbey of Fruttuaria in Lombardy, Anno and Siegfried had their own vision of monastic reform and its relationship to the episcopacy.[74] Far from being completely deracinated from all episcopal and lay control, the monks of Saalfeld were placed under the supervision of Archbishop

---

[68]   *Regesten Mainz*, p. 181. However, see Büttner, "Das Erzstift Mainz und die Klosterreform," p. 48, who argues for a later date, *c.*1080.

[69]   Günther Christ, "Territoriale Entwicklung in Erfurt und im thüringischen Raum," in *Handbuch der Mainzer Kirchengeschichte*, ed. Günther Christ and Georg May, vol. 2 (Würzburg, 1997), pp. 395–96.

[70]   Bernd Kluge, *Deutsche Münzgeschichte von der späten Karolingerzeit bis zum Ende der Salier: Ca. 900 bis 1125*, Römisch-Germanisches Zentralmuseum, Forschungsinstitut für Vor- und Frühgeschichte 29 (Sigmaringen, 1991), pp. 43–45, 275.

[71]   *Chronicon Lippoldesbergense*, ed. Wilhelm Arndt, MGH SS 20 (Hannover, 1868), pp. 546–58, at pp. 547–48.

[72]   *MUB*, no. 331, pp. 223–26; Büttner, "Das Erzstift Mainz und die Klosterreform," pp. 38–39.

[73]   Lampert, *Annales*, pp. 132–33 (s.a. 1071).

[74]   Josef Semmler, "Die Klosterreform von Siegburg (11. und 12. Jahrhundert)," in *Germania Benedictina*, vol. 1, *Die Reformverbände und Kongregationen der Benediktiner im deutschen Sprachraum*, ed. Ulrich Faust and Franz Quarthal (St Ottilien, 1999), pp. 141–51, esp. at pp. 144–45.

Siegfried and given authority to preach and establish parish churches in the area, which, in the words of the foundation charter, was only then in the process of being Christianized.[75] They were, however, expressly granted the right of free abbatial elections and did not have to provide *servitium* to the bishop, as did some of the other churches discussed above.

The connection to Cluny in this process was not entirely superficial, however. Siegfried demonstrated an abiding, if eclectic, interest in Cluniac reformed monasticism throughout his episcopacy, including his brief abdication in 1072, when he actually fled to Cluny and attempted to become a monk there. In 1081, Siegfried also reformed the hilltop collegiate church in Hasungen, which for several decades had been a popular pilgrimage spot dedicated to the early eleventh-century eremitic monk Haimerad, as a Benedictine-Cluniac monastery.[76] The surviving copy of the foundation charter talks about Cluniac reform not in terms of ecclesiastical liberty or the severing of all external lay and episcopal ties to the church, but as a kind of *vita perfectior*, "in which voluntary poverty and contempt for the world presides, and in which charity reigns with obedience and humility."[77] This was, as (Hasungen's future abbot) Lampert wryly noted in the account of his visitation to Saalfeld, precisely the image that the monks wished to cultivate in the public imagination and the reason they played such a significant role for Siegfried during his episcopacy.

Siegfried's vision of the well-ordered diocese often involved collaborations with the local aristocracy in reforming the clergy in private churches and integrating them into the diocesan tithe and pastoral care regime.[78] In 1063, he granted tithes in more

---

[75]   "Igitur gentem terre huius rudem et divini germinis incultam [reperi; monsterium] primo ritu canonico institui. Deinde divino perurgente desiderio magis spiritualibus intendens, canonicis huiusmodi ad me Coloniam [transvectis], vitam monasticam et monasterium in pago ultra Salam, qui dicitur Salavelt, de novo institui et construxi abbatem eisdem monarchis preficiens secundum regulam sancti Benedicti viventibus, ut errore gentilitatis eliminato [gentem huius terre ad] fidem inducere[nt] sancte trinitatis": *MUB*, no. 331, p. 224. The original charter has been lost, but Stimming makes an effort to reconstruct its main points based on surviving copies and a twelfth-century papal confirmation that preserved much of the original. Elements of it, particularly the listing of properties and privileges retained by the monks in the portion dictated by Siegfried, are idiosyncratic and ought to be treated with caution. On the Siegburg reform generally, see Semmler, "Die Klosterreform von Siegburg."

[76]   *MUB*, no. 358, pp. 253–58. The foundation charter is a forgery, but the basic historic narrative it contains is not in doubt. The forgeries stem from twelfth-century efforts to secure certain properties. See Walter Heinemeyer, "Die Urkundenfälschungen des Klosters Hasungen," *Archiv für Diplomatik* 4 (1958), 226–63. See, too, "Hasungen," in Regina Elisabeth Schwerdtfeger, Friedhelm Jürgensmeier, and Franziskus Büll eds, *Die benediktinischen Mönchs- und Nönnenkloster in Hessen*, Germania Benedictina 7 (St Ottilien, 2004), pp. 535–59. On the cult of Haimerad, see Phyllis G. Jestice, *Wayward Monks and the Religious Revolution of the Eleventh Century* (Leiden, 1997), pp. 146–51.

[77]   ". . . in quo cum mundi huius contemptu voluntaria paupertas principatur, in quo cum humilitate et oboedientia caritas dominatur": *MUB*, no. 358, p. 257. Like Saalfeld, Hasungen was also guaranteed free abbatial elections and exemption from episcopal and secular *servitium*.

[78]   Büttner, "Das Erzstift Mainz und die Klosterreform," pp. 37–39. On reassessing the important role played by the nobility in church reform during this period, see the seminal

than a dozen nearby villages to a collegiate church in Sulza in Thuringia, which had been founded by Frederick, the count palatinate of Saxony, and his wife, Hedwig.[79] In return, Frederick and the community at Sulza agreed to supply the bishop's itinerant court with food and clothing. That same year, according to Lampert of Hersfeld, margrave Otto of Meissen agreed to pay tithes on his estates in Thuringia and persuade the other lords in Thuringia to do the same.[80] A copy of a charter from the early 1080s suggests that Otto's tithe agreement with Siegfried followed upon the dedication of the altar in a church of St. Pancratius in Orlamünde in a manner very much similar to Sulza.[81] Siegfried dedicated the church for Otto and his wife, Adelheid, and confirmed for it the tithes from a number of surrounding villages. In return, Otto agreed, as did Frederick, that the church should supply the bishop or his itinerant court with provisions as needed. There is no mention of the personal tithe issue, but all the evidence seems to point to the fact that Siegfried and Otto did come to some kind of agreement around this time. Shortly before his death in 1084, Siegfried issued a confirmation for the church in Orlamünde, remembering in it that the late Otto and his wife were "the first in Thuringia" to agree to pay the lawful tithe to God's church.[82]

In 1074, in the midst of the Saxon rebellion against Henry IV and his own severe difficulties in raising tithes from the monasteries and lords of Thuringia, Siegfried again dedicated an aristocratic foundation, this time in Ravengiersburg (in the Hunsrück between Mainz and Trier), for a count Berthold and his wife, Hedwig, who the charter tells us was a relative (*consanguinea*) of Siegfried.[83] As earlier, he also confirmed for it property donated by the count, in particular tithes. The charter continues: the foundation was from that point forward to be a collegiate church and the couple subsequently donates it to St. Martin of Mainz, that is, the episcopal

---

article by John Howe, "The Nobility's Reform of the Medieval Church," *The American Historical Review* 93 (1988), 317–39.

[79]   *MUB*, no. 306, pp. 195–96.

[80]   Lampert, *Annales*, pp. 79, 104 (s.a. 1062[?]).

[81]   *MUB*, no. 365, pp. 264–65.

[82]   The notice survives in a partial copy made in the cartulary of Bishop Conrad of Orlamünde in 1194, but the original date remains conjectural. It seems that because the text speaks in the past tense, we can assume that it was a confirmation or reissuing of an agreement made sometime prior to Otto's death in 1067. Lampert places the date of Otto's tithe concessions around 1062, but might not be entirely precise. Since Siegfried's agreement with Otto is so similar to that made with the count palatinate Frederick, they may have been part of the same reform campaign of the early 1060s in which Siegfried convinced regional nobles to allow their churches to be confirmed by the bishop and receive tithes.

[83]   Büttner, "Das Erzstift Mainz und die Klosterreform," p. 45. See, too, *MUB*, no. 341, pp. 236–38. This Hedwig is not related to Hedwig, the wife of Count Frederick. On the counts of the Nahegau and their political position between Mainz and Trier, see Winfried Dotzauer, *Geschichte des Nahe-Hunsrück-Raumes von den Anfängen bis zur Französischen Revolution* (Stuttgart, 2001), pp. 110–12.

church, along with all its appurtenances. Berthold is then declared to be a knight (*miles*) of the bishop and will serve as advocate of the new monastery.[84]

As Cinzio Violante observed, reforming clerical life in otherwise independent or loosely-organized rural churches was part of a process of centralization and rationalization that can be seen throughout western Europe at this time, and was pursued with particular alacrity by bishops as well as reformist popes like Alexander II.[85] However, bringing local clergy under a common life also brought the church's property and resources under closer episcopal supervision and served to enhance the role and stature of the bishop in local ecclesiastical affairs. As secular lordship began to focus more on territorial and hierarchical structures in a region, bishops, too, sought ways of translating episcopal power into more clearly articulated and organized forms of control over churches, land, and people.[86] We see evidence of this not only in the growing prominence of armed militias and knights in the service of bishops, but in the way bishops sought to create more formally defined spaces of control. Reformed monks and Augustinian canons were an important component in the construction of episcopal power, particularly in a diocese like Mainz where the bishops did not exercise direct secular, or comital, lordship over large areas.[87] In the cases of Sulza and Orlamünde, the benefits of reorganizing these churches and placing them on a firm economic footing are clear: clerical life and discipline were regularized and the bishop's ability to exercise his authority and justice through an itinerant court better secured. In Saalfeld, the monks were to play a leading role in establishing parochial institutions in a frontier area and organizing religious life—a function that older abbeys like Fulda had once performed under the Carolingians. In Ravengiersburg, an important church was incorporated into the diocese, along with the resources and services of Siegfried's family in the Hunsrück.

As is evident in Siegfried's local collegiate church and monastic reforms, concomitant reform of the tithe system was part and parcel of ending the old practices of private patronage and supervision of churches and renewing episcopal authority.[88]

---

[84]   "Bertoldus etiam comes miles noster effectus est, quem rogatu canonicorum eiusdem loci advocatum substitutimus": *MUB*, no. 341, p. 237; Gerlich, "Aufbau der Mainzer Herrschaft," pp. 13–15.

[85]   Cinzio Violante, "La vita commune del clero," in *Studi sulla cristianità medioevale: Società, istituzioni, spiritualità*, ed. Piero Zerbi (Milan, 1972), pp. 111–26; Cosimo Damiano Fonseca, "Il movimento canonicale a Lucca e nella diocesi lucchese tra XI e XII secolo," in *Allucio da Pescia (1070 ca.–1134), un santo laico dell'età postgregoriana: Religione e società nei territori di Lucca e della Valdinievole* (Rome, 1991), pp. 147–58, esp. pp. 150–55. On the social appeal of a communal lifestyle for the secular clergy in particular, see Staab, "Reform und Reformgruppen," pp. 122–23.

[86]   Wolfgang Metz, "Wesen und Struktur des Adels Althessens," in *Die Salier und das Reich*, ed. Weinfurter, 1:331–66.

[87]   Karl Heinemeyer, "Territorium ohne Dynastie: Der Erzbischof von Mainz als Diözesanbischof und Landesherr," *Hessisches Jahrbuch für Landesgeschichte* 44 (1994), 1–15, at pp. 8–9.

[88]   Compare, however, Staab, "Reform und Reformgruppen," at p. 143, where he states that Siegfried's reforms do not reflect much concern for pastoral care. I think the attention to tithes, which Staab generally does not mention, suggests otherwise, ensuring a permanent

Churches and clergy which supported themselves with tithes paid by local farmers and landowners, as guaranteed by episcopal writ, effectively belonged to the diocesan regime, and their resources could be placed at the bishop's disposal more effectively than if they came from the largess of lay patrons or monasteries. Certain laymen, like the counts Frederick and Otto, were willing to voluntarily submit their churches and tithes to the bishop as acts of piety. Others, like Berthold of Ravengiersburg, entered into a military alliance with the bishop and gained new legitimacy as the advocate of his formerly private church.

As Siegfried learned when he confronted the issue in Thuringia, however, shifting the tithe and tax regime in a particular area opened the door to a wide range of conflicts over lordship and power. His attempts to force Hersfeld and Fulda to pay tithes from property and churches under their control was only marginally successful, and resulted in a drawn-out conflict over a several-year period that included episodes of outright warfare.[89] At a royal assembly in Mühlhausen in 1069, Fulda finally yielded to an agreement with Siegfried over the tithes owed by the monastery's dependents in Thuringia, particularly those of the *milites*, or knights.[90] In a privilege for St. Peter's in Mainz, probably issued not long after the agreement at Mühlhausen, Siegfried states that his predecessors had "struggled to the point of bloodshed" to recoup the church's tithes in Thuringia, but that he had finally "acquired [them] more fully and securely."[91] Despite the dramatic rhetoric in his privilege, however, it is unclear if reality corresponded particularly well with the ideal. In 1073 and again in 1074— amid a violent uprising against Henry IV in Saxony and Thuringia—Siegfried held at least two major synods in which he attempted to compel the Thuringians, along with the two monasteries, to completely recognize his rights to tithes from their churches and property.[92] The synod in March 1073, held in the episcopal stronghold of Erfurt before Henry IV and a number of Mainz and Cologne's suffragan bishops, was only marginally successful from Siegfried's perspective, largely because his ability to enforce the agreements was obviated by the Saxon War.

Lampert of Hersfeld transmits a detailed account of the proceedings, including Siegfried's oration to the assembly justifying his claims. Even if we accept the words as Lampert's, and not literally Siegfried's, they nonetheless reflect a strong sense of reform as an idea of history unfolding in a preconceived direction. Responding to the argument that no bishops of Mainz before Liutpold had infringed upon the rights of either monastery regarding their tithes, Siegfried states that:

---

income stream for the church and placing previously rather fungible revenue under episcopal supervision.

[89]   See, for example, Lampert, *Annales*, pp. 107–8 (s.a. 1069).

[90]   *MUB*, no. 321, pp. 209–10.

[91]   "Unde ego Sigefridus dei gratia Magunt. sedis archiepiscopus notum facio omnibus tam futuris quam presentibus, quomodo decimationem illam super Thuringiam, pro qua antecessors mei maximeque proximus predecessor meus beate in Christo memorie Luidbaldus pene usque ad sanguinem certando laboravit, plenius et perfectius acquisivi": *MUB*, no. 323, p. 212.

[92]   On the synod of Erfurt, see Eldevik, "Ecclesiastical Lordship," pp. 53–54.

his predecessors, using their best judgment, had been moderate in their day towards the church of God, and had given those still new to the faith milk to drink rather than solid food, indulging many things with wise dispensation which, with the progress of time, and when they had grown stronger in their faith, would be eliminated through the efforts of their successors.[93]

Tithe reform entailed recognizing that a new stage in the Christian history of the region had been reached that effectively invalidated received tradition. Given Siegfried's view of the tithe affair as one of a long-term, and often violent, process fought by him and his predecessors, it seems likely that Lampert's account captures at least some aspect of Siegfried's argumentation at the synod. Of course, both Lampert and Siegfried's memories are selective reconstructions. There had been conflicts between the bishops of Mainz and the two monasteries over tithes going back to the ninth century,[94] which had been selectively remembered in the current revision of history proposed by each side. The monasteries—and, indeed, the Thuringians— envisioned their privileges as an unbroken protective umbrella over their possessions which extended back to their founding, while Siegfried saw the past in terms of an ongoing struggle to have the bishops' rights recognized, at first indulgently, and now with greater strictness. Eventually, Siegfried and the synod obliged the abbots to accept a compromise, dividing the tithe revenue between themselves and the bishop. The Thuringians, seeing that the issue was not going to be resolved in their favor, capitulated shortly afterward and agreed to submit their tithes as well.

In October of the following year, however, after an uneasy truce between Henry IV and the rebellious lords had been reached at Gerstungen, Siegfried held another synod at Erfurt where he announced to his clergy that he would be implementing new rules on clerical celibacy. He demanded that priests leave their wives and concubines or resign their offices.[95] According to Lampert, he then reopened the debate on the Thuringian tithes, which were still not being submitted, and the attending lords and knights nearly killed him and drove him from the church.[96] This is the last we hear of the tithe dispute under Siegfried, although he still attempted to excommunicate those who had disrupted the synod.[97]

---

[93]　". . . id atroci responso archiepiscopus repulit, scilicet predecessores suos sua aetate pro suo arbitratu aecclesiae Dei moderatos fuisse, eosque rudibus in fide auditoribus et pene adhuc neophitis lac potum dedisse, non escam, et sapienti dispensatione multa indulsisse, quae processu temporis, dum in fide convaluissent, successorum suorum industria resecari vellent": Lampert, *Annales*, pp. 142–43 (s.a. 1073). Giving milk to the uninitiated and solid food to the spiritually mature is an allusion to Heb. 5.12, as well as 1 Cor. 3.2.

[94]　Lübeck, "Zehntrechte und Zehntkämpfe des Klosters Fulda" (above, n. 42).

[95]　Lampert, *Annales*, pp. 200–1 (s.a. 1074). Siegfried here appears to have preempted the official pronouncement of these reforms by Gregory VII in a series of letters to the German episcopate in March of 1075; see *Das Register Gregors VII.*, ed. Erich Caspar, MGH Epistolae Selectae 2/1 (Berlin, 1920; repr. Berlin, 1955), 2.66–68, pp. 221–26. Either Siegfried had actually anticipated the papal policy by some months, or (more likely) Lampert intentionally conflated the tithe and the celibacy topics as a way of underscoring Siegfried's irrational disregard for custom and traditional law.

[96]　Lampert, *Annales*, pp. 200–1 (s.a. 1074).

[97]　*Regesten Mainz*, p. 203.

Siegfried and the Reform Papacy

While one might assume that Siegfried's efforts to assert the church's control over tithes would have been greeted warmly by the reform papacy, the opposite appears to be the case, particularly where papally-immunized monasteries were concerned. The reluctance of popes Alexander II and Gregory VII to endorse Siegfried's campaign against the Thuringians and the two monasteries is revealing in that it demonstrates the obvious fissures between Siegfried's vision of episcopal power and the far more subordinate role the reform popes expected him to play in ecclesiastical affairs.[98] Siegfried had tried repeatedly since the mid-1060s to attract the papacy's support for his tithe reform, but without success. Indeed, his campaign against Fulda elicited a fairly nasty rebuke from Alexander II which survives as an excerpt in a papal letter to the abbot Widerad.[99] Likewise, his efforts to assert his metropolitan rights in a dispute over the bishopric of Prague, as we shall see below, put him at cross-purposes with Gregory VII's theory of papal supremacy.[100] In 1072, he attempted to resign his episcopacy entirely and become a monk at Cluny, probably in no small part because of the withering reprimand he received from Alexander regarding the tithes.[101]

In April of 1073, about five months after Siegfried returned from his short-lived exile in Burgundy, Alexander II died and the archdeacon Hildebrand was elected as Pope Gregory VII. Later that same year, Siegfried sent a belated greeting to Gregory VII congratulating him on his election and requesting aid against the *inveterata obduratio* of the Thuringians, who were still refusing to submit to the bishop.[102] As noted above, the archbishop had forced a settlement upon both the monasteries and inhabitants of Thuringia in March of 1073, but the outbreak of a revolt later that summer had nullified its results.[103] Siegfried tried to set a conciliatory tone in this letter, but after complaining about the continued resistance in Thuringia, he went on to denounce the pope's interference in another affair that had also clouded his relationship with Alexander, namely the bitter feud between Gebhard, the bishop

---

[98]   I.S. Robinson, "'Periculosus Homo': Gregory VII and Episcopal Authority," *Viator* 9 (1978), 103–31.

[99]   *Germania pontificia*, vol. 4/4, *Provincia Maguntinensis*, ed. Hermann Jakobs (Göttingen, 1960), nos 86–87, pp. 386–87, found also in Jaffé and Wattenbach eds, *Regesta pontificum Romanorum*, nos 4658–59, p. 584. For the text of the letter, see PL 146:1409.

[100]   Tellenbach, *Church in Western Europe*, pp. 201–2.

[101]   *Regesten Mainz*, p. 195. Compare the account in Lampert, *Annales*, p. 139 (s.a. 1072), as well as the letter from the people of Mainz from the *Udalrici Babenbergensis Codex*, ed. Jaffé, no. 39, pp. 81–84. Marianus Scottus adds that Siegfried felt compelled to return when he heard that the "mercenarii" of Mainz were preparing to sell the episcopacy to the highest bidder; see his *Chronicon*, ed. Georg Waitz, MGH SS 5 (Hannover, 1844), p. 560 (s.a. 1094 [1072]).

[102]   *MUB*, no. 335, pp. 230–31, also in *Udalrici Babenbergensis Codex*, ed. Jaffé, no. 40, pp. 84–87.

[103]   "Hoc anno post exortum bellum Saxonicum nulla deinceps exactio facta est decimarum in Thuringia, gaudentibus Thuringis, quod occasionem invenissent, ut traditas sibi a patribus leges manu militari tuerentur": Lampert, *Annales*, p. 172 (s.a. 1073).

of Prague, and another prelate, John of Olmütz.[104] The origins of the dispute involved Gebhard's allegedly violent attempts to force Olmütz under his control and the subsequent resistance from John as well as his own brother, Duke Wratislav. Siegfried, who had consecrated both John and Gebhard, demanded that the matter be settled under his auspices, but Wratislav and John considered their chances better before the pope and sought redress in Rome. Alexander II had attempted for several years to mediate the dispute through papal legates, much to Siegfried's dismay. Although Prague was traditionally a suffragan bishopric of Regensburg, Siegfried still claimed jurisdiction in the affair as the supreme metropolitan in all Germany. Siegfried complained to Gregory that papal intervention in Gebhard's case threatened to undermine the authority and honor of the episcopacy itself, because it was the duty of bishops to appoint and depose other bishops within the framework of canon law.[105] He further cautioned that the maintenance of church discipline was particularly important in recently Christianized regions like Bohemia, where the people could easily revert to paganism if they saw dissension in the ranks of their Christian pastors.[106]

Gregory, however, summarily rejected Siegfried's claim to jurisdiction in the Prague matter and did not offer any opinion on the Thuringians.[107] As a proponent of a fundamentally hierocratic church, Gregory asserted the central role of the episcopacy, but that it should be strictly subordinate to the highest bishop, the pope in Rome. Siegfried's exclusive jurisdictional claims in the Prague case disrupted this line of authority, and his attacks on papally immunized monastic institutions surely disturbed Gregory as much as they had Alexander. It was not Siegfried's disregard for Roman authority that raised troubling issues for the popes, but rather how he saw papal authority operating in conjunction with his own, rather than over it. To be sure, Siegfried acknowledged the papacy as the head of the church, yet this is not the same as humble submission to Roman primacy in all respects; Siegfried expected the papacy to acknowledge and reinforce his own authority, not merely suggest that he refer all potential controversies or questions to final arbitration in Rome. As with monastic reform, Siegfried envisioned his diocese—and indeed all of Germany and its subject territories—as a unified whole under the guiding and renewing hand of his spiritual leadership. This view of Siegfried's world is brought into sharper focus when we consider the way in which it was couched in a certain view of history that

---

[104] A Bohemian perspective on the conflict is found in Cosmas of Prague, *Chronica Boemorum*, cc. 27–30, ed. Bertold Bretholz, MGH SS rer. Germ., n.s., 2 (Berlin, 1923), pp. 120–26. See, too, Tellenbach, *Church in Western Europe*, pp. 216–17.

[105] "Porro ecclesia illa iam multis diebus pastorali caret amministratione et vivente pastore vidua episcopali vacat benedictione; nisi quod episcopus ille (John of Olmütz), qui expulsionis et perturbationis huius auctor est, eius sibi usurpat officium et, quod omnibus conciliis et decretis maxime cautum est, consecrando et confirmando eundem circuit episcopatum": *MUB*, no. 335, p. 231.

[106] "Quod maxime ob hoc periculosum est, quod gens illa catholicae fidei novella est plantatio et nondum radicata et fundata in christianismo; et facile ad antiquum paganismi revolabit errorem, si inter pastores suos tantam viderit durare dissensionem": Ibid.

[107] *MUB*, no. 337, pp. 232–33, also in *Register Gregors VII.*, ed. Caspar, 1.60, pp. 87–88.

reinforced the centrality of Mainz in German history, as well as the centrality of spiritual leadership by the bishop.

History, Memory, and the Bishop as its Guide

In 1069, Siegfried brought the renowned Irish recluse Marianus Scottus to Mainz.[108] Marianus at the time was composing a major world chronicle and included certain details about events in Mainz that are not mentioned elsewhere, such as Siegfried's dedication of the Liebfrauenkirche monastery near to the main cathedral in November of that same year.[109] While Marianus does not give a detailed explanation for his move from Fulda to Mainz in his own history, the fact that it does appear to have been the result of an invitation—if that is how we might generously construe *iussio*—from Siegfried makes a great deal of sense given the latter's ongoing interest in both monastic reform as well as new foundations of institutional and local memory.

Heinz Thomas has cogently argued that Siegfried attempted to intensify Mainz's position within the German kingdom by reinvigorating the see's identification with the legacy of St Alban, the fourth-century martyr and eponymous patron of Mainz's oldest and most prestigious monastery.[110] Boniface, of course, had always been central to Mainz's identity as an archbishopric, and sometime during the first half of the eleventh century the *vita* of Boniface was re-composed to reflect new concerns about the authority of the see and the role of its bishops as leaders of the church within the German kingdom.[111] However, in the late 1060s or early 1070s,

---

[108]   "Ego miser Marianus, iusione episcopi Mogontini et abbatis Fuldensis, feria 6. ante palmas, 3. non. Aprilis, post annos 10 meae inclusionis solutus, de clausola in Fulda ad Mogontiam conductus": Marianus Scottus, *Chronicon*, p. 560 (s.a. 1091 [1069]).

[109]   "Consecratio novi monasterii sanctae Mariae in Mogontia, 9. Kal. Decembris, feria secunda, die sancti Clementis": Ibid.

[110]   See especially Thomas, "Erzbischof Siegfried von Mainz" (above, n. 1).

[111]   *Vita quarta Bonifatii auctore Moguntini*, in *Vitae sancti Bonifatii archiepiscopi Moguntini*, ed. Wilhelm Levison, MGH SS rer. Germ. 57 (Hannover, 1905; repr. Hannover, 2003), pp. 90–106. The date of composition is uncertain, but lies somewhere between the pontificate of Willigis (975–1011) and the composition of Othloh of St Emmeram's version of the *Vita Bonifatii*, which draws upon it (1060–1062). Compare Staab, "Mainzer Kirche," pp. 40–44, as well as the remarks by Levison ed., pp. xlix–l. A later, rather than an earlier date may be called for. In chapter seven, the author of the *Vita quarta* liberally reworks chapter eight of Willibald's *Vita Bonifatii* in describing the consecration of Lull as Boniface's successor. Note the following texts:

Willibald, *Vita Bonifatii*, c. 8, p. 45:	*Vita quarta Bonifatii*, c. 7, p. 98:
Et Lul suum ingeniosi indolis discipulum ad erudiendum tantae plebis numerositatem constituit et in episcopatus gradum provehit atque ordinavit eique hereditatem, quam in Christo instanti adquesierat labore, implicavit. . . .	Synodali auctoritate et consensu principis Pippini Lullum Mogontie ordinavit, secum primitus ad Thuringeam deduxit et omnibus in illa regione nobilibus illum commendavit uti fidei catholicae astipulatores ei assisterent. . . .

the celebrated schoolmaster Gozwin of St. Alban's in Mainz composed a new *passio* for Mainz's proto-martyr and dedicated it to Siegfried.[112] In it, the see of Mainz is described as primate of all Christians in Germany and Gallia, thereby establishing the tradition of Mainz's privileged place among the German bishoprics.[113] But, Gozwin also incorporated new details about Alban's mentor, Theonast, into the story, casting him, too, as a "prefiguration of Boniface."[114] Gozwin's *Passio* may have also served to help Siegfried configure his own identity in terms reflecting this new vision of Mainz's sainted past. In the *subscriptio* of his 1069 privilege for St. Peter's tithes, which we examined above, Siegfried signs *Sigefrido archipresule currum Dei aurigante*, a phrase alluding to Psalm 67.18.[115] He used the same *intitulatio* in the charter for Berthold and Hedwig of Ravengiersburg in 1074, as well as in the protocols of the 1071 synod that decided the case of Charles of Constance.[116] The notion of a bishop as the "driver of the chariot of God" first appears in the *Passio sancti Albani*, but refers to Paulinus of Trier, who "at that time was serving as the driver of the chariot of God as bishop among the Treverines."[117] Commentators from Augustine to Gregory the Great construed the idea of the "chariot of God" as a metaphor for the church—a vehicle transporting the community of saints to its final

---

The changes made in the later *vita* clearly suggest that the story's message was targeted in part to the Thuringians who are reminded of their ancestor's vows of loyalty to the bishop of Mainz.

[112]   *Passio sancti Albani*, MGH SS 15/2:984–90 (excerpts only, with the *Prologus* and dedication). The full text, minus the prologue, is available in *Thesaurus monumentorum ecclesiasticorum et historicorum*, ed. Basnage, pp. 157–66 (above, n. 23).

[113]   "Quia vero ab urbe Mogonciaca eo tempore primus veri solis radius per magnum illum Bonifacium Galliae Germanaeque illuxit, et perfidiae tenebras luce veridicae praedicationis exclusit, cunctorum assinsu adiudicavit apostolicus pontifex Gregorius, deinde Zacharias magnum Bonifacium, et sedem illi creditam primates dignitate et pallii honore perpetualiter insigniri, et per totam Galliam Germaniamque in omnibus concillis et ecclesiasticis conventibus Apostolica vice fungi": *Passio sancti Albani*, in *Thesaurus monumentorum ecclesiasticorum et historicorum*, ed. Basnage, c. 24, p. 164. See, too, ibid., c. 38, p. 166: "Vere felix tali patrono Mongontia, quae tanti martyris sanguine purpuratur, quae tam pretiosi cineric theca consecratur, quae victoriosi huius agonistae triumpho coronatur, in cuius veneratione Regina assurgit Gallia; nobilis applaudit Germania; imo tota congaudet ecclesia. . . ."

[114]   Staab, "Mainzer Kirche," pp. 64–77, with edition and commentary of a fragmentary *Passio Albani*, including the passages featuring Theonast, in New York, Columbia University Library, Plimpton Collection, No. 175. The cult of Theonast had been part of Mainz's commemorative literature since at least the mid-ninth century, where it appears in the *Martyrologium* of Rabanus Maurus, PL 110:1152 (X. Kal. Jun.).

[115]   ". . . currus Dei decem milibus multiplex milia laetantium Dominus in eis in Sina in sancto": Psalm 67.18.

[116]   *Acta synodi Moguntinae* in *Udalrici Babenbergensis Codex*, ed. Jaffé, no. 37, pp. 70–77, at p. 70.

[117]   "Qui videlicet Paulinus eo tempore apud Treviros Episcopali functus dignitate currum Dei aurigabat": *Passio sancti Albani*, ed. Basnage, c. 22, p. 162. The phrase was later picked up by Sigebert of Gembloux in his *Vita Deoderici episcopi Mettensis*, ed. Georg Pertz, MGH SS 4 (Hannover, 1841), c. 7, pp. 461–83, at p. 467: "Treviris auigabat currum Dei Henricus, post eum Egbertus. . . ."

reward.[118] It was an innovative and dynamic title for a bishop like Siegfried, who seemed, as so many in his day, increasingly conscious of both the past and the future and the fissures between the two. As the church fathers taught, the chariot of God, bearing the "multitude" of the saints, was destined for salvation. At the head of that vehicle were bishops like Siegfried—carrying forward with their prerogatives but also mindful of how those prerogatives were grounded in a careful cultivation and renovation of past memories and precedents.

The Ends of History and Memory

Although Siegfried was among the twenty-six bishops who joined Henry IV in calling for Gregory VII's resignation at the royal assembly in Worms in January of 1076, by the fall of the same year, he had abandoned the royal party and openly endorsed the efforts of Rudolf of Swabia to claim the crown.[119] The reasons behind Siegfried's dramatic switch are unclear, but undoubtedly linked to the fact that Rudolf agreed to be crowned in Mainz, thus formally restoring the ancient privilege of the archbishops of Mainz to anoint and crown the German king.[120] The decision was politically disastrous for Siegfried at home; the populace of Mainz remained fiercely loyal to Henry and both the bishops and the new anti-king were forced to flee when the inhabitants revolted during the coronation festivities in March 1077. Siegfried never entered Mainz again. When he died in 1084, he was buried in Hasungen, the monastery which he had reformed in 1081 and where, at least up to that point, Lampert of Hersfeld had served as abbot.[121]

Neither Siegfried's tenure as archbishop, nor the character of the changes he brought to Mainz, can be summed up in a single paragraph or article—and, indeed, I shall not try to do so here. Historians ought to resist the attempt to programmatize or systematize things too much. We can tease out from the above a few tendencies or trends, however, that can help put not only Siegfried's episcopacy, but also the tremendous religious, social, and political transformations of the eleventh century into a new context. The first is that, as Gerhart Ladner reminded us, reform and renewal were both historically contingent processes, but at the same time represented a persistent ideal fundamental to Christian institutions and society.[122]

---

[118]   Compare Gregory the Great, *Expositiones in Canticum Canticorum*, ed. Pierre-Patrick Verbraken, CCSL 144 (Turnhout, 1963), c. 45, pp. 43–44; Augustine, *Enarrationes in Psalmos*, vol. 2, *LI-C*, ed. Eligius Dekkers and Johannes Fraipont, CCSL 39 (Turnhout, 1956), p. 887.

[119]   *Regesten Mainz*, p. 209.

[120]   Thomas, "Erzbischof Siegfried von Mainz," pp. 395–96.

[121]   Struve, "Lampert von Hersfeld, Teil A" pp. 95–96, speculates that it was probably upon the death of Lampert that the monks invited Siegfried to impose a reform there.

[122]   Gerhart B. Ladner, *The Idea of Reform: Its Impact on Christian Thought and Action in the Age of the Fathers*, rev. edn (New York, 1967), p. 35: ". . . the idea of reform may now be defined as the idea of free, intentional and ever perfectible, multiple, prolonged and ever repeated efforts by man to reassert and augment values pre-existent in the spiritual-material compound of the world."

That is, there was, and always will be, "reform" in the Christian church of one kind or another. The historian's task is to understand how various strains of reformist thought evolve or interact with differing social, political, and cultural traditions over time. For Siegfried, reform of the church centered on redefining the meaning of the church's authority, possessions, and position in an historical context, and less around perceived moral deficiencies, like simony and clerical celibacy. While he displayed a certain deference to the papacy depending on the situation, it is clear that his image of a well-ordered and well-reformed church did not always elide easily with the one being promoted in Roman circles. The reassertion of Mainz's position as the primary see of Germany—a cornerstone of Mainz reforms since the time of Bardo—was a particular sticking point and one that underscores the diversity of reform ideology within the church during this period. Imposing common life on local clergy, as well as reforming monasteries, restored a kind of order that both laymen and ecclesiastics found comforting and useful. Restoring the proper structure to the tithe regime fulfilled a historical pastoral mandate and gave territorial and economic coherence to episcopal power. Patronage of new historical works reinforced the idea that a bishop like Siegfried worked within the legitimate traditions of the past and fulfilled them in an appropriate way. It was a view of the world in which the bishop occupied the driver's position in both time and place, in memory and in deed.

Chapter 10

Pastoral Care as Military Action: The Ecclesiology of Archbishop Alfanus I of Salerno (1058–1085)

Valerie Ramseyer
Wellesley College

Ad salutem fidelium,
cleri simul et civium,
venit corpus apostoli;
sit laus divinae soboli!

Lauda, felix ecclesia,
pange Christi praeconia,
claris vocibus intona;
sint vox et corda consona.

Plaude divinae gratiae,
quia coniunctus gloriae
Mathaeus nos non deserit,
nos servat, hostes conterit.[1]

Sometime before his death in 1085, Archbishop Alfanus I of Salerno composed a series of songs in celebration of the translation of the relics of St Matthew to the newly-constructed cathedral church.[2] Funded by the Norman duke Robert Guiscard, who less than a decade earlier had taken the city by force from the Lombard prince Gisolf II after a long and arduous siege, the new church was built on an elevated spot in the middle of the city. Surrounded by walls, with a tall bell tower soaring above, the church looks very much like a fortress, with a commanding view of the city itself as well as the port and adjacent countryside.[3] The songs composed by Alfanus likewise stressed Matthew's role as urban protector. According to the archbishop,

---

[1]   Alfanus I of Salerno, *I Carmi di Alfano I, arcivescovo di Salerno*, ed. Anselmo Lentini and Faustino Avagliano, Miscellanea Cassinese 38 (Montecassino, 1974), no. 58, pp. 225–26.

[2]   Alfanus, *I Carmi*, nos 58–62, pp. 225–32.

[3]   For a discussion of the cathedral church of Salerno, see Generoso Crisci and Angelo Campagna, *Salerno Sacra: Ricerche Storiche* (Salerno, 1962), pp. 118–24; and Valentino Pace, "La cattedrale di Salerno. Committenza programma e valenze ideologiche di un monumento di fine XI secolo nell'Italia meridionale," in *Desiderio di Montecassino e l'arte della riforma gregoriana*, ed. Faustino Avagliano (Montecassino, 1997), pp. 189–230.

the body of the saint was brought to Salerno specifically for the welfare and safety of the citizens, both clergy and laity ("Ad salutem fidelium, cleri simul et civium, venit corpus apostoli"), and Alfanus exhorted the Salernitans to give praise to God because St Matthew would never let down his loyal followers but would always protect them and annihilate their enemies. ("Plaude divinae gratiae, quia coniunctus gloriae Mathaeus nos non deserit, nos servat, hostes conterit.")

Such a composition will not seem unusual to historians of medieval Europe. Religious houses and the relics of saints played an important defensive role in cities throughout Italy and Europe in this period, and churches and monasteries often doubled as fortresses and centers of worship.[4] Nonetheless, in the case of Salerno the poem reflects a transformation in the role of the archbishops, who before the eleventh century played a negligible role in the Principality's administration and even had limited authority over religious life and organization. Unlike Carolingian territories, where bishops were an integral part of the government, Lombard rulers relied on secular officials to govern their realms. In addition, bishops in southern Italy were not an important component of pastoral care. They never created ecclesiastical hierarchies, never exercised authority over a system of parish churches, and never claimed a monopoly over certain religious functions. They neither participated in the education or training of the clerics in the diocese, nor did they focus on preaching or *cura animarum*. Instead, other types of institutions, including monasteries, private churches, and princely foundations, oversaw religious life and provided pastoral

---

[4]   For an excellent study of fortress-churches in the Languedoc, see Sheila Bonde, *Fortress-Churches of Languedoc: Architecture, Religion, and Conflict in the High Middle Ages* (Cambridge, 1994). Also see the recent study by Louis Hamilton, who talks about the strategic importance of churches in Rome during Robert Guiscard's conquest of the city in 1084; Louis I. Hamilton, "Memory, Symbol, and Arson: Was Rome 'Sacked' in 1084?" *Speculum* 78 (2003), 378–99. In the Principality of Salerno, evidence also suggests that churches served military purposes. For example, when the bishop of Paestum moved his cathedral church from Paestum to Capaccio sometime in the tenth century, the new site chosen was a well-fortified hilltop village referred to as a *castellum*; see Paolo Delogu, "Storia del sito," in *Caputaquis medievale*, vol. 1, *Ricerche 1973* (Salerno, 1976), pp. 23–32, at p. 24. In addition, churches were often built next to towers. In Salerno, for example, the church of San Felice was located next to the city's main citadel, while the church of San Michele Arcangelo in Capriglia and two churches in Cava, dedicated to Saints Liberatore and Vito, all had towers adjacent to them; Cava Archives, Arca XXIII, 20. (The archives of the abbey of the Holy Trinity of Cava, located just outside of Salerno, contain parchment charters dating back to the late eighth century. Charters in the archive are divided into two sections, based on a system created by monastic archivists working in the sixteenth through eighteenth centuries: the "Armario Magno," which contains what the archivists viewed as the most important documents of the monastery, and the "Archae," for all remaining charters. Charters from the Armario Magno are identified by a capital letter, followed by an Arabic numeral, with approximately 40–50 documents per letter. Charters in the Archae are identified by a Roman numeral followed by an Arabic one, with 120 documents per numeral. Editions of the charters up through 1080 are available in 10 vols, in the *Codex diplomaticus Cavensis* [below, nn. 8 and 53]. In this article, I will identify all post-1080 charters at Cava according to the archival system described above, which is still in use at the monastery today. For charters dated 1080 and earlier, I will provide a reference to the *Codex diplomaticus Cavensis*.)

care to the population in the form of religious services and the administration of the sacraments.[5]

Over the course of the eleventh century, however, and particularly during the episcopacy of Alfanus I, the role of the cathedral church in the Principality of Salerno would change as the archbishops initiated a slow reorganization of their

Fig. 10.1   The Principality of Salerno

[5]   On bishops in southern Italy in the early Middle Ages, see Giovanni Vitolo, "Vescovi e Diocesi," in *Storia del Mezzogiorno*, ed. Giuseppe Galasso, vol. 3 (Naples, 1990), pp. 73–151; Jean-Marie Martin, "L'ambiente longobardo, greco, islamico, e normanno," in *Storia dell'Italia religiosa*, vol. 1, *L'antichità e il Medioevo*, ed. Gabriele De Rosa, Tullio Grogy, and André Vauchez (Rome, 1993), pp. 193–242; Cosimo Damiano Fonseca, "Aspetti istituzionali dell'organizzazione ecclesiastica meridionale dal VI al IX secolo," in *Montecassino: Dalla prima alla seconda distruzione. Momenti e aspetti di storia cassinese (Secc. VI–IX). Atti del II Convegno di studi sul Medioevo meridionale (Cassino-Montecassino, 27–31 maggio 1984)*, ed. Faustino Avagliano, Miscellanea Cassinese 55 (Montecassino, 1987), pp. 297–316; repr. in Cosimo Damiano Fonseca, *Particolarismo istituzionale e organizzazione ecclesiastica del Mezzogiorno medievale*, Università degli Studi di Lecce, Saggi e Ricerche 25 (Galatina, 1987), pp. 3–20; Hans-Walter Klewitz, "Zur Geschichte der Bistumsorganisation Campaniens und Apuliens im 10. und 11. Jahrhundert," *Quellen und Forschungen aus italienischen Archiven und Bibliotheken* 24 (1932–1933), 1–61; Hans Erich Feine, "Studien zum langobardisch-italischen Eigenkirchenrecht," *Zeitschrift der Savigny-Stiftung für Rechtsgeschichte, Kanonistiche Abteilung* 30 (1941), 1–95, and 31 (1942), 1–105.

archdiocese, in tandem with papal reformers in Rome and the Lombard princes of Salerno, and began to participate more intensely in the religious life and organization of their archdiocese.[6] First, they constructed an ecclesiastical hierarchy made up of bishops and archpriests, with the archbishop exercising control at the top. Alfanus himself founded at least four new bishoprics and began to supervise more closely the religious houses and clergy that made up his archdiocese. Next, they received donations of lands and built up an episcopal lordship based on their castle of Olevano located in the Tanagro River Valley. They also sought to regain lands and churches that had been part of their diocese in an earlier period, but were now controlled by others. Finally, they promoted the reform of clerical lifestyles, calling for an end to simony and advocating for better education for the clergy. By the end of the eleventh century, the cathedral church of Salerno had become an important religious, political, and economic force in the region.

Traditionally, historians have viewed Alfanus's program of reform in purely religious terms.[7] They have interpreted the establishment of new bishoprics as part of a push by the archbishop to improve pastoral care by constructing churches for a growing population, especially in rural areas, and participating more directly in church organization and *cura animarum*. Indeed, evidence shows that Alfanus sought to involve himself more actively in the religious life of his archdiocese.[8] Yet Alfanus's reform program also had important political implications. With the establishment of the episcopal lordship in Olevano sul Tusciano and the creation of new suffragan bishoprics in his archdiocese, the archbishop became one of an emerging group of territorial lords who participated directly in the political administration of the Principality of Salerno, first under the Lombard princes and then under the Norman dukes.[9] These lords would form the primary basis of

---

[6]   On the reorganization of the archdiocese of Salerno, see Bruno Ruggiero, "'Parrochia' e 'Plebs' in alcune fonti del Mezzogiorno longobardo e normanno," *Campania Sacra* 5 (1974), 5–11, reprinted in his *Potere, istituzioni, chiese locali: Aspetti e motivi del Mezzogiorno medioevale dai Longobardi agli Angioini* (Bologna, 1977), pp. 175–81; Huguette Taviani-Carozzi, *La principauté lombarde de Salerne (IXe–XIe siècle): Pouvoir et société en Italie lombarde méridionale*, Collection de l'École française de Rome 152, 2 vols (Rome, 1991), 2:949–1036; and Vitolo, "Vescovi e Diocesi," pp. 116–41.

[7]   See, for example, Michelangelo Schipa, *Alfano I., arcivescovo di Salerno* (Salerno, 1880); Giorgio Falco, "Un vescovo poeta del secolo XI: Alfano di Salerno," *Archivio della società romana di storia patria* 35 (1912), 439–81; Nicola Acocella, "La figura e l'opera di Alfano I di Salerno," *Rassegna Storica Salernitana* 19 (1958), 1–74, and 20 (1959), 17–90; and, more recently, Vitolo, "Vescovi e Diocesi," pp. 126–27.

[8]   See, for example, his investiture of the new suffragan bishop of Sarno in 1066 and the *charta libertatis* issued to the new church of San Nicola de Palma in Salerno. Ferdinando Ughelli, *Italia sacra*, 10 vols (Venice, 1717–1722), 2:571–72; *Codex diplomaticus Cavensis*, ed. Simeone Leone and Giovanni Vitolo, vol. 9 (Cava dei Tirreni, 1984), no. 103, pp. 318–22. His numerous liturgical compositions written in honor of local saints also demonstrate his interest in the religious life of his archdiocese.

[9]   The archbishop's expansion of wealth and political clout can be seen most clearly in the diploma issued by Duke Robert Guiscard in 1080; see Léon-Robert Ménager, *Recueil des actes des ducs normands d'Italie (1046–1127)*, vol. 1, *Les premiers ducs (1046–1087)*, Società di Storia Patria per la Puglia, Documenti e monografie 45 (Bari, 1981), no. 35,

local government in the region in the twelfth century and beyond.[10] In addition, Alfanus's activities had a military dimension.[11] In particular, Alfanus's church building can be directly linked to military exigencies, and his establishment of new bishoprics had much more to do with protecting the archdiocese from the Normans' advance than with providing additional churches or clerics for the population. Moreover, after the Norman conquest of Salerno in 1077, Alfanus would continue to exercise political and military power through his bishoprics.

In many ways, Alfanus's program of reform had more political than religious ramifications for the cathedral church. Although the number of religious houses in the archdiocese directly under archiepiscopal control increased substantially in the twelfth and thirteenth centuries, proprietary churches and monasteries outside of episcopal jurisdiction continued to dominate the religious landscape of the Principality. Most rural churches were neither built nor administered by the archbishop, and religious sacraments such as baptism, burial, and penance never became an episcopal prerogative.[12] Alfanus's reform program thus neither aimed to place all religious houses and clergy under the authority of the cathedral church nor to make certain religious rites an episcopal monopoly.

A study of Alfanus's activities and extant writings brings to light an ecclesiology that unites the various elements of the archbishop's reform program and elucidates the meaning of pastoral care for the archbishop, highlighting what Alfanus saw as the primary duties and responsibilities of prelates.[13] For Alfanus, pastoral care meant more than just providing religious services for the population. It meant actively involving himself in the health and well-being of the citizens of his archdiocese, in this world and the next. One of the main ways Alfanus undertook such a responsibility was as custodian of the relics of St Matthew, whose power could be harnessed to provide protection for the Christian population. Other suffragan churches of the archdiocese of Salerno could similarly rely on the supernatural power of their patron saints to protect and defend their cities. In addition, the bishops and archbishops could rely on

---

pp. 110–13. In addition to the *castrum* of Olevano, the archbishop also controlled the *castellum* of Battipaglia at the mouth of the Tusciano River, as well as numerous lands, villages, and churches between the Tusciano and Sele rivers, making the archbishop one of the leading economic and political powers in the region.

[10] Valerie Ramseyer, "Territorial Lordships in the Principality of Salerno, 1050–1150," *The Haskins Society Journal* 9 (2001), 79–94.

[11] Pietro Caiazza, "Aspetti e problemi dell'opera di Alfano I arcivescovo salernitano," *Benedictina: Fascicoli di Studi Benedettini* 22 (1975), 347–58; Errico Cuozzo, "Un vescovo della Longobardia minore: Alfano arcivescovo di Salerno," *Campania Sacra* 6 (1975), 15–29; Gerardo Sangermano, "Nicola Acocella (Itinerario interrotto di un medievista)," *Rassegna Storica Salernitana*, n.s., 2 (1985), 179–202.

[12] Valerie Ramseyer, "Ecclesiastical Reorganization in the Principality of Salerno in the Late Lombard and Early Norman Period," *Anglo-Norman Studies* 17 (1995), 203–22, at pp. 211–12; Crisci and Campagna, *Salerno Sacra*, pp. 146–54.

[13] For a discussion of Alfanus's ecclesiology, see Benedetto Vetere, "Cattedrale, santo patrono, e cives," in *Salerno nel Medioevo*, ed. Huguette Taviani-Carozzi et al., Le città del Mezzogiorno medievale 3 (Galatina, 2000), pp. 55–95.

man-made defenses in the form of fortresses and walls. In this way the prelates became guardians of the safety of their flocks, protecting them against enemies who threatened their souls as well as those who threatened their city.[14] In so doing, they worked alongside lay rulers, who also relied on both human and divine assistance in their military undertakings. Thus, Alfanus's military actions did not in any way stand in opposition to his religious duties. Instead, they formed a key component to Alfanus's vision of pastoral care.

Alfanus was born *c.*1020 into a noble family which was perhaps related to the princely family of Salerno.[15] In his youth, he was an avid student of a variety of subjects, including Latin, Greek, medicine, and theology. In fact, Alfanus is known primarily for his intellectual achievements, which included medical treatises, translations from Greek, and a large collection of poetry, consisting mainly of hymns and offices composed for the celebration of martyrs and saints. In particular, his medical knowledge was renowned, and, according to Leo of Ostia, Desiderius, future abbot of Montecassino and Pope Victor III, first met Alfanus when he traveled to Salerno seeking a medical cure. Soon after, Alfanus fled his native city out of fear that he would be suspected of complicity in the assassination of Prince Guaimarius IV, in which his brothers had taken part. At the request of Desiderius, he took the monastic habit at the abbey of Santa Sofia in Benevento for a time. Still fearing that he would be implicated in his brothers' activities, he went to Florence, where Pope Victor II was sojourning. The two quickly became friends, but at Desiderius's behest Alfanus once again returned south. With the pontiff's permission, Alfanus and Desiderius entered the monastic community at Montecassino, where Alfanus remained until 1057, when Prince Gisolf II asked him to return to Salerno to become abbot of the monastery of San Benedetto.[16] Shortly thereafter he was elected archbishop, and in March 1058 he traveled to Rome where Pope Stephen IX ordained him a priest and then consecrated him archbishop of Salerno.[17]

When Stephen ordained Alfanus as archbishop, he issued him a bull reconfirming the cathedral church's privileges.[18] In many ways, Stephen's privilege resembles those

---

[14]   Vetere notes how in the poem quoted above, Alfanus used the plural form of "hostes," suggesting more than one type of enemy; Vetere, "Cattedrale, santo patrono," p. 73. In another poem, Alfanus more explicitly delineates between the two types of enemies that saints can protect against: those visible and those invisible. See Alfanus, *I Carmi*, no. 11, pp. 92–93.

[15]   Information on Alfanus's early life is found in two sources, both written at Montecassino: *Chronica Monasterii Casinensis / Die Chronik von Montecassino*, ed. Hartmut Hoffmann, MGH SS 34 (Hannover, 1980), 3.7–8, pp. 367–69; and Peter the Deacon, *De viris illustribus Casinensibus*, ed. and trans. Giuseppe Sperduti (Cassino, 1995), c. 19, pp. 84–85. Also see Acocella, "La figura," pp. 1–20, which summarizes and analyzes the information found in these sources and reviews the various theories about Alfanus's early life found in the secondary literature. Cuozzo distrusts the information found in the Montecassino sources, believing Alfanus to be a mere hagiographical construct in them: the ideal friend who accompanies Desiderius on his way to Montecassino. Cuozzo, "Un vescovo," pp. 16–17.

[16]   *Chronica Monasterii Casinensis*, 3.7–8, pp. 368–69.

[17]   *Chronica Monasterii Casinensis*, 2.96, pp. 354–55.

[18]   Julius von Pflugk-Harttung ed., *Acta pontificum Romanorum inedita*, 3 vols (Tübingen and Stuttgart, 1881–1886; repr. Graz, 1958), no. 116, 2:82–84.

Fig. 10.2   The Archdiocese of Salerno under Alfanus I (1058–1085) (new bishoprics in italics)

granted by his predecessors beginning in the late tenth century, when the cathedral of Salerno was elevated to the status of a metropolitan church and the newly-elected archbishops began to travel to Rome on a regular basis for consecration at the hands of the pope.[19] However, Stephen's bull also contained something novel. It listed four

---

[19]   For summaries of the confirmation bulls of previous archbishops, see Paul Fridolin Kehr ed., *Italia pontificia*, vol. 8, *Regnum normannorum, Campania* (Berlin, 1935; repr. Berlin, 1961), pp. 346–50, and Maria Galante, "La documentazione vescovile Salernitana: Aspetti e problemi," in *Scrittura e produzione documentaria nel Mezzogiorno longobardo: Atti del Convegno internazionale di studio, Badia di Cava, 3–5 ottobre 1990*, ed. Giovanni Vitolo and Francesco Mottola, Acta Cavensi 1 (Cava dei Tirreni, 1991), p. 239 and pp. 247–49. For editions, see Ughelli, *Italia sacra*, 7:376–77 (for Grimoald's 994 investiture); Ughelli, *Italia sacra*, 7:377 (for Michael's 1012 investiture); Pflugk-Harttung ed., *Acta pontificum Romanorum*, nos 95 and 97, 2:61–63 (for Benedict's 1016 investiture and Amatus II's 1019 investiture); Pflugk-Harttung ed., *Acta pontificum Romanorum*, no. 99, 2:64–65 (for Amatus III's 1036 investiture); and Ughelli, *Italia sacra*, 7:378–80 (for John's 1047 and 1051 investitures).

new bishoprics recently established by Alfanus I, in Marsico, Policastro, Martirano, and Cassano, and gave the archbishop permission to create more dependencies if he so desired. By the end of the eleventh century, three additional bishoprics had been added to the archdiocese in Sarno, Nusco, and Acerno (see Fig. 10.2).

Policastro and Marsico, both located in the southern part of the Principality, had been bishoprics in the late Roman period and would remain suffragans of Salerno up till the present day.[20] In contrast, Martirano and Cassano were completely new creations and both were located in Calabria, which was effectively outside the control of the prince of Salerno. By 1058 most of northern Calabria was in the hands of the Norman count of Apulia, Robert Guiscard, who had been campaigning in the region since his arrival in southern Italy ten years earlier. The inhabitants of Martirano had been paying Robert tribute since at least 1056.[21] Thus it is doubtful that Alfanus ever had control over these bishoprics or their bishops, and Stephen's bull is the only one to mention Martirano and Cassano as suffragans.

So why did Alfanus and Stephen attempt to establish new bishoprics in the area? Most likely it was part of the papacy's anti-Norman policy. Pope Stephen IX was a staunch enemy of the Normans in southern Italy, as his predecessor Leo IX had been. Stephen had been Leo's legate during the papal military expedition to southern Italy in 1053, when the pope joined forces with Emperor Henry III and various Lombard counts and dukes in an attempt to halt Norman expansion in the region. The venture ended in the disastrous defeat at Civitate, and Leo himself was taken prisoner. Afterward the Norman leaders easily continued their conquests, and it was the period immediately after Civitate that saw Robert's most stunning gains in Calabria.[22]

In 1058, however, a number of factors weakened Robert's position in Calabria. First, he had to spend time in Apulia making good his claim to succeed his brother Humphrey as count of Apulia. In addition, he fell out with his brother Roger, whose aid had been indispensable to Robert's conquests in Calabria. Finally, his marriage to Sichelgaita, Prince Gisolf II's sister, meant that he had to travel to Salerno. As a result, Robert Guiscard was completely absent from Calabria between April and the fall of 1058, during which time a famine broke out in the region as well.[23] Thus, Robert's hold over Calabria was precarious, making 1058 a propitious year for mounting a counter-offensive, and all four new suffragans mentioned in Stephen's bull were located in areas of strategic importance for preventing any further expansion on Robert's part, either in Calabria or into the Principality of Salerno itself. Policastro, in fact, became a region of intense fighting between the Normans and the Lombards

---

[20] Although at different locations, Policastro replaced the ancient see of Buxentum, while Marsico replaced the one at Grumentum; see Kehr ed., *Italia pontificia*, vol. 8, *Regnum normannorum, Campania*, pp. 371–76.

[21] G.A. Loud, *The Age of Robert Guiscard: Southern Italy and the Norman Conquest* (Harlow, 2000), p. 123.

[22] For more information on the battle of Civitate and its aftermath, see Loud, *Age of Robert Guiscard*, pp. 119–30.

[23] For a detailed account of Robert Guiscard's conquest of Calabria, see ibid., pp. 123–26.

beginning at this time, and would remain so until Robert's conquest of Salerno in 1077.[24]

When Nicholas II became pope in 1059, he reversed papal policy and allied himself with the Normans of southern Italy. He recognized Robert Guiscard as duke of Apulia, and Richard, the Norman count of Aversa who had captured Capua in 1058, as prince of Capua.[25] Up to the end of the eleventh century, popes continued to remain on more or less good terms with the new Norman rulers of southern Italy, with the exception of some difficult moments during the pontificate of Gregory VII. Interestingly enough, at the same time the popes went from enemies to allies of the Normans, the Lombard prince of Salerno, Gisolf II, did just the opposite, moving from friendship to antagonism. By 1060 the prince had embarked on his long, but ultimately futile, attempt to stop Robert Guiscard's expansion into his Principality and save it from the fate of the rest of southern Italy.

At the beginning of Gisolf's reign in 1052, the Norman leaders were important allies of the prince. Gisolf's father Guaimarius IV had formed strong bonds of friendship with the Normans, and it was largely due to Norman manpower that Guaimarius was able to expand his power.[26] Guaimarius was by far the most powerful ruler in southern Italy in the 1040s, controlling large sections of both Lombard and Byzantine territories. With a combined Norman-Salernitan army, he conquered Amalfi, Sorrento, and parts of Apulia. He received lordship over the Principality of Capua from Emperor Conrad II, who led a military expedition to southern Italy in 1038 and placed the Principality under Guaimarius's power in order to punish Prince Pandolf of Capua.[27] Then, in 1042, when the Normans divided lands they had conquered in Apulia and Calabria, they named Guaimarius as their sovereign.[28] Guaimarius, in turn, gave a niece in marriage to the newly-elected Norman count of Apulia, William, and shortly thereafter married off his daughter Gaitelgrima to William's brother Drogo, who became count of Apulia in 1046 after William's death.[29]

In 1052 the four brothers of Guaimarius IV's wife stirred up a rebellion against the prince. They entered his bedroom while he was sleeping, assassinated him, and

[24] Alfanus, *I Carmi*, no. 20, pp. 150–52; Amatus of Montecassino, *Storia de'Normanni*, ed. Vincenzo de Bartholomaeis, Fonti per la Storia d'Italia, Scrittori Secolo XI 76 (Rome, 1935), 8.30, p. 371; Prescott N. Dunbar, trans., with G.A. Loud, *The History of the Normans* (Woodbridge, 2004); Ferdinand Chalandon, *Histoire de la domination normande en Italie et en Sicile*, 2 vols (Paris, 1907), 1:148.

[25] For a detailed analysis of the 1059 investitures, see Loud, *Age of Robert Guiscard*, pp. 186–94.

[26] Vera von Falkenhausen, "I Longobardi meridionali," in *Storia d'Italia*, vol. 3, *Il Mezzogiorno dai Bizantini a Federico II* (Turin, 1983), pp. 251–365, at p. 283; Chalandon, *Histoire*, 1:80–87.

[27] Loud, *Age of Robert Guiscard*, p. 76. Emperor Conrad II was evidently upset that Pandolf had failed to provide hostages and pay tribute to the emperor as promised.

[28] Amatus of Montecassino, *Storia de'Normanni*, 2.29–31, pp. 93–97; William of Apulia, *La geste de Robert Guiscard*, ed. and trans. Marguerite Mathieu, Istituto Siciliano di Studi Bizantini e Neoellenici, Testi e Monumenti 4 (Palermo, 1961), lines 229–40, pp. 110–13.

[29] Amatus of Montecassino, *Storia de'Normanni*, 2.29, pp. 93–95; 2.35, pp. 101–3.

imprisoned Gisolf, his son and heir. Pandolf, the oldest of the four brothers, named himself prince, but he held office only for six days. Guido, Prince Guaimarius's brother, sought Norman aid against the usurpers, and Humphrey count of Apulia arrived promptly in Salerno. The Normans quickly overwhelmed the conspirators and placed Guaimarius's son Gisolf II on the throne.[30] Although the assassination seems to have been merely a palace coup, and not the result of Guaimarius's support of the Normans, Gisolf's reestablishment as prince was due solely to Norman help.[31] In return for their aid, Gisolf rewarded the Normans with both money and gifts. He also invested them in lands that they had captured and now held.[32] In addition, the prince remained neutral during the battle of Civitate in 1053.[33]

After Civitate, however, the friendship between Gisolf and the Normans started to break down. According to Amatus of Montecassino, a contemporary who wrote one of the most detailed accounts of the Norman conquest of southern Italy, the first signs of friction appeared sometime around 1054–1055, when Count Richard of Aversa and Humphrey, who became count of Apulia after the death of his brother Drogo in 1051, began to demand tribute from Gisolf, attacking the Principality of Salerno when payment was not forthcoming.[34] Richard, in fact, led an assault on the city of Salerno itself, killing 105 Salernitans in the process, while Humphrey gave military aid to his half-brother, William son of Tancred, who was beginning to carve out a lordship in the southern parts of Gisolf's Principality, referred to in the sources as the County of the Principate. In 1055 William and Humphrey captured the castle of San Nicandro, located two kilometers from Sicignano in the Tanagro River Valley, along with two other villages. Soon thereafter Count Humphrey made William "count of the Principate" and invested him in the lands he had conquered in the region.[35] In response, the inhabitants of Gisolf's southern territories began to fortify their villages, and small landholders began to donate their lands to religious houses in return for protection.[36] The whole region would remain a battleground for more than twenty years, as various Norman leaders fought Gisolf as well as each other in their quest to consolidate power.

Despite the conflicts between Gisolf and the three Hauteville brothers, Richard, Humphrey, and William, Gisolf at the same time attempted to form an alliance with a fourth Hauteville brother, Robert Guiscard, who arrived in southern Italy in around 1046–1047 and was elected count of Apulia in 1057 after the death of Humphrey.[37] Sometime around 1055, Gisolf sought to enlist Robert's aid in his battle against the

---

[30]   Ibid., 3.26–32, pp. 141–48.

[31]   Loud, *Age of Robert Guiscard*, p. 117.

[32]   Amatus of Montecassino, *Storia de' Normanni*, 3.32–34, pp. 148–49.

[33]   Loud, *Age of Robert Guiscard*, p. 117.

[34]   Amatus of Montecassino, *Storia de' Normanni*, 3.45–46, pp. 161–63.

[35]   Geoffrey Malaterra, *De rebus gestis Rogerii Calabriae et Siciliae Comitis et Roberti Guiscardi Ducis fratris eius*, ed. Ernesto Pontieri, Rerum Italicarum Scriptores, n.s., 5/1 (Bologna, 1928), 1.15, p. 16.

[36]   Amatus of Montecassino, *Storia de' Normanni*, 3.45, pp. 161–62; Ramseyer, "Territorial Lordships," pp. 90–91.

[37]   On the date of Robert's arrival in southern Italy, see Loud, *Age of Robert Guiscard*, p. 105.

rulers of Amalfi, who, in turn, were allied with Count Richard of Aversa.[38] Richard at this time was quickly becoming master of lands north of Salerno and demanding tribute from Gisolf.[39] The prince thus needed a powerful ally to help stop Richard's expansion southward into the Principality. Since Robert and Richard were the two most powerful Norman leaders in southern Italy in the 1050s, Gisolf's choice to ally with Robert Guiscard was a sound one.[40] At the same time, Gisolf fell out with his uncle Guido, who made a pact with Count William of the Principate sometime in the late 1050s and gave his daughter in marriage to the count.[41] Shortly thereafter, Gisolf's sister Sichelgaita married Robert Guiscard, who then convinced his brother, William count of the Principate, to make peace with Gisolf, although the reconciliation did not last long.[42] Presumably, through his alliance with Robert Guiscard, Gisolf hoped to share power with the count, allowing the Norman leader to rule over Calabria and Apulia while he kept control over the lands of the Principality that he had inherited from his father.

The alliance between Gisolf and the Norman duke was short-lived, as it became clear that Robert wanted nothing less than complete control over all of southern Italy, including the Principality of Salerno itself. By 1060, Gisolf had begun his long but unsuccessful battle against Robert Guiscard. A reconstruction of Gisolf's activities is difficult, not only because the sources for Robert's conquest of southern Italy were written by Norman supporters and thus tend to focus on Norman victories, but also because the chronicles spend little time on events in the Principality before the conquest of Salerno itself. Nonetheless, we know that in 1062 Gisolf took possession of some additional strongholds in Salerno and two nearby towns, Cava and Capriglia.[43] In addition, Gisolf traveled to Constantinople sometime in the early 1060s to ask for aid from the emperor against Robert Guiscard, who was attacking Byzantine as well as Lombard territory in Italy.[44] He also sent his brothers, Guido, Guaimarius, and Landulf, to Cilento to fight Robert's expansion from Calabria

---

[38] Amatus of Montecassino, *Storia de'Normanni*, 3.44, pp. 159–61.

[39] Ibid., 3.46, pp. 162–63; 4.9, pp. 188–89.

[40] According to Amatus, Richard alone of all the Normans was not subject to Robert's power at this time; Amatus of Montecassino, *Storia de'Normanni*, 4.7, p. 188.

[41] Ibid., 4.22, p. 197.

[42] Ibid., 4.18–19, pp. 194–96; 4.25, p. 199. According to Amatus of Montecassino, William became Gisolf's knight and the two of them were to share the castles located in the Principate.

[43] Cava Archives, Arca XXIII, 20. The 1062 document is transcribed in a later 1132 charter, although a 1067 papal bull acknowledged the archbishop's possession of San Vito "given by Prince Gisolf." An edition of the document is found in Salvadore Maria de Blasi, *Series principum qui Langobardorum aetate Salerni imperarunt* (Naples, 1785), pp. liv–lviii.

[44] Amatus of Montecassino, *Storia de'Normanni*, 4.39, pp. 209–12. On the date of Gisolf's trip to Constantinople, see Dunbar trans., *History of the Normans*, pp. 123–24, nn. 49 and 52.

northward into the Principality.[45] Finally, he allied himself with Gregory VII when the pope began to build a coalition against Robert in the early 1070s.[46]

In Amatus's chronicle, which contains the most detailed information on Gisolf's activities in the 1060s and 1070s, the prince of Salerno is seen switching his alliances constantly throughout the two decades preceding the conquest of Salerno, but always with the goal of finding partners to help him stave off Robert's expansion. The tenacity of Gisolf and his arduous struggle to stop Robert can also be gleaned from the conquest of Salerno itself. The siege lasted over seven months, and Gisolf refused to capitulate even as he watched his citizenry starve to death. When Robert finally entered the city, Gisolf continued to fight, holing up with his two brothers in a citadel where he remained for another few months.[47]

So where does Archbishop Alfanus fit into all of this? During Gisolf's seventeen-year struggle against Robert Guiscard and Norman expansion, Alfanus remained a loyal friend and ally to the prince. Alfanus accompanied Gisolf on his voyage to Constantinople, and although Amatus insinuates that the archbishop was tricked into going on the pretext of a pilgrimage to Jerusalem, and that the prince treated him so badly on the trip that the archbishop sought an alliance with Robert Guiscard upon his return to Italy, such assertions must be taken with a pinch of salt given the chronicler's strong animus toward the Lombard prince.[48] In fact, Alfanus's poetry

---

[45]   Alfanus, *I Carmi*, no. 20, pp. 150–52; Amatus of Montecassino, *Storia de'Normanni*, 8.30, p. 371.

[46]   H.E.J. Cowdrey, *Pope Gregory VII, 1073–1085* (Oxford, 1998), p. 430.

[47]   Amatus of Montecassino, *Storia de'Normanni*, 8.24–28, pp. 364–70.

[48]   Ibid., 4.36–39, pp. 207–12. The journey, in fact, is mentioned not during the author's chronological summary of Duke Robert's conquest but in a section devoted to demonstrating Prince Gisolf's evil nature; ibid., 4.33–49, pp. 206–20. Amatus saw Gisolf as the embodiment of everything sinful, and his trip to Constantinople to seek aid from the Byzantine emperor was proof of his dissimulation, arrogance, and greed. In addition, the suggestion in Amatus that, on his way back to Salerno, Alfanus approached Duke Robert Guiscard in an attempt to establish an alliance with him, could be the result of a poor rendering of Amatus's eleventh-century Latin into fourteenth-century French. The text (p. 211) reads as follows: "Et lo Impereor constreint lo Prince o tout terrible sacremens liquel il avoit juré. Et retorna riche de li don de li Empereor. Et li Archevesque prist autre voie, pour partir soi da sa compaingnie. Et vint droit à lo duc Robert, de loquel no fu receü come anemi, mès comme ami. Et non l'ot en reverence pour santtité qu'il venoit de Jherusalem, mès se mervailla que vint o grant barbe, comme s'il fust de Costentinoble. Et Gisolfe, qui avoit tout son penser en iniquité, toutez foiz contre li Grez se pensa malice." Most scholars have interpreted the passage to mean that Alfanus, after falling out with the prince, sought out Robert Guiscard. However, Lentini has made a convincing argument that an alternative reading could be that Gisolf, not Alfanus, came to Guiscard after his mission in Byzantium, feigning to be his friend. As the passage above shows, the old French text is often unclear about a sentence's subject. For example, it is clearly Gisolf who returned rich with gifts from the emperor, despite the fact that he is not named, and from a grammatical standpoint, the emperor could be construed as the subject of the second sentence. Moreover, elsewhere in Amatus's text Gisolf approached Duke Robert, falsely claiming a desire to become a friend and ally. Anselmo Lentini, "Sul viaggio di Gisulfo di Salerno con l'arcivescovo Alfano," in *Atti del terzo Congresso internazionale di studi sull'alto Medioevo: Benevento, Montevergine, Salerno, Amalfi, 14–18 Ottobre 1956*, vol. 3

reveals the archbishop's strong support of Gisolf and the Lombard defensive. Two poems composed by Alfanus around this time praised the military activities of Prince Gisolf and his brother Guido, and their success at beating down the Norman invaders, who had been wreaking havoc and causing much destruction in the area of Velia and Policastro.[49] Most significantly, Alfanus was directly involved in the defense of the Principality. It was he who in 1062 gave the prince the three fortresses mentioned above in exchange for the monastery of San Vito, located just outside the walls of Salerno near the sea.[50] These three *roccae* formed an important part of Salerno's defensive system. The first stronghold was located in Salerno itself, and it had served as the city's main citadel dating back to the reign of Arechis II (758–787).[51] The fortress of Capriglia was on the road that went from Rota to Salerno, while the one in Cava was located on Mt Burtuninu, above the road that led from Nocera to Vietri and Salerno.[52] Nocera was a region where Norman activity was widespread early on, and a charter at the abbey of Cava dated 1041 claimed that the Normans actually held the *comitatus* of Nocera.[53] The strategic importance of these three fortresses is thus clear.

In addition, the four or five bishoprics founded by Alfanus I in the Principality of Salerno, in Policastro, Marsico, Sarno, Nusco, and possibly Acerno,[54] were all in key strategic locations, with commanding views of the major roads entering into the Principality. Currently there are two hypotheses about the route Robert Guiscard's army took to Salerno, and, in fact, there were really only two ways to travel to Salerno from the south.[55] The first runs along the coastal route from Policastro and

---

(Spoleto, 1959), pp. 437–43; Caiazza, "Aspetti," pp. 351–52. Although it is possible that Alfanus and Gisolf had fallen out, it is our only indication of tension between the two men. All other evidence suggests mutual support and alliance.

[49] Alfanus, *I Carmi*, no. 17, pp. 143–44, and no. 20, pp. 150–52.

[50] Cava Archives, Arca XXIII, 20.

[51] Acocella, "La figura," p. 53.

[52] Taviani-Carozzi, *La principauté lombarde*, p. 302.

[53] *Codex diplomaticus Cavensis*, ed. Michele Morcaldi et al., 8 vols (Naples, 1873–1893), vol. 6, nos 985 and 1041.

[54] Kehr ed., *Italia pontificia*, vol. 8, *Regnum normannorum, Campania*, p. 303 and pp. 377–79; Cosimo Damiano Fonseca, "L'organizzazione ecclesiastica dell'Italia normanna tra l'XI e il XII secolo: I nuovi assetti istituzionali," repr. in *Particolarismo istituzionale e organizzazione ecclesiastica*, pp. 77–103 (above, n. 5); Vitolo, "Vescovi e Diocesi," p. 126; Elindoro Capobianco, *S. Amato da Nusco: Monografia storico-critica* (Avellino, 1935–1936). Acerno may have been established as a bishopric after Alfanus I's death. The first reference to it is found in the *Liber confratrum* of the cathedral church of Salerno, which lists the date of death of a Mirandus bishop of Acerno as either 1091 or 1106; see Kehr ed., *Italia pontificia*, vol. 8, *Regnum normannorum, Campania*, p. 379; Acocella, "La figura," pp. 36–37. Sarno, on the other hand, may have been a cathedral church before Alfanus's time, with the archbishop merely establishing it as a suffragan of Salerno, rather than creating it *ex novo*; see Galante, "La documentazione vescovile," pp. 233–34.

[55] Based on chronicle evidence, historians have traditionally thought that Robert's army traveled from Santa Severina in Calabria to Sant'Agata di Bianco near Gerace, then Cosenza, then a place on the Calabrian-Lucanian border called Rotunda, and finally up the coastal road to Salerno (see Fig. 10.3). More recently historians such as Cuozzo and Sangermano have

Fig. 10.3   Possible Path of Robert Guiscard – Coastal Route

through Velia and Paestum, approaching the city from the south (see Fig. 10.3). The second cuts through the Valley of Diano and the Picentine mountains to the Irpine Valley and then crosses to the Irno River Valley, approaching the city from the east (see Fig. 10.4). As the map clearly shows, all five new bishoprics were located along one or the other route. In addition, Sarno was located on the Via Popilia, leading to Nocera and Salerno, and was also on the border between the Principality of Salerno and the two major Norman realms of the time: the Duchy of Apulia and the Principality of Capua. Marsico was likewise located on the Via Popilia in the Valley of Diano, where Norman expansion was rife.[56] Places such as Atena, Brienza, and Teggiano became centers of Norman lordship in the eleventh and twelfth centuries.

made a convincing argument that the path taken by Robert started in a different Santa Severina in Calabria, and then traveled up through the Valley of Diano to Sant'Agata di Puglia, on to Conza, and then to a place called Castrum Rotunda located near Acerno, and then finally to Salerno itself (see Fig. 10.4). Errico Cuozzo, "Riflessioni in Margine all'Itinerario di Roberto Guiscardo nella Spedizione contro Salerno del 1076," *Rivista Storica Italiana* 81 (1969), 706–20; Sangermano, "Nicola Acocella," pp. 192–93.

   [56]   Ramseyer, "Territorial Lordships," pp. 85–86.

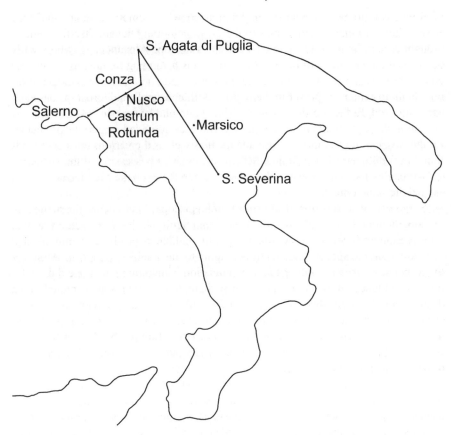

Fig. 10.4   Possible Path of Robert Guiscard – Inland Route

Furthermore, the new churches were located on some of the highest elevations in the area, overlooking roads and the surrounding countryside.

The new bishoprics established by Alfanus I not only aided Gisolf in his battle against Robert Guiscard, but also served to advance the archbishop's own ambitions by protecting the possessions of Salerno's cathedral church. As mentioned above, the archbishops of Salerno rapidly expanded their wealth and power over the course of the eleventh century. They established a lordship based on the *castrum* of Olevano sul Tusciano and received donations of land in both the Tanagro River Valley and the Irno River Valley.[57] In both of these areas, Alfanus had run-ins with Norman soldiers who were similarly carving out lordships in the Principality. He also clashed with the archbishop of Benevento over lands on the border of the two archdioceses.

In the Tanagro River Valley, conflict occurred between Alfanus and William, count of the Principate. Sometime around 1055, William, along with his knight Guimond

---

[57]   For information on the episcopal lordship of Olevano sul Tusciano, see Carlo Carucci, *Un feudo ecclesisatico nell'Italia meridionale: Olevano sul Tusciano* (Subiaco, 1937), and Taviani-Carozzi, *La principauté lombarde*, pp. 963–69.

of Molise, captured lands in and around Sicignano, while sometime before 1067 they took additional villages and castles in the area, including Olevano itself. Alfanus I brought a complaint about the men's activities to Pope Alexander II, who swiftly denounced the two perpetrators for usurping lands belonging to Salerno's cathedral church.[58] Although the two men gave back the land soon after, they nonetheless both built up centers of power in the region: William established lordships based on Sicignano and, further north, on Conza, while Guimond became lord of Eboli.[59] The cathedral churches built in Nusco and Acerno thus provided important protection for the *castrum* of Olevano sul Tusciano itself as well as the various episcopal lands found in the Tanagro River Valley. Alfanus also gained possession of the *castellum* of Battipaglia, located at the mouth of the Tusciano River on the Mediterranean Sea, around the same time.[60]

Sarno was well positioned to protect archiepiscopal lands being threatened by Troisio, the founder of the powerful Sanseverino family. In 1067, the same year that Pope Alexander II denounced William and Guimond, the pope also excommunicated Troisio for having appropriated lands belonging to the archbishop in Rota. Although the response of Troisio to the papal condemnation is unknown, the pope did confer the usurped lands on the archbishop shortly thereafter.[61] Alfanus also entered into a dispute with the archbishop of Benevento, Roffrid, over lands, churches, and castles in Forino on the border between the two archdioceses, which, according to the 849 division of the Lombard Duchy of Benevento, fell within the borders of Salerno's diocese.[62] Alfanus won his case and both Nusco and Sarno were well placed to provide protection for these lands.

Thus, the bishoprics created by or placed under Alfanus's authority in the 1050s and 1060s were all in locations of strategic importance for protecting the Principality against further Norman expansion. In addition, the new suffragans formed part of Alfanus's quest to increase the political and economic power of the cathedral church of Salerno. Moreover, once Alfanus and Robert Guiscard had made peace after the Norman conquest of Salerno in 1077, Alfanus continued to exercise authority over his suffragans and lordship, and the cathedral church became an integral part of the

---

[58] Kehr ed., *Italia pontificia*, vol. 8, *Regnum normannorum, Campania*, no. 25, p. 351.

[59] On the counts of the Principate and the lords of Eboli, see Errico Cuozzo, "'Milites' e 'testes' nella contea normanna di Principato," *Bullettino dell'Istituto Storico Italiano per il Medio Evo* 88 (1979), 121–63; Joanna H. Drell, *Kinship and Conquest: Family Strategies in the Principality of Salerno during the Norman Period, 1077–1194* (Ithaca, NY, 2002), pp. 177–84; Léon-Robert Ménager, "Les fondations monastiques de Robert Guiscard, duc de Pouille et de Calabre," *Quellen und Forschungen aus italienischen Archiven und Bibliotheken* 39 (1959), 1–116, at pp. 65–82.

[60] Both the *castrum* of Olevano and the *castellum* of Battipaglia are mentioned in the 1080 privilege issued by Robert Guiscard to Alfanus; see Ménager, *Recueil des actes des ducs normands*, no. 35, pp. 110–13.

[61] Kehr ed., *Italia pontificia*, vol. 8, *Regnum normannorum, Campania*, nos 24–25, pp. 351–52; Ughelli, *Italia sacra*, 7:382–84. Cuozzo, "Un vescovo," p. 22.

[62] Hartmut Hoffmann, "Die älteren Abtslisten von Montecassino," *Quellen und Forschungen aus italienischen Archiven und Bibliotheken* 47 (1967), 224–354, at pp. 352–54; Taviani-Carozzi, *La principauté lombarde*, pp. 993–96.

new Norman government in the region. Unlike Lombard and Byzantine rulers, the Norman dukes of southern Italy relied upon large religious foundations to govern their realm, and the reorganization of bishoprics as well as the establishment of Benedictine abbeys in the region formed part of the consolidation of Norman power in the second half of the eleventh century.[63] As a result, the cathedral church of Salerno and its suffragan bishoprics became centers of political power during Alfanus's episcopacy, and over the course of the twelfth century archpresbiterial churches established by archbishops would further expand the cathedral church's political reach. The new dependent churches in Campagna, Eboli, Olevano, Montecorvino, Giffoni, Ogliara, San Severino, San Giorgio, Montoro, Forino, Serino, and Nocera were all placed in fortified villages that became important nuclei of local power in the twelfth century.[64] Thus, as in other areas of southern Italy, Alfanus's program of ecclesiastical reform led to greater political authority and increased military responsibilities for the cathedral church of Salerno.

In addition, Alfanus was an important political figure not only within his archdiocese, but outside as well. He was a friend and ally to many reformers in Rome, and attended at least five papal councils during his career, including the Lateran Council of 1059, which issued new regulations for papal elections; the Council of Melfi in 1059, when Pope Nicolas II recognized Richard as prince of Capua and Robert Guiscard as duke of Apulia; and the Roman Council of 1073, when Hildebrand was elevated to the papacy. He was present at the dedication of the new basilica of Montecassino in 1071 and composed a series of odes in honor of it.[65] Alfanus also took part in important theological debates, such as the Berengar controversy regarding the eucharist, and supported reformers such as Gregory VII, who advocated a stronger political role for prelates.[66] In a poem composed to

---

[63]   Vitolo, "Vescovi e Diocesi," pp. 131–32; Norbert Kamp, "Vescovi e diocesi nell'Italia meridionale nel passaggio dalla dominazione bizantina allo stato normanno," in *Il passaggio dal dominio bizantino allo stato normanno nell'Italia meridionale: Atti del secondo Convegno internazionale di Studi sulla civiltà rupestre medioevale nel Mezzogiorno d'Italia, Taranto-Mottola, 31 ottobre–4 novembre 1973*, ed. Cosimo Damiano Fonseca (Taranto, 1977), pp. 165–87, at pp. 176–79.

[64]   Bruno Ruggiero, "Per una storia della pieve rurale nel Mezzogiorno medievale," in *Potere, istituzioni, chiese locali* (above, n. 6), pp. 59–106, at pp. 65–66.

[65]   Acocella, "La figura," pp. 40–44; Giuseppe Paesano, *Memorie per servire alla storia della chiesa Salernitana*, vol. 1 (Naples, 1846), pp. 117–21, 128–29; H.E.J. Cowdrey, *The Age of Abbot Desiderius: Montecassino, the Papacy, and the Normans in the Eleventh and Early Twelfth Centuries* (Oxford, 1983), pp. 74–75.

[66]   Cowdrey, *Age of Abbot Desiderius*, p. 91. Interestingly, during the debate over transubstantiation, Alfanus condemned Berengar of Tours against his better judgment. A letter written by a friend or pupil of Berengar to Alfanus shortly after the 1059 Lateran council claimed that the archbishop not only found Berengar's theory on the eucharist to be perfectly orthodox, but even went so far as to say that anyone who had read and understood Augustine would have no choice but to side with Berengar. Nonetheless, according to the letter, Alfanus decided to support the pope and go along with the majority. For an edition of the letter, see R.W. Southern, "Lanfranc of Bec and Berengar of Tours," *Studies in Medieval History Presented to Frederick Maurice Powicke*, ed. R.W. Hunt et al. (Oxford, 1948), pp. 27–48, at p. 48.

Hildebrand before his election to the papacy, he praised the future pope and glorified Rome as the center of the world, advocating a renewal of the Roman polity under the leadership of St Peter and reformers like archdeacon Hildebrand.[67] Clearly, Alfanus was more than just a pious monk and brilliant scholar. He was a man at the center of the important political events of his time.[68]

Moreover, Alfanus's reorganization of his archdiocese did not have a solely military or political meaning. Alfanus was interested in the *cura animarum*, and in ensuring that the Christian populace in the new dioceses had properly trained clerics to serve in the churches. When Alfanus invested Risus as the new bishop of Sarno in 1066, for example, the archbishop checked to make sure that Risus was educated, literate, and morally upright. He also instructed the new bishop on the correct way to celebrate religious holidays and carry out baptisms and the ordination of new clerics.[69] In emancipation charters to new proprietary foundations, Alfanus similarly showed concern that proper procedure be followed. In a 1070 *charta libertatis* issued to the church of San Nicola de Palma in Salerno, for example, Alfanus required the owners to appoint clerics according to canonical practice and stated that the clerics themselves had to behave in an orthodox manner.[70] Finally, Alfanus's numerous liturgical compositions demonstrate his attention to the proper ordering of religious celebrations in his archdiocese. Thus, Alfanus participated intensely in the religious life of his city and archdiocese, seeking to establish common standards for clerical lifestyles and the celebration of religious services.

Alfanus's religious and political activities did not oppose, but rather complemented one another. They formed part of his vision of pastoral care in which prelates, princes, and patron saints worked together to protect Christians in this world and guide them to salvation in the next. Military activity was an integral part of the equation, and this is clearly seen in Alfanus's poetry, which is infused with military vocabulary and imagery. For example, Alfanus referred to the martyrs Fortunatus, Gaius, and Anthes, whose relics were located in Salerno, as "soldiers of Christ," able to drive away enemies both visible and invisible.[71] In a hymn dedicated to the monks at Montecassino, he spoke of the "army of saints" who resided side-by-side with the monks and participated in their activities.[72] Prelates also become *milites Christi* in Alfanus's poetry. For example, in a eulogy dedicated to Bernard, cardinal-bishop of Palestrina, Alfanus praised Bernard for destroying the enemies of the church.[73] Alfanus even composed a whole hymn in honor of all of Christ's soldiers, entitled *Oda excitativa militis Christi*.[74]

Furthermore, lay rulers were a third element in the equation, similarly playing an important role in the defense of the *populus christianus*. In two poems dedicated to

---

[67] Alfanus, *I Carmi*, no. 22, pp. 155–57.
[68] Caiazza, "Aspetti," pp. 350–51.
[69] Ughelli, *Italia sacra*, 2:571–72.
[70] *Codex diplomaticus Cavensis*, ed. Leone and Vitolo, vol. 9, no. 103, pp. 318–22.
[71] Alfanus, *I Carmi*, no. 11, pp. 92–93.
[72] Ibid., no. 39, p. 191.
[73] Ibid., no. 30, p. 169.
[74] Ibid., no. 52, p. 215.

Prince Gisolf II and his brother Guido, for example, he praised the two brothers for protecting the realm and restoring order by means of laws and military prowess.[75] In a poem composed in honor of the Twelve Brethren, whose relics Duke Arechis II brought to the city of Benevento in the eighth century, he paid tribute to the complementary role of duke and saint, who worked together to bring victory to their people.[76] In addition, in Alfanus's poetry, military activity could take on an explicitly religious character. In the poem dedicated to Gisolf's brother, Guido, Alfanus compared Guido's decision to concentrate on military activity to a monk's choice to embrace a religious life, because both chose to sacrifice a tranquil life in order to serve the public good.[77] Thus, in Alfanus's vision of pastoral care, prelates, princes, and saints worked together to protect and take care of the Christians under their care, which meant that fortresses, churches, and relics served complementary purposes.

Historians have often exaggerated the supposed dichotomy between religious duties and political undertakings, between the sacred and the mundane, and even between the roles of secular and regular clergy. Alfanus's career demonstrates well how all of these elements blended together. Pastoral care and the exercise of political and military power were two sides of the same coin for Alfanus, and he would have seen no contradiction in using churches and clerics for military and political ends. Political goals were infused with religious meaning, and vice versa, which meant that military activity was a central component of pastoral care.

In addition, Alfanus is an excellent representative of the spirit of monastic reform characteristic of southern Italy. Unlike centers of reform such as the abbey of Cluny, southern Italian abbeys did not focus on the promotion of an exemplary monastic lifestyle, did not introduce spiritual, devotional, or liturgical reforms, and did not seek to reform other monasteries in the region.[78] Instead, for men like Desiderius and Alfanus, reform meant above all a return to the ancient Roman world, and the type of government set in place by Emperor Constantine.[79] As a result, church reformers in southern Italy sought a new Christian polity based on a partnership between lay and ecclesiastical leaders, and Alfanus and the other monks at Montecassino saw no dichotomy between a monastic and secular existence. They were expected to participate in the establishment and administration of the new Christian order, and Alfanus was not the only monk from Montecassino who later became a bishop and episcopal reformer. Many church leaders in southern Italy were trained in large

---

[75] Ibid., no. 17, pp. 143–44, and no. 20, pp. 150–52.

[76] Ibid., no. 13, p. 125. The link between the military power of lay rulers and relics can also be seen in Robert Guiscard's actions after his conquest of Salerno: he demanded the return of St Matthew's tooth, which Gisolf had taken from the cathedral church, because he wanted to ensure that the city did not lose the precious relic; Amatus of Montecassino, *Storia de'Normanni*, 8.29, pp. 370–71.

[77] Alfanus, *I Carmi*, no. 20, pp. 150–52.

[78] Cowdrey, *Age of Abbot Desiderius*, pp. 29–30.

[79] A good example of this view can be seen in the inscriptions composed by Alfanus for the new basilica of Montecassino, which mirrored closely the ones inscribed in Constantine's Roman basilica of Saint Peter that depicted Emperor Constantine as the model ruler; Cowdrey, *Age of Abbot Desiderius*, pp. 73–75.

Benedictine monasteries, demonstrating how a monastic education often led to a politically active career.[80]

Such a vision of reform even led reformers from elsewhere to level criticisms against the monks and abbots at Montecassino. Peter Damian, for example, while praising the abbey for its fame and grandeur, at the same time chastised Abbot Desiderius for his involvement in the world and warned him to free himself from worldly distractions. He also disapproved of what he perceived as lax spiritual standards found in the abbey, and wrote letters to the monks in which he implored them to fast more frequently and pay more attention to their religious duties.[81] Thus, monastic reform in southern Italy was different from that in other parts of the Latin West, and Alfanus's career reminds us of the diverse forms that church reform could and did take in eleventh-century Latin Christendom.

---

[80]   Norbert Kamp, "The Bishops of Southern Italy in the Norman and Staufen Periods," trans. G.A. Loud and Diane Milburn, in *The Society of Norman Italy*, ed. G.A. Loud and Alex Metcalfe, The Medieval Mediterranean 38 (Leiden, 2002), pp. 191–93.

[81]   Cowdrey, *Age of Abbot Desiderius*, pp. 34–38.

Chapter 11

What Made Ivo Mad? Reflections on a Medieval Bishop's Anger

Bruce C. Brasington

West Texas A&M University

That word "individualism" which we have coined for our own requirements was unknown to our ancestors, for the good reason that in those days every individual necessarily belonged to a group and no one could regard himself as an isolated unit.[1]

Alexis de Toqueville, *The Old Regime and the French Revolution*

Alexis de Tocqueville reminds us of the dangers of imposing modern terminology on the past.[2] Such reservations have, however, frequently been ignored. Since the Enlightenment, there has been periodic reflection on how "modern" temperament differs from the emotions of medieval people.[3] Marc Bloch judged that medieval, "unrestrained" emotions, accompanied often by seemingly irrational behavior, revealed a worldview still shaped by nature, not institutions.[4] Others, notably

---

[1]   Alexis de Toqueville, *The Old Regime and the French Revolution*, trans. Stuart Gilbert (Garden City, NY, 1955), p. 96, quoted in John Jeffries Martin, "The Myth of Renaissance Individualism," in *A Companion to the Worlds of the Renaissance*, ed. Guido Ruggiero (Oxford, 2002), pp. 208–24, at p. 220.

[2]   Karl F. Morrison, *History as a Visual Art in the Twelfth-Century Renaissance* (Princeton, NJ, 1990), p. 247: "To historians of our day it seems self-evident that once a critic begins with the assumption that there is more to a work than can be seen, inquiries have to be bridled; for, at some point in the inquiry, there may be less, or something other, in the text than the critic sees."

[3]   A search of the JSTOR database (11 August 2005) revealed 691 citations of "medieval mind" in articles and reviews. In the popular press, a relatively recent example is William Manchester's *A World Lit only by Fire: The Medieval Mind and the Renaissance. Portrait of an Age* (Boston, 1993). For a learned and critical review, see Jeremy DuQuesnay Adams, *Speculum* 70 (1995), 173–74. See also, among many studies, Robin Fleming, "Picturesque History and the Medieval in Nineteenth-Century America," *The American Historical Review* 10 (1995), 1061–94; Paul Freedman and Gabrielle M. Spiegel, "Medievalisms Old and New: The Rediscovery of Alterity in North American Medieval Studies," *The American Historical Review* 103 (1998), 677–704; Fred C. Robinson, "Medieval, The Middle Ages," *Speculum* 59 (1984), 745–56.

[4]   Stephen D. White, "The Politics of Anger," in *Anger's Past: The Social Uses of An Emotion in the Middle Ages*, ed. Barbara Rosenwein (Ithaca, NY, 1998), pp. 127–52, at pp. 130–31, commenting on Bloch's *Feudal Society* and Johan Huizinga's *The Waning of the Middle Ages*. See also Benedicta Ward, *Miracles and the Medieval Mind: Theory, Record*

Colin Morris, have been apologists, arguing that the twelfth-century "Renaissance" championed by Charles Homer Haskins was the moment when self-reflection anticipated the modern, introspective personality.[5] In either case, however, the point of comparison is with our modernity.

Such explorations impose modern psycho-social constructs on the past. Without sensitivity to historical context—not the least being a textual record in medieval Latin—inflexible modes of interpretation lead to the tyranny of the model.[6] The medieval world does not easily submit itself to psychological analysis. Stephen White's comments on Marc Bloch should be kept in mind:

> Finally, because he tried to identify and explain the emotional style of feudal society *generally* without regard to such variables as class, status, gender, or regional identity, he neither located medieval emotions in particular political settings nor studied the emotional setting of political actions.[7]

When these variables are considered, remarkable insights are possible.[8] Scholars have revealed how the elaborate rhetorical formulae of charters and letters help us better understand why medieval men and women acted, spoke, even felt the way

---

and Event 1000–1215 (Philadelphia, 1987), especially the introduction and chapter one. The replacement of the ordeal by "rational" proof has attracted much attention, on which see recently Edward L. Rubin, "Trial by Battle and Trial by Argument," *Arkansas Law Review* 56 (2003), 261–94, and Trisha Olson, "Of Enchantment: The Passing of Ordeals and the Rise of the Jury Trial," *Syracuse Law Review* 50 (2000), 109–96, both accessed via Lexis-Nexis on 30 July 2003.

[5] Colin Morris, *The Discovery of the Individual (1050–1200)* (New York, 1972). On Morris, Southern, and other advocates for this emergence of individualism, see Susan R. Kramer and Caroline W. Bynum, "Revisiting the Twelfth-Century Individual: The Inner Self and the Christian Community," in *Das Eigene und das Ganze: Zum Individuellen im mittelalterlichen Religiosentum*, ed. Gert Melville and Markus Schürer, Vita Regularis 16, (Münster, 2002), pp. 57–85. Haskins's own interest in the medieval individual as revealed in surviving letters was apparent early in his career, as seen in "The Life of Medieval Students as Illustrated by their Letters," *The American Historical Review* 3 (1898), 203–29.

[6] Charles M. Radding, "Superstition to Science: Nature, Fortune, and the Passing of the Medieval Ordeal," *The American Historical Review* 84 (1979), 945–69. More persuasive is Arno Borst, "Heretics and Hysteria," in *Medieval Worlds: Barbarians, Heretics, and Artists in the Middle Ages*, trans. Eric Hansen (Chicago, 1996), pp. 91–100.

[7] White, "The Politics of Anger," in *Anger's Past*, ed. Rosenwein, p. 130.

[8] Stephen D. White, "*Pactum . . . Legem Vincit et Amor Judicium*: The Settlement of Disputes by Compromise in Eleventh-Century Western France," *The American Journal of Legal History* 22 (1978), 281–308, with discussion of *concordia* and its cognates in charters resolving disputes. On the rhetorical code in letters from bishops from the late eleventh and early twelfth centuries, see Marylou Ruud, "Unworthy Servants: The Rhetoric of Resignation at Canterbury, 1070–1170," *The Journal of Religious History* 22 (1998), 1–13, which discusses how pleas by the archbishops of Canterbury about "unworthiness" served to strengthen their position. See also Antonia Harbus, "The Medieval Concept of the Self in Anglo-Saxon England," *Self and Identity* 1 (2002), 77–97, discussing forms of lament in elegiac poetry.

they did. [9] The results are far more sensitive than the above-mentioned categorical judgments of "irrational" or "religious" applied to "the medieval mind."

The following is one such attempt to encounter a medieval individual, Bishop Ivo of Chartres (c.1040–1115). It is a particularly difficult task. In addition to the challenges of encountering a medieval author on his own terms, we confront screens of rhetorical conventions, [10] and a discourse shaped by exegesis, patristic admonition, and canon law. [11]

Nevertheless, Ivo's correspondence permits glimpses of the author. These occur when he becomes angry. Scholars have noted that anger could be expressed in various ways, from formal monastic protests against those who disturbed a community's rights or properties, to letters advancing claims and counter-claims of dispute among the religious and political elite. [12] Ivo will draw upon these rhetorical strategies in his angry letters; he will also, at one point, uniquely express his anger.

Reading Ivo's Anger

Educated at Bec, Ivo became bishop of Chartres in 1090 after some years as provost of Saint-Quentin in Beauvais. [13] The alumni of Bec were particularly enthusiastic correspondents, and Ivo was no exception. [14] Their letters formed and maintained

---

[9]   Geoffrey Koziol, *Begging Pardon and Favor: Ritual and Political Order in Early Medieval France* (Ithaca, NY, 1992); Philippe Buc, *The Dangers of Ritual: Between Early Medieval Texts and Social Scientific Theory* (Princeton, NJ, 2001); and Koziol, "The Dangers of Polemic: Is Ritual Still an Interesting Topic of Historical Study?" *Early Medieval Europe* 11 (2003), 367–88.

[10]   For an introduction, see Terence O. Tunberg, "Prose Styles and *Cursus*," in *Medieval Latin: An Introduction and Bibliographical Guide*, ed. F.A.C. Mantello and A.G. Rigg (Washington, DC, 1996), pp. 111–21. On *dictamen* and its relationship to "proto-humanism," see Ronald Witt, "Medieval *Ars dictaminis* and the Beginnings of Humanism: A New Construction of the Problem," *Renaissance Quarterly* 35 (1982), 1–35.

[11]   Constance Brittain Bouchard, *Spirituality and Administration: The Role of the Bishop in Twelfth-Century Auxerre,* Speculum Anniversary Monographs 5 (Boston, 1979), especially its introduction and conclusion; see also Robert L. Benson, *The Bishop-Elect: A Study in Medieval Ecclesiastical Office* (Princeton, NJ, 1968).

[12]   In addition to White, "The Politics of Anger," see Lester K. Little, "Anger in Monastic Curses," in *Anger's Past*, ed. Rosenwein, pp. 9–35, especially the discussion at pp. 27–28 of how anger was expressed in "a shared culture of speech acts." See also his *Benedictine Maledictions: Liturgical Cursing in Romanesque France* (Ithaca, NY, 1993).

[13]   Rolf Sprandel, *Ivo von Chartres und seine Stellung in der Kirchengeschichte*, Pariser historische Studien 1 (Stuttgart, 1962). On Ivo's views toward the laity, see Michel Grandjean, *Laïcs dans l'Église: Regards de Pierre Damien, Anselme de Cantorbéry, Yves de Chartres*, Théologie historique 97 (Paris, 1994), especially pp. 310–37; Kimberly LoPrete, "Adela of Blois and Ivo of Chartres: Piety, Politics, and the Peace in the Diocese of Chartres," *Anglo-Norman Studies* 14 (1991), 131–52.

[14]   Most recently, see Sally N. Vaughn, *St. Anselm and the Handmaidens of God: A Study of Anselm's Correspondence with Women* (Turnhout, 2002); also Thomas Michael Krüger, *Persönlichkeitsausdruck und Persönlichkeitswahrnehmung im Zeitalter der*

ties of friendship, patronage, and power.[15] His correspondence chronicles an exceptionally active career; for over two decades, he was one of the leading figures not only in France but also in the wider Church.[16] Well over eighty manuscripts survive that transmit his letters in varying collections, proof of their reception during the twelfth century.[17]

Often, Ivo spoke with the traditional voice of episcopal authority, betraying few signs of personal frustration or anger at the matter in question. Typical is letter 234, sent to the newly-installed abbot of Marmoutier, William, sometime around 1104, in which Ivo asserted that the abbot must submit to his bishop.[18] By demanding that William render due obedience (*obedientiam debitam*), Ivo supported his colleague at Tours and emphasized episcopal solidarity. What mattered was achieving peace.

Other letters, however, reveal a greater degree of agitation. Ivo expressed this through the term *inauditum*, "unheard of."[19] Condemnations of events as novelties abound in medieval texts.[20] When fortified by claims that they were "unheard of," they became even clearer signs of how the present had declined from the golden past.[21]

Investiturkonflikte: Studien zu den Briefsammlungen des Anselm von Canterbury, Spolia Berolinensia 22 (Hildesheim, 2002).

[15] Giles Constable, *Letters and Letter-Collections*, Typologie des sources du moyen âge occidental 17 (Turnhout, 1976), and, more recently, the chapter "The Rhetoric of Reform" in his *The Reformation of the Twelfth Century* (Cambridge, 1996). See also, among many studies, Morris, *Discovery of the Individual*, pp. 97–107, treating expressions of *amicitia*, and I.S. Robinson, "The Friendship Network of Gregory VII," *History* 63 (1979), 1–22.

[16] For a contemporary appreciation, see Sigebert of Gembloux, *Liber de scriptoribus ecclesiasticis*, c. 167 (PL 160:586), who notes Ivo's *utiles valde epistolas*.

[17] The *editio princeps* is D. *Ivonis: Opera omnia*, ed. Jean Fronteau, 2 vols (Paris, 1647), with the letters in vol. 2. This was reprinted with no essential change in PL 162. Neither edition was based on an analytical or extensive selection of the surviving manuscripts. A partial edition of the letters by Jean Leclercq now enables us to compare at least some of the letters in Fronteau's edition with a more recent version based on fresh manuscript collations: Jean Leclercq ed. and trans, *Yves de Chartres: Correspondance*, Les classiques de l'histoire de France au moyen âge 22 (Paris, 1949). The forthcoming Cambridge dissertation of Christof Rolker offers a major reevaluation of both the transmission of Ivo's letters and their relationship to Ivo's work in canon law. See also Bruce C. Brasington, "New Perspectives on the Letters of Ivo of Chartres," *Manuscripta* 37 (1993), 168–78.

[18] "Cum ab inferioribus membris praelatis suis plena fuerit obedientia exhibita; quam quia multo tempore non exhibuistis, prout": Letter 234, PL 162:237. Sprandel, *Ivo von Chartres*, p. 194.

[19] Ivo did not employ *ira* and *malevolentia*, which were typical terms used by contemporaries, as Stephen White has noted: "The Politics of Anger," in *Anger's Past*, ed. Rosenwein, pp. 132–39.

[20] See, in general, Beryl Smalley, "Ecclesiastical Attitudes to Novelty c. 1100–c. 1250," in *Church, Society and Politics*, ed. Derek Baker, Studies in Church History 12 (Oxford, 1975), pp. 113–31, reprinted in *Studies in Medieval Thought and Learning: From Abelard to Wyclif* (London, 1981), pp. 97–115.

[21] For examples from Ivo's day, see Koziol, *Begging Pardon and Favor*, pp. 194–202, especially at p. 197 n. 73 in a monastic charter.

Ivo employed the term when angry. A particularly good example is found in letter 236, which dates from around 1111. Written shortly after news had reached him concerning Pope Paschal II's imprisonment and the promulgation of his controversial Investiture Privilege, Ivo responded to Archbishop John of Lyon. John had called a council to meet at Anse (near Lyon) to treat Paschal's privilege. Ivo refused to attend, citing a procedural defect:

> . . . but we fear to overstep the ancient limits [i.e. rules], rules our fathers placed.[22] On no occasion did the revered authority of the Fathers sanction this, nowhere was antiquity accustomed to observe that the bishop of the first see [which would be Lyon in this case] would invite to a council bishops outside his own province, unless either the apostolic see commanded this or one church from the provincial churches called the audience of the first see on account of disputes which it could not decide within its province.[23]

Ivo then cites a decretal of Nicholas I stating that archbishops claiming patriarchal status had no more power over their fellow bishops than permitted by tradition.[24]

Archbishop John's call for an unprecedented council would probably have provoked a response from the learned canonist at Chartres regardless of the circumstances, but the state of the Church was particularly unsettled in 1111. Ivo was not merely being legalistic. What had taken place at Rome, followed now by the proposed irregular council, was *inauditum*: "Fortified by these authorities, we do not wish to introduce unheard of novelty in your churches or to alter their laws instituted of old."[25] The language of transgressing the Fathers continues: "Furthermore, though in this council you are disposing to treat the investitures of laymen, which certain ones judge to be heresies, you will rather uncover the hidden things of your father [Paschal II]."[26] This is strong language. Rather than "disposing" of the subject of

---

[22]   Letter 236, PL 162:238–42. On this maxim see Edward Peters, "Transgressing the Limits Set by the Fathers: Authority and Impious Exegesis in Medieval Thought," in *Christendom and its Discontents: Exclusion, Persecution, and Rebellion, 1000–1500*, ed. Scott L. Waugh and Peter D. Diehl (Cambridge, 1996), pp. 338–62.

[23]   " . . . sed terminos quos posuerunt patres nostri, terminos antiquos transgredi formidamus. Nusquam enim reverenda Patrum sanxit auctoritas, nusquam hoc servare consuevit antiquitas, primae sedis episcopus episcopos extra provinciam propriam positos invitaret ad concilium, nisi hoc aut apostolica sedes imperaret, aut una de provincialibus Ecclesiis pro causis quas intra provinciam terminare non poterat, primae sedis audientiam appellaret": PL 162:238.

[24]   "Primates enim vel patriarchas nihil privilegii habere prae caeteris episcopis, nisi quantum sacri canones concedunt, et prisca consuetudo illis antiquitus contulit": PL 162:238. The letter of Nicholas I was written to Archbishop Radulf of Bourges: Philipp Jaffé and Paul Ewald eds, *Regesta pontificum Romanorum*, vol. 1 (Leipzig, 1885; repr. Graz, 1956), no. 2765. On the complicated history of this letter, see Detlev Jasper and Horst Fuhrmann, *Papal Letters in the Early Middle Ages*, History of Medieval Canon Law (Washington, DC, 2001), pp. 140–41 n. 11.

[25]   "His auctoritatibus muniti, nolumus Ecclesiis vestris inauditatem novitatem inducere, vel jura earum antiquitus instituta permutare": PL 162:238–39.

[26]   "Praeterea quia in hoc concilio de investituris laicorum, quas quidam inter haereses computant, tractare disponitis, potius pudenda patris vestri nudabitis": PL 162:239.

lay investiture, John will be exposing what should remain discretely hidden. If the council still convenes, Ivo warns that this "exposure" of the Father's "part," connecting Paschal's controversial privilege with Noah's nakedness (Genesis 9:21–27), would cause *strages populorum*. *Strages* refers to schism and civil strife; the term is frequently found in Augustine's writings against the Donatists, and often used by Ivo in his own works.[27] Ivo's response is clear: respect the pontiff's decision and be patient; this council would only expose the error made at Rome.

It is suggestive that Ivo employed *inauditum/a* only when communicating with fellow ecclesiastics. These, presumably, were the ones who, like Archbishop John, were supposed to know the canons and would thus recognize the censure conveyed by this term. For they were innovating, violating sacred norms and customs. In letter 157 to Paschal II from 1105 concerning the disputed episcopal election at Lisieux,[28] Ivo complained about the *inaudito invasionis genere* of the see by Ranulf Flambard, bishop of Durham, supported by King William Rufus. Flambard's son, *judaico more*, had followed his father. Such crimes were *inaudita*.[29] Ivo also declared incidents closer to home to be *inaudita* and deserving of his wrath. In letter 135, he condemned the "unheard-of" violence of a returned crusader, Rambold.[30] Elsewhere, he advised John of Orléans about an equally unprecedented case of an apparently cross-dressing priest.[31] These, however, did not concern Ivo personally.

Letter 182, conversely, seems to do just that, and provides us with what I believe is a revealing use of *inauditum/a*. Sometime shortly before 1108, an exasperated Ivo wrote to his metropolitan, Daimbert of Sens, about the troubled cathedral chapter at Chartres. Ivo had long advocated, and had attempted to introduce, the regular life among his clergy. He had often met resistance. Never before, however, had he expressed his frustration in quite this way:

> Recently, while I was in our chapter taking care of certain matters according to the custom of the church and, with open book, wished to make an investiture of a subdeanery to the cleric Fulco, a matter very necessary for the affairs of our church, men arose against me, inflamed by old hatred . . . and that deacon, with two old men, the cantor, and his brother, joined with some young men who came from their houses, began to cause a scene and opposed me, that I should not do this, objecting that I should do nothing unless it was with their counsel. I, however, knew that this is simply not the custom of the church and

---

[27]   See Bruce C. Brasington, *Ways of Mercy: The Prologue of Ivo of Chartres*, Vita regularis: Ordnungen und Deutungen religiosen Lebens im Mittelalter, Editionen 2 (Münster, 2004), pp. 61–62.

[28]   Sprandel, *Ivo von Chartres*, p. 192.

[29]   Letter 157, PL 162:162–63; see also Carolyn P. Schriber, *The Dilemma of Arnulf of Lisieux: New Ideas versus Old Ideals* (Bloomington, IN, 1990), pp. 26–27.

[30]   Letter 135, PL 162:144–45. Rambold had had a monk castrated, on which see Bruce C. Brasington, "Crusader, Castration, Canon Law: Ivo of Chartres' Letter 135," *The Catholic Historical Review* 85 (1999), 367–82.

[31]   Letter 162, PL 162:166–67, on which see Bruce C. Brasington, "Memory, Anger, Oblivion: Ivo of Chartres and the Presbyter of Orléans," in *Medieval Paradigms: Essays in Honor of Jeremy DuQuesnay Adams*, ed. Stephanie Hayes-Healy, 2 vols (London, 2005), 1:177–90.

observed that they had certainly not been opposed when they had received their own honors, so, lest I diminish my power, I did not stop what I had begun.[32]

The clerics' objections turned to violence:

> But though these were my men both through their ordination (*per manum*) and vow (*per sacramentum*), they angrily and loudly swarmed my seat, ripping the book out of my hand (*furiose et clamose sedem meam circumdederunt*), hurling at me foul, false, and disgraceful words, words extremely contrary to [my] holy order.[33]

Ivo goes on to say that he feared for his life (*mortem timens obmutui*), and thus had called on Daimbert for help. In his choice of *circumdederunt*, he may have made a biblical allusion to emphasize his outrage more strongly. Psalm 118 declares: "The pagans were swarming around me, in the name of Yaweh I cut them down; they swarmed around me closer and closer, in the name of Yahweh I cut them down; they swarmed around me like bees, they blazed like a thorn fire. . . ."[34]

Ivo concludes by noting the gravity of the transgression: "This is not a slight injury. It is an unheard-of injury (*injuria inaudita*) brought against the episcopal order (*pontificali ordini*)." As in the letter to William of Marmoutier discussed above, this was an affront to all bishops, not just himself. Ivo's language was utterly traditional, the voice of episcopal dignity offended. Even his retelling of the uprising in his chapter house emphasized that what had taken place had been an affront not only to himself—indicated by *ego*—but also to his *ordo*, highlighting his sense of office and solidarity with his colleagues.

Anger and an *Egodocument*

It remains to be seen whether there might be evidence of a more personal nature in Ivo's anger, a moment when Ivo's *ego* reveals more of the man and less of the bishop. We search for an *egodocument*. Coined in the 1950s by the Dutch scholar Jacques Presser, this term has been used most frequently by historians of early modern and

---

[32] "Nuper, cum in capitulo nostro quaedam officia secundum ecclesiae consuetudinem dispensarem, et porrecto libro investituram subdecaniae Fulconi clerico strenuo et in agendis causis ecclesiasticis valde necessario facere vellem, veteri odio inflammati insurrexerunt in me . . . et ipse decanus, cum duobus senibus cantore et fratre ejus, ascitis sibi quibusdam juvenculis qui de domibus eorum prodierant, et tumultuose contradicere coeperunt ne facerem, nihil aliud certum objicientes, nisi quia id eorum consilio non facerem. Ego autem sciens quod hanc consuetudinem in Ecclesia non inveni, nec in ipsis contradictoribus quando suos honores acceperunt observavi, ne potestatem meam minuerem, ab incoepto non destiti": Letter 182, PL 162:183.

[33] "Ipsi igitur quamvis mei homines essent et per manum et per sacramentum, furiose et clamose sedem meam circumdederunt, librum de manibus meis rapientes, verba turpia, falsa, probosa, et sacro ordini valde contraria in me protulerunt": PL 162:183.

[34] Translation from the *Jerusalem Bible*. The *Vulgate* reads: "omnes gentes circumdederunt me et in nomine Domini ultus sum eas circumdederunt me et obsederunt me sed in nomine Domini ultus sum eas circumdederunt me quasi apes extinctae sunt quasi ignis spinarum." See http://speedbible.com/vulgate/B19C117.htm (accessed 29 April 2003).

modern Europe to describe self-reflective texts such as diaries.[35] Recently, scholars such as Wilfried Hartmann have applied it to research on medieval conceptions of self.[36] Among the various medieval texts that have been examined as *egodocuments* are letters, although they present a particular challenge, for they are neither fully public nor fully private. However self-revelatory they may be, they have an intended audience, which is not necessarily true with diaries. As Roberta Mullini notes, the rhetorical and social conventions of medieval epistolography also shaped, and restrained, how the self could be expressed.[37] When, however, those conventions were broken, this was an especially autobiographical moment.[38]

Letter 195, directed to Abbot Geoffrey of Vendôme, is, I believe, such an instance in Ivo's correspondence. In the lengthy, contentious correspondence between Ivo and Geoffrey concerning episcopal rights and monastic immunities there is no other letter quite like it. It conforms to what was considered the familiar style, which, since Antiquity, had been the type of address most similar to conversation.[39] This is not to say that it was intended as a private communication, a category that would probably have made little sense to either bishop or abbot.[40] But its frank tone highlights its highly personal nature:

> Ivo, by the grace of God, minister of the Church of Chartres, to Geoffrey, abbot of the monastery of Vendôme, who should not seek to know higher things but instead consent to more humble matters. I received your letter, flattering and contentious, fragrant with the sweetness of honey, sprinkled with bitter poison. You complain to me that I am giving those things committed to you over to robbers and evildoers and that, in words and deeds, I am undertaking many evil things against you. I tell you . . . that, when I have dealt with another person, I have not molested you or your properties nor have the possessions of your monastery committed to you been mishandled. Yet, since I frequently drink from your bitterness, it is not surprising if I cannot offer sweetness to you in return nor show

---

[35]   Rudolf Dekker, "Jacques Presser's Heritage: Egodocuments in the Study of History," *Memoria y Civilización* 5 (2002), 13–37. See http://www.egodocument.net/homeframe.html (accessed 22 August 2005); also see the essay by Andreas Rutz, "Ego-Dokument oder Ich-Konstruktion? Selbstzeugnisse als Quellen zur Erforschung des frühneuzeitlichen Menschen," *Zeitenblicke* 1 (2002), at http://www.zeitenblicke.historicum.net/2002/02/rutz/ (accessed 22 August 2005).

[36]   For example, in 2005 Professor W. Hartmann taught a seminar at the University of Tübingen entitled "Ego-Dokumente" im frühen Hochmittelalter: Von Hermannus Contractus (†1054) bis zu Hermannus quondam iudaeus († nach 1181)."

[37]   Roberta Mullini, "Tradition and Innovation in the Paston Women's Ego-Documents," at http://www.women.it/cyberarchive/files/mullini.htm (accessed 17 August 2005).

[38]   Ibid.; see also Carol Dana Lanham, *Salutatio Formulas in Latin Letters to 1200: Syntax, Style, and Theory*, Münchener Beiträge zur Mediävistik und Renaissance-Forschung 22 (Munich, 1975), pp. 48, 50–52 (noting similar forms of *salutatio* used by Ivo, Anselm of Canterbury, and Bernard of Clairvaux).

[39]   On the familiar and formal styles, see Witt, "Medieval *Ars dictaminis*," pp. 6–8.

[40]   Witt, "Medieval *Ars dictaminis*," pp. 8–9.

myself to be your father, since in you I do not find a son. Therefore it is not unjust, if I take the mother's milk away from you, for you do not show me the honor due to a father.[41]

Ivo then notes that, as Pope Paschal had backed his claims against Geoffrey, Geoffrey was defying both his ordinary and the pope. As in the other letters discussed, Ivo's anger has declared itself through a command to obedience, which he then strengthens by citing Matthew 16.18–19, a text that immediately highlighted the abbot's defiance of Rome.[42]

Thus far, Ivo's anger has been conventional. However, he then continues:

Whence I briefly respond to all your objections . . . and will forgo all useless words: Do your own business and I will do mine. (*Fac quod tuum est, et ego faciam quod meum est.*) Because so long as you delay to do this, do not be surprised if I also delay to do those things which concern you.[43]

The *fac-faciam* clause makes his anger and resolve abundantly clear. The expression *fac quod tuum est et ego faciam quod meum est* is also unique in Ivo's correspondence. There also does not seem to be any precedent for it in earlier literature.[44] There might, however, be an echo here of an Augustinian maxim: "Have charity and do what you will."[45] Certainly Ivo knew it well, for he used it in the opening section of his famous treatise on canonistic jurisprudence, the *Prologue* to the *Panormia* and the *Decretum*.[46] The inversion of the precept is suggested by the *fac-faciam* construction. Geoffrey has defied his bishop and, more importantly, charity itself. Thus, Ivo declares him free to "do his own thing," cut off from the fraternal bond of love.

---

[41] "Accepi litteras tuas palpantes et pungentes, in quibusdam mellis dulcedinem redolentes, in quibusdam fellis amaritudinem respergentes, objicientes mihi quod te et tibi commissa praedonibus et malefactoribus exposuerim, et multa tibi mala factis et dictis ingesserim. Hoc prorsus dico teste veritate, quae Deus est, et conscientia mea, quia nec te nec tua cuiquam exposui, neque ut res monasterii tibi commissi male tractarentur, cum aliquo tractavi. Verum quia frequenter ex te bibo amara, non est mirandum si non possum tibi propinare dulcia, nec exhibere me patrem, qui te non invenio filium. Non ergo est injustum, si tibi subtraho lac matris, qui mihi debitum honorem non exhibes patris": Letter 195, PL 162:204. For the context of the letter, see Grandjean, *Laïcs dans l'Église*, p. 371.

[42] "Noveris enim vanas esse excusationes quas obtendis, te propter obedientiam Romanae Ecclesiae, Carnotensis Ecclesiae professionem refutasse, cum Ecclesia Romana a Deo nullam injustam acceperit potestatem, fidem violandi videlicet, debita sua cuique non reddendi, sed tantum quae sunt liganda ligandi, et quae sunt solvenda solvendi": PL 162:204.

[43] "Unde ad omnia objecta tua vel praemissa breviter respondeo, postpositis omnibus verbis supervacuis: Fac quod tuum est, et ego faciam quod meum est. Quod quandiu facere distuleris, si distulero facere ea quae tua sunt, non mireris": PL 162:204.

[44] Based on a search of the Chadwyck-Healy *Patrologia Latina* database, accessed at the British Library. I thank the British Library for the opportunity to use the database.

[45] "Habe caritatem et fac quicquid vis," on which see Giles Constable, *"Love and Do What You Will." The Medieval History of an Augustinian Precept*, Morton W. Bloomfield Lectures on Medieval English Literature 4 (Kalamazoo, MI, 1999).

[46] Brasington, *Ways of Mercy*, p. 27.

Ivo's use of *ego* does suggest that this is a particularly personal expression of anger. If not an *egodocument* like a modern diary—by definition a discursive exercise in self-exploration and revelation—this letter to Abbot Geoffrey of Vendôme does stand out when compared to the remainder of the bishop's correspondence. That Ivo became angry with the stubborn abbot is no surprise; as we have seen, his frustration could be caused by a variety of subjects. What is striking here is its expression. Highly personal, emphasized by a rare use of direct speech, it indicates a moment of self-revelation. I suggest that closer attention to the use of *ego* in other bishops' letters may enlarge our understanding of the discourse of emotion in the twelfth century and, through that, better our sense of the affective world of the "Twelfth-Century Renaissance."

Conclusion

There must be humility and caution in our search for the individuals behind the texts. The confidence with which older scholarship relegated the "medieval mind" to a primitive emotional and cognitive stage now seems utterly without foundation. While more attractive and seemingly more applicable, modern anthropological and sociological readings of our medieval authors are no less open to criticism.[47] For these are products of our modernity, not medieval creations.

Despite these reservations, the letters of a medieval bishop surely reveal something of the individual and not just his office. Despite the filters of rhetoric and exegesis, expectations of office and sensitivity to tradition, letters were the product of an individual, whose emotions, however differently understood and expressed than ours, were no less real. When Ivo of Chartres chose on several occasions to refer to himself directly in his writings, his *ego* was a moment of self-revelation. It reminds us that bishops like Ivo were men, no matter how hard they attempted to cloak themselves with their office.

---

[47]   See the works of Koziol and Buc (above, n. 9). See also Elizabeth A.R. Brown, "The Tyranny of a Construct: Feudalism and Historians of Medieval Europe," *The American Historical Review* 79 (1974), 1063–88. The debate continues, recently in connection with Susan Reynolds's *Fiefs and Vassals: The Medieval Evidence Reinterpreted* (Oxford, 1994).

Chapter 12

The Bishops of Piacenza, Their Cathedral, and the Reform of the Church

Dorothy F. Glass
Professor Emerita, University at Buffalo

During the first week of March, 1095, Urban II convened a council at Piacenza.[1] Although its significance has been overshadowed by the momentous council held at Clermont in November of the same year, during which Urban II preached the First Crusade, the gathering at Piacenza marked a significant moment in both Urban's papacy and in the checkered history of the city itself. In the first instance, Urban II was emerging from the exceedingly trying early years since his election in 1088. Assailed by Henry IV, as well as by Clement III, the antipope, he could neither hold Rome securely under his control nor initiate his own program of activities.[2] Indeed, he was often absent from Rome. In the second instance, Piacenza, having been in both the imperial and reform camps, was now a firm papal ally and was, of course, eager to benefit from this new, resolutely-forged alliance.

Piacenza was a site of extraordinary significance well before the high Middle Ages.[3] Lying in the northernmost part of the Emilia-Romagna at the border with

---

[1]   On the Council of Piacenza, see Bernold of Constance's account in *Die Chroniken Bertholds von Reichenau und Bernolds von Konstanz, 1054–1100*, ed. Ian S. Robinson, MGH SS rer. Germ., n.s., 14 (Hannover, 2003), pp. 518–21; *Urbani II. Concilium Placentinum, 1095, Mart. 1–7*, ed. Ludwig Weiland, MGH Legum 4, Constitutiones et acta publica imperatorum et regum 1 (Hannover, 1893), pp. 560–63; Giovanni Domenico Mansi ed., *Sacrorum conciliorum nova et amplissima collectio*, 53 vols (Florence and Venice, 1759–1798; repr. Paris, 1899–1927; repr. Graz, 1961–), 20:801–16; and Robert Somerville, "The Presentation of the Canons of Piacenza (March, 1095): An Overview, Baronius to Weiland," *Annuarium Historicae Conciliorum* 27–28 (1995–1996), 193–207. Additionally, the Council of Piacenza was of sufficient significance that it was commented upon by Donizo, the biographer of Matilda of Tuscany. See his *Vita Mathildis, celeberrimae principis Italiae*, ed. Luigi Simeoni, Rerum Italicarum Scriptores, n.s., 5/2 (Bologna, 1940), lines 27–28, p. 80; lines 1–11, p. 81.

[2]   The standard biography of Urban II is that of Alfons Becker, *Papst Urban II. (1088–1099)*, 2 vols (Stuttgart, 1964–1988).

[3]   Among the useful early historians of Piacenza, see especially *Iohannis Codagnelli Annales Placentini*, ed. Oswald Holder-Egger, MGH SS rer. Germ. 23 (Hannover, 1901); Johannes de Mussis, *Chronicon Placentinum ab anno CCXXII. usque ad annum MCCCCII*, ed. Lodovico Antonio Muratori, Rerum Italicarum Scriptores 16 (Milan, 1730), cols 448–

Lombardy, at least as those borders are defined today, it is located on the famed Via Emilia and the mighty River Po flows just outside its borders. Piacenza's strategic location thus made it ripe for the picking; that situation encouraged attention from both papal and imperial forces. Its economy, fueled by textiles, was prosperous, as were its citizens, both those living in the city proper and those in the outlying areas. The extent to which trade and craft were of the utmost importance to the economic health of the city is given visual witness by the mid-twelfth-century reliefs of the trades that are sculpted on the columns of the interior of the cathedral.[4] Throughout the eleventh and twelfth centuries, the bishops of Piacenza were both actively involved in the economy and major owners of property both in the city and in the *contado*. Medieval Piacenza thus offers an interesting contrast between economic stability and religious upheaval. Indeed, during the latter half of the eleventh century, Piacenza and her religious leaders vacillated between the papal and imperial parties. It was, in fact, not until the beginning of the third decade of the twelfth century, at the time of the Concordat of Worms, that a pro-papal bishop and the requisite financial resources resulted in the commissioning of a new and glorious cathedral for the city.

The story is best begun with Bishop Dionysius, who occupied the see for a lengthy period in the mid-eleventh century, from 1048 until 1077, an era that embraces both the first stirrings of the reform of the church and the early years of the papacy of Gregory VII (1073–1085), for whom that very reform is named.[5] Well-born and attached to the Lombard aristocracy, Dionysius was the son of a count, as well as the nephew of Riprand, bishop of Novara. Dionysius clearly revealed his attachment to the imperial cause when, in Basel, on 28 October 1061, he served as one of the electors of the antipope, Cadalus, the ambitious bishop of Parma. The latter, who

---

634; and, especially, Pietro Maria Campi, *Dell'historia ecclesiastica di Piacenza*, 3 vols (Piacenza, 1651–1662). The first volume treats the medieval era. On Campi's work, see Simon Ditchfield, *Liturgy, Sanctity, and History in Tridentine Italy: Pietro Maria Campi and the Preservation of the Particular* (Cambridge, 1995). More recent pertinent works include the essays in Piero Castignoli ed., *Storia di Piacenza*, vol. 2, *Dal vescovo conte alla signoria (996–1313)* (Piacenza, 1984); and Pierre Racine, *Plaisance du Xème à la fin du XIIIème siècle: Essai d'histoire urbaine*, 3 vols (Lille, 1979). Racine is primarily concerned with social and economic history. An historiographical overview is provided by Piero Castignoli, "La storiografia medievale piacentina nell'ultimo quarto di secolo," *Bollettino storico piacentino* 87 (1992), 3–35. Also useful is Luca Ceriotti et al. eds, *Storia della Diocesi di Piacenza*, vol. 1/1, *Guida alle Fonti: Archivi e biblioteche di Piacenza*, and vol. 1/2, *Guida alle Fonti: Repertorio delle pubblicazioni dal 1870* (Brescia, 2004).

4   See, for example, Bruno Klein, *Die Kathedrale von Piacenza: Architektur und Skulptur der Romanik* (Worms am Rhein, 1995), figs. 298–305.

5   On Bishop Dionysius, see Paul Fridolin Kehr ed., *Italia pontificia*, vol. 5, *Aemilia sive provincia Ravennas* (Berlin, 1911; repr. Berlin, 1961), nos 21–24, p. 447; Racine, *Plaisance du Xème à la fin du XIIIème siècle*, 1:209–12; Werner Goez, "Bischof Dionysius von Piacenza (1048/49–1082/85)," in idem, *Gestalten des Hochmittelalters: Personengeschichtliche Essays in allgemeinhistorischen Kontext* (Darmstadt, 1983), pp. 132–49; Giuseppe Fornasari, "La riforma gregoriana nel 'Regnum Italiae,'" *Studi gregoriani* 13 (Rome, 1989), 281–320, at pp. 297–305; Werner Goez, "Riforma ecclesiastica–Riforma gregoriana," in ibid., pp. 167–78; and Ivo Musajo Somma, "Un vescovo e la sua città nella lotta tra Papato e Impero: Dionigi di Piacenza (1048–1082)," *Bollettino storico piacentino* 94 (1999), 35–63.

took the name Honorius II, was to torment the canonically-elected pope, Alexander II (1061–1073), for more than a decade. The council at Basel, a gathering of the imperialist faithful, had been convened by the Empress Agnes, then serving as regent for her young son, Henry IV.

Alexander II was quick to retaliate: sometime between 1063 and 1067, a document now lost records that the pope excommunicated Dionysius.[6] Piacenza's wayward bishop must have returned to the orthodox fold at some point, for on 27 November 1074, Gregory VII wrote to Dionysius to ask him to oversee the election of a new abbot to rule over the monastery of San Savino as a replacement for the simoniacal abbot, Rigizo. In the same letter, Gregory VII urged Dionysius to allow some of his own disputes to be settled by papal legates. One of these disagreements was with the subdeacon Bonizo, who—if indeed this was Bonizo of Sutri, a polemical figure of the reform era—would have great importance for the diocese of Piacenza at a later date. Whatever Dionysius did or did not do, it is clear that Gregory VII was unsatisfied with his behavior, for he removed the errant bishop from episcopal office in February 1075, and followed this action with a letter, written on 3 March 1075 to the people of Piacenza, in which he not only informed them of the deposition of their bishop, but also revealed the harshness of the terms imposed:

> Accordingly, by the immutable sentence of the holy synod and with the irrevocable consent of all the brothers who were seated round, we have deposed brother Dionysius, formerly so-called bishop, from his entire episcopal honour without any hope of reconciliation at any time, and we have decreed that a hearing should in perpetuity be denied to him.[7]

Clearly, then, the leader of the diocese of Piacenza did not find favor with the reform papacy. After the deposition of Dionysius, the situation concerning the episcopal succession in Piacenza becomes murky because of the virtual absence of surviving documents. The eager historian can, however, pick up the trail in 1088, the first year of the papacy of Urban II, who early on showed an interest in Piacenza and its episcopal leadership. It will be recalled that Gregory VII, when reprimanding Bishop Dionysius, noted a dispute with "subdeacon Bonizo" who became bishop of Piacenza in 1088, seemingly under strange circumstances.[8]

---

[6]   On the lost document, see Kehr ed., *Italia pontificia*, vol. 5, *Aemilia sive provincia Ravennas*, no. 20, p. 446.

[7]   H.E.J. Cowdrey, *The Register of Pope Gregory VII, 1073–1085: An English Translation* (Oxford, 2002), p. 147.

[8]   On Bonizo of Sutri, see Bernold of Constance's comments in *Die Chroniken Bertholds von Reichenau und Bernolds von Konstanz*, lines 16–17, p. 429; lines 1–2, p. 430; lines 1–4, p. 477; Kehr ed., *Italia pontificia*, vol. 5, *Aemilia sive provincia Ravennas*, nos 25–26, 28, p. 448; Paul Fournier, "Bonizo de Sutri, Urbain II et la comtesse Mathilde d'après le *Liber de vita christiana* de Bonizo," *Bibliothèque de l'École des chartes* 76 (1915), 1–34; Emilio Nasalli Rocca di Corneliano, "Osservazione su Bonizone vescovo di Sutri e di Piacenza come canonista," *Studi gregoriani* 2 (Rome, 1947), 151–62; Ludovico Gatto, *Bonizone di Sutri e il suo Liber ad amicum: Richerche sull'età gregoriana* (Pescara, 1968); Giovanni Miccolo, "Bonizone," in *Dizionario biografico degli Italiani*, vol. 12 (Rome, 1970), pp. 246–59; Walter Berschin, *Bonizo di Sutri: La vita e le opere*, trans. Andrea Tabarroni (Spoleto, 1992) (original

Indeed, it would be fair to say that Bonizo, one of the most loyal and well-published of the reformers, was, to some extent, shrouded in mystery from his birth, the place and date of which are not securely known, to his death, about which there is disagreement concerning both the date and its means. Walter Berschin, whose monograph on Bonizo, written more than three decades ago, is still the standard work, avers that he was born sometime around 1045, probably in the province of Milan into a lower-class family.[9] A student of canon law, Bonizo may have grown up in Milan among the Patarenes, the local reform movement that campaigned especially against simony among the clergy. In his *Liber ad amicum*, Bonizo writes of the diffusion of the Patarene movement in cities near the Po and its relationship with the papacy, especially with the Milanese pope, Alexander II.[10]

By 1078, Bonizo had moved south, for he is noted in that year as the bishop of Sutri, located just north of Rome and south of Viterbo. Indeed, on 1 November 1078, Bonizo was in Rome taking part in a synod during which, among other matters, the heretical doctrines of Berengar of Tours concerning the eucharist were discussed. While nothing is known of Bonizo's specific activities when he was bishop of Sutri, the chronicler Bernold of Constance states that in 1082, Bonizo was arrested by Henry IV, who was besieging Rome.[11] Sutri was later to become a stronghold of Wibert, who, as Clement III, served as antipope from 1080 until his death at Cívita Castellana in 1100. In any case, Bonizo must surely have been out of prison by 1086, if not before, because it is known that he was present in Mantua shortly before the death of Anselm of Lucca, which occurred in that year. By this point Bonizo, long active in papal circles, was a well-known figure in the reform movement, a man whose opinion was listened to with care.

After Bonizo's time in Mantua, his exact whereabouts, like so much else about his life, are unknown until 1088, when he appeared in Piacenza, perhaps for the second time in his career, and where he seems to have enjoyed being. Indeed, between April and June of 1088, Urban II wrote three letters in which he agreed with Bonizo's desire to be in Piacenza. After some fussing from Urban about the propriety of his election, Bonizo seems to have actually become bishop of Piacenza. Thus, that city, long an imperial stronghold, was at least temporarily in the hands of the reformers, indeed in the hands of Bonizo of Sutri, one of the most eloquent and persuasive voices of that movement.

Bonizo's tenure was exceedingly brief, for he seems to have served for just six months before he was driven out by his enemies in 1089. Moreover, Bernold of Constance reports for that year that Bonizo's enemies attacked him so violently that they blinded him.[12] While some early interpreters thought that he died from this brutal assault, others believed that he left Piacenza and lived for a few more

---

edition: *Bonizo von Sutri: Leben und Werk*, Beiträge zur Geschichte und Quellenkunde des Mittelalters 2 [Berlin, 1972]).

[9]   See above, n. 8.

[10]   For the text of Bonizo of Sutri's *Liber ad amicum*, see the edition of Ernst Dümmler, MGH Ldl 1 (Hannover, 1891), pp. 568–620.

[11]   *Die Chroniken Bertholds von Reichenau und Bernolds von Konstanz*, p. 429.

[12]   Ibid., p. 477.

years, finally dying at Cremona, perhaps in 1095, where he was buried in that city's monastery of San Lorenzo. Thus, for a brief period, the episcopacy of Piacenza was held by a figure who was intimately involved in the reform movement. Although Bonizo's activities and their chronology are but sparsely documented, his ideas are articulated in his two major works, the *Liber ad amicum*, probably written in 1085–1086, and the *Liber de vita christiana*, written toward the end of his life. The first work, containing many polemical treatises addressing such issues as the use of arms by Christians to defend the faith, is essentially a history of the church from the conversion of Constantine to the death of Gregory VII. In it, Bonizo discusses the presence of God in history and thus the church itself. The second work, as its title suggests, offers rules for the Christian life and suggests the ways in which that life might be obtained. Significantly, given his own difficulties, he defines the first virtue of a good Christian as obedience.

Despite Bonizo of Sutri's prominence and the currency of the ideas expressed in his writings, his influence in Piacenza did not endure. Again, records of any kind are lacking for the two years immediately following the scandalous attack on Bonizo that drove him from the city. Thereafter, in 1091, and continuing until 1093, Piacenza was once more in imperial hands, for the bishop was none other than Wenric, librarian of the church at Trier between 1068 and 1075, and again between 1080 and 1083. Additionally, he was without doubt a canon of the chapter at Verdun.[13] Wenric, who referred to Henry IV as "dominus meus rex," is best known for a letter that he wrote to Gregory VII in the name of Bishop Thierry of Verdun.[14] Therein, he rehearsed the imperial charges against the pope and was particularly critical of Gregory VII's actions at the synod held during Lent, 1080, when the pope deposed Henry IV and "enthroned" Rudolf of Swabia in his place. Thus, Piacenza, geographically so crucially located, continued to vacillate between imperial and papal forces, the representatives of which were seemingly never in office long enough to concern themselves with the physical development and embellishment of their city.

Thus, the council held at Piacenza in March 1095, the mention of which began this essay, can now be seen to have been of enormous significance because it marked, finally, the triumph of the orthodox forces of Urban II, who would not have dreamed of holding a council of such importance in an imperial stronghold. The ecclesiastical affairs of the diocese of Piacenza then became more secure through the efforts of two bishops whose long tenures assured stability. Aldo, born in Rivergaro in the Piacentine Apennines, assumed office in either 1095 or 1096, and served for about a quarter of a century, until 1121.[15] During that era, Aldo accomplished much. Well-

---

[13]   On Wenric, see I.S. Robinson, *Authority and Resistance in the Investiture Contest: The Polemical Literature of the Late Eleventh Century* (Manchester, 1978), esp. pp. 152–56; H.E.J. Cowdrey, *Pope Gregory VII, 1073–1085* (Oxford, 1998), pp. 216–17; and Pierre Racine, "La civitas precommunale," in *Il Concilio di Piacenza e le Crociate* (Piacenza, 1996), pp. 3–18, at p. 18 n. 77.

[14]   For Wenric's letter, see *Epistola sub Theoderici episcopi Virdunensis nomine composita*, ed. Kuno Francke, MGH Ldl 1:280–99.

[15]   Opinion varies as to whether Aldo was elected prior to the council and installed during the council, or elected in the course of the council. On Aldo, see: Vincenzo Pancotti, *Aldo, vescovo di Piacenza* (Piacenza, 1922); Emilio Nasalli Rocca, "Aldo vescovo di Piacenza," in

traveled, he not only was instrumental in raising funds for the First Crusade, but he also actually went to the Holy Land in support of that crusade and was absent from his diocese between the years 1100 and 1103.[16] Aldo, who served under four popes (Urban II, Paschal II, Gelasius II, and Calixtus II), also ventured to France in 1107 and again in 1118, when he accompanied the then pope, Gelasius II. He was, moreover, in Rome in 1111, along with Bishops Bernard of Parma and Bonsenior of Reggio Emilia, to take part in the negotiations between Paschal II and Henry V concerning the concessions that the pope had made in regard to matters concerning investiture. Finally, along with the bishops of Asti and Acqui, he is noted as being present at the dedication of the cathedral of Genoa by Gelasius II in 1118.

Aldo's frequent absences from his diocese may have inadvertently served a useful purpose, for they allowed the officials of the commune to exercise their authority. Although certainly present earlier, the commune was first documented in 1126. The transition from absolute episcopal power to cooperation with the commune may be noted in the fact that Aldo was the last bishop of Piacenza to use the title "bishop-count" throughout his reign.[17] His successor, Arduin, employed that title only very early in his episcopate and then abandoned it. The increased political equilibrium in Piacenza, its continuing economic prosperity, and the leadership of Aldo, a strong and long-lived bishop, all may have encouraged Paschal II to make a momentous resolution at the council held in Guastalla in 1106. There, the pope proclaimed that the dioceses of Parma, Piacenza, Reggio Emilia, Modena, and Bologna, all burgeoning cities, were no longer subject to the diocese of Ravenna, a diocese no doubt weakened by the death of the Ravennate antipope Clement III, a fierce imperialist, at the beginning of Paschal II's papacy in 1100. The separation was ultimately finalized during the papacy of Alexander III.[18]

Il Duomo di Piacenza (1122–1972): Atti del Convegno di studi storici in occasione dell'850° anniversario della fondazione della Cattedrale di Piacenza (Piacenza, 1975), pp. 133–44; G. Cerati, "Per una biografia di Aldo vescovo di Piacenza (eletto 1096?–morto 1121)," *Annali Canossani* 1 (1981), 9–29; Luigi Canetti, *"Gloriosa Civitas": Culto dei santi e società cittadina a Piacenza nel Medioevo* (Bologna, 1993), esp. pp. 150–64; and Simona Rossi, "Il Vescovo Aldo. Problematiche e linee interpretative del suo episcopato," in *Il Concilio di Piacenza e le Crociate*, pp. 63–70. The last source mentioned regrettably lacks footnotes.

[16]   On Piacenza's participation in the crusades, see A.G. Tononi, "Actes constatant la participation des Plaisançais à la Ire Croisade," *Archives de l'orient latin* 1 (1881), 395–401; and *Il Concilio di Piacenza e le Crociate*, passim.

[17]   According to Pierre Racine, "La chiesa piacentina nell'età del Comune," in *Storia di Piacenza*, ed. Castignoli, p. 351, the bishop of Piacenza was referred to as a bishop-count beginning in 1065 with Dionysius, who is noted by that designation in a document dated 1 July 1065. For the document, see Cesare Manaresi ed., *I placiti del 'Regnum Italiae'*, Istituto storico italiano per il Medio Evo, Fonti per la storia d'Italia 97/3 (Rome, 1960), no. 418, p. 278. For the use of the title by Bishop Aldo and by Bishop Arduin, see Emilio Nasalli Rocca, "Aldo vescovo di Piacenza," p. 136. For the document dated 20 July 1123, in which Arduin uses the title for the last time, see Simona Rossi, "Arduino vescovo di Piacenza (1121–1147) e la chiesa del suo tempo," *Aevum* 66 (1992), 197–232, at p. 225.

[18]   On the Council of Guastalla, see Uta-Renate Blumenthal, *The Early Councils of Pope Paschal II, 1100–1110*, Pontifical Institute of Mediaeval Studies, Studies and Texts 43 (Toronto, 1978), pp. 32–73. For the text of the second decree of the council, which concerned

While at home in his diocese, Aldo was certainly not inactive, for it is known that he dedicated the Benedictine abbey of San Savino on 15 October 1107.[19] San Savino was strategically located outside the walls of Piacenza, at the point where the Via Postumia led to Cremona and the Via Emilia to Parma. Decorated by Lombard sculptors, it embodies a rather old-fashioned medieval aesthetic that differentiates it from Piacenza's new cathedral, begun fifteen years later. A few months after he dedicated San Savino, Bishop Aldo dedicated the church of Sant'Eufemia on 3 February 1108. He was less successful in his attempt to reform the abbey of San Sisto. Initially, at the instigation of the reform-minded Matilda of Tuscany (and Canossa), the badly behaved nuns, including the abbess, Febronia, were removed for both immoral conduct and the corruption of monastic customs. They were replaced by nuns from the reformed Benedictine congregation at Clermont-Ferrand, a change confirmed by Paschal II on 30 October 1115, just a few months after Matilda herself died.[20] Toward the end of Aldo's episcopate, however, the deposed nuns, supported by Henry V, tried to return to San Sisto, but it was Arduin, Aldo's successor, who eventually resolved the issue.

Like Aldo, a native of the area around Piacenza, Arduin, too, had had long experience in Piacenza, for he had served as the abbot of the aforementioned monastery of San Savino from 1107 until 1119.[21] Also like Aldo, Arduin served a lengthy term as bishop of Piacenza, for he died in either 1146 or 1147.[22] Arduin, seemingly less well-traveled than Aldo, was greatly concerned with matters within the diocese and was particularly attentive to such issues as the role of the cathedral as the baptismal church of the city; the affirmation of his episcopal rights, especially in regard to the ordination of clerics and the consecration of churches; and the protection of the *pievi* in his diocese. Arduin's efforts are visible even today, for he commissioned a new cathedral for his city. It was begun in 1122.[23] In the very next

---

independence from the diocese of Ravenna, see no. 2, p. 52. See also Kehr ed., *Italia pontificia*, vol. 5, *Aemilia sive provincia Ravennas*, no. 28, p. 448; Racine, "La chiesa piacentina nell'età del Comune," p. 356. Racine incorrectly gives the date of Paschal II's edict as 1109.

[19]   On San Savino, see Roberto Salvini and Enrichetta Cecchi Gattolin, *La basilica di San Savino e le origini del romanico a Piacenza* (Modena, 1978); and Franz Neiske, *Das ältere Necrolog des Klosters S. Savino in Piacenza: Edition und Untersuchung der Anlage*, Münstersche Mittelalter-Schriften 36 (Munich, 1979).

[20]   Kehr ed., *Italia pontificia*, vol. 5, *Aemilia sive provincia Ravennas*, no. 17, p. 493; nos 20–21, 23–24, p. 494.

[21]   On Arduin, see Rossi, "Arduino vescovo di Piacenza," pp. 197–232, and her "Piacenza dal governo vescovile a quello consolare. L'episcopato di Arduino (1121–1147)," *Aevum* 68 (1994), 323–38.

[22]   For the controversy concerning the date of Arduin's death, 1146 or 1147, see Rossi, "Arduino vescovo di Piacenza," p. 198 and n. 8.

[23]   The most recent monograph on the cathedral at Piacenza is that by Klein, *Die Kathedrale von Piacenza*. Still useful are the essays in *Il Duomo di Piacenza (1122–1972)*. Also relevant are the earlier studies of the cathedral by A.M. Romanini, "Die Kathedrale von Piacenza. Der Bau des 12. und 13. Jahrhunderts," *Zeitschrift für Kunstgeschichte* 17 (1954), 129–62; trans. as "La cattedrale di Piacenza dal XII al XIII secolo," *Bollettino storico piacentino* 51 (1956), 1–45. Only Arturo Carlo Quintavalle has proposed an earlier date for the cathedral; see his "Piacenza Cathedral, Lanfranco and the School of Wiligelmo," *Art Bulletin* 55 (1973), 40–57.

Dorothy F. Glass

Fig. 12.1   Facade, Piacenza Cathedral (photo: Bildarchiv Foto Marburg)

year, 1123, Arduin chose to emphasize the significance of the cathedral by asserting that it was to be the sole baptismal church for the entire city as well as for seven suburban churches.[24]

Of particular interest, in the context of the reform of the church, is the facade of Piacenza's cathedral (Fig. 12.1). Although restored rather brutally just over a century ago, the three portals still have much to offer the attentive viewer.[25] The tripartite facade is dominated by three double-storeyed porches, of which the center one is wider and higher than the lateral porches. It is important to note that the double-storeyed porch portal, used so extensively on the facade of the cathedral at Piacenza, was a relatively recent innovation in the Emilia-Romagna.[26] The center portal, the most heavily restored, has only a small part of its original sculpture remaining, primarily an elaborate cosmological archivolt consisting of zodiacal signs, personifications of the winds, and the hand of God protruding from the center of the archivolt. The lower storey of the left, or north, porch has a decorative archivolt above which is St John the Evangelist at the left and St John the Baptist at the right (Figs. 12.2–3). Between the two figures, at the apex of another decorative archivolt, is depicted the Lamb of God with a cross bisecting its body and resting on its right forequarter. The lintel of the left portal, believed to have been carved by Wiligelmus of Modena or a closely related member of his school, houses scenes from the early life of Christ, beginning with the Annunciation to Mary and ending with the Adoration of the Magi. The lintel of the right portal, carved by the young Nicholaus, active primarily in the Emilia-Romagna between *c*.1120 and *c*.1145, is similarly constructed. It begins with the depiction of the Presentation in the Temple, continues with the Flight into Egypt and the Baptism of Christ, and ends, most unusually, with the representation of all three of Christ's Temptations. The contents of each of the six scenes on the south lintel, unlike those on the north lintel, are clearly identified by inscriptions on their upper edge. The lower edge bears an inscription reading: HOC OPVS INTENDAT QVISQVIS BONVS EXIT ET INTRA[T]. Above the lintel, on the outer face of the lower part of the porch, in a position similar to St John the Baptist and St John the

---

[24]   Augustine Thompson, *Cities of God: The Religion of the Italian Communes, 1125–1325* (University Park, PA, 2005), p. 17.

[25]   On the restorations, see Camillo Guidotti, *Consolidamento e restauro del nostro duomo, 1894–1902* (Piacenza, 1906). For an historiographical analysis of the restoration, see Roberto Cassanelli, "L'osso di Cuvier. Aspetti e protagonisti del restauro romantico a Piacenza," *Bollettino storico piacentino* 77 (1982), 170–87.

[26]   Christine Verzár Bornstein has argued that the porch portal in the Emilia-Romagna, itself a complex form, was derived at least in part from Roman sources and associated with the reform papacy. See her "Matilda of Canossa, Papal Rome, and the Earliest Italian Porch Portals," in *Romanico padano, Romanico europeo: Atti del Convegno internazionale di studi, Modena-Parma, 26 ottobre–1 novembre 1977* (Parma, 1982), pp. 143–58; and "Sources and Function of the Earliest Italian Porch Portals: Matilda of Canossa and Papal Rome," in eadem, *Portals and Politics in the Early Italian City-State: The Sculpture of Nicholaus in Context* (Parma, 1988), pp. 31–50. In my view, Verzár Bornstein greatly over-emphasizes the role of Matilda as a patron of the arts.

Figs. 12.2–3 Facade, Piacenza Cathedral, North Portal, St John the Evangelist (left), St John the Baptist (right) (photos: author)

Evangelist on the left porch portal, are the Old Testament figures Enoch and Elijah, the latter on the left, the former on the right (Figs. 12.4–5).[27]

Here, then, I would propose that not only did Bishop Arduin and his advisers create a thoroughly "modern" facade, at least in terms of the early twelfth century, but that some of the images carved on the facade, that is, the two St Johns, Enoch and Elijah, and the Three Temptations of Christ, reflect both a deep knowledge of the art of medieval Rome and of other sites in the Emilia-Romagna, as well as a desire to adopt, create, and emulate themes that closely linked Piacenza with the ideals pertinent to the reform of the church. Piacenza's identity with the Rome of the popes was particularly significant at this juncture, not only because the city was now securely in the papal camp, but also because twice during the early years of the episcopacy of Arduin, in 1126 and again in 1132, the possessions

---

[27] Arthur Kingsley Porter, *Lombard Architecture*, vol. 3 (New Haven, CT, 1917), p. 252, records the inscriptions as HENOC and HELIAS, as does Klein, *Die Kathedrale von Piacenza*, p. 186, n. 745. Joachim Poeschke, *Die Skulptur des Mittelalters in Italien*, vol. 1, *Romanik* (Munich, 1998), p. 83, declares that the inscriptions are modern, a view not discussed elsewhere.

Figs. 12.4–5 Facade, Piacenza Cathedral, South Portal, Elijah (left), Enoch (right)
(photos: author)

of Piacenza's cathedral chapter were put under papal protection, an arrangement renewed periodically throughout the twelfth century.[28]

Let us begin, then, with the depiction of the two St Johns in the spandrels of the lower storey of the porch of the north portal (Figs. 12.2–3). Each is carved from a separate block of stone whose outer edges form a frame and whose lower edge projects to create a platform for each figure. Additionally, the drill holes in the book held by John the Evangelist, doubtless his gospel, and in John the Baptist's nimbus, suggest the possibility that both objects may have had metal inserts. John the Evangelist stands at the left. Nimbed, short-haired, and holding the aforementioned book in his right hand, he is dressed in a simple garment, the lower part of which falls gently to his ankles while the upper part descends in a series of tubular pleats to just below his knee. With his left hand flat, palm outward, John the Evangelist gestures toward the Lamb of God, who appears at the center of the floreated archivolt. On the opposite side, the right side of the porch, stands John the Baptist, whose appearance contrasts

[28] Kehr ed., *Italia pontificia*, vol. 5, *Aemilia sive provincia Ravennas*, nos 2 and 4, p. 461; nos 16–18, p. 464; no. 26, p. 466; Racine, "La chiesa piacentina nell'età del Comune," p. 356.

greatly with that of John the Evangelist. John the Baptist, bearded as always, is not clad in camel's hair (Mark 1.6) but rather in drapery that swirls in an agitated manner. In his left hand, John the Baptist holds a scroll that seems to be blowing in the wind; it bears the words from the Gospel of John 1.29: HECCE AGNUS DEI ("Behold the Lamb of God [who takes away the sin of the world]"). With his right hand, index finger extended, John the Baptist gestures forcefully toward the Lamb of God in the center of the archivolt, thereby emphasizing the words from the gospel of John the Evangelist, who stands opposite him. Thus, John the Baptist, who first announced Christ's coming, and John the Evangelist, whose gospel announces Christ's second coming, are paired both theologically and visually.

The motif of the two St Johns is without precedent in the Emilia-Romagna or elsewhere in North Italy. Why, then, at a church dedicated to the Virgin and St Giustina, should the two Johns appear prominently on the porch of the north portal? The explanation lies, I would argue, in the need of Bishop Arduin, during whose tenure the first building campaign of the cathedral was brought to fruition, to proclaim his alliance with Rome and the reform papacy, no doubt still reveling in the success of the Concordat of Worms, concluded in the same year in which Piacenza's cathedral was begun. Indeed, the two St Johns were featured prominently in Latin Christendom's most sacred edifices, most especially at Saint John Lateran.[29] Documentary evidence concerning that church, the cathedral of the pope, who, during the Middle Ages, resided in the adjacent Lateran palace, makes abundant reference to the importance of John the Baptist and John the Evangelist. The Lateran Basilica was identified as the "basilica Salvatoris" until just after 600, when the name "Sancti Johannis" appears. Although it is not clear at this point whether both St Johns or only one are meant, later it is demonstrable that both are meant, for notice of their patronage is taken in liturgical texts and in the inscription concerning the restoration of the basilica during the papacy of Sergius III (903–911). Additionally, in reference to Saint John Lateran, the names "basilica Salvatoris," "basilica Constantiniana," and "Sancti Johannis" existed together at the same time during the seventh and eighth centuries. Moreover, from the fifth century, the church had relics of both St Johns. In letters, Pope Gregory the Great (590–604) speaks of a tunic of John the Evangelist and the hair of John the Baptist.[30]

The visual evidence concerning the presence of John the Baptist and John the Evangelist at Saint John Lateran is equally convincing. Pope Hilary (461–468) built three chapels around the baptistery of Saint John Lateran: one dedicated to St John the Baptist, one dedicated to St John the Evangelist, and one dedicated to the

---

[29]   The literature on Saint John Lateran is abundant. The depiction of the two St Johns is treated by Christian Heck in his regrettably unpublished dissertation: "Les deux saints Jean: Étude de l'iconographie jumelée de saint Jean-Baptiste et de saint Jean l'Evangéliste en Occident, des origines à la fin du Moyen Âge," 2 vols (Diss., University of Aix-Marseille, 1979). I am grateful to Professor Heck for providing me with citations to his articles in which the material on Saint John Lateran is published.

[30]   On the Lateran and its relationship to the two St Johns, see Sible de Blaauw, *Cultus et Décor: Liturgia e architettura nella Roma tardoantica e medievale*, vol. 1, *Basilica Salvatoris, Sanctae Mariae, Sancti Petri*, Biblioteca Apostolica Vaticana, Studi e Testi 355 (Vatican City, 1994), pp. 161–62.

Holy Cross. The two chapels dedicated to the St Johns had the Lamb as their principal theme. The last mentioned, destroyed but known through ancient descriptions, had a cross at the center and eight figures, grouped two-by-two, of which one pair was the St Johns. Later, Pope John IV (640–642) transformed the fourth side, the portico of the baptistery, into the chapel of Saint Venantius. The apse mosaic of that chapel, still extant, represents the Virgin surrounded by eight figures, two of whom are the St Johns.[31] Further, it has been hypothesized by Francesco Gandolfo that St John the Baptist and St John the Evangelist appeared standing opposite each other on the apsidal arch of Saint John Lateran during the earlier Middle Ages.[32]

The interest in the depiction of the two St Johns continued in such early medieval churches in Rome as the rather recently discovered and reconstituted aedicula fresco in Santa Susanna and the much abraded fresco on an arch between rooms L and M in the early medieval lower church of San Martino ai Monti.[33] Both have John the Baptist on the left and John the Evangelist on the right; the porch at Piacenza thus reverses the placement of the two Johns. In both Roman churches, the Lamb of God is in the center of the arch (or aedicula); at Santa Susanna, the Lamb clasps a roll with the seven apocalyptic seals. It would thus seem that Bishop Arduin of Piacenza, or whoever planned the facade program of the new cathedral, was eager to introduce

---

[31] This material is summarized in Christian Heck, "Rapprochement, antagonisme, ou confusion dans le culte des saints: Art et dévotion à Katharinenthal au quatorzième siècle," *Viator* 21 (1990), 229–38, at pp. 232–33. More recently, see, on the St Venantius Chapel in the Lateran Baptistery, Gillian Valance Mackie, *Early Christian Chapels in the West: Decoration, Function and Patronage* (Toronto, 2003), pp. 212–30; see fig. 98A for a plan of the Lateran Baptistery chapels.

[32] Francesco Gandolfo, "I programmi decorativi nei protiri di Niccolò," in *Nicholaus e l'arte del suo tempo: In memoria di Cesare Gnudi*, ed. Angiola Maria Romanini, vol. 2 (Ferrara, 1985), pp. 515–59; idem, "Il protiro romanico: Nuove prospettive di interpretazione," *Arte medievale* 2 (1984), 67–78, at p. 69. Gandolfo's hypothesis is supported by Ursula Nilgen. See, most recently, her "Eine neu aufgefundene Maria Regina in Santa Susanna, Rom. Ein römisches Thema mit Variationen," in *"Bedeutung in den Bildern": Festschrift für Jörg Traeger zum 60. Geburtstag*, ed. Karl Möseneder and Gosbert Schüssler, Regensburger Kulturleben 1 (Regensburg, 2002), pp. 231–45, at p. 240. Verzár Bornstein cites Gandolfo's hypothesis as a fact. See her *Portals and Politics*, pp. 60, 62.

[33] For the discovery, reconstitution, and preliminary analysis of the frescoed aedicula at Santa Susanna, see Margherita Cecchelli, "Scavi e scoperte di archeologia cristiana a Roma dal 1983 al 1993," in *1983–1993: Dieci anni di archeologia cristiana in Italia. Atti del VII Congresso nazionale di archeologia cristiana, Cassino, 20–24 settembre 1993*, ed. Eugenio Russo, 3 vols (Cassino, 2003), 1:335–57, esp. pp. 344–45; and, in the same volume, Alessandro Bonanni, "Scavi e ricerche in S. Susanna a Roma," 1:359–74; and Maria Andaloro, "I dipinti murali depositati nel sarcofago dell'area di Santa Susanna a Roma," 1:377–86. The decade-long gap between the conference and the publication of the acts should be noted. For an exacting stylistic and iconographic analysis of the Santa Susanna frescoes, see Ursula Nilgen, "Eine neu aufgefundene Maria Regina," pp. 231–45. For the San Martino ai Monti fresco, see Caecelia Davis-Weyer and Judson J. Emerick, "The Early Sixth-Century Frescoes of S. Martino ai Monti in Rome," *Römisches Jahrbuch für Kunstgeschichte* 21 (1984), 3–60. Despite the title of the article, the authors date the fresco under discussion here to the first half of the ninth century.

a Roman motif, one that had not appeared previously on other recent edifices, like the cathedral at Modena, that were begun after their bishops and inhabitants had left the imperial fold and become pro-papal.[34] It is arguable, then, that those charged with planning the cathedral at Piacenza sought to liken it to Saint John Lateran, not only by creating a visual analogue to the apsidal arch figures once possibly there, but also by honoring the two saints so highly revered at the pope's own cathedral and in its baptistery.[35]

The figures standing on the south porch portal in the same position as the two St Johns are equally revealing of the intentions of the planner(s) of the facade of Piacenza's new cathedral. They depict two Old Testament figures, Elijah at the left and Enoch at the right (Figs. 12.4–5). The figures, perhaps at first seemingly out of place, are instead, I would argue, part of the artistic vocabulary of the reform in North Italy, for they had previously appeared as a duo at the cathedrals of Modena (*c.*1100–1110) and Cremona (*c.*1107–1115). In both these cases, they are clearly identified by inscription and hold the dedicatory plaque referring to their respective cathedrals. At the cathedral of Piacenza, however, they do not hold a dedicatory plaque, but instead occupy the same position as the two St Johns on the north porch portal. To understand the significance of Enoch and Elijah during the earlier years of the twelfth century, it is necessary to examine both canonical and apocryphal biblical texts, as well as medieval interpretations such as that of Augustine.

The most commonly known exegesis of the figures of Enoch and Elijah concerns their immortality. In Genesis 5.24, in regard to Enoch, it is noted that "he walked with God, and was seen no more because God took him." In the case of Elijah, who had been battling idolatrous cults in Canaan, 2 Kings 2.11 states: "And as they [Elisha and Elijah] went on, walking and talking together, behold a chariot of fire and fiery horses parted them both asunder: and Elijah went up by a whirlwind into heaven." While this interpretation is certainly valid, it does not begin to explain their presence on the facades of three cathedrals.[36] One must delve more deeply into the texts, for both are perceived not only as men of faith, but also as instrumental in the events preceding the Last Judgment. Of Enoch, Hebrews 11.5 avers: "By faith Henoch was translated, that he should not see death," while the epistle of Jude 1.14–15 adds that: "Now of these Enoch also, the seventh from Adam, prophesied, saying: 'Behold, the Lord cometh with thousands of his saints, to execute judgment upon all, and to reprove the ungodly for all the works of their ungodliness. . . .'" Thus Enoch, a man of faith, would assist at the Last Judgment. Similarly, Elijah is seen as associated with the coming Last Judgment, not in the New Testament, but in the words of the prophet Malachi 4.5: "Behold, I will send you Elias the prophet before the coming of the great and dreadful day of the Lord." Malachi's words were well known and

---

[34]   On the underside of the lintel of the Porta dei Principi of the cathedral at Modena (*c.*1110), a roundel containing a Lamb is supported by two angels. The motif is flanked by St John the Baptist and St Paul.

[35]   Gandolfo, "I programmi decorativi," p. 530, discusses the significance of depictions of the Lamb in twelfth-century Rome.

[36]   Richard K. Emmerson, *Antichrist in the Middle Ages: A Study of Medieval Apocalypticism, Art, and Literature* (Seattle, WA, 1981), pp. 95–99.

often cited by such medieval exegetes as St Augustine. In the twenty-ninth chapter of book twenty of *The City of God*, Augustine cites Malachi's prophecy and then goes on to say:

> It is a belief frequently present in the speech and hearts of the faithful that, in the last time, before the judgment, the great and wondrous prophet Elijah will expound the law to the Jews who will thereby come to believe in the true Christ: that is, in our Christ. And it is not without reason that we hope that, before the coming of our Judge and Saviour, Elijah will come.[37]

Enoch and Elijah, on the south portal, are thus associated with John the Baptist and with John the Evangelist, on the north portal, who also prophesied the coming of Christ.

But the aforementioned texts do not form the only basis for the notion that Elijah, often accompanied by Enoch, will appear before the Last Judgment. The two Old Testament figures are also closely associated with the Antichrist, a well-known interpretation based on the Apocalypse 11.3–13, in which it is noted that two witnesses will preach for 1,260 days and, through preaching and performing miracles, will convert many from the Antichrist to Christ.[38] But the Antichrist will kill the two witnesses, who, after having been brought back to life, will then join God in heaven. Although the Apocalypse does not name the witnesses, they have long been believed to be Enoch and Elijah. The two Old Testament figures are prominent early on in Christian apocalyptic writing and commentary, for they appear, for example, in the apocryphal *Gospel of Nicodemus*, where, during the account of Christ's Descent into Limbo, Enoch and Elijah are discovered there. They note that they were sent to combat the Antichrist and were killed by him. Paralleling Christ himself, Enoch and Elijah are meant to rise in three days.[39] In a like manner, *The Apocalypse of Peter* notes Enoch and Elijah's work in combating the Antichrist.[40] Of equal importance in the category of non-canonical texts is the prophecy of the Tiburtine sibyl. Like so many of the aforementioned texts, the Tiburtine sibyl tells us that Enoch and Elijah will fight the Antichrist and will be slain. Then, "He who was crucified on the wood of the cross" will resurrect them, wage war on the Antichrist, and slay him. Christ and his holy angels will then rule. The prophecy of the Tiburtine sibyl was of particular significance because, in the late tenth or early eleventh century, probably in Italy, the old Latin translation of the text was edited and brought up to date. The names of Lombard and German rulers were inserted. The text thus achieved a

---

[37] Augustine, *The City of God against the Pagans*, ed. and trans. R.W. Dyson, Cambridge Texts in the History of Political Thought (Cambridge, 1998), p. 1036.

[38] For a highly informative study of the Antichrist, see Emmerson, *Antichrist in the Middle Ages*.

[39] J.K. Elliott, *The Apocryphal New Testament: A Collection of Apocryphal Christian Literature in an English Translation* (Oxford, 1993), p. 189.

[40] Ibid., p. 601. The *Apocalypse of Paul*, p. 628, however, places Enoch and Elijah in paradise where they happily greet Paul upon his arrival.

modern currency and certainly remained in circulation.[41] Its contents were doubtless well known to churchmen of the era.

While the wide diffusion of texts concerning the role of Enoch and Elijah in battling the Antichrist clearly abounds in the non-canonical literature, the legend is equally well known from an exceedingly early date in canonical literature. For example, both Tertullian in *De anima* and Irenaeus in *Adversus haereses*, commenting on the eleventh chapter of the Apocalypse, identify the two prophets, or witnesses, who battle the Antichrist as Enoch and Elijah.[42] The same account also appears in Gregory's *Moralia in Iob* and Pseudo-Isidore of Seville's *De ortu et obitu patrum*.[43] Once established, the significance of Enoch and Elijah certainly continued into the era of the Gregorian reform, as witnessed by the words of Bruno of Segni, who, in commenting on Apocalypse 11.3–5, notes that the witnesses are to be identified as Enoch and Elijah.[44]

The notion that Enoch and Elijah were witnesses of and participated in the slaying of the Antichrist was thus well known not only in apocryphal literature, patristic literature, and in the era of the Gregorian reform, but was also current in visual images. Best known, perhaps, is the presence of Enoch and Elijah in the numerous illustrations of the commentary on the Apocalypse written by Beatus of Liébana. There, in numerous individual illuminations, Elijah and Enoch appear together as illustrations to chapter eleven of the Apocalypse.[45] Similarly, the Pamplona Bibles (Amiens, Bibliothèque municipale, MS 108, and Augsburg, Universitätsbibliothek, 1.2. qu. 15), dated *c.*1200 and commissioned by King Sancho el Fuerte of Navarra (1194–1234), also illustrate the notion that Enoch and Elijah will be killed by the Antichrist and announce the coming of the Lord.[46]

Their appearance on the facade of the cathedral at Piacenza thus serves to announce the victory over heresy, a message particularly appropriate to that city, which had vacillated for so long between imperial and papal loyalties. While the two St Johns in the spandrels of the north portal of the facade of Piacenza cathedral speak to a direct relationship with

---

[41]   On the prophecy of the Tiburtine sibyl, see Ernst Sackur, *Sibyllinische Texte und Forschungen: Pseudomethodius, Adso und die Tiburtinische Sibylle* (Halle, 1898), pp. 117–87; and Paul Julius Alexander, *The Oracle of Baalbek: The Tiburtine Sibyl in Greek Dress*, Dumbarton Oaks Studies 10 (Washington, DC, 1967).

[42]   See Emmerson, *Antichrist in the Middle Ages*, p. 97. See also Tertullian, *De anima*, c. 50, PL 2:735; and Irenaeus of Lyon, *Libros quinque adversus haereses*, ed. W. Wigan Harvey, 2 vols (Cambridge, 1857; repr. Ridgewood, NJ, 1965), 2:330.

[43]   Emmerson, *Antichrist in the Middle Ages*, p. 97. See also Gregory the Great, *Moralia in Iob* 15.58, PL 75:1117; and Pseudo-Isidore of Seville, *De ortu et obitu patrum*, c. 3, PL 83:131–32.

[44]   *Expositio in Apocalypsim* 3.11, PL 165:662.

[45]   On the Beatus illustrations, see Peter K. Klein, *Der ältere Beatus-Kodex Vitr. 14–1 der Biblioteca Nacional zu Madrid: Studien zur Beatus-Ill. u. d. span. Buchmalerei d. 10. Jh.*, Studien zur Kunstgeschichte 8, 2 vols (Hildesheim, 1976), 1:100–1, 204–9; 2:82–90 and fig. 49; and John Williams, *The Illustrated Beatus: A Corpus of the Illustrations of the Commentary on the Apocalypse*, vol. 1, *Introduction* (London, 1994), Table of Apocalypse Illustrations, p. 5.

[46]   François Bucher, *The Pamplona Bibles*, 2 vols (New Haven, CT, 1970), 1:286 and 2, fig. 557.

the church at Rome, the figures of Enoch and Elijah speak more generally to the church's triumph over heresy, which was embodied, for example, in the imperial claims regarding investiture. In the context of the reform of the church, the German emperor was, of course, thought of as an Antichrist, one who could and would threaten the papacy.[47]

The third motif on the cathedral of Piacenza that is significant in the context of the reform of the church, and hence of concern to Bishop Arduin, is the emphasis on the Temptation of Christ that appears on the lintel of the south portal as the three culminating scenes in the early life of Christ (Fig. 12.6). Indeed, they comprise half of the six scenes on that lintel, a most unusual arrangement. The appearance of all three Temptations of Christ is an extraordinarily rare phenomenon, for there are no comparisons in monumental sculpture in Italy prior to, or during, the Romanesque era.[48] The only other contemporaneous example of which I know is that contained on fols 42v–43r of the so-called Gospels of Matilda of Tuscany, made at the nearby Benedictine Abbey of San Benedetto Po, most likely during the last decade of the eleventh century, and now New York, Morgan Library, M. 492.[49] It contains, over two folios, the Three Temptations of Christ as individual scenes.

Far more sophisticated than the rather schematic images on the lintel at Piacenza, the manuscript illuminations are replete with both detailed settings and scrolls having quotations from the account of the Temptations in the Gospel of Matthew 4.1–11.[50] That such images should have been produced at San Benedetto Po is not in the least surprising, for the monastery stood not only at the very center of the reform movement, but was also so favored, both spiritually and financially, by

Fig. 12.6   Facade, Piacenza Cathedral, South Portal, lintel (photo: author)

---

[47]   On the political use of the sibylline prophecies, see Robinson, *Authority and Resistance*, pp. 74, 100–3.

[48]   On the iconography of the Three Temptations, see Vasanti Kupfer, "The Iconography of the Tympanum of the Temptation of Christ at The Cloisters," *Metropolitan Museum Journal* 12 (1977), 21–31; and Lucy A. Adams, "The Temptations of Christ: The Iconography of a Twelfth-Century Capital in the Metropolitan Museum of Art," *Gesta* 28 (1989), 130–35.

[49]   On the Gospels of Matilda, see most recently the extensive catalogue entry by Giuseppa Zanichelli in Arturo Carlo Quintavalle, *Wiligelmo e Matilde: L'officina romanica* (Milan, 1991), pp. 535–44. For excellent illustrations of the manuscript, see George F. Warner, *Gospels of Matilda, Countess of Tuscany, 1055–1115* (Oxford, 1917).

[50]   Verzár Bornstein, *Portals and Politics*, p. 63, notes the presence of the scenes of the Temptations on the south lintel of the cathedral of Piacenza and in the Gospels of Matilda of Tuscany, but attributes the similarity to Matilda's patronage of the cathedral at Piacenza, even though the countess had died in 1115, seven years before the cathedral was begun.

Matilda of Tuscany, that she chose the abbey's church to be her burial site.[51] It is worth noting that images of all three Temptations of Christ appear only once in the oeuvre of Nicholaus and his school, that is, at the cathedral of Piacenza.[52] At the cathedral of Ferrara, for example, begun in 1135, the cycle of Christ's early life on the lintel of the center portal of the facade ends with his Baptism. By the time that the work at Ferrara was carved, the exigencies of reform and investiture had receded. The meaning of the Three Temptations is further amplified by the aforementioned inscription running along the lower edge of the entire lintel: HOC OPVS INTENDAT QVISQVIS BONVS EXIT ET INTRA[T], that is: "May any good person who exits and enters look upon this work."[53] Christ's resistance to temptation thus serves as an exemplar of the good life in a general sense. More specifically, it may well speak to the clergy about the need to avoid the sins of simony and nicolaitism, both so fiercely battled by the reformers of the church. By refusing to yield to Satan, the reformed clergy, following the example of Christ on the lintel, thus serve as behavioral models for the citizens of Piacenza as the latter enter their new cathedral.

It would thus seem that the cathedral at Piacenza, begun in 1122 at an auspicious moment when the Concordat at Worms had smoothed, at least temporarily, the relations between the imperial and papal powers, also stands as witness to the wealth of the diocese and the power of Arduin, then bishop of the city. Clearly, the diocese, having been freed from servitude to the diocese of Ravenna, where the imperial forces dominated, and having the property of its cathedral chapter protected by the pope, felt sufficiently confident to undertake the building of a new cathedral. Thereon, Arduin and his advisers placed images that spoke to the church at Piacenza's close relationship to Rome, as seen in the figures of the two St Johns flanking the Lamb of God; to the defeat of the Antichrist in the person of the German emperor, as seen in the figures of Enoch and Elijah; and, finally, to the need to avoid both specific and general temptations, as seen in the highly unusual depiction of all three of Christ's Temptations.

---

[51]   On Matilda's tomb, see Beth L. Holman, "'*Exemplum* and *Imitatio*': Countess Matilda and Lucrezia Pico della Mirandola at Polirone," *Art Bulletin* 81 (1999), 637–64; and Paolo Piva, "La tomba della Contessa Matilda (nota filologica)," in *Studi matildici: Atti e memorie del III Convegno di studi matildici, Reggio E., 7–8–9 ottobre 1977* (Modena, 1978), pp. 243–54.

[52]   For a brief account of the career of Nicholaus, as well as pertinent bibliography through 1994, see Christine Verzár, "Nicolò (o Niccolò, Nicolao)," *Enciclopedia dell'arte medievale*, vol. 8 (Rome, 1997), pp. 699–703.

[53]   Verzár Bornstein translates the inscription erroneously as: "This work may be understood by those who enter and leave as good people." See her *Portals and Politics*, p. 63. I am grateful to John Ott, Elizabeth Parker, and Maria Henderson Wenglinsky for lively discussions concerning the inscription.

Chapter 13

Urban Space, Sacred Topography, and Ritual Meanings in Florence: The Route of the Bishop's Entry, *c.*1200–1600

Maureen C. Miller
University of California, Berkeley

From at least the thirteenth century, every new bishop of Florence ceremonially entered the city and took possession of the diocese through an elaborate ritual.[1] The clergy and religious of the city processed from the cathedral to one of the city's southern gates to meet the new prelate, who kissed their processional crosses in greeting, donned the miter and vestments signifying his office, and mounted a white horse. Representatives of the Visdomini families, who were considered the guardians of the see and who administered its properties during episcopal vacancies, raised a special baldachin over the mounted bishop and served as his honor guard (*adestratores*). The procession then led the bishop into the city, through the Oltrarno, over the river, to various stops in the old urban center, and finally to the episcopal palace behind the baptistery of San Giovanni. There the representatives of the Visdomini families swore their loyalty to the new bishop, gave him the keys to the palace, and turned over a register recording their administration of the see's properties during the vacancy.

While the basic outlines of the ritual remained stable over several centuries, the route of this entry procession did change in response to political transformations. The changes pragmatically acknowledged shifts in power, but they did not radically alter the representation of the bishop. Indeed, the development of this ritual was extremely conservative; it remained a distinctly ecclesiastical rite, especially in comparison to other entries, such as those of popes, kings, and other secular dignitaries. It was structured around processions to churches and the commemoration of saints and their miracles. Throngs of clergy and religious, arrayed solemnly behind the processional crosses of their institutions, accompanied the bishop on this urban pilgrimage. Prayers, invocations, and hymns punctuated his progress from the city's southern gate to the episcopal palace. Other ceremonial entries into Florence increasingly

[1] I would like to thank the Office of the Provost at George Mason University for a summer research fellowship that allowed me to return to Florence in 2001 to complete this research and the community of scholars at the Harvard University Center for Italian Renaissance Studies at Villa I Tatti for stimulation and support in just the right quantities. I am also grateful to the editors of this volume for their comments and suggestions.

invoked antique themes, with buildings draped in classicizing ornamentation and pauses for Latin orations on secular Roman models. The bishop's *adventus* never followed these fashions. This conservatism is highly significant. The ritual of episcopal entry that emerged in thirteenth-century Florence was an expression of the new position of the bishop in the post-reform era. The endurance of this expression and its stability underscore the importance of developments in the episcopal office over the period covered by this volume. They set the pattern for centuries to come.

Sources

While some historians have described the Florentine ritual of episcopal entry or *adventus* as an "ancient" ritual,[2] our earliest record of it comes in a document of 1286. This charter, which recorded a dispute between the cathedral canons and the Visdomini over where Bishop Jacopo Rainucci said his first mass in the city, is typical of the early documentation for the rite.[3] Conflict over participation and precedence in the ceremony was particularly intense in the fourteenth century and illuminates interesting details. In 1302, for example, the abbess of San Pier Maggiore—who was joined with the bishop in a symbolic marriage as part of the ritual entry—protested that Bishop Lotterio della Tosa had brought more than the customary number of *familiares* to dine with him in the convent during his entry. The bishop acknowledged that his inclusion of members of the cathedral chapter along with his Visdomini escorts did not establish any right of these additional individuals to be received or fed at the monastery.[4] Other documents reveal contention over which families received the saddle and stirrups of the horse the bishop rode during the entry and over who escorted the bishop when he entered certain churches.[5]

The Visdomini families played a major role in the ritual and their defense of these prerogatives accounts for our fullest descriptions. These families were descendants of Davizio, the first layman to be *vicedominus* of the Florentine see. Appointed by Bishop Ildebrand in 1009, Davizio's administration of the see's patrimony continued

---

[2]   Emilio Sanesi, for example, called the ritual entry "una tradizione antico e costante": Emilio Sanesi, *L'Antico ingresso dei vescovi fiorentini* (Florence, 1932), p. 15.

[3]   *Archivio Arcivescovile di Firenze* (hereafter *AAF*), Mensa Arcivescovile Bulletoni (hereafter MAB) I, 1: Bulletone, fols 255r–257r. A transcription of the document is published in Giovanni Lami ed., *Sanctae ecclesiae Florentinae monumenta*, 4 vols (Florence, 1758), 3:1709–11, and George Dameron has studied this particular controversy in depth in his article "Conflitto rituale e ceto dirigente fiorentino alla fine del Duecento: L'Ingresso solenne del vescovo Jacopo Rainucci nel 1286," *Ricerche storiche* 20 (1990), 263–86.

[4]   *Archivio di Stato, Firenze* (hereafter *ASF*), Diplomatico, Normali, S. Pier Maggiore, 1301 [1302] Feb. 24 (00027634). In brackets are the years in the modern style where they differ from the year on the document (the Florentines began their year on the feast of the Annunciation, 25 March). The numbers in parentheses are the barcodes assigned to individual parchments when they were recently scanned as part of a major digitalization project at the Florentine state archive. On the ritual marriage, see Maureen C. Miller, "Why the Bishop of Florence Had to Get Married," *Speculum* 81 (2006), 1055–91.

[5]   *ASF*, Diplomatico, Normali, S. Pier Maggiore, 1309 Dec. 20 (00031111); Lami ed., *Sanctae ecclesiae Florentinae monumenta*, 3:1711–12, 1731–33.

under several bishops down to 1054 when he successfully passed the office on to his sons.[6] By the thirteenth century, the Visdomini had defined a "right" to administer the see during vacancies and members of the clan actually took up residence in the episcopal palace until a new bishop arrived. These rights meant that they organized (and starred in) the entry of a newly consecrated bishop. There were two main branches to the lineage in the thirteenth century: the Visdomini (or Bisdomini) and the Della Tosa (or Tosinghi). By the mid-fourteenth century, the Aliotti are also identified as one of the Visdomini families, and in the sixteenth century, there were four families sharing these rights: the Tosi, the Tosinghi, the Bisdomini, and the Cortigiani.[7]

The Visdominis' tenacious defense of their roles in the episcopal *adventus* produced an important, but peculiarly biased, body of sources. They reveal every detail of Visdomini participation, down to the color of their gloves and the type of *erba* used in their garlands. The bishop, indeed, often seems no more than a supporting actor in these narratives. Regardless of this particular lay bias, the ritual that emerges from these sources is clearly an ecclesiastical rite. The spaces in which the Visdomini were most concerned to preserve their roles were churches; the honorable actions they competed for were holding candles, handing the bishop his crosier, and escorting him to altars, in addition to acting as groomsmen.[8] It is also a rite that reveals only a notional relationship to ancient and early medieval rituals of *adventus*. It differed in two significant ways. First, it was complex and highly scripted. The Florentine rite took two days to complete and had a precise order, specific roles, and prescribed prayers, gestures, and costumes. Descriptions of early medieval episcopal entries attest only to disorganized but enthusiastic crowds greeting their bishop at the gates of the city and accompanying him to his residence. Second, early medieval communities performed this spontaneous *adventus* any time their bishop returned to the city. The rituals of episcopal *adventus* that emerge in the twelfth and thirteenth centuries were only enacted when a new bishop first entered his see. They were rituals of *possesso*, taking possession of the see, and were modeled on papal rituals of this type that emerged in the late twelfth century.[9]

The Entry Route in the Thirteenth and Fourteenth Centuries

The ceremony of episcopal entry in the thirteenth and fourteenth centuries took at least two days to complete. On the first day, the clergy, religious, and people of the city processed to the city gate to receive their new pastor. The 1286 account of the Florentine entry specifies that they met the bishop at the city's southernmost gate, the Porta San Pietro Gattolino (close to the gate today called the Porta Romana—see Fig. 13.1).

---

[6]   For the history of this Visdomini lineage see Carol Lansing, *The Florentine Magnates: Lineage and Faction in a Medieval Commune* (Princeton, NJ, 1991), pp. 65–66, 70–72, 78–80; Carlo Celso Calzolai, *S. Michele Visdomini* (Florence, 1977), pp. 15–22.

[7]   *ASF*, Manoscritti, no. 167, fol. 40r, and no. 129 (Settimanni, Diario Fiorentino IV), fol. 326v.

[8]   *ASF*, Manoscritti, no. 167, fols 44r–47r.

[9]   Maureen C. Miller, "The Florentine Bishop's Ritual Entry and the Origins of the Medieval Episcopal *Adventus*," *Revue d'histoire ecclésiastique* 96 (2002), 5–28.

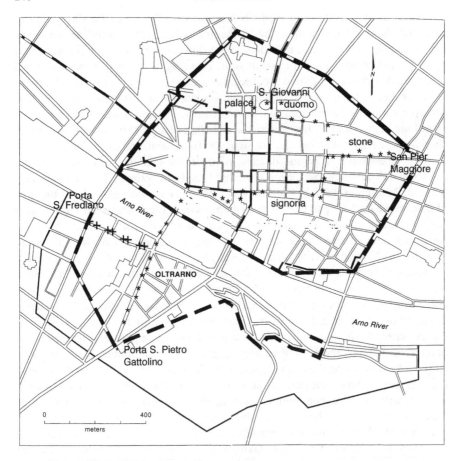

Fig. 13.1   The Route of Florentine Episcopal Entry

The earliest document (1286) recording the *adventus* gives only the following indications of the route: Porta S. Pietro Gattolino; S. Pier Maggiore (Piazza, church, and monastery); the stone commemorating the miracle of St Zenobi; S. Reparata (altar of St Zenobi); S. Giovanni; Episcopal Palace (chapel, sala). A description from 1384 gives more detailed information about the processional route (roughly indicated here with asterisks): Porta S. Pietro Gattolino; Via S. Pietro Gattolino; Via Maggio; Ponte S. Trinità; Borgo SS. Apostoli; "viam Variariorum" [Via Vacchereccia]; Piazza della Signoria; "per viam ante Pallatium Executionis & ante domum illorum de Magaloctis & ante illorum de Pazzis"; Piazza S. Pietro Maggiore; "ante domus illorum de Albitiis"; stone commemorating the miracle of St Zenobi ("ante domo illorum del Tanagli"); "viam Balestariorum" [Via del Proconsolo]; S. Reparata; S. Giovanni; Episcopal Palace (chapel). The 1532 shift to the Porta San Frediano changed only the Oltrarno portion of the route.

A document from 1384 also designates this gate, asserting that the bishop's entry here was "their custom and most ancient tradition."[10] This point of entry assumes that the new bishop was coming from the south and, indeed, these high medieval rituals of episcopal *adventus* were in part necessitated by the post-reform role of Rome in making bishops: the papacy increasingly provided bishops for sees and insisted upon consecration in Rome even for those elected within their dioceses.[11] After the new Florentine bishop actually entered the walls, he and all the clergy, religious, and people crossed the city to the monastery of San Pier Maggiore. The bishop rode a white horse, or a horse draped in white, and his Visdomini attendants held a special gold brocade baldachin over him. In the piazza before the church of San Pier Maggiore, the bishop dismounted and the horse was given to the abbess while the saddle and stirrups went to a prominent family in the neighborhood.[12] The Visdomini escorted him into the church where the bishop said a special prayer at the high altar and then was enthroned. Afterwards, he entered the convent where he was shown the room and special bed prepared for his stay. Lunch followed in the cloister, provided at the expense of the monastery, and then the ritual marriage of the new bishop with the abbess, the bishop placing a gold ring on her finger.[13] The new bishop then spent the night at the monastery in the room and bed specially prepared for him by the abbess.

This first day of the rite is clearly dominated by St Peter. The bishop entered at the Porta San Pietro and then went to San Pier Maggiore where he prayed at the altar dedicated to the apostle. The choice of this gate, church, and monastery used preexisting elements in the urban topography of Florence to generate several meanings. First, it underscored the papal, Roman mandate of the new leader. The prelate went from Saint Peter's in Rome to the various Saint Peters in Florence.[14] Second, the choice of these sites reiterated the apostolic origins of the bishop's power. For centuries, ecclesiology and episcopal culture had traced the authority of each and every bishop back to the twelve apostles, particularly highlighting connections to

---

[10]   " . . . ut eorum moris & antiquissime consuetudinis est": *AAF*, MAB I, 1: Bulletone, fol. 255r; Lami ed., *Sanctae ecclesiae Florentinae monumenta*, 3:1722.

[11]   See Miller, "Why the Bishop of Florence Had to Get Married" (above, n. 4).

[12]   In the late thirteenth and early fourteenth centuries, the Bianchi claimed this right. *ASF*, Diplomatico, Normali, San Pier Maggiore, 1309 Dec. 20 (00031111). In the fifteenth and sixteenth centuries the Strozzi received these items. Richard C. Trexler, *Public Life in Renaissance Florence* (New York, 1980), p. 273; Alessandra Macinghi negli Strozzi, *Lettere di una gentildonna fiorentina del secolo XV ai figliuoli esuli*, ed. Cesare Guasti (Florence, 1877), pp. 168, 174–76; Luca Landucci, *A Florentine Diary from 1450 to 1516*, trans. Alice De Rosen Jervis (London, 1927), p. 229; *Ingresso dell'Arcivescovo Antonio Altoviti in Firenze* (Florence, 1868), p. 14.

[13]   Bishop Lotterio della Tosa specified that he gave her a golden ring with a sapphire, although this was only after the abbess's protest: *ASF*, Diplomatico, Normali, S. Pier Maggiore, 1301 [1302] Feb. 24 (00027634). On this most peculiar aspect of the Florentine *adventus* see Miller, "Why the Bishop of Florence Had to Get Married."

[14]   The 1384 description also details that the new bishop traversed the neighborhood of SS. Apostoli on his way to San Pier Maggiore, underscoring the apostolic theme of the day. Lami ed., *Sanctae ecclesiae Florentinae monumenta*, 3:1722.

Peter. Thus in lists, frescos, and other representations of their predecessors, bishops articulated a genealogy of power connecting the present incumbent of any see with the original disciples of Christ.[15] Finally, the ritual marriage to the abbess—whom later documents identify as a representative of the Florentine people—asserts that the union of the bishop with his flock is presided over or brought about through St Peter (another reiteration of papal authority).

Having been united with his Florentine flock, the bishop was associated with more local saints during the second day of the ritual entry while his power over salvation was underscored. Day two began in the church of San Pier Maggiore: while enthroned near the altar, the bishop's shoes were removed. Special cloths were spread over his entire route to the cathedral. This part of the ritual took on the character of a sort of pilgrimage to sites associated with one of Florence's earliest bishops, St Zenobi. San Pier Maggiore was an appropriate starting point because local tradition held that Bishop Zenobi had kept a hermit's cell at the monastery.[16] The new bishop walked first to a stone in Via Borgo degli Albizi commemorating one of St Zenobi's most famous miracles. Supposedly here the saintly bishop restored to life a boy who had taken ill and died on a pilgrimage to Rome. The cries of his distraught mother summoned Bishop Zenobi, who brought the boy back to life. Indeed, St Zenobi is credited with two miracles of resurrecting the dead and his own relics made a dead tree sprout new leaves (this miracle is commemorated by the column still standing in Piazza San Giovanni).[17] The bishop's homage to St Zenobi thus also underscored the bishop's gift of eternal life through his power over the sacraments. When the new bishop arrived at the stone commemorating the site of this miracle (today at Via Borgo degli Albizi 18), he kneeled and said a special prayer. He then continued his barefoot pilgrimage down Borgo degli Albizi, turning northward on

---

[15]   Maureen C. Miller, *The Bishop's Palace: Architecture and Authority in Medieval Italy* (Ithaca, NY, 2000), pp. 50–53, 182–83, 236–37.

[16]   The earliest *vita* of Zenobi dates from the eleventh century, and to make sense of where people believed the saint performed his miracle of restoring a boy to life and the idea that the bishop heard the boy's mother's cries, it identified the church where Zenobi was at the time as San Pier Maggiore. This, of course, has led to the belief that the church and monastery date from the fourth century. In fact, the monastery dates from the mid-eleventh century, although the church may have already existed in the tenth century. On the *cella sancti Zenobii* see Giuseppe Richa, *Notizie istoriche delle chiese fiorentine divise ne' suoi quartieri*, 10 vols (Florence, 1754–1762), 1:138. The earliest life of Zenobi is by Laurentius, archbishop of Amalfi: *Opera*, ed. Francis Newton, MGH Die deutschen Geschichtsquellen des Mittelalters 500–1500, Quellen zur Geistesgeschichte des Mittelalters 7 (Weimar, 1973), pp. 50–70.

[17]   AASS May, vol. 6, pp. 60–61; see also Anna Benvenuti, "I culti patronali tra memoria ecclesiastica e costruzione dell'identità civica: L'esempio di Firenze," in *La religion civique à l'époque médiévale et moderne (Chrétienté et Islam)*, ed. André Vauchez, Collection de l'École française de Rome 213 (Rome, 1995), pp. 99–118, at pp. 102–3. The inscription on the commemorative stone in Borgo degli Albizi is barely legible today, but Domenico Moreni transcribed it as "ΣΥΝ ΘΕΨ / B. Zenobius puerum sibi a matre Gallica Romam eunte / creditum, atque interea mortuum dum sibi urbem / lustranti eadem reversa hoc in solo conquerens / occurrit signo crucis ad vitam revocavit. / An. Sal. CCCC." Domenico Moreni, *De ingressu Antonii Altoviti* (Florence, 1815), p. 90 n. 36, in Florence, Biblioteca Moreniana, misc. 279.4.

Via Balestariorum (today Via del Proconsolo), past Santa Maria in Campo, and to Santa Reparata (later Santa Maria del Fiore). Upon entering the cathedral, the new bishop went immediately to the altar dedicated to St Zenobi and said a series of prayers. Having venerated his holy predecessor, the new bishop was enthroned and his Visdomini escorts put his shoes back on.

The last part of the ritual was enacted in episcopal space. From Santa Reparata, a space dominated by the cathedral canons, the bishop went to his church, the baptistery of San Giovanni, where he was enthroned yet again. Here he said his first mass in the city. He exited the baptistery on the north side, processing past the column commemorating the miracle of St Zenobi, and up the staircase of the episcopal palace. Within the palace, he changed vestments and then entered the chapel of San Salvatore where he was enthroned for a fourth and final time. Here he received the keys of the palace from the Visdomini and the register recording their administration of the patrimony during the vacancy. The new bishop also received oaths of fidelity from all the male members of the Visdomini lineages. These episcopal "guardians" and other guests then shared a special meal with the bishop in the hall of the palace. During or just after the meal, the abbess of San Pier Maggiore made a visit to the palace to deliver the bedding that had been prepared for and used by the bishop during his stay at the monastery. In most accounts, this exchange concludes the ritual entry, although the 1286 document mentions that it was customary on the day following this for the bishop to go out to the monastery of San Miniato. He said a mass at the church and was treated to a festive meal by the abbot and monks.

It seems important to recognize three distinct segments to the original *adventus* ritual. The first, from the Porta San Pietro to the monastery of San Pier Maggiore, emphasized the apostolic origins of the bishop's authority and the direct Roman-papal dependence of the prelate. Places already dedicated to St Peter in the urban landscape were used to articulate these ties. After the bishop was joined to the see in the ritual marriage, a second part of the ritual positioned him as a penitential pilgrim paying homage to his saintly predecessor in the see, St Zenobi. Again, specific places in the urban center—the stone marking the miracle of St Zenobi and the altar dedicated to him in the duomo—are central to the route and the meaning of the rite. Finally, the new bishop entered space associated with his lordship: the baptistery of San Giovanni, where his tenants came to pay their rents and offer candles on the feast of St John, and the episcopal palace, where the bishop held court.[18] The chapel of San Salvatore, where the Visdomini consigned the keys and register and swore fidelity, was the space in which the normal administrative business of the see was transacted. Notice that the exercise of lordship is positioned after the prayerful cultivation of universal (St Peter) and local (St Zenobi) saints. Temporal power derives from spiritual power in the ritual.

The overall form of the ritual is a procession punctuated by stops for prayers at specific sacred places. While many religious processions in the city were organized around a relic—the periodic processions with the image of Our Lady of Impruneta

---

[18]   George Dameron, *Episcopal Power and Florentine Society, 1000–1320* (Cambridge, MA, 1991), pp. 62–63, 67, 149; *AAF*, MAB 6, "Libro Affitti e Rendite dal 1329 al 1342," fol. 161v.

being a good example—the bishop himself in the *adventus* is the sacred presence at the center of the rite. The places where he stopped to pray were already sacred in local tradition (the stone commemorating St Zenobi's miracle) or by the presence of relics (the altars in San Pier Maggiore and the duomo), but certainly this ritual of visitation and prayer re-inscribed a set of relationships and a sacred topography in the city.

Changes in the Route from the late Fourteenth to the Sixteenth Century

Two changes in the route occurred, one in 1384 and the other in 1532. In 1384, with the entry of Angelo II Acciaiuoli, a stop at the communal palace, the seat of civic government, is recorded for the first time as part of the ritual (Fig. 13.1). When the bishop and his Visdomini attendants arrived,

> before the palace of the lords Priors of the Arts and of the Standard Bearer of Justice of the Popolo and Commune of Florence, there the lords Priors and the Standard Bearer of Justice of the said Popolo and Commune then in office, having descended from the Palace, before its door greeted the lord bishop with great reverence. And the said lord bishop, putting both hands on his miter, bowed to them on arrival and on departure, greeting them courteously and reverently.[19]

Previously, the city's leaders had taken part in the general procession of clergy and people out to greet the bishop at the Porta San Pietro Gattolino. This change in 1384 seems to take the city's elected officials from being among the joyful subjects of the new prelate to being among the individuals and places reverenced by the bishop on the processional route. The imputation of sacrality to communal leaders and their seat of power in the urban landscape was an important change.

Two years later, the commune intervened directly in the definition of the entry ritual. In the days preceding the entry of Bartolomeo da Padova—citing many conflicts between the canons, the Visdomini, and the parishioners of San Pier Maggiore as well as the desire to avoid scandal—the priors appointed a four-man committee of inquiry to settle all disputes and define the roles in the ritual so that no further controversies might arise. This committee, like the regime that appointed it, was conservative. It upheld the dominant role of the Visdomini families in the rite but did sanction roles for the chaplains of San Pier Maggiore and the cathedral canons: when the bishop entered these two churches, representatives of their clergy, with the Visdomini, escorted him.[20]

---

[19]   " . . . ante Pallatium dominorum Priorum Artium & Vexilliferi Iustitie Populi & Communis Florentie ubi domini Priores & Vexillifer Iustitie dicti Populi & Communis, tunc in officio presidentes descensi de Pallatio ante ianuam dicti Pallatii, cum reverentia salutarunt prefatum dominum episcopum. Et ipse dictus dominus episcopus ambas ponens manus suas ad mitriam & se flectendo in advenctu & recessu eos benigne & reverenter salutavit": Lami ed., *Sanctae ecclesiae Florentinae monumenta*, 3:1722–23.

[20]   Ibid., 3:1731–34. The entry occurred on Sunday, 28 January 1386: "vene i.Firenze il venerabile padre messer Bartolomeo da Padova veschovo di Firenze. Fugli fatto grandissimo onore da tutti e' cittadini, e tutti e' cittadini e 'l chericato e' religiosi gli andorono incorto, e

Why did the route of the *adventus* shift to sacralize communal space and officials in 1384? And why did the commune itself intervene so directly in the definition of the ritual in 1386? The 1386 document repeatedly emphasizes the desire to avoid scandal and other sources verify that unseemly contention had plagued the entry across the fourteenth century.[21] In 1358 the entry of Bishop Filippo dell'Antella was interrupted by a dispute between Piero Bellagio and Bartolommeo (called Golfo) del fu Masseo di Chiarissimo over the right to receive the saddle, and a similar conflict disrupted the entry of Bishop Angelo da Ricasoli in 1370.[22] In June of 1385, an episcopal procession carrying the head of St Zenobi crossed paths with another bearing the image of Our Lady of Impruneta and the resultant struggle over precedence turned so violent that Bishop Angelo II Acciaiuoli had to seek refuge in a nearby house.[23] Thus, when in January 1386 preparations were underway for the entry of Bishop Bartolomeo, the commune appointed its commission to clarify roles and *preheminentie* in the ritual so that similar conflicts could be avoided.

The instability, real or feared, of the Florentine regime in this period suggests that we take seriously these protestations of concern over conflict and "scandal." The Ciompi revolt of 1378 was a not-too-distant memory, as was the overthrow in 1382 of the guild regime that followed it. "The twin themes of pacification and reconciliation," Gene Brucker noted, "occurred again and again in the *pratiche*" of the more conservative regime that came to power in 1382, but the government's attempt to pursue a middle course was threatened by the return of aristocratic exiles and the resurgence of the Guelph party.[24] Several conspiracies, popular and aristocratic, came to light in 1383, and in the closing months of the year the Guelph party stepped up pressure for a new scrutiny (the designation of those eligible for specific offices) and screening of nominees. Although the regime withstood this concerted pressure for much greater exclusivity, conflict over the rules for a new scrutiny continued into 1385.[25] This political context is essential to understanding the new affirmation and reverence offered to the commune in the entry ritual. Just as important is the crippled financial situation of the Florentine church. During Florence's war against Pope Gregory XI, the "War of the Eight Saints" (1375–1378), the commune confiscated a huge portion of the church's patrimony, and although it had begun to return properties in the 1380s, much of the compensation came not in real estate but in shares of the

---

smontò i.Santo Piero Magiore. E lunedì mattina entrò i.veschovado chon grandissimo honore e chantò messa in Sancto Giovanni." *Alle Bocche della Piazza: Diario di Anonimo Fiorentino (1382–1401) (BNF, Panciatichiano 158)*, ed. Anthony Molho and Franek Sznura (Florence, 1986), p. 61.

[21] " . . . propter quas lites, & questiones multa scandala poterant oriri inter cives . . . in detrimentum pacifici & tranquilli status Civitatis Florentie & scandalum omnium predictorum & plurium aliorum": Lami ed., *Sanctae ecclesiae Florentinae monumenta*, 3:1731.

[22] Trexler, *Public Life*, p. 273; Strozzi, *Lettere* (above, n. 12), p. 175.

[23] Trexler, *Public Life*, p. 272.

[24] Gene Brucker, *The Civic World of Early Renaissance Florence* (Princeton, NJ, 1977), p. 62.

[25] Ibid., pp. 60–75.

government's funded public debt.[26] Thus, in 1384 when the route of the bishop's entry came to include a stop at the palace, the communal regime needed legitimizing support and the church needed good relations with the city's secular leaders.

The commune's definition of the ritual in 1386 seems to have silenced disputes over the various roles and rights in the *adventus* and, as a result, the character of our documentation changes dramatically. From 1386 we are dependent upon accounts in chronicles for our knowledge of the ritual and its development. Meager as some of these are, it seems clear that the stop at the communal palace continued to be part of the processional route.[27] The next major change in the ritual came in 1532, when the point of entry was shifted from the Porta San Pietro Gattolino to the Porta San Frediano (Fig. 13.1).

As the date of this change might suggest, the return of the Medici and the establishment of the Grand Duchy figure in the abandonment of the Porta San Pietro. The archbishop entering in 1532, Andrea Buondelmonte, was a strong Medici supporter and his ecclesiastical career, not to mention his financial fortunes, had soared under the Medici popes, Leo X and Clement VII.[28] Archbishop Buondelmonte opted to stay just outside the city before his entry at the monastery of San Bartolomeo a Monteoliveto, instead of at the Certosa, where most of the bishops in the Quattrocento had been received. It is possible that Monteoliveto had sustained less damage than the Certosa during the siege that preceded the Medici's return. Both had been occupied by papal–imperial forces, the Certosa by the Prince of Orange, but most of the besieging forces were camped southeast of the city in the

---

[26]	David S. Peterson, "Conciliarism, Republicanism and Corporatism: The 1415–1420 Constitution of the Florentine Clergy," *Renaissance Quarterly* 42 (1989), 183–226, at p. 189; idem, "Archbishop Antoninus: Florence and the Church in the Earlier Fifteenth Century" (Ph.D. diss., Cornell University, 1985), pp. 246–64.

[27]	When Bishop Nofri (or Onofrio) de' Visdomini entered on 13 March 1390, the honor done him by "le signorie" was noted. Cosimo dei Pazzi's entry in 1508 (Wednesday 27 September) stopped at the "plateam magnificorum dominorum, ubi super ringeria erant sedentes excelsi Domini & Vexilifer Iustitie Reipublice & Populi Florentini & ibidem maximo cum sonitu campanarum, tubarum, & aliorum instrumentorum, fuit ab eis honorabiliter receptus & honoratus & salutatus ex ringeria predicta a magnifico & excelso Petro Soderino ad vicem Vexilifero Iustitie Populi Florentini & idem Reverendissimus Dominus Archiepiscopus inclinato capite & posita manu ad mitriam in signum reverentie resalutavit eos." Giulio de' Medici's entry on Sunday 15 August 1513 is similarly described. Benedetto Varchi reported that Archbishop Andrea Buondelmonte (24 October 1532) was received at the *ringhiera* by a "luogotenente e consiglieri del duca," as was Archbishop Antonio Altoviti (15 May 1567) in Domenico Moreni's account. Alessandro de' Medici's entry on 12 March 1584 also included a stop at the Piazza Vecchia: *Alle Bocche della Piazza*, ed. Molho and Sznura (above, n. 20), p. 90; Lami ed., *Sanctae ecclesiae Florentinae monumenta*, 3:1744, 1760; Benedetto Varchi, *Storia fiorentina*, ed. Lelio Arbib, 3 vols (Florence, 1843–1844), 3:10; Moreni, *De ingressu Antonii Altoviti* (above, n. 17), p. 47, or the Italian translation: *Ingresso dell'Arcivescovo Antonio Altoviti in Firenze* (above, n. 12), pp. 13–14; Agostino Lapini, *Diario fiorentino di Agostino Lapini dal 252 al 1596*, ed. Gius[eppe] Odoardo Corazzini (Florence, 1900), pp. 231–32; and *ASF*, Manoscritti, no. 129 (Settimani, Diario Fiorentino IV), fols 326r–327r.

[28]	*Dizionario Biografico degli Italiani*, ed. Alberto Maria Ghisalberti (Rome, 1960–), 15:191–92.

hills between the Via Romana and San Miniato.[29] More likely, however, the change was influenced by the strong relationship between the Medici and Monteoliveto. Cosimo il Vecchio had been the key patron in the monastery's reconstruction in the fifteenth century and the family continued to fund its expansion and development.[30] Archbishops Antonio Altoviti and Alessandro de' Medici also stayed here before their entries and they, too, met their welcoming processions at the adjacent Porta San Frediano.

Despite these changes in route to accommodate political realities, the character of the episcopal *adventus* remained markedly ecclesiastical and relatively unpretentious in the context of the increasingly elaborate and classicizing tendencies of sixteenth-century secular entries. The shift to San Frediano had diminished the strong Petrine associations of the first day of the rite, but Alessandro de' Medici in 1584 used the stay at Monteoliveto before descending into the city to construct new meanings. He timed his *adventus* for the Sunday just preceding Palm Sunday, emphasizing the role of the bishop as successor to and representative of Christ. Contemporaries did not miss the parallels created between his entry into the city on 12 March, the Palm Sunday procession the next week, and then the Easter rites: in all of these, the new archbishop represented Christ.[31] The new beginning of the entry from Monteoliveto added Passion overtones to the bishop's union with his see and the assumption of his duties as lord and pastor. This invocation opened up meaningful parallels: just as Christ's humiliation, suffering, and death were necessary for the salvation of mankind, so the burdens of episcopal administration were necessary for the salvation of souls in the diocese. And certainly in the late sixteenth century, after the Council of Trent, as bishops were increasingly pressured to take up residence in their sees, the entry into one's diocese may have seemed the beginning of suffering to prelates accustomed to the delights of Rome or other European courts.

The episcopal ritual of entry also never embraced the use of festive *apparati* such as the temporary triumphal arches, statuary, and theatrical constructions that became typical of secular and even papal entries in the sixteenth century.[32] This seems to have been a conscious choice, rather than any lack of classicizing possibilities. The episcopal entry was, at root, an *adventus*. This terminology and other details (particularly the characterization of the Visdomini escorts as *adestratores*) link the

[29]   Silvia Meloni Trkulja and Giampaolo Trotta, *Via di Monteoliveto: Chiese e ville di un colle fiorentino* (Florence, 2000), p. 55; *La Certosa del Galluzzo a Firenze*, ed. Caterina Chiarelli and Giovanni Leoncini (Milan, 1982), p. 21; Aldo Valori, *La Difesa della Repubblica Fiorentina* (Florence, 1929), p. 261 and map between pp. 210–11.

[30]   Trkulja and Trotta, *Via di Monteoliveto*, pp. 22–55.

[31]   Maureen C. Miller, "Architecture, Representation, and Presence: Alessandro de' Medici's New Façade for the Archiepiscopal Palace of Florence (1581–1584)," *Mélanges de l'École française de Rome: Italie et Méditerranée* 115 (2003), 13–28, at pp. 21–24.

[32]   Silvia Mantini has also noted the distinctive character of the episcopal *entrata*: *Lo spazio sacro della Firenze medicea* (Florence, 1995), p. 235. On secular and papal entries in sixteenth-century Florence, see "Triumphalism: The Sala Grande in Florence and the 1565 Entry," in *Arts of Power: Three Halls of State in Italy, 1300–1600*, ed. Randolph Starn and Loren Partridge (Berkeley, CA, 1992), pp. 151–89; John Shearman, "The Florentine *Entrata* of Leo X, 1515," *The Journal of the Warburg and Courtauld Institutes* 38 (1975), 136–54.

Florentine rite to papal rituals of entry codified in the late twelfth century that clearly drew upon and referenced the model of the late imperial *adventus*.[33] But while the papacy during the Renaissance transformed its entry ritual into a *triumphus*, the archbishops of Florence preserved the religious tone and visual simplicity of their traditional rite.

This conservatism is important to note. First, it should remind us that not all entries are alike. At least in Florence, but very likely elsewhere too, episcopal rituals of entry were quite distinctive from secular *entrate*. Even after the changes in the route explored here, the Florentine ritual remained a religious procession to various sacred places in the urban center. It constructed the power of the entering prelate as rooted in relations with the apostolic authority of Rome and with saints especially venerated in the city. Even in the sixteenth century it incorporated none of the festive props that celebrated the arrival of a royal bride or a visiting potentate. Second, this difference underscores diversity within the visual culture of urban ceremonial in medieval and renaissance Italy. Contemporaries certainly remarked most upon the novelties occurring in festive life and historians of ritual have focused their attention on these changes. But the refusal to change is also a statement. Florentine bishops, for example, not only distinguished their entries from secular processions by preserving their own traditions, but they also cultivated a different ritual "look" than their papal overlords. Thus, conservatism in urban ritual seems just as important a force as novelty in the visual articulation of relationships in the medieval and renaissance city.

The consistency and chronology of the Florentine ritual of episcopal entry, moreover, suggests the significance of the re-making of the episcopal office through the reform movements of the eleventh and early twelfth centuries. The ritual emerged in the thirteenth century and articulated some of the key changes that the reform movements had wrought. The bishop was no longer a creature of kings, emperors, or local lay strongmen; he was a delegate of the pope and linked his particular community to the church universal. He acknowledged and venerated local ecclesiastical institutions, customs, and cults, and this alliance with the community was, like his relationship with Rome, important to his power. The ritual gave primacy to a spiritual lordship constituted by these two traditions, the Roman and the local. The bishop's temporal lordship, his power over lands and men, came after; it was positioned as a result of his relationship with St Peter and the local patrons of the see: Zenobi and John. It was also related in the ritual to the bishop's sacramental powers. The bishop only entered his palace after saying mass in the baptistery, a space in which he made Christians and citizens through the waters of baptism. The ritual's construction of the relationship between the spiritual, priestly powers of the bishop and his temporal lordship articulated a central contention of the reformers: that priestly authority (*sacerdotium*) was of a higher order than temporal power (*regnum*). This representation of authority and of the bishop's relationship with his

---

[33]   Susan Twyman, "Papal *Adventus* at Rome in the Twelfth Century," *Historical Research* 69 (1996), 233–53, at p. 244; *Le Liber Censuum de l'Église Romaine*, ed. Paul Fabre and Louis Duchesne, 3 vols (Paris, 1910–1952), 1:311–13; Miller, "The Florentine Bishop's Ritual Entry" (above, n. 9).

see endured in Florence with remarkably few changes for more than three centuries. It seems to have been a highly compelling model.

The changes we have considered here in the route of the entry, however, do presage the major transformation that led to the ritual's demise. Both changes accommodated secular power in the city and acknowledged its increasing importance in relation to the see. The consolidation and expansion of Grand Ducal authority in the city from the mid-sixteenth century made the ritual's assertions about authority untenable. It was performed for the last time in 1584 by the first member of the ruling Medici family to hold the see: Alessandro di Ottaviano de' Medici (1574–1605). When this archbishop of the city became pope in 1605, taking the name Leo XI, he was succeeded in Florence by another Medici, Alessandro Marzi Medici. With the conquest of both the see and the papacy by this ruling family, the ritual became superfluous. New reform movements had the challenge of re-forming the bishop once again.

Chapter 14

Postscript: The Ambiguous Bishop

Thomas Head

Hunter College and the Graduate Center, City University of New York

Near the beginning of a bitter attack on fellow bishops for their faults, Rather of Verona (*c.*887–974) emphasized that twin ideals, those of the active and the contemplative lives, framed their duties:

> [W]hom in this did [God] instruct more than you, who ought to mock the devil's wiles with wise forethought and to bear rich offspring of your works by the practice of an active life of pastoral concern, but [also] through your intention of ethereal contemplation ever cling to God in seeking, knowing, and loving the things which belong to contemplation? For no rank or order do these two types of life alike suit more than the bishop's majesty.[1]

The then-exiled bishop of Verona thus concisely phrased a question explored in a formative manner by Gregory the Great in his *Rule of Pastoral Care*, as well as by many other thinkers in the intervening three-and-a-half centuries.[2] In a slightly different key, the editors of this volume have highlighted "the twin ideals of noble resourcefulness and pastoral solicitude [which] combined in the figure of the bishop."[3]

Using different terminology, both medieval theorists and modern scholars recognize that a bishop of the central Middle Ages (a term discussed further below) found himself almost necessarily in an ideological bind. Neither pair of ideals is absolutely polarized, but there is an enormous tension implicit in each. To be a bishop was to engage in not just one, but a number of delicate balancing acts. The contributors to this volume have described many specific instances in which a bishop navigated a difficult channel bounded by—to return to the words of the editors—

---

[1] Rather of Verona, *Praeloquia*, in *The Complete Works of Rather of Verona*, ed. and trans. Peter L.D. Reid, Medieval and Renaissance Texts and Studies 76 (Binghamton, NY, 1991), 5.1, p. 157. The entire Latin text of the *Praeloquia*, of which more below, may be found in *Ratherii Veronensis Opera, Fragmenta, Glossae*, ed. Peter L.D. Reid, François Dolbeau, Bernard Bischoff, and Claudio Leonardi, CCCM 46A (Turnhout, 1984), pp. 3–196.

[2] Gregory the Great, *Règle pastorale*, ed. and trans. Bruno Judic, Floribert Rommel, and Charles Morel, Sources chrétiennes 381–82, 2 vols (Paris, 1992), 1.5–7, 1:144–55. On the elaboration of this idea, see Jacques Fontaine, "L'évêque dans la tradition littéraire du premier millénaire en Occident," in *Les évêques normands du XIe siècle: Colloque de Cerisy-la-Salle (30 septembre–3 octobre 1993)*, ed. Pierre Bouet and François Neveux (Caen, 1995), pp. 41–51. In this volume, see John S. Ott's analysis of Bishop Lietbert of Cambrai (Chapter 8).

[3] John S. Ott and Anna Trumbore Jones, "Introduction: The Bishop Reformed," p. 1.

"[l]ocal and regional concerns [which] molded episcopal identities and established administrative agendas."[4] They deftly demonstrate that no succinct definition of the bishop in this period is possible. The bishop was by nature ambiguous.

Rather of Verona: Ambiguous Product of the "Middle Kingdom"

Few bishops of the period were more acutely aware of such ambiguities than Rather.[5] Born in the county of Hainaut (located in modern Belgium) in the late 880s, he spent the eighty-odd years of his life in lands within or bordering the recently extinct Middle Kingdom of the Carolingian Empire, where rulership remained uncertain, contested, and malleable—in short, ambiguous. The Middle Kingdom, essentially created in the Treaty of Verdun of 843 for Lothar I (795–855), was the very embodiment of the political problems that flowered during the slow demise of the Carolingian Empire.[6] It was the "local and regional concerns" of that dissolving Middle Kingdom—hemmed in by the powers of West Frankland (Carolingian, later Capetian, France) and East Frankland (Ottonian Germany), as well as by the fractured but still potent regions of Provence and Lombardy—which informed Rather's identity and agenda as a bishop. Like some bishops of his time, he was first a monk, becoming a child oblate in the abbey of Lobbes in Hainaut around the year 900 and eventually taking his monastic vows under Abbot Hilduin. As Hilduin's family rose in power, the abbot was nominated to the bishopric of Liège, but was successfully opposed by a candidate supported by King Charles the Simple of West Frankland. Hilduin then journeyed to Italy, where his cousin Hugh of Provence had seized the throne; the abbot of Lobbes became in turn bishop of Verona and archbishop of Milan. Rather had followed his mentor in his travels, and he replaced Hilduin on the see of Verona in October 931. This began a stormy career as a prelate, both bishop and abbot, which was to last more than forty years. Rather unadvisedly supported an unsuccessful coup against Hugh, and in February 934 he was banished for five years of arrest, first in Pavia and then in Como. During his time in Pavia, Rather composed the *Praeloquia*, a treatise on the duties of the varied orders of human society, which included the long invective against contemporary bishops described above. Following his release in

---

[4]   Ott and Trumbore Jones, "Introduction: The Bishop Reformed," p. 19.

[5]   The following biographical sketch is based on Peter L.D. Reid in *The Complete Works of Rather*, pp. 3–16, and Erich Auerbach, *Literary Language and its Public in Late Latin Antiquity and in the Middle Ages*, trans. Ralph Manheim (Princeton, NJ, 1993; German original, Bern, 1958), pp. 133–52. For more on the bishops of Verona in the period following Rather's struggles, see Maureen C. Miller, *The Formation of a Medieval Church: Ecclesiastical Change in Verona, 950–1150* (Ithaca, NY, 1993).

[6]   The "Middle Kingdom" of Lothar I had extended from the North Sea through the Alps to Rome. It included such regions as Lotharingia, Provence, and northern Italy. For a convenient summary of the rise and fall of the Middle Kingdom, see Johannes Fried, "The Frankish Kingdoms, 817–911: The East and Middle Kingdoms," in *The New Cambridge Medieval History*, vol. 2, *c.700–c.900*, ed. Rosamond McKitterick (Cambridge, 1995), pp. 142–68. For reflections on Cambrai as a "border diocese" to the Middle Kingdom see John S. Ott (Chapter 8) and T.M. Riches (Chapter 7).

February 939, Rather traveled the lands of the old Middle Kingdom, pressing his claims to the see of Verona, but also seeking some suitable ecclesiastical office as an alternative. Considering the *Praeloquia* to be an indictment of contemporary secular and ecclesiastical society that supported his own position, Rather sent copies to, among others, Archbishops Gui of Lyon, Sobbo of Vienne, and Rodbert of Trier, as well as to Brun, the brother and chancellor of Emperor Otto I. His efforts were, in the short term, successful: he regained the see of Verona in 946 with the support of Hugh of Provence, but was arrested in 948 by Berengar II—marquis of Ivrea and future king of Italy—and went once more into exile. He found comfort once again in Lotharingia, where Brun, now archbishop of Cologne, nominated him to the see of Liège in 953. Within the year, however, Rather was once more forced from office, this time by Rodbert of Trier, who successfully sought that see for his nephew.

Now in his sixties, the self-styled "bishop of the Church of Verona but monk of Lobbes" had been forced from episcopal office three times by political exigencies and had spent much of his adult life in exile, scrounging for support through the spoken and written word.[7] In 955, Brun of Cologne managed to provide renewed patronage, but it was an office of relatively small value, the abbacy of Aulne-sur-Sambre, located close to Lobbes. Aging and near despair, Rather began writing a series of dyspeptic jeremiads against contemporary clerical vices, including simony and clerical marriage. Disillusioned as he claimed to be, however, he continued to involve himself in ecclesiastical politics. During the final two decades of his life, he briefly held—but lost or abandoned—the see of Verona (for a third time) and the abbacies of Saint-Amand, Hautmont, and Lobbes. In the frequent interludes of exile, imposed by himself or by others, he returned to Aulne, whose abbacy he retained and where he died in 974.

Rather's self-image was that of a humble and spiritual monk who entered the active life of the episcopacy, only to be defeated time and again by forces of political patronage and clerical corruption. He was a victim of the secular and ecclesiastical vices of his time. Historians, seduced by Rather's own words, have described him as a "Gregorian reformer" *avant le lettre*. By his own account, however, he profited almost as often as he suffered from the vagaries of political patronage. He played the game of power politics in the Middle Kingdom continually and vigorously, if not always adeptly. In July 968, during the waning days of his final tenure as bishop of Verona, Rather sent a desperate appeal to the imperial chancellor in Italy.[8] He described himself as the victim of "violence, provocation, and conspiracy" whose enemies were "falsely accusing me since I will not stop attacking them." His own recital of the circumstances, however, implied that Rather seized the land of some canons of his diocese, tried unsuccessfully to bribe others, and spent lavish amounts on his episcopal palace. Even more damningly, Folcuin of Lobbes—admittedly an adversary—portrayed him as a rich man who returned from Italy to gain

---

[7]   See the preface to the *Praeloquia* in *Ratherii Veronensis Opera*, ed. Reid et al., p. 3; English translation in *The Complete Works of Rather*, ed. and trans. Reid, p. 21.

[8]   *Die Briefe des Bischofs Rather von Verona*, ed. Fritz Weigle, MGH Die Briefe der deutschen Kaiserzeit 1 (Weimar, 1949), no. 33, pp. 183–88; English translation in *The Complete Works of Rather*, ed. and trans. Reid, pp. 527–30.

various church offices in Lotharingia through simony, a vice Rather had publicly condemned.[9]

The son of a Lotharingian noble family and sycophantic friend of ecclesiastical and secular nobles, Rather often benefited from the so-called corruption he decried in contemporary society. He did not always live as the penurious exile described in his writings. He was, in short, an ambiguous man: a critic of simony who bought ecclesiastical office; a monk who subverted the independence of monastic communities; a critic of political infighting who supported a coup; a "reforming" bishop who used his critique of secular canons to meddle extensively and partially for his own gain in the finances of his diocese. His career was defined by a number of dyads or "twin ideals," including the spiritual and the active life, ecclesiastical corruption and reform, local and imperial politics.

Rather of Verona provides an excellent complement to the bishops described in this volume. All of them were beset by ambiguity. The bishops of the central Middle Ages were men "in the middle" of competing ideals and loyalties.[10] While this inherent ambiguity makes bishops difficult to define in absolute terms, it does not rule out the possibility of a thick description that provides some real precision. Indeed, the contributors to this volume have shown how attention to the local circumstances of individual bishops can map the competing ideals that compelled and controlled their actions. All of the bishops discussed in this volume, however, were also affected by the gradual transformation of the place of the bishop in western Christendom that occurred during the central Middle Ages.

The Central Middle Ages: From Carolingian Legislation to Roman Centralization

The chronological scope of this volume is the period "from the fragmentation of the Carolingian Empire to the Fourth Lateran Council" (that is, roughly 900–1200), which the editors sensibly call the central Middle Ages.[11] The term is an awkward one, but it is as good as any to denominate the centuries of change from the "early" to the "late" Middle Ages. The authors in this volume, quite understandably, have frequent recourse to the language of transition: John Eldevik subtitles his essay "Siegfried I of Mainz (1060–1084) and Episcopal Identity in an Age of Transition;" John S. Ott notes that the death of Gerard II of Cambrai in 1092 "brought momentous strife and change to the diocese"; Greta Austin describes her chosen period of 900–1050 as "crucial centuries of transition and transformation"; Renée R. Trilling discusses

---

[9] Folcuin of Lobbes, *Gesta abbatum Lobiensium*, ed. Georg Pertz, MGH SS 4 (Hannover, 1841), c. 28, pp. 69–70.

[10] It is not by chance that Sean Gilsdorf, the editor of a volume of essays on bishops of the period under discussion, which makes a fine complement to the present volume (albeit covering a shorter period), chose the following title for his own work: "Bishops in the Middle: Mediatory Politics and the Episcopacy," in *The Bishop: Power and Piety at the First Millennium*, ed. Sean Gilsdorf, Neue Aspekte der europäischen Mittelalterforschung 4 (Münster, 2004), pp. 51–73.

[11] Ott and Trumbore Jones, "Introduction: The Bishop Reformed," p. 4.

how Wulfstan of York, in the early decades of the eleventh century, tried to prescribe renewal for an England "ravaged by more than three decades of continuous Viking attacks" and in "an almost constant state of war."[12]

What are the boundaries of this time of transitions? The events which establish the chronological limits for this book are, implicitly at least, the deposition of Emperor Charles the Fat from the Carolingian throne in 885 and the Fourth Lateran Council called by Pope Innocent III in 1215. These two events, however, are not easily comparable, like the proverbial apples and oranges. As far as the place of the bishop in church and society goes, it is far better to see the boundaries of this volume as being set by two loosely defined movements for the regulation (or, perhaps better, regularization) of church practice: the first carried out in the ninth century under the Carolingian emperors, the second in the thirteenth century under Innocent III, his successors, and the curia which served them. Each had a vision of and legislation for a Christian society, in which the bishop had an essential position.

The royal capitularies and ecclesiastical councils of the Carolingian period, most importantly the *Admonitio Generalis* of 789 and the *Capitula proprie ad episcopos* of 817, provided bishops with clear duties and powers to be administered in conjunction with secular magnates, and (in the Aachen legislation of 817) perhaps more autonomy than bishops had ever possessed in western Christendom.[13] It was not that Carolingian legislation ignored the power of the pope, who was in ideological terms at the top of the ecclesiastical hierarchy. Papal power, however, was mediated through archbishops and bishops, over whom the pope had little direct control.[14] Papal autonomy was itself fragile. As Thomas F.X. Noble has noted, "In the end papal freedom collapsed in the political and social strife of the tenth century and papal autonomy became meaningless in view of the weakening of the imperial office."[15] In sharp contrast, bishops largely retained their local power and autonomy as imperial and papal power fragmented. Timothy Reuter applied the phrase, cited several times in this volume, "a Europe of bishops" to the post-Carolingian period.[16] Bishops often, but far from always, continued to act in close concert with

---

[12]   John Eldevik, "Driving the Chariot of the Lord: Siegfried I of Mainz (1060–1084) and Episcopal Identity in an Age of Transition," p. 176; John S. Ott, "'Both Mary and Martha': Bishop Lietbert of Cambrai and the Construction of Episcopal Sanctity in a Border Diocese around 1100," p. 154; Greta Austin, "Bishops and Religious Law, 900–1050," p. 40; Renée R. Trilling, "Sovereignty and Social Order: Archbishop Wulfstan and the *Institutes of Polity*," pp. 58 and 62.

[13]   See, for example, Jean Imbert, *Les temps Carolingiens (741–891)*, Histoire du droit et des institutions de l'Église en Occident 5, 2 vols (Paris, 1994–1996), 1:94–99 and 128–42, and Jean Heuclin, *Hommes de Dieu et fonctionnaires du roi en Gaule du Nord du Ve au IXe siècle (348–817)* (Villeneuve-d'Ascq, 1998), pp. 289–93 and 347–50. For the texts of the *Admonitio Generalis* and the *Capitula proprie ad episcopos*, see *Capitularia regum Francorum*, ed. Alfred Boretius, MGH Legum 2, 2 vols (Hannover, 1883–1897), 1:51–62 and 275–80.

[14]   Imbert, *Les temps Carolingiens*, 1:91–94.

[15]   Thomas F.X. Noble, "The Papacy in the Eighth and Ninth Centuries," in *The New Cambridge Medieval History*, vol. 2, *c.700–c.900*, ed. McKitterick, pp. 563–86, at p. 574.

[16]   Timothy Reuter, "Ein Europa der Bischöfe. Das Zeitalter Burchards von Worms," in *Bischof Burchard von Worms, 1000–1025*, ed. Wilfried Hartmann, Quellen und Abhandlungen

lay magnates, as Anna Trumbore Jones has shown with admirable nuance for the bishops and dukes of Aquitaine.[17] Many of the individual disputes of the Investiture Controversy focused on the attempts by emperors and popes to bring bishops more directly under their specific control.[18] It remained, however, for Innocent III and his formulation of the papal *plenitudo potestatis* for the papacy to regain a viable claim to supremacy over bishops. To a degree never attained by the Gregorian ideologues of the eleventh century, the "Roman centralization" of the early thirteenth century drew bishops away from the sort of local autonomy and entente with secular rulers, which had been envisioned in Carolingian legislation, into a thoroughly "Roman" hierarchy.[19]

The change in the position of the bishop is reflected in the development of canon law. Within the context of imperial capitularies and conciliar decrees, bishops of the Carolingian empire composed an impressive number of *capitula episcoporum*, that is, legislation on ecclesiastical and moral matters compiled by a bishop for his diocese, although they were often adapted by other bishops for use in their own dioceses. The latest datable examples of this genre were issued in the early tenth century by such contemporaries of Rather of Verona as Ruotger of Trier (d. 931) and Atto of Vercelli (d. *c.*960).[20] While several episcopal capitularies, such as those of Theodulf of Orléans (d. 821), continued in circulation and use, the production of this sort of independent episcopal legislation virtually ceased after the middle of the tenth century.[21] Taking their place, in a process well described by Greta Austin, were

---

zur mittelrheinischen Kirchengeschichte 100 (Mainz, 2000), pp. 1–28. Cited in Ott and Trumbore Jones, "Introduction: The Bishop Reformed," n. 10; Austin, "Bishops and Religious Law," n. 1; Riches, "Bishop Gerard I of Cambrai-Arras, the Three Orders, and the Problem of Human Weakness," n. 74.

[17] Anna Trumbore Jones, "Lay Magnates, Religious Houses, and the Role of the Bishop in Aquitaine (877–1050)."

[18] See, for example, I.S. Robinson, *Authority and Resistance in the Investiture Contest: The Polemical Literature of the Late Eleventh Century* (Manchester, 1978), pp. 163–79.

[19] For a convenient sketch of these developments, see "La centralisation romaine et l'unification de la chrétienté," in Jean-Marie Mayeur, Charles and Luce Pietri, André Vauchez, and Marc Venard eds, *Histoire du Christianisme des origines à nos jours*, vol. 5, *Apogée de la papauté et expansion de la chrétienté (1054–1274)* ([Paris], 1993), pp. 519–734, particularly pp. 543–50 on the importance of the Fourth Lateran Council and pp. 587–94 on the *plenitudo potestatis*. The "Rome" in question was not the city itself, but the Roman papacy and curia; see p. 560.

[20] The surviving corpus of this legislation has been published in *Capitula episcoporum*, ed. Peter Brommer and Rudolf Pokorny, MGH Capitula episcoporum, 4 vols (Hannover, 1984–2005). On the genre itself, see Peter Brommer, *Capitula episcoporum: Die bischöflichen Kapitularien des 9. und 10. Jahrhunderts*, Typologie des sources du moyen âge occidental 43 (Turnhout, 1985).

[21] The capitularies of Theodulf, for example, were copied or used by (among others): Ademar of Chabannes (989–1034), a monk probably working in this case for the bishop of Angoulême; Regino of Prüm (d. 915), an influential compiler of canon law; and Bishop Wulfstan of York. See *Capitula episcoporum*, ed. Brommer, 1:145–46; Patrick Wormald, "Archbishop Wulfstan: Eleventh-Century State-Builder," in *Wulfstan, Archbishop of York: The Proceedings of the Second Alcuin Conference*, ed. Matthew Townend, Studies in the

carefully compiled and copied collections of letters written by bishops in which they commented on their practice of pastoral care, on trials which they adjudicated, and on legal proceedings in which they participated.[22] Rather of Verona's own letters were collected and transmitted in this manner, as were those of many other influential bishops and their chancellors, including Dunstan of Canterbury (d. 988), Gerbert of Aurillac (d. 1003), Fulbert of Chartres (d. 1028), Ivo of Chartres (d. 1116), and John of Salisbury (d. 1180).[23] Such case law was essential to, and eventually replaced by, papal letters (or decretals) and collections of canon law compiled by academic lawyers such as Gratian, who were not bishops (and a few, such as Burchard of Worms, who were). The formation and use of an allegedly universal canon law was one of the keys to the consolidation of power by popes and the curia in the early thirteenth century.

One of the clearest markers of the shift from episcopal autonomy to papal authority is provided by legislation governing the authorization of saints' cults—the process that has come to be known as canonization.[24] Carolingian legislation clearly gave bishops control over the practice of the cult of saints in their own dioceses.[25] One of the most important canons was issued at the Council of Mainz in 813: "Henceforth let no one presume to move the bodies of saints from one place to another without the counsel of the prince (*princeps*) or license from a holy synod of bishops."[26] (The ritual of the translation of relics, described here, implicitly authorized the cult of a saint.) The *princeps* in question was certainly a secular magnate, an excellent example of the close cooperation of the ecclesiastical and secular nobilities. Over the next three centuries, this text was included in the canonical collections of Burchard of Worms, Ivo of Chartres, and Gratian.[27] Slowly the understanding of the term *princeps* changed so that by the late twelfth century it was assumed to be the pope, not a secular ruler. Eventually the Carolingian text, bearing this interpretation, was

---

Early Middle Ages 10 (Turnhout, 2004), pp. 9–27, at pp. 18–19; Trilling, "Sovereignty and Social Order," p. 61–62.

[22]   Austin, "Bishops and Religious Law," pp. 53–54.

[23]   On the importance of the collection of Ivo's letters, see Bruce C. Brasington, "What Made Ivo Mad? Reflections on a Medieval Bishop's Anger." These collections could be of mixed origin: the letters of Gerbert were variously written while he was chancellor of the archbishop of Reims, archbishop of Reims in his own right, and pope (as Sylvester II).

[24]   The fullest account of the development of the process of canonization remains, despite its problems, Eric Waldram Kemp, *Canonization and Authority in the Western Church* (Oxford, 1948). I have offered a critique of Kemp's account of the developments between 800 and 1200 in "The Genesis of the Ordeal of Relics by Fire in Ottonian Germany: An Alternative Form of 'Canonization,'" in *Procès de canonisation au Moyen Âge: Aspects juridiques et religieux/Medieval Canonization Processes: Legal and Religious Aspects*, ed. Gábor Klaniczay, Collection de l'École française de Rome 340 (Rome, 2004), pp. 19–37. I also discuss there the development of the term "canonization" and how its use is anachronistic for much of the period discussed in the present volume.

[25]   Imbert, *Les temps Carolingiens*, 1:163–65; Heuclin, *Hommes de Dieu*, pp. 259–61 and 333–35; Kemp, *Canonization and Authority*, pp. 36–43.

[26]   See canon 51 in the edition of Albert Werminghoff: *Concilium Moguntinense*, MGH Concilia 2/1, 2 vols (Hannover and Leipzig, 1896), 1:272.

[27]   The precise references are provided by Kemp, *Canonization and Authority*, p. 42.

included in canon 62 of the Fourth Lateran Council. Innocent III made a number of solemn declarations that demonstrated his confidence that, under the *plenitudo potestatis*, the papacy alone possessed the authority to recognize saints.[28] In terms of the authorization of sanctity, the bishop changed, over the course of the central Middle Ages, from an independent actor to a deputy of the papacy.

Nonetheless, certain traditional ideals and practices of the episcopal office remained constant. Gregory the Great's *Rule of Pastoral Care*, for example, was an essential text for Gratian in compiling the section on bishops in the *Decretum*.[29] Codices that contained prayers and rituals specific to the office of bishop, such as pontificals and benedictionals, multiplied over the course of the central Middle Ages.[30] As Eric Palazzo points out, the "first fully-fledged episcopal liturgical book" was produced as late as 962, but it literally incorporated an ideal of episcopal authority over certain rituals that derived from Carolingian and Ottonian legislation.[31] Evan Gatti has neatly shown how an eleventh-century benedictional which belonged to Bishop Engilmar of Parenzo was later fully incorporated into a thirteenth-century liturgical codex.[32] Maureen Miller has detailed how the stational liturgy, a ritual with its ultimate roots in the fourth century, continued to be adapted and reinterpreted well after the Fourth Lateran Council.[33] Certain ritual responsibilities of a bishop had changed hardly at all over the course of the central Middle Ages.

The Ambiguity of Being Both Mary and Martha

Perhaps the most obvious lesson taught by the reformulation offered by this volume is that no single definition or ideal of the bishop existed for the central Middle Ages. The ambiguities of the careers of the individual bishops described here defy the imposition of absolute, monistic ideals and categories. The long-term changes in the position of the episcopate outlined above served as a context, but generally not a direct cause, for these ambiguities. Instead it was the tensions inherent in dyadic, "twin ideals" such as the spiritual and the active life or noble and pastoral duties that gave rise to the ambiguous behaviors described in these essays. The recognition of the dynamic and dyadic qualities which framed the actions of a bishop of the central Middle Ages is the central insight which the authors share. And without a doubt the

---

[28] Kemp, *Canonization and Authority*, pp. 101–3, and André Vauchez, *Sainthood in the Later Middle Ages*, trans. Jean Birrell (Cambridge, 1997; French original, Rome, 1988), pp. 27–29.

[29] Jean Gaudemet, "Patristique et pastorale: La contribution de Grégoire le Grand au 'Miroir de l'évêque' dans le Décret de Gratien," in *Études d'histoire du droit canonique dédiées à Gabriel Le Bras*, 2 vols (Paris, 1965), 1:129–39.

[30] For a concise statement of the evidence, see Eric Palazzo, *L'Évêque et son image: L'illustration du Pontifical au Moyen Âge* (Turnhout, 1999), pp. 119–28.

[31] Eric Palazzo, "The Image of the Bishop in the Middle Ages," p. 88.

[32] Evan Gatti, "Building the Body of the Church: A Bishop's Blessing in the Benedictional of Engilmar of Parenzo," pp. 102–4.

[33] Maureen C. Miller, "Urban Space, Sacred Topography, and Ritual Meanings in Florence: The Route of the Bishop's Entry, *c.*1200–1600."

single most important achievement of this volume is the rejection of "reform" as a monolithic ideal that can be used to describe and judge the actions of bishops (or, for that matter, popes, princes, abbots, noblewomen, and others). "Reform" only exists in tension with other categories, or perhaps more accurately is itself an ambiguous product of the tensions inherent within various "twin ideals," such as pious gift-giving and sinful simony, or peace-keeping and war-making.

If no two bishops acted in exactly the same manner and with the same idiosyncratic ambiguity, there was still a coherent universe—possessing its own specific if unwritten rules—within which the bishops acted.[34] And so it seems that the best way to describe the bishop of the central Middle Ages is to explore some of the dyads or contending ideas which the contributors to this collection have expertly laid out before us.

Let us start with that presented by Rather of Verona in the passage quoted at the beginning of this essay: the need for a bishop to combine the contemplative and active lives, that is, in contemporary terms, to be both Mary and Martha. (The biblical figures Mary and Martha of Bethany were taken to be symbols respectively of the contemplative and active lives, based on Luke 10:38–42.)[35] It was an ideal that figured prominently in biographical sketches of bishops as a means of asserting their holiness. Writing in the first decades of the eleventh century, Theodoric, a monk of Saint Eucharius in Trier, described Archbishop Egbert of Trier (d. 993) in these terms:

> He was a man of blessed memory and a lamp of virtue, of high standing due to the generous bequest of his deceased parents, but of even higher standing due to the priceless dowry of complete uprightness. His reverence surpassed that of all the bishops and magnates of the kingdom [and] . . . he was the principle teacher and sustainer of monks, a special lover of the discipline of the *Rule* [of St. Benedict]. The humble heart of a devoted monk hid under the costume of a bishop, as if he frequently paraded with Martha in public in order to carry out the ministry of God, but nevertheless turned himself with Mary completely over to the study of the divine word. He made of himself a free sacrifice to the Godhead, in practical matters like a rock dove, but in contemplative matters like a turtledove.[36]

Like Siegfried I of Mainz (d. 1084) and Anno II of Cologne (d. 1075), Egbert had been a monk, and that experience seems to have driven those bishops in their support and oversight of monasteries in their dioceses. These dioceses were also, during the tenth and eleventh century, locked in a struggle to be recognized as the primatial see of Germany. All three prelates used actions that might be categorized as "reformist"

---

[34]   The discussion of unwritten "rules of the game" or *Spielregeln* in early medieval politics stems from the work of Gerd Althoff, particularly *Family, Friends, and Followers: Political and Social Bonds in Early Medieval Europe*, trans. Christopher Carroll (Cambridge, 2004; German original, Darmstadt, 1990) and *Spielregeln der Politik im Mittelalter: Kommunikation in Frieden und Fehde* (Darmstadt, 1997).

[35]   On medieval views of the relationship of the active and contemplative lives more generally, see Giles Constable, *Three Studies in Medieval Religious and Social Thought* (Cambridge, 1995), chapter one.

[36]   Theodoric of Saint Eucharius, *Inventio s. Celsi*, in AASS February, vol. 3, c. 5, p. 403.

to assert that politically potent claim on behalf of his see.[37] One did not need to be monk, however, to bring contemplative ideals and practice into the episcopal office. Writing almost a century after Theodoric, the monk Raoul described Bishop Lietbert of Cambrai in similar terms: "you would see in [Lietbert] Mary and Martha, now going about the business of the ministry, now humbly laying at Jesus's feet . . . with tears and attentive prayers."[38] Many bishops of late Anglo-Saxon England, including Dunstan of Canterbury (d. 988) and Oswald of Worcester (d. 992), had once been monks. Wulfstan of York (d. 1023), however, never entered the cloister, but as Renée Trilling points out, he was "[g]reatly influenced by the tenth-century Benedictine Reform, [and his] life's work can be viewed as a single-handed attempt to bring the ecclesiastical reform begun in the monasteries to the people of the secular church."[39] For Wulfstan, practice of the contemplative life tempered people in the active life to be more identifiably Christian in their engagement with the world.

Attempting to bring the virtues of Mary and Martha together did not simply mean becoming a monk in preparation for election as a bishop. In fact, some thought it almost impossible to combine the two lives. Remember that Rather of Verona made his statement of an ideal as a preface to a bitter attack on the vices of contemporary bishops, and presented his own monastic simplicity as one of the reasons why he was so often abused by the more worldly and politically astute. Abbot Guibert of Nogent (d. *c.*1125) frankly doubted whether the contemplative life was compatible with any form of ecclesiastical administration.[40] And Abbot Abbo of Fleury (d. 1004), in a description of the ideal of Christian society, flatly stated that monks (both men and women) who pursued the contemplative life were superior to all clerics, including bishops.[41] Abbo did, however, think—in partial agreement with Wulfstan—that the imitation of monastic virtues was desirable for their clerical and lay inferiors.

There is a tendency among historians to label monks-turned-bishops as "reformers," in part because of the prominence of reforming movements in the monasticism of this period and in part because of the attempt by the Gregorian party to impose some monastic virtues, such as celibacy, on the entire clergy. Indeed, the number of monks nominated to episcopal office increased in the late eleventh and twelfth century, at least in France and Germany. But it goes without saying that all bishops, including those who had once been monks, had a family, and the great majority hailed from the nobility.[42] Bishops were caught between their natal families and their spiritual families—that is, the flock whom they shepherded.

---

[37]   Eldevik, "Driving the Chariot of the Lord," pp. 175–78; Thomas Head, "Art and Artifice in Ottonian Trier," *Gesta* 36 (1997), 65–82, at pp. 68–71; Jonathan Rotondo-McCord, "Body Snatching and Episcopal Power: Archbishop Anno II of Cologne (1056–75), Burials in St Mary's *ad gradus*, and the Minority of King Henry IV," *Journal of Medieval History* 22 (1996), 297–312.

[38]   Ott, "'Both Mary and Martha,'" p. 149.

[39]   Trilling, "Sovereignty and Social Order," pp. 59–60.

[40]   Jay Rubenstein, *Guibert of Nogent: Portrait of a Medieval Mind* (New York, 2002), pp. 176–82.

[41]   Abbo of Fleury, *Apologeticus*, PL 139:464.

[42]   Bernard Guillemain, "Les origines des évêques en France aux XIe et XIIe siècles," in *Le istituzioni ecclesiastiche della "societas christiana" dei secoli XI–XII: Papato,*

While bishops were expected to be celibate and not produce direct heirs, they still had many relatives. Historians have emphasized the attempts by noble dynasties to impose their will and candidates on specific sees.[43] Less attention has been paid to the implications of actual episcopal dynasties, in which a nephew succeeded his paternal uncle. These were relatively common during the tenth and eleventh centuries in France and Spain.[44] A few striking examples in which nephew followed uncle for at least three generations include: Urgell from 914 to 1075 (with one interruption); Orléans from c.956 to c.1010 and (a different family) from c.1020 to 1067; Poitiers from 975 to 1087; and Cambrai from 1012 to 1092. With rare exception, members of these episcopal dynasties had not been monks.[45] In the case of Orléans, the bishop who separated the two episcopal dynasties was a monk from Sens named Theodoric, who was supported as a "reformer" against the local nobility by King Robert the Pious and the monks of Fleury. His tenure was disastrous and ended somewhat bizarrely in the events surrounding the famous trial of heretics at Orléans in 1022, with its dire political consequences for the king.[46] Anna Trumbore Jones, T.M. Riches, and John S. Ott have all shown in these pages how difficult it is to characterize members of the episcopal dynasties of Poitiers and Cambrai as either "reform" or "anti-reform." Indeed, Trumbore Jones has shown how the fact that the bishops of Poitiers were from a different family than the counts of Poitou (that is, the dukes of Aquitaine) benefited the bishops of the province and their attempts at such "reform" efforts as the Peace of God and support of monasteries.[47] The biographer

---

cardinalato ed episcopato. Atti della quinta Settimana internazionale di studio (Mendola, 26–31 agosto 1971), Miscellanea del Centro di studi medioevali 7 (Milan, 1974), pp. 374–402; Carlrichard Brühl, "Die Sozialstruktur des deutschen Episkopats im 11. und 12. Jahrhundert," and Gabriella Rossetti, "Origine sociale e formazione dei vescovi del 'Regnum Italiae' nei secoli XI e XII," in *Le istituzioni ecclesiastiche della "societas christiana" dei secoli XI–XII: Diocesi, pievi e parrocchie. Atti della sesta Settimana internazionale di studio (Milano, 1–7 settembre 1974)*, Miscellanea del Centro di studi medioevali 8 (Milan, 1977), pp. 42–56 and 57–84.

[43] For France, see, for example, Jacques Boussard, "Les évêques en Neustrie avant la réforme grégorienne (950–1050 environ), *Journal des savants*, s.n. (1970), 161–96; Guillemain, "Les origines des évêques"; Guy Devailly, "Les grandes familles et l'épiscopat dans l'Ouest de la France et les Pays de la Loire," *Cahiers de civilisation médiévale* 27 (1984), 49–55; Pierre Bouet and Monique Dosdat, "Les évêques normands de 985 à 1150," in *Les évêques normands du XIe siècle*, ed. Bouet and Neveux, pp. 19–37.

[44] In addition to the studies listed in the previous two notes, see also Jeffrey Bowman, "The Bishop Builds a Bridge: Sanctity and Power in the Medieval Pyrenees," *The Catholic Historical Review* 88 (2002), 1–16, at pp. 3–5, and the bibliography he cites in n. 10, as well as the family trees in Thomas Head, *Hagiography and the Cult of Saints: The Diocese of Orléans, 800–1200* (Cambridge, 1990), pp. 228 and 260.

[45] In contrast, episcopal dynasties were much less common in Anglo-Saxon England and Ottonian Germany, where proportionally more bishops had passed through monasteries on their way to their see.

[46] Head, *Hagiography and the Cult of Saints*, pp. 255–70.

[47] Trumbore Jones, "Lay Magnates, Religious Houses, and the Role of the Bishop," esp. pp. 37–39; Riches, "Bishop Gerard I of Cambrai-Arras," pp. 123–24; Ott, "'Both Mary and Martha,'" pp. 138–40.

of Lietbert of Cambrai emphasized how much Lietbert had learned both about the episcopal office and the spiritual life from his uncle Gerard I; he had not needed to enter a monastery to learn about balancing the lives of Mary and Martha.[48] Scholars need to pay more attention to what bishops may have learned at their uncles' knees.

Even if they did not succeed their uncles, bishops generally inherited much from their natal families. Egbert of Trier's biographer, although he preferred to emphasize the spiritual, noted that the archbishop had received "a generous bequest of his deceased parents." Egbert undertook an ambitious program of building, patronage of saints' cults, and support of monastic reform. Although he had been for a while a monk, he still had sufficient wealth to follow the lead of his father and maternal grandfather (respectively the counts of Holland and of Flanders) in grandiose expenditure on gifts to ecclesiastical institutions.[49] Over a century after his death, a cleric of Trier specifically remembered Egbert for his donation "of silver and gold crosses, missals, chasubles, dalmatics, tunics, stoles, reliquaries, and draperies" to his see.[50] Such magnanimity was expected from bishops. The phrase "poor bishop" would have been a virtual oxymoron until the middle of the twelfth century, when members of orders such as the Cistercians were nominated to sees in significant numbers.[51] The gifts of bishops doubtless did much to support liturgical ritual and pastoral care in their dioceses. To adapt the words of the editors of this volume, quoted earlier, the "noble resourcefulness" of bishops made possible much of their "pastoral solicitude." As in the case of most gifts, however, these were intended to benefit the donor as well.[52] Evan Gatti and Dorothy Glass have, in their studies of the bishops of Parenzo and Piacenza, tellingly contributed to the growing literature on how the ornate objects (such as buildings, sculpture, books, and liturgical vestments) commissioned by bishops served as expressions of their self-understanding and props for their authority. As Glass notes, "It would thus seem that the cathedral at Piacenza, begun in 1122, at an auspicious moment when the Concordat at Worms had smoothed, at least temporarily, the relations between the imperial and papal powers, also stands as witness to the wealth of the diocese and the power of Arduin, then bishop of the city."[53] The interpretation of the iconography and the economics of this

---

48   Ott, "'Both Mary and Martha,'" pp. 144–45. It is interesting to note that Gerard's maternal uncle was Archbishop Adalbero of Laon, although Gerard was probably too young ever to have benefited from Adalbero's knowledge and experience.

49   Head, "Art and Artifice," pp. 68–70.

50   *Gesta Treverorum*, ed. Georg Pertz, MGH SS 8 (Hannover, 1848), c. 29, p. 169.

51   Guillemain, "Les origines des évêques," pp. 385–91.

52   We must take seriously, however, Barbara Rosenwein's brilliant suggestion that donations to ecclesiastical institutions were not considered so much as gifts to God and his saints, but as counter-gifts in exchange for the gift of salvations provided by God: *To Be the Neighbor of Saint Peter: The Social Meaning of Cluny's Property, 909–1049* (Ithaca, NY, 1989), pp. 136–41.

53   Dorothy F. Glass, "The Bishops of Piacenza, Their Cathedral, and the Reform of the Church," p. 261.

wealthy material culture, particularly within the framework of kinship relations and gift giving, can still provide much opportunity for future work by medievalists.[54]

In the calculus of social position, violence was always a factor. The giving of gifts was measured against the taking of plunder. As pastors and nobles, bishops regularly had to consider the tension between the keeping of peace and the making of war. Virtually all writers of the central Middle Ages would have agreed with the Carolingian theory that the king was responsible for the maintenance of peace and justice. In practice, however, royal government often failed in this task.[55] Bishops often had to step into the breach. Perhaps the most famous example is the movement called the Peace of God, which had its origin among the Aquitanian bishops discussed by Anna Trumbore Jones.[56] She describes how this effort to contain attacks on ecclesiastical property (largely by noblemen, including the duke) involved a delicate negotiation between the bishops of the region (themselves mostly noblemen) and the duke.[57] Despite the ambiguities involved, there is no masking the fact that the bishops acted to keep the peace in part for their self-interests.[58] In similar circumstances, but writing theoretically rather than acting practically, Wulfstan of York made the bishop chiefly responsible for keeping the peace in his part of the kingdom. As Renée Trilling observes, this "reveal[s] a fundamental contradiction at the heart of Wulfstan's *Polity*: the irreconcilability of divine and secular sovereignty in the administration of civil society."[59] And so bishops—ambiguously, not paradoxically—at times had

---

[54] Some idea of the riches of this evidence can be provided by catalogues for three museum exhibitions celebrating the artistic patronage of individual Ottonian bishops: Anton Legner ed., *Monumenta Annonis: Köln und Siegburg, Weltbild und Kunst im hohen Mittelalter. Eine Ausstellung des Schnütgen-Museums der Stadt Köln in der Cäcilienkirche vom 30. April bis zum 27. Juli 1975* (Cologne, 1975); Franz Ronig ed., *Egbert, Erzbischof von Trier, 977–993: Gedenkschrift der Diözese Trier zum 1000. Todestag*, Trierer Zeitschrift für Geschichte und Kunst des Trierer Landes und seiner Nachbargebeite 18, 2 vols (Trier, 1993); Michael Brandt and Arne Eggebrecht eds, *Bernward von Hildesheim und das Zeitalter der Ottonen: Katalog der Ausstellung, Hildesheim 1993*, 2 vols (Hildesheim, 1993). On the question of self-representation in Ottonian art and politics, see Gerd Althoff and Ernst Schubert eds, *Herrschaftsrepräsentation im ottonischen Sachsen*, Vorträge und Forschungen 46 (Sigmaringen, 1998).

[55] See, among others, Hans Hattenhauer, *Pax et iustitia*, Berichte aus den Sitzungen der Joachim Jungius-Gesellschaft der Wissenschaften 3 (Hamburg, 1983), on the theory; and Janet L. Nelson, "Kings With Justice, Kings Without Justice: An Early Medieval Paradox," in *La giustizia nell'alto Medioevo (secoli IX–XI), 11–17 aprile 1996*, Settimane di studio del Centro italiano di studi sull'alto Medioevo 44 (Spoleto, 1997), pp. 797–826, on the practice.

[56] It is a subject on which I have commented (as Trumbore Jones graciously acknowledges). See, most recently, Thomas Head, "The Development of the Peace of God in Aquitaine (970–1005)," *Speculum* 74 (1999), 656–86.

[57] Trumbore Jones, "Lay Magnates, Religious Houses, and the Role of the Bishop," esp. pp. 26–28 and 37–39.

[58] A point made particularly well by Hans-Werner Goetz, "Protection of the Church, Defense of the Law, and Reform: On the Purposes and Character of the Peace of God, 989–1038," in *The Peace of God: Social Violence and Religious Response in France around the Year 1000*, ed. Thomas Head and Richard Landes (Ithaca, NY, 1992), pp. 259–79.

[59] Trilling, "Sovereignty and Social Order," p. 60.

to fight. Here Valerie Ramseyer catches the tension perfectly in the title of her essay on Archbishop Alfanus I of Salerno (d. 1085): "Pastoral Care as Military Action." In parallel with the other contributors to this volume, she shows how Alfanus's "reform program" was not part of a monolithic Gregorian movement, but was formed by the specific circumstances of southern Italy and Alfanus's monastery of Montecassino.[60]

Conclusion: Holy Bishops or Episcopal Saints?

One of the consistently important duties of a bishop was to serve as the arbiter of the holy in his corner of Christendom. Many rituals—as chronicled in pontificals, which were a product of the central Middle Ages—were a specifically episcopal prerogative. The consecration of kings was such an important duty that the archbishoprics of Mainz, Cologne, and Trier squabbled over primacy, and thus the right to consecrate the German king, for centuries. Preaching—the *viva voce* interpretation of God's word for a live audience—was a right that was not, in theory, ceded by bishops until the late twelfth century, although in practice others had taken it over much earlier. The rituals which provided God's grace, codified at the Fourth Lateran Council as the seven sacraments, were part and parcel of the bishop's oversight of pastoral care. Bishops controlled the veneration of saints in their own diocese, even after the development of the procedures of papal canonization. They were the watchdogs of orthodoxy, able to condemn—although not to execute, a power reserved to secular rulers—heretics. Carolingian legislation prescribed for the bishop a role as mediator between heaven and earth, which, from the point of view of the bishop's flock, changed relatively little over the course of the central Middle Ages, just as the position of the bishop to his royal and papal superiors was being vigorously debated and radically transformed.

One of the most important, and problematic, sources for the ideals and practice of the episcopacy during the central Middle Ages is the corpus of the *vitae* of individual bishops of this period written by their contemporaries. They and the scholarship on them have been cited repeatedly in this volume. Although in one sense quite numerous, they are in another sense rare: a significant percentage of the narrative literature composed in Latin during the central Middle Ages consists of contemporary bishops' lives, but only a small percentage of bishops were recorded in such works. Scholars tend to describe these works generically as *vitae episcoporum*.[61]

---

[60] Ramseyer, "Pastoral Care as Military Action," esp. pp. 193–94 and 205–7.

[61] Amongst the vast amount of scholarship on this topic, see particularly: Friedrich Lotter, *Die Vita Brunonis des Ruotger: Ihre historiographische und ideengeschichtliche Stellung*, Bonner historische Forschungen 9 (Bonn, 1958); C. Stephen Jaeger, "The Courtier Bishop in *Vitae* from the Tenth to the Twelfth Century," *Speculum* 58 (1983), 291–325; Reinhold Kaiser, "Die *Gesta episcoporum* als Genus der Geschichtsschreibung," in *Historiographie im frühen Mittelalter*, ed. Anton Scharer and Georg Scheibelreiter, Veröffentlichungen des Instituts für Österreichische Geschichtsforschung 32 (Munich, 1994), pp. 459–80; Stephanie Haarländer, *Vitae episcoporum: Eine Quellengattung zwischen Hagiographie und Historiographie,*

Therein lies a problem. The *vitae episcoporum* from the central Middle Ages present a staggeringly broad spectrum. Some—such as the lives of Gauzlin of Bourges (d. 1030) and Meinwerk of Paderborn (d. 1036)—are little more than a catalogue of the man's achievements. Most—such as those of Ulrich of Augsburg (d. 973), Ermengold of Urgell (d. 1035), and Lanfranc of Canterbury (d. 1089)—depict men struggling with the contrasting demands of the religious and the secular. Many scholars have commented on the ambiguities presented by these texts.[62] The mere existence of a *vita*, however, does not imply that its subject was considered a saint. Only nine bishops of the central Middle Ages were canonized by papal bull before the Fourth Lateran Council.[63] Of those, Thomas Becket was the only one to be accorded a widespread posthumous cult, although it was, to be sure, one of the most important pilgrimages of the later Middle Ages. The Latin *sanctus* (*-a*) is a richly ambivalent term, sometimes used as an adjective denoting holiness, other times as an honorific or title denoting an official "saint" worthy of public veneration. English, with its dual Romance and Germanic roots, is unique among modern European languages in being able to make this distinction. Writers of the central Middle Ages made use of this ambiguity: other than works about the great martyr, Thomas Becket, the authors of the *vitae episcoporum* were careful not to assert the official sanctity of their subjects. Despite their obvious similarities, the life of Meinwerk of Paderborn is listed in the standard scholarly catalogue of works of hagiography, but the life of Gauzlin of Bourges is not.[64] Many *vitae episcoporum* were intended by their authors to be guides to the office—*specula episcoporum*, if you will—more than the description of a saint for the purposes of liturgy and cult. Perhaps the most significant ambiguity of the bishops of the central Middle Ages is that all were arbiters of the holy, but very few were saints.

---

untersucht an Lebensbeschreibungen von Bischöfen des Regnum Teutonicum im Zeitalter der Ottonen und Salier, Monographien zur Geschichte des Mittelalters 47 (Stuttgart, 2000).

[62]   See, most recently, Bowman, "The Bishop Builds a Bridge," and Maureen C. Miller, "Masculinity, Reform and Clerical Culture: Narratives of Episcopal Holiness in the Gregorian Era," *Church History* 72 (2003), 25–52.

[63]   Gerard of Toul (by Leo IX in 1050), Theobald of Vicenza (by Alexander II or III after 1066), Peter of Anagni (by Paschal II in 1109/10), Conrad of Constance (by Calixtus II in 1123), Godehard of Hildesheim (by Innocent II in 1131), Thomas Becket (by Alexander III in 1173), Bernward of Hildesheim (by Celestine III in 1192/3), Ubald of Gubbio (by Celstine III in 1192), and Wulfstan of Worcester (by Innocent III in 1203). For details, see Kemp, *Canonization and Authority*, pp. 86–106. The bull of canonization for Ulrich of Augsburg is probably a forgery: Bernhard Schimmelpfennig, "Afra und Ulrich. Oder: Wie wird man heilig?" *Zeitschrift des historischen Vereins für Schwaben* 86 (1993), 23–44, and Günther Wolf, "Die Kanonisationsbulle von 993 für den Hl. Oudalrich von Augsburg und Vergleichbares," *Archiv für Diplomatik* 40 (1994), 85–104. I acknowledge having previously argued for the authenticity of this document.

[64]   *Bibliotheca hagiographica latina antiquae et mediae aetatis*, Subsidia hagiographica 6, 2 vols (Brussels, 1898–1901), no. 5884, p. 860; see also the new supplement ed. Henryk Fros, Subsidia hagiographica 70 (Brussels, 1986), no. 5884, p. 639. Andrew of Fleury, *Vie de Gauzlin, abbé de Fleury: Vita Gauzlini abbatis Floriacensis monasterii*, ed. and trans. Robert-Henri Bautier and Gillette Labory, Sources d'histoire médiévale publiées par l'Institut de Recherche et d'Histoire des Textes 2 (Paris, 1969).

Index